The
Law of Damages

The
Law of Damages

by

A. I. OGUS, B.C.L., M.A.
Fellow of Mansfield College, Oxford

LONDON
BUTTERWORTHS
1973

ENGLAND: BUTTERWORTH & CO. (PUBLISHERS) LTD.
              LONDON: 88 KINGSWAY, WC2B 6AB

AUSTRALIA: BUTTERWORTHS PTY. LTD.
              SYDNEY: 586 PACIFIC HIGHWAY, CHATSWOOD, NSW 2067
              MELBOURNE: 343 LITTLE COLLINS STREET, 3000
              BRISBANE: 240 QUEEN STREET, 4000

CANADA: BUTTERWORTH & CO. (CANADA) LTD.
              TORONTO: 14 CURITY AVENUE, 374

NEW ZEALAND: BUTTERWORTH & CO. (NEW ZEALAND) LTD.
              WELLINGTON: 26-28 WARING TAYLOR STREET, 1

SOUTH AFRICA: BUTTERWORTH & CO. (SOUTH AFRICA) (PTY.) LTD.
              DURBAN: 152-154 GALE STREET

ISBN 0 406 63350 9

Made and printed in Great Britain by
William Clowes & Sons, Limited, London, Beccles and Colchester

To

S.J.O.
S.P.O.

Preface

In the days when the assessment of damages lay exclusively within the province of the jury, one might have been excused for ignoring the problems raised by the process of quantification. It would indeed have been presumptuous and unrealistic to have undertaken an analysis of the "law of damages". But once the process has been transferred to a judge, the position is very different. He is expected to formulate and apply principles of law. There must emerge a rational body of rules which is appropriate both to accommodate a wide variety of factual situations, and to pursue the broad policies implicit in the notion of compensation. For his part, the teacher of law must become aware that to instruct his students on the circumstances in which one party must assume responsibility for another's misfortunes without indicating the extent of that responsibility is to leave the story but half told. How and why the defendant is liable for one type of loss rather than another is as important an issue as that which determines whether he is to bear any responsibility at all.

In 1961 Professor Street felt compelled to observe that "hitherto the law of damages has been quite remarkable for the lack of interest shown by jurists in its fundamental rules". In the field of personal injuries, the law has developed rapidly since then, and there has been a widespread interest in such problems as the role of punishment in a damages award, and the relationship between a common law remedy and other sources of compensation. But the observation remains valid for the law of damages as a whole. There is still evident a tendency to focus on the doctrine of remoteness in the forlorn hope that its broad and necessarily vague formula will solve the many problems which the process of quantification creates. Conversely, in an effort to state satisfactory rules for particular areas of the law of contract and tort, specialists have been prone to lose sight of the broad principles of compensation.

This book has been written from the conviction that there is a need for a work which gives a comprehensive and critical account of the law within a broad framework of principle and policy. The hope is that the reader will as a result be instructed not only on the principles themselves but on the process of reasoning from general doctrine to par-

vii

ticular rule. Within the area of the law of contract, it was felt that this could be achieved only within a framework of discussion which departed from traditional lines. Experience has suggested that the conventional method of describing the "object of damages" in vague terms, and then jumping adroitly from the rules of remoteness to the "market rules" of the Sale of Goods Act leaves the reader both bewildered as to the relationship between the rules and uninformed on some of the important aspects of the assessment process.

Comments on developments occurring since the manuscript went to press can be briefly made. The decision of the Court of Appeal in *Jarvis* v. *Swans Tours, Ltd.* appears to have set a new trend for non-pecuniary damages in contractual actions and, as such, necessitated the rewriting of part of Chapter Eight. On the other hand *Lyndale Fashion Manufacturers* v. *Rich*, an important case on the incidence of tax liability, came too late to be accommodated in the text. Within the field of death and personal injuries the future holds some prospects of substantial reform. The Law Commission is expected to publish its report on this area in Summer 1973—the existing text contains references to and observations on its Published Working Paper No. 41—and it is clear from the statement made by the Prime Minister (H.C.Deb. Vol. 919, Col. 1127) that the terms of reference of the recently established Royal Commission on Compensation for Personal Injuries will include the question of quantification.

I have benefited from the valuable advice and criticism of many since I commenced work on this subject some five years ago. In particular, I wish to acknowledge my gratitude to Otto Kahn-Freund, who originally inspired my interest in it, to Stephen Desch, Michael Furmston, Edward Griew, Don Harris, Philip Lewis, Bernard Rudden and Guenter Treitel, who read and criticized various parts of the book; and to Dan Ellis who courageously read the whole work in proof. The Editor of the Modern Law Review has kindly given me permission to draw on material originally published in that journal. Butterworths have offered me guidance and encouragement and have spared me the task of preparing the index and tables.

A. I. OGUS

Mansfield College, Oxford
  March, 1973

Table of Contents

Table of Statutes

References in this Table to *"Statutes"* are to Halsbury's Statutes of England (Third Edition) showing the volume and page at which the annotated text of the Act will be found.

Table of Cases

In the following Table references are given where applicable to the English and Empire Digest where a digest of the case will be found.

A

PAGE

I

Table of Abbreviations

CHAPTER ONE

An Introduction to the Law of Damages

I DEFINITION AND SCOPE

1 Definition

For the purposes of this work, an award of damages is to be considered as the sum of money payable as compensation for an injury resulting from a tort or breach of contract.[1]

2 "Liability" and "Damages"

In any action for tort or breach of contract, the court may have to resolve a conflict on one or more of four different issues:

   (i) whether the defendant was in breach of contract or has committed a tort;

  (ii) whether the breach of contract or tort inflicted an injury on the plaintiff's person or property, or gave rise to a purely economic injury;

 (iii) the extent of the plaintiff's losses (pecuniary and non-pecuniary) consequent on his injury and whether such losses are recoverable at law;

 (iv) the amount of money to be paid as compensation for the legally recoverable pecuniary and non-pecuniary losses.

In broad terms it may be said that (i) and (ii) are issues of *"liability"* and therefore outside the *law of damages* which is concerned with (iii) and (iv). This is not a perfect classification.[2] Questions of "liability"

---

[1] Cf. *Halsbury's Laws of England*, Vol. 11, p. 216; McGregor, § 1; Walker, *Law of Damages in Scotland*, p. 1; and see PEARSON, J. in *Jabbour* v. *Custodian of Israel's Absentee's Property*, [1954] 1 W.L.R. 139, at p. 143–144.

[2] It differs from that usually adopted in the conflicts of law, which treats (iii) as an issue of liability. See, e.g. Cheshire, *Private International Law*, 8th Edn., pp. 680–684. For the purposes of a conflict of law situation this seems justifiable, for the object is to sever questions of "substantive law", to be governed by the *lex causae*, from questions of "procedural law", to be governed by the *lex fori*.

and "damages" cannot always be kept distinct[1]—in particular, where the tort or breach of contract gives rise to a purely economic injury, the division between (ii) and (iii) remains somewhat obscure. But, though sometimes imprecise, the distinction carries a force beyond that of a mere academic exercise. It reflects the difference between two major tasks of legal science. The first seeks to prescribe the quality of conduct necessary to make a man or an enterprise answerable for injuries caused. It must have recourse to a certain set of moral, economic and social factors. The second determines the extent of the injured party's redress, the types of loss which may properly be made the subject of an award, and the general level of compensation. The factors which influence the incidence of liability may be relevant here but more often different considerations prevail, notably those representing the economic standards of the community.[2]

II TERMINOLOGY

The failure of the law more clearly to delimit the various aspects of the compensation process has led to ambiguities in terminology. Two areas of confusion require immediate[3] attention.

1 "Damage" and "damages"

The terms "damage" and "damages" have suffered from loose usage. Some writers[4] and judges[5] have used them as if they were synonymous. But "damages" should connote the *sum of money payable by way of compensation* (issue (iv), *supra*), while the use of "damage" is best confined to instances where it refers to the *injury inflicted* by the tort or breach of contract (issue (ii), *supra*).[6] "Damage" has frequently been used to describe also the *losses for which compensation is payable* (issue (iii), *supra*). This, as will be seen,[7] has tended to blur the distinction between questions of liability and compensation, and in this book it has been sought to avoid this particular usage.

This distinction has no bearing on the internal law of damages, the principles of which, it is submitted, can more easily be understood within the framework proposed in the text.
   [1] McGregor, § 7; McCormick, § 1 and see further *infra*, pp. 61–62.
   [2] Atiyah, *Accidents, Compensation and the Law*, p. 520.
   [3] There are of course other problems of terminology but these will be dealt with as they arise in the course of exposition.
   [4] E.g. Jowitt, *Dictionary of English Law*, p. 563.
   [5] E.g. LORD SUMNER in *Weld-Blundell* v. *Stephens*, [1920] A.C. 956, at p. 983; LORD WRIGHT in *Liesbosch, Dredger* v. *Edison S.S.*, [1933] A.C. 449, at p. 469.
   [6] *Per* LORD DONOVAN, *Perestrello* v. *United Paint*, [1969] 1 W.L.R. 570, at p. 579.
   [7] *Infra*, p. 61.

2 "General" and "special"

The ambiguous use of "damage" and "damages" is partially responsible for the confusion created by the distinction between "general" and "special" damages.[1] Four different meanings require explanation.

(a) Actionability

Originally the distinction was between general damage and special damage and therefore referred to an issue of liability. To establish a cause of action in certain torts (e.g. negligence, slander, public nuisance) the plaintiff had to show that he had suffered an *injury* which resulted from the tort: he must prove "special damage". In contrast, he could successfully sue for breach of contract or a tort actionable *per se* without proof of injury; "general damage" was implied.[2]

(b) Remoteness

As will be seen,[3] in the classic case of *Hadley* v. *Baxendale*[4] a distinction was drawn between those losses which "arise naturally" from a breach of contract, and those which are incurred as a result of special or extraordinary circumstances. A plaintiff could recover damages for the latter only if the special circumstances had been communicated to the defendant. The distinction has sometimes been referred to in terms of "general damages" and "special damages".[5]

(c) Pleading

The same distinction between ordinary and extraordinary losses has been applied in quite a different context. It is a clear and convenient principle of procedural law that,

> "if a plaintiff has suffered damage of a kind which is not the necessary and immediate consequence of the wrongful act, he must warn the defendant in the pleadings that the compensation claimed will extend to this damage, thus showing the defendant the case he has to meet and assisting him in computing a payment into court."[6]

Not surprisingly, the terminology of "general" damage(s) and "special" damage(s) has been used to distinguish between those cases where the loss must be specifically pleaded, and those cases where it need not.[7]

---

[1] McGregor, § 16–20; Street, pp. 18–22; Jolowicz, [1960] C.L.J. 214.
[2] See BOWEN, L.J.'s judgment in *Ratcliffe* v. *Evans*, [1892] 2 Q.B. 524, at pp. 527–534.
[3] *Infra*, pp. 72–78.
[4] (1854), 9 Exch. 341.
[5] By e.g. LORD WRIGHT in *Monarch S.S.* v. *A/B Karlshamns Oljefabriker*, [1949] A.C. 196, at p. 221.
[6] *Per* LORD DONOVAN, *Perestrello* v. *United Paint, supra*, at p. 579.
[7] See, e.g. BOWEN, L.J. in *Ratcliffe* v. *Evans, supra*; LORD DUNEDIN in *The Susquehanna*, [1926] A.C. 655, at p. 661.

(d) Proof

Some losses are susceptible of exact quantification, for example, medical expenses or loss of earnings incurred up to the date of the trial. Compensation for such losses, known as "special damages", must be specifically pleaded and proved. Other losses either have no pecuniary equivalent, as, for example, pain and suffering, or their quantification involves a substantial amount of guesswork, as with future pecuniary losses. All these are treated as "general damages" and need not be specifically pleaded.

There will, inevitably, be some overlap between these four meanings. For example, what is regarded as a special loss for the purposes of the doctrine of remoteness may well have to be specifically pleaded. But there is a substantial difference between losses which are the "necessary and immediate consequences" of the tort or breach of contract and those which are capable of exact quantification.[1] The danger is that if these anomalies are not eliminated, the requirements of "special damage" falling within one of the four meanings will be applied to losses coming under the head of "special damage" in quite another context.

III HISTORY OF THE LAW OF DAMAGES[2]

Historically two themes have dominated the law of damages. In both cases evolution has been neither uniform nor complete.

1 Punishment or compensation?

In a legal system in which public wrongs are indistinguishable from private wrongs,[3] the distinction between "punishment" and "compensation" will hardly exist. In the earliest period of our legal history a sum was fixed for each category of injury[4] and the injured party was in no way entitled to plead his actual loss.[5] Indeed, it was probably not until the thirteenth century that the plaintiff could claim "mere damages", that is monetary compensation assessed by a jury independently of specific relief.[6] Even then, compensation in the modern sense was only one of several different purposes which the award might seek to achieve. It might represent the state's interest in punishing the

---

[1] See *Perestrello* v. *United Paint, supra.* Cf. in *British Transport Commission* v. *Gourley,* [1956] A.C. 185, at p. 206 LORD GODDARD seems to have been unaware of shifting from one meaning to another.

[2] Sedgwick, *Damages,* 9th Edn., Vol. 1, §§ 7–19; Washington (1931), 47 L.Q.R. 345, (1932), 48 L.Q.R. 90.

[3] Plucknett, *Concise History of the Common Law,* 5th Edn., pp. 421–423.

[4] Called the "bot" under Anglo-Saxon law. See *infra,* p. 206.

[5] Pollock and Maitland, *History of English Law,* 2nd Edn., Vol. II, pp. 458–460.

[6] *Ibid.,* at pp. 522–524.

wrongdoer;[1] it might seek to deter the plaintiff from taking the law into his own hands and wreaking private vengeance on the defendant.[2] The time came when the divorce between crime and tort was fully evident, but the ability to use damages in a civil action as a means of punishing the defendant lingered on. Within the wide ambit of the jury's discretion exercisable when damages were "at large", that is where an exact pecuniary loss was not claimed, there was ample room for a punitive element in the award. Indeed, in the eighteenth century, the power of the jury to express its view of the defendant's conduct by awarding large damages was regarded as a constitutional right.[3] In this overt form, generally referred to as *exemplary* damages, punishment as an element in damages survived until 1964 when its application was severely restricted by the House of Lords.[4] But punitive considerations have continued to infiltrate into the law of damages by more oblique methods. Under the law of defamation, there is no doubt that the judge or jury awarding damages may advert to the grossness of the defendant's conduct up to and during the trial.[5] In actions of deceit, it seems that the plaintiff may be awarded more because the defendant intended to inflict the harm.[6] The same influence may be traced in the view that each infringement of a patent is a "wrong" and the patentee may recover a sum of money for each such "wrong" independently of the loss actually sustained by him.[7] There is more than a hint of punishment in the leading cases which decided that an unconscious but severely injured plaintiff may recover large awards even though he cannot appreciate his loss.[8] Finally, in determining whether a plaintiff must set-off against his award those compensating advantages which resulted from the tort or breach of contract, the courts have sometimes adopted an argument that the wrongdoer should not be allowed to benefit from the conduct of a third party.[9] In 1956 the House of Lords firmly rejected this view and restated the basic principle of compensation,[10] but some

---

[1] E.g. under the Statute of Westminster the Second 1285 (c. 13) a false appellor would be "punished by Imprisonment and Restitution of Damages". Other provisions, e.g. c. 25–26, imposed a penalty of double damages.

[2] As late as 1814 a judge could say, "it goes to prevent the practice of duelling, if juries are permitted to punish insult by exemplary damages"; HEATH, J. in *Merest* v. *Harvey* (1814), 5 Taunt. 442, at p. 444.

[3] E.g. *Huckle* v. *Money* (1763), 2 Wils. 205, *infra*, p. 28.

[4] *Rookes* v. *Barnard*, [1964] A.C. 1129 affirmed in *Cassell & Co., Ltd.* v. *Broome*, [1972] A.C. 1027. See generally *infra*, pp. 30–34.

[5] *Infra*, p. 238.

[6] *Doyle* v. *Olby*, [1969] 2 Q.B. 158, *infra*, p. 71.

[7] *Per* FLETCHER MOULTON, L.J., *Meters* v. *Metropolitan Gas Meters, Ltd.* (1911), 28 R.P.C. 157, at p. 164, *infra*, p. 259.

[8] *Wise* v. *Kay*, [1962] 1 Q.B. 638; *West & Son* v. *Shephard*, [1964] A.C. 326; *infra*, pp. 210–211.

[9] *Infra*, pp. 223–225.

[10] *British Transport Commission* v. *Gourley*, [1956] A.C. 185, *infra*, p. 107.

fourteen years later, by holding that a pension benefit should be ignored, it seems to have reversed the swing of the pendulum away from compensation.[1]

2 Fact or law?

So long as the award of damages is regarded as a function of the jury, it is obvious that assessment is primarily a factual inquiry and there is little room for the operation of legal principles.   Indeed, the "law" emerging from the first four hundred years of damages awards in this country reveals little more than the circumstances in which a court might disturb a jury's assessment.   Until the fifteenth century, the only method of setting aside an award lay in the writ of attaint,[2] a procedure by which a grand jury of twenty-four knights was enjoined to review a verdict.   But this was hardly review in the modern sense.   The proceedings were in effect a prosecution of the first jury for perjury.   The grand jury was not a permanent body and could not be influenced by the view of the court.   It could not, it seems, *increase* the award, and, at least by the fifteenth century, the rule emerged that attaint would not lie if the amount awarded was within that claimed by the plaintiff.[3] The power of the court to upset awards was only slowly assumed.   Up to the eighteenth century there had to be something like misconduct on the part of the jury or some breach of procedural rules before interference was permitted.[4]   The position was changed by an important development which was completed in the middle of the eighteenth century: the crystallization of the rule that the jury must decide the case according to the evidence, not on the basis of their own knowledge.[5] Now the way was open for the court to order a new trial on the ground of erroneous assessment.   But one important limitation remained: for review to be available the loss pleaded by the plaintiff had to be certain, that is capable of exact pecuniary quantification.[6]   In practice this meant that there was some control over awards for breach of contract where the losses pleaded were often in an accountable form, but that in tort actions where damages were generally at large the award had to be "excessive and outrageous" before the court would order a new trial.[7]   The strictness of this test was at length diluted so that when we enter the modern era, the court may interfere where "having regard to

---

[1] *Parry* v. *Cleaver*, [1970] A.C. 1.
[2] Washington (1931), 47 L.Q.R. 345, at pp. 346–351.
[3] See, e.g. *Anon* (1580), Dyer 369a.
[4] Holdsworth, *H.E.L.*, Vol. I, pp. 225–226.
[5] See the study of Jenks in *Cambridge Legal Essays* (1926), pp. 191–205.
[6] *Wilford* v. *Berkeley* (1758), 1 Burr. 609.
[7] Per DE GREY, C.J., *Sharpe* v. *Brice* (1774), 2 Wm. Bl. 942, at p. 943.

all the circumstances of the case, the damages are so excessive that no twelve men could reasonably have given them".[1]

The law of damages as it is known today is a creature of judical practice over the last ninety or so years and has resulted from the joint effect of three developments.

(a) Usurpation of jury's role

Apart from defamation actions the jury has virtually disappeared from civil litigation. The position was reached by three steps. The first was the Common Law Procedure Act 1854 which permitted trial by judge alone, provided that the parties consented. Secondly, section 6 of the Administration of Justice (Miscellaneous Provisions) Act of 1933 gave a right to either party to claim a jury in actions for libel, slander, malicious prosecution, false imprisonment, seduction or breach of promise of marriage but in all other cases left the matter to the discretion of the court. The final development resulted from judicial interpretation. For several years it was assumed that the discretion conferred by the 1933 Act was absolute.[2] But the principle could not remain intact for long: either a litigant was to be allowed a jury whenever he claimed one, or the judiciary would evolve some criteria for deciding the point.[3] In practice, juries were granted only where special circumstances existed, for example where there was an acute conflict of evidence or the infliction of exceptionally severe injuries.[4] The practice was endorsed by a full Court of Appeal in *Ward* v. *James*.[5] It was also extended in two directions. Even in cases where the judge thought that the issue of *liability* should be tried by jury, he might order that the damages be assessed by judge alone.[6] Secondly, the Court of Appeal would not in future feel the same hesitation in disturbing a jury award.[7] As a result both of the directions issued and the general sentiments expressed, the jury has virtually disappeared from all but defamation actions.

(b) Elaboration of principles of assessment

The reason for the decline of the jury is not hard to find. Quite apart from questions of expense and delay, jury awards could be referable only to the broadest of general principles and were therefore completely unpredictable. A law of damages aimed at precise rules of

---

[1] *Per* LORD ESHER, M.R., *Praed* v. *Graham* (1890), 24 Q.B.D. 53, at p. 55.
[2] See, especially, *Hope* v. *Great Western Rail Co.*, [1937] 2 K.B. 130.
[3] Devlin, *Trial by Jury*, p. 181.
[4] *Sims* v. *William Howard*, [1964] 2 Q.B. 409.
[5] [1966] 1 Q.B. 273.
[6] *Ibid.*, at p. 303.
[7] *Ibid.*, at p. 301.

quantification could evolve only when the jury has been replaced as assessor. Judicial assessors or expert arbitrators would tend to calculate damages according to established practical guidelines. In time, these guidelines would evolve into rules of law.[1] Significantly it was in the Admiralty court where no jury sat that principles of quantification first emerged. From the middle of the nineteenth century maritime collisions provoked some careful and methodical analyses of losses and the methods of indemnifying them.[2] These judgments still form the basis for assessing damages in property injury cases.[3] Commercial cases were the next to free themselves from the arbitrariness of the jury, and, building on the structure of the "market rules" in the Sale of Goods Act 1893 (themselves the product of earlier case-law)[4] the courts sought to establish a body of rules at once uniform and comprehensive.[5] Retention of the jury meant that the law of damages for death and personal injuries was slower to develop. But since the Second World War a very large body of law has been created as a result of the efforts of the Court of Appeal to achieve uniformity and predictability in awards.[6] The rapid expansion of this area of law prompted the publication and republication of specialist monographs.[7]

In 1926 LORD SUMNER had said:

> "Damages may be a 'jury question', that is a question of fact for the jury, if there is one, but they must be measured under a proper direction, as to what the law requires. . . . The measure of damages ought never to be governed by mere rules of practice, nor can such rules override the principles of law on this subject."[8]

But not all judges have shared his view. On the one hand, there was, especially in contract, an almost exclusive preoccupation with the rules of remoteness. What is at most a vague guide to the boundaries of compensation came to be regarded as an omnipotent criterion, capable of solving all problems arising in the law of damages.[9] On the other

---

[1] *Per* LORD ESHER, M.R., *Joyner* v. *Weeks*, [1891] 2 Q.B. 31, at p. 43 and see *Ward* v. *James, supra, per* LORD DENNING, M.R., at p. 300.
[2] See, e.g. *The Hebe* (1847), 2 Wm. Rob. 530 and *The Northumbria* (1869), L.R. 3 A. & E. 6 and generally *infra*, pp. 124–127.
[3] Cf. *infra*, pp. 124–141.
[4] E.g. *Barrow* v. *Arnaud* (1846), 8 Q.B. 595.
[5] For what amount to almost encyclopaedic surveys of rules see, especially, the judgments of BAILHACHE, J. in *Melachrino* v. *Nickoll*, [1920] 1 K.B. 693, at pp. 696–699 and DEVLIN, J. in *Biggin & Co.* v. *Permanite*, [1951] 1 K.B. 422, at pp. 426–440.
[6] *Infra*, pp. 208–210.
[7] Kemp & Kemp, 1st Edn. 1954; Munkman, 1st Edn. 1956.
[8] *Admiralty Commissioners* v. *S.S. Chekiang*, [1926] A.C. 637, at p. 643.
[9] Street, pp. 236–237 and see VISCOUNT SANKEY in *Banco de Portugal* v. *Waterlow & Sons, Ltd.*, [1932] A.C. 452, at pp. 474–476; LORD WRIGHT in *Monarch S.S.* v. *A/B Karlshamns Oljefabriker*, [1949] A.C. 196, at p. 224; UPJOHN, L.J. in *Charterhouse Credit* v. *Tolly*, [1963] 2 Q.B. 683, at p. 712.

hand some judges were hesitant to particularize the rules governing quantification. As recently as 1963 UPJOHN, L.J. was moved to remark that "the assessment of damages has never been an exact science; it is essentially practical."[1] Yet these and other observations to the same effect[2] must be read in the light of the circumstances which provoked them. In a transitional stage, when some but not all the rules appropriate to a particular category of loss have been evolved a judge is sometimes faced with a principle, emanating from another decision, which clearly does not fit the circumstances of the case before him. In such a situation he may be tempted to react against the legal principles that do exist within the area in question and reach his conclusion according to instinct or "common sense". His proper task, however, should be the rationalization of the exception to the general rule, consistent with the ordinary principles of the law of damages.

(c) Quest for scientific precision

The final development is much more speculative and, for the most part, has taken place outside of the courts. The demand for greater precision in damages awards has attracted experts from other disciplines. Medical practitioners,[3] economists,[4] and actuaries[5] have impressed their learning on a legal world which, as yet, seems somewhat reluctant to listen to them[6]. Indeed, it may legitimately be argued that there are features in the process of quantification for which the lawyer's expertise is not well suited,[7] and that a more appropriate forum for expediting these problems would be a damages tribunal manned by a lawyer, an actuary, and, if a personal injuries case, a medical practitioner.[8] There is, however, one aspect of this matter which tends to be overlooked.[9]

---

[1] *Charterhouse Credit* v. *Tolly, ibid.*, at p. 711.
[2] E.g. *per* FLETCHER MOULTON, L.J., *Meters* v. *Metropolitan Meters* (1911), 28 R.P.C. 157, at p. 163; *per* VISCOUNT HALDANE, L.C., *British Westinghouse Electric and Manufacturing Co., Ltd.* v. *Underground Railways Co., of London, Ltd.*, [1912] A.C. 673, at pp. 688–689.
[3] Olender, [1962] Duke, L.J. 344 and the periodical literature cited there.
[4] Peck and Hopkins (1969), 44 Wash.L.R. 311; Leonard (1970), 31 Ohio S.L.J. 687.
[5] Prevett (1972), 35 M.L.R. 140, at p. 257 and *infra*, pp. 190–192.
[6] See especially *Mitchell* v. *Mulholland (No. 2)*, [1972] 1 Q.B. 65.
[7] In *The Greta Holme*, [1897] A.C. 596, at p. 604 LORD WATSON admitted to "a dislike, which I have reason to believe is shared by other judges, to the task of assessing damages".
[8] The Evershed Committee on Supreme Court Practice and Procedure Cmnd. 8878 (1953), paras. 366–368 and the Winn Committee on Personal Injury Litigation Cmnd. 3691 (1968), paras. 406–408 both rejected such a suggestion but W. Australia has set up a semi-lay tribunal to try motor accident claims: see Braybrooke (1967), 8 W. Aust. L.R. 204.
[9] But see SWINFEN EADY, J. in *Leeds Forge* v. *Deighton's Patent Flue* (1907), 25 R.P.C. 209, at p. 213 and WINN, L.J. in *Doyle* v. *Olby*, [1969] 2 Q.B. 158, at p. 169.

Accuracy and precision can generally only be bought at a price. A balance must be struck between the desire to achieve a high degree of precision in the assessment process and the expenditure of time and money.

IV FORM OF AWARD

Only one award of compensation can be recovered for each cause of action. Damages for all losses flowing from the tort or breach of contract must be assessed once for all in a lump sum. This proposition gives rise to four different principles.

1 No damages for losses arising from a cause of action on which judgment has already been given

The classic illustration is *Fitter* v. *Veal*.[1]

In an action for battery and assault P recovered £11 damages against D. His disabilities proved to be more serious than at first realized and an operation on his skull was carried out. It was held that he could not recover in a new action for this further loss.

The object of the rule is, of course, to prevent continual and vexatious litigation. But there are two exceptions.

(a) Different cause of action

The plaintiff may recover for his subsequent loss if he is able to ground the defendant's liability on a different cause of action. This will arise where the defendant has violated two separate legally protected interests. But what, for the purposes of this rule, are "separate interests" is difficult to define. Certain broad distinctions are clear. In *Gibbs* v. *Cruikshank*[2]

D entered P's land and wrongfully distrained his goods. In an action for replevin, P recovered £2 8s. 6d. In subsequent proceedings, P claimed further damages for (1) trespass to goods and (2) trespass to land. It was held that his claim for (1) was barred by the previous award for replevin—the cause of action was the same—but that damages could be awarded under (2): the action of replevin has "no relation to the trespass to land".[3]

Clearly there is one interest in goods and another in land, but this obviously sound approach hardly helps to explain the distinction in

---

[1] (1701), 12 Mod. Rep. 542.
[2] (1873), L.R. 8 C.P. 454.
[3] *Per* BOVILL, C.J., *ibid.*, at p. 460.

Ash v. *Hutchinson & Co. (Publishers), Ltd.*[1] where it was held that judgment in an action for infringement of copyright by authorizing the republication of the plaintiff's literary work was held to be no bar to a similar but subsequent action for infringement of copyright by actually reproducing the work. They were regarded as infringements of "distinct and separate rights".[2] It might be easier to accommodate this decision under the alternative proposition that two causes of action will arise on the separate violation of the same interest.[3] This explains why separate causes of action arise on successive publications of the same libel.[4]

(b) Continuing wrong

The rule does not apply to losses caused by a continuing breach of contract (e.g. the continued use of property for a purpose prohibited under a restrictive covenant) or a continuing tort (e.g. a trespasser remaining on the plaintiff's land). As regards breaches of contract and torts actionable *per se*, a fresh cause of action arises *de die in diem* until the unlawful activity ceases.[5] Where the tort is actionable only on proof of actual harm, a fresh cause of action will arise for every fresh incidence of harm.[6] The corollary to this exception is that in an action for a continuing wrong the plaintiff may recover compensation only for those losses accruing up to the date of judgment.[7] It follows also that in assessing the harm inflicted, the court is not entitled to take into account the risk of the injury exacerbating.[8]

2 The award must be in the form of a lump sum

English law, like all other common law systems except one,[9] has from the earliest times insisted that the award be in the form of a lump sum.[10] Unlike its counterpart in continental and socialist systems,[11] the court has no power to order a series of periodical payments.[12] Now

---

[1] [1936] Ch. 489.
[2] *Per* ROMER, L.J., *ibid.*, at p. 502.
[3] See *Darley Main Colliery* v. *Mitchell* (1886), 11 App. Cas. 127.
[4] *Associated Newspapers* v. *Dingle*, [1964] A.C. 371.
[5] See, e.g. *Cameron-Head* v. *Cameron*, 1919 S.C. 627 (contract); *Holmes* v. *Wilson* (1839), 10 Ad. & El. 503 (tort).
[6] *Crumbie* v. *Wallsend Local Board*, [1891] 1 Q.B. 503.
[7] *Battishall* v. *Reed* (1856), 18 C.B. 696 as modified by R.S.C. Ord. 37 r. 6.
[8] *West Leigh Colliery Co.* v. *Tunnicliffe*, [1908] A.C. 27.
[9] See Fleming (1969), 19 U. of Toronto L.J. 295; McGregor 11 I.E.C.L. 9–49 *et seq.*
[10] *Fournier* v. *Canadian National Rail Co.*, [1927] A.C. 167.
[11] Rudden (1967), 42 N.Y.U.L.R. 583, at pp. 610–612 and Fleming, *supra*, n. 9.
[12] There is a suggestion in *Metcalfe* v. *London Passenger Transport Board*, [1938] 2 All E.R. 352, at p. 355 that such a power may exist where the parties consent but it does not seem to have been adopted.

as compensation for most types of losses, the lump sum is without doubt the only appropriate form of award, but where the plaintiff claims for lost future income, as most notably in personal injury and fatal accident cases, the conclusion is not so obvious. Indeed in recent times there has developed a lively discussion as to whether, in these cases, the court should have power to award damages by way of periodical payments.[1] Arguments tend to focus on the following issues.

(a) Capitalism or paternalism

Some socialist systems have a strict rule forbidding the award of a lump sum for future lost income.[2] The objection is that it tends to encourage capitalism. At the other political extreme it will be argued that too tight a control of the plaintiff's compensation smacks of paternalism—that a man should be free to do what he likes with his damages.[3] Whichever ideological view is taken it must be recognized that by substituting periodical indemnities for lost income the periodical payment system comes closer to the fundamental principle of restoring to the plaintiff what he has lost.

(b) Long-term provision or dissipation

The opponents of the lump-sum advert to the risk of the plaintiff dissipating his award and having to fall back on social security. Further, it is argued, even the most prudent man may be caught out by unexpectedly high rates of inflation against which the lump sum award offers little protection.[4] The answer made to this is that the proper assessment of the lump sum should enable the plaintiff to protect himself: he can invest against inflation, or he can purchase a small business to mitigate his loss. The difficulty in evaluating the merits of these arguments is that there is hardly any empirical evidence on what successful plaintiffs do with their money and how quickly damages are spent.[5]

---

[1] The proposal was rejected by the Winn Committee, *supra*, n. 8, p. 9, paras. 374–377 and the provisional conclusions of the Law Commission (Working Paper No. 41 paras. 222–256) are the same. In 1971 LORD DIPLOCK moved an amendment to the Law Reform (Miscellaneous Provisions) Bill which would have empowered the court to order periodical payments to widows in Fatal Accident cases (H.L. Deb. Vol. 318, cols. 522–523). It was later withdrawn as the machinery to implement the reform was not available. See also, generally, Fleming, *supra*, n. 9, p. 11 and Samuels (1968), 17 I.C.L.Q. 443.

[2] Rudden, *supra*, n. 11, p. 11; Fleming, *supra*, n. 9, p. 11.

[3] See further *infra*, pp. 216–218.

[4] Cf. *infra*, pp. 192–193.

[5] A hint dropped by LORD PARKER, C.J. in 18 Current Legal Problems 1, at p. 5 suggests that the incidence of early dissipation is more serious than most assume.

(c) Finality or variability

The calculation of future losses in personal injury and fatal accident cases is notoriously haphazard. The judge must attempt to predict what the future holds on such matters as the plaintiff's physical condition, his health and happiness,[1] his employment potential,[2] the economic climate,[3] the pattern of taxation.[4] The plaintiff has no second chances; he may be subjected to a subsequent exacerbation of his loss against which the award can offer him no protection. A system of periodical payments could adapt the level of compensation to meet changed circumstances. It would not, of course, eliminate all instances of conjecture—the court would still have to predict what would have happened to the plaintiff if he had not been injured—but it would offer him security against unpredictable changes. Yet, it is urged, there are still some advantages to finality. Foreign experience shows that a plaintiff who knows that an improvement in his condition will lead to a fall in his payments does not recover rapidly.[5] This difficulty could be partially met by allowing only upward variations to be made. Then, it is said that if a widow's payments will cease on remarriage, she will be encouraged to "live in sin", and though the law might take cognizance of cohabitation, the methods of investigating this matter can, as social security practice has shown, be unsavoury. It is further claimed that the enforcement of periodical payment orders might create difficulties. The defendant might go bankrupt, go into liquidation or disappear. This contingency could be met by compelling the defendant to pay a lump sum into the court (which would then administer the periodical payments) and combine with it an insurance policy to cover the risks of any increases. Finally resort must be had to the relative cost of the two methods. Of course if the existing machinery for trying cases were to administer a periodical payments system it would be prohibitively expensive. The present writer's own view is that though, on balance, there seems to be a stronger case for the periodical payments system, it could only function economically if it were harnessed to new machinery for assessment. The concept of a "damages tribunal" referred to earlier[6] might provide the solution.

3 The award of damages must be unconditional

As a general principle the court cannot order that the damages be payable only on the occurrence of a certain event. Nor can it control

---

[1] *Infra*, p. 187.
[2] *Infra*, p. 188.
[3] *Infra*, p. 188.
[4] *Infra*, p. 111.
[5] Law Commission Working Paper no. 41, para. 238.
[6] *Supra*, p. 9.

what the plaintiff does with his money. In *Banbury* v. *Bank of Montreal*[1]

> The D Bank was held liable for negligently advising P to invest in certain securities. The jury found damages "for £25,000 and all securities to be returned to the defendant bank." On appeal D was held not liable but *obiter* the House of Lords observed that the jury (and therefore in appropriate cases the court) had no power to give such a verdict. An award must be final and unconditional.

To this principle there would appear to be three exceptions. First, where the successful plaintiff is under a disability (e.g. is an infant or insane), the court assumes control of the award.[2] Secondly, where the plaintiff is under a legal or perhaps moral obligation to indemnify a third party for assistance given the court has sometimes insisted that he hold part of the award for the benefit of the third party.[3] Thirdly, in an action for personal injuries or death the court may, under section 20 of the Administration of Justice Act 1969, make an order for the interim payment of damages.[4] This provision implemented a recommendation of the Winn Committee.[5] It was concerned with the plight of the plaintiff who sustains severe pecuniary losses but who must await the outcome of perhaps prolonged litigation before he receives any indemnity. The Law Commission has canvassed the possibility of an even more radical departure from the principle of unconditional awards. In personal injury cases where there is a possibility (but only a possibility) of a serious deterioration in the plaintiff's condition, it considers that the court should have power to make a provisional award. The award would be variable within a specified time limit to increase compensation should the misfortune occur.

4   Losses must be assessed as at the date of judgment

In *Philips* v. *Ward*,[6] DENNING, L.J. said "the general principle of English law is that damages must be assessed as at the date when the

---

[1] [1918] A.C. 626.

[2] R.S.C. Ord 80 r. 12.

[3] *Allen* v. *Waters*, [1935] 1 K.B. 200; *Dennis* v. *London Passenger Transport Board*, [1948] 1 All E.R. 779; *Schneider* v. *Eisovitch*, [1960] 2 Q.B. 430. See generally *infra*, pp. 175–177. Where as in the first and last of these cases, there is no contract between the plaintiff and the third party, the exact nature of the obligation to pay is questionable. Perhaps it is a constructive trust.

[4] The necessary conditions are that either (1) the defendant has admitted liability or (2) the plaintiff has obtained judgment for damages to be assessed or (3) if the action were to proceed to trial the plaintiff would succeed on liability without any reduction for contributory negligence: R.S.C. Ord. 29, r. 12.

[5] Cmnd. 3691 (1968), paras. 71–110.

[6] [1956] 1 W.L.R. 471, at p. 474. To the same effect see LAWSON, J. in *Clark* v. *Woor*, [1965] 1 W.L.R. 650, at p. 656 and Halsbury Vol. 11, p. 237.

damage occurs". This is, with respect, misleading. The true principle is that damages are assessed on the basis of the plaintiff's loss at the *date of judgment*.[1] This means that the trial judge can avail himself of evidence relating to any change in the plaintiff's position from the date of the injury to the date of judgment, including such factors as the death of a widow claiming under the Fatal Accidents Acts,[2] or a rise in wages[3] or in profits[4] that would have been earned but for the accident. There are three qualifications to the general principle. The first two ostensibly shift the time for assessment to the date of the injury and thus account for the dictum quoted at the head of this paragraph.

(a) Mitigation

Under the doctrine of mitigation a plaintiff must take reasonable steps to avoid the loss inflicted by the defendant's activity. Sometimes he will be expected to repair property which has been damaged or find a substitute for property which has not been delivered on the *date of the defendant's breach*. In such circumstances his measure of damages will be the cost of the repairs[5] and the cost of the substitute[6] respectively at that date. Subsequent variations in the cost will be ignored.[7]

(b) Damages or debt calculable in foreign currency

It is a rule of English law that damages or debt calculable in a foreign currency must be converted into English currency at the rate prevailing at the time of the breach of contract[8] or tort.[9] This is a special rule that it has been sought to justify in terms of the doctrine of remoteness[10]—it is the "foreseeable" loss—or the doctrine of certainty[11]—it is the only certain means of ascertaining the true loss. It would, however, seem to depend more on the now discredited (and somewhat ironical) assumption that while sterling remains stable other currencies tend to

---

[1] See among many other judicial statements Lord Macnaghten in *Bwllfa and Merthyr Dare Steam Collieries (1891), Ltd. v. Pontypridd Waterworks Co.*, [1903] A.C. 426, at p. 431.

[2] *Williamson v. Thorneycroft & Co., Ltd.*, [1940] 2 K.B. 658. Also the re-marriage of a widow (*Mead v. Clarke Chapman & Co.*, [1956] 1 All E.R. 44 though under s. 4(1) of Law Reform (Miscellaneous Provisions) Act 1971 this must now be ignored: *infra*, pp. 269–271.

[3] *The Swynfleet* (1941), 81 Ll.L.Rep. 116.

[4] *Bwllfa case, supra.*

[5] *Infra*, pp. 132–135.

[6] *Infra*, pp. 138–139.

[7] E.g. *Philips v. Ward, supra* and on the analogous problem in compulsory purchase compensation cases see *Birmingham Corporation v. West Midland Baptist (Trust) Association*, [1970] A.C. 874.

[8] *Di Ferdinando v. Simon Smits & Co.*, [1920] 3 K.B. 409.

[9] *S.S. Celia v. S.S. Volturno*, [1921] 2 A.C. 544; cf. *Suchcicka v. Grabowski* (1972), Sol. Jo. 58.

[10] *Ibid., per* LORD PARMOOR at pp. 559–560.

[11] *Ibid., per* LORD SUMNER at p. 558.

depreciate, and that therefore the plaintiff must be protected.[1] The rule is peculiar to the common law systems and has been severely criticized.[2]

(c) Changes subsequent to judgment

There are, finally, circumstances in which an appellate court will admit evidence of changes occurring since judgment by the court of first instance. Under the Rules of the Supreme Court,[3] the Court of Appeal[4] has the discretion to admit such evidence where "special grounds exist". It is, of course, a question of balancing the desire to do justice in the particular case with the need for finality and certainty. It is not surprising therefore that different views have been expressed as to where such special grounds exist and when the discretion is to be exercised.

(i) *Damages on wrong basis* In *Jenkins* v. *Richard Thomas and Baldwins*[5]

Damages were awarded to P, injured in an industrial accident, on the assumption that he would be employed as a grinder. After the trial it was found that he had no aptitude for the work and his earnings were thereby reduced. Evidence of this was admitted and damages increased. In the words of SALMON, L.J., "if the basis on which the damages have been assessed proves to be wrong very shortly after the trial and the point is promptly taken up with the other side, then, in the exceptional circumstances, there may be good grounds for this court giving leave . . . to call further evidence".[6]

(ii) *Basis of award falsified by defendant's conduct* Despite the caution evident in this dictum, it may still be too wide. In *Murphy* v. *Stone Wallwork*[7]

P recovered damages from Ds for personal injuries sustained while in their employment. Ds continued to employ P for some time after the accident but shortly after the case had been heard on appeal they dismissed him. The House of Lords admitted the evidence and the award was increased. Their Lordships tended to focus on the fact that here the basis of the award had been falsified by Ds' own conduct. As LORD PEARCE said, "to allow them to obtain an advantage from the assumption that their conduct (although not *mala fide*) induced and

---

[1] *Per* LORD DENNING, *Re United Railways of Havana and Regla Wharfhouses*, [1961] A.C. 1007, at p. 1069.
[2] Mann, *The Legal Aspect of Money*, 3rd Edn., Chap. 10.
[3] Ord. 59, r. 10.
[4] The rule is applied by analogy to appeals to the House of Lords: *Murphy* v. *Stone Wallwork*, [1969] 2 All E.R. 949.
[5] [1966] 1 W.L.R. 476.
[6] *Ibid.*, at p. 479.
[7] [1969] 2 All E.R. 949.

then falsified would be inequitable."[1] This was the exceptional circumstance which was necessary for the court to exercise its discretion and admit further evidence. At least one judge[2] doubted whether such circumstances had existed in *Jenkins'* case.

(iii) *No precise formula* In its latest pronouncement on the matter[3] the House of Lords while confirming the approach taken in *Murphy* began to doubt the value of formulating a precise criterion on which the court should exercise its discretion to admit further evidence.[4] LORD WILBERFORCE, however, was prepared to lay down some guidelines:

"Negatively, fresh evidence ought not to be admitted when it bears upon matters falling within the field or area of uncertainty, in which the trial judge's estimate has previously been made. Positively, it may be admitted if some basic assumptions, common to both sides, have clearly been falsified by subsequent events, particularly if this has happened by the act of the defendant. Positively, too, it may be expected that courts will allow fresh evidence where to refuse it would affront common sense, or a sense of justice. All these are only non-exhaustive indications. . . ."[5]

It would appear that this dictum, combining the flexibility of *Jenkins* with the hesitancy of *Murphy*, now represents the law on this subject.

V THE OBJECT OF DAMAGES—THE FUNDAMENTAL PRINCIPLE OF COMPENSATION

1 General

The underlying theme of damages, the fundamental object of an award, has been restated many times:

"It is well settled that the governing purpose of damages is to put the party whose rights have been violated in the same position, so far as money can do so, as if his rights had been observed."[6]

If this principle is applied to actions in tort, the object becomes: to put the plaintiff in the position he would have been in if the tort had not been committed—the *restitutio in integrum* doctrine.[7] In actions

---

[1] [1969] 2 All E.R. 949, at p. 954.
[2] LORD UPJOHN at p. 956. See also LORD PEARCE at p. 953 and LORD PEARSON at p. 960.
[3] *Mulholland* v. *Mitchell*, [1971] A.C. 666.
[4] *Ibid., per* LORD HODSON at p. 676, *per* LORD WILBERFORCE at p. 679.
[5] *Ibid.*, at pp. 679–680.
[6] *Per* ASQUITH, L.J., *Victoria Laundry (Windsor), Ltd.* v. *Newman Industries, Ltd.*, [1949] 2 K.B. 528, at p. 539.
[7] E.g. *per* LORD WRIGHT, *Liesbosch, Dredger* v. *Edison S.S.*, [1933] A.C. 449, at p. 459.

for breach of contract, the prima facie[1] object is to put the plaintiff in the position he would have been in if the contract had been satisfactorily performed.[2]

2   Types of compensation

The varying types of compensation can be classified according to the nature of the loss pleaded and whether the claim is in tort or contract.

(a)   Tort

Three categories may be distinguished:

(i) *Positive Losses*, compensation for the extent to which existing assets have been diminished by expenses incurred or a change of position;

(ii) *Consequential losses*, compensation for being deprived of the advantages, profits and earnings which would have accrued to the plaintiff if the tort had not been committed;

(iii) *Non-pecuniary losses*, compensation for the loss of such assets as have no pecuniary equivalent or market "value": human happiness and sentiment.

(b)   Breach of contract

The distinction between the object of tort damages and that of contract damages has already been drawn. In consequence the various types of compensation for breach of contract are best viewed within a different conceptual framework:

(i) *Expectation interest award*, compensation for the loss of the benefits which would have accrued to the plaintiff if the contract had been satisfactorily performed;

(ii) *Reliance interest award*, compensation for the wasted expenditure incurred by the plaintiff in reliance on the defendant's promise to perform;

(iii) *Indemnity interest award*, compensation for the diminution in the plaintiff's existing assets (cf. positive losses in tort, *supra*);

---

[1] The plaintiff may, it seems, opt for a measure of damages which seeks to put him in the position he would have been if he had not made a contract with the defendant: *Anglia Television, Ltd.* v. *Reed*, [1972] 1 Q.B. 60. This and the relationship between the tort and contract measure are fully discussed *infra*, pp. 283–288.

[2] *Per* PARKE, B., *Robinson* v. *Harman* (1848), 1 Ex. 850.

(iv) *Restitution interest award,* restitution[1] of any benefits conferred by the plaintiff on the defendant in reliance on the defendant's promise to perform.

This classification and the relationship between the various interests will be explained at greater length in the chapters on contract damages.[2]

3 Qualifications to the fundamental principle of compensation

The principle of compensation is the beginning rather than the end of the assessment process. It is subject to a number of qualifications.

(a) Literal restitution impossible

Most obviously *restitutio in integrum* in a literal sense cannot be applied to non-pecuniary losses.[3] The lost years of life, a severed limb, the shattered remains of a unique vase, none of these can be restored. No amount of money can transform a "thalidomide" invalid into a healthy individual.[4] In such situations, "compensation" must be understood in a different sense.[5] Its object becomes rather to provide the plaintiff with some alternative form of happiness, or solace for his misfortunes.[6] For certain forms of pecuniary loss exact restitution is equally impossible. A capital sum, for example, represents only the approximate present value of future, and therefore necessarily uncertain, lost income.[7] Even where, as in the case of a damaged chattel, restitution is possible, the court may decide that in the circumstances it would be impracticable or unreasonable and instead award damages based on the "diminished value" of the asset.[8]

(b) Limiting doctrines

The principle of compensation is itself qualified by a number of doctrines which operate to limit the amount payable. A plaintiff may

---

[1] Usually by an action in quasi-contract and thus not strictly an award of damages: *infra*, pp. 367–370.

[2] *Infra*, Chaps. 8–9.

[3] *Per* EARL JOWITT, *British Transport Commission* v. *Gourley*, [1956] A.C. 185, at p. 197; *per* LORD MORRIS, *West & Son* v. *Shephard*, [1964] A.C. 326, at p. 346 and *Parry* v. *Cleaver*, [1970] A.C. 1, at p. 22.

[4] Cf. *S.* v. *Distillers Co.*, [1969] 3 All E.R. 1412.

[5] *Per* LORD GODDARD, *British Transport Commission* v. *Gourley*, *supra*, at p. 208; *per* LORD DENNING, M.R., *Fletcher* v. *Autocar and Transporters*, [1968] 2 Q.B. 322, at pp. 335–336.

[6] *Per* HARMAN, L.J., *Warren* v. *King*, [1964] 1 W.L.R. 1, at p. 10, and see Ogus (1972), 35 M.L.R. 1. German law has the word "*Ausgleichsfunktion*" to express this type of compensation: McGregor 11 I.E.C.L. 9–13.

[7] *Infra*, pp. 182–185.

[8] For tort, see *infra*, pp. 131–133 and for contract *infra*, pp. 335–337.

not recover compensation for a loss which was not, legally, caused by the defendant's tort or breach of contract, or which was too remote, or which could reasonably have been avoided. Damages may have to be reduced because the loss was uncertain, or because the plaintiff has enjoyed the benefit of a compensating advantage. These doctrines will form the subject-matter of Chapter Three.

(c) Non-compensatory awards

There are four types of award which ostensibly are not based on the compensatory principle: nominal, contemptuous, exemplary and liquidated damages. These will be examined in Chapter Two. In fact, as will be seen, the only genuine exception to the compensatory principle lies in the court's power to award exemplary damages and this has been severely limited by recent decisions of the House of Lords.[1]

---

[1] *Rookes* v. *Barnard*, [1964] A.C. 1129; *Cassell & Co., Ltd.* v. *Broome*, [1972] A.C. 1027.

CHAPTER TWO

Non-Compensatory Damages

I INTRODUCTION

In the first chapter, it was stated that the primary function of an award of damages is to compensate the plaintiff for the loss he has suffered.[1] In subsequent chapters we shall see how the courts have allowed certain non-compensatory elements to creep in behind the façade of the compensatory principle.[2] In this chapter, we shall consider those situations in which the quantification of the award is explicitly not based on compensation, in which the law of damages has sought to achieve other ends.

Yet even in these situations the courts have been wary of straying too far from the well-defined path of compensation. Of the types of awards now to be discussed, only one, exemplary damages, constitutes a true exception, and its scope has been much restricted during recent years.[3] A case for nominal or contemptuous damages arises only when the plaintiff has suffered no loss for which he can be compensated. In the remaining categories, in which the quantum of damages has been fixed by the contracting parties, the agreed sum will, in general, only be upheld where it constitutes a genuine pre-estimate of the compensation necessary to satisfy the expected loss. We may, indeed, legitimately find in the cases "a progression which should lead to the early total acceptance of the principle of compensation over the whole range of the law of damages".[4]

---

[1] *Supra*, p. 18.
[2] E.g. (a) collateral benefits, *infra*, pp. 225–230; (b) personal injuries *infra*, pp. 213–215; and see, generally McGregor (1965), 28 M.L.R. 629.
[3] *Rookes* v. *Barnard*, [1964] A.C. 1129, *Cassell & Co., Ltd.* v. *Broome*, [1972] A.C. 1027.
[4] McGregor, *loc. cit.*, at p. 653.

II NOMINAL DAMAGES

1 Nature and definition

Nominal damages have been defined as "a trivial sum of money awarded to a litigant who has established a cause of action but has not established that he is entitled to compensatory damages".[1] In most cases, to establish a cause of action, the plaintiff must prove not only that the defendant was under an obligation towards him, and was in breach of that obligation, but also that he (the plaintiff) had sustained some loss as a result of the breach. In a limited number of cases, however, he need not prove loss. His right of action accrues on the mere breach of obligation: it is actionable *per se.* "So a man shall have an action against another for riding over his ground, though it do him no damage; for it is an invasion of his property and the other has no right to come there."[2]

At common law there was, effectively, only one judical remedy for the breach of an obligation: an action for damages.[3] In all cases of tort and contract, therefore, even where the cause was actionable without proof of the actual loss, the court's only method of recording the plaintiff's success was to award him damages. If the claim was actionable *per se* and the plaintiff had suffered no loss, he would be awarded nominal damages, a token sum, which has varied in size,[4] but is now generally £2.[5] This is not, it may be emphasized a case of damages being quantified on a non-compensatory principle, but a method of recording a verdict where no compensation is required.

2 Cases giving rise to nominal damages

(a) Torts actionable per se

Nominal damages will be awarded against a defendant who has committed a tort actionable *per se*, where loss to the plaintiff is neither proved nor presumed. There are, thus, two conditions to be satisfied.

(i) *The tort in question must be actionable* per se It is difficult to find the common feature which distinguishes these from other torts. Viewed historically, they mostly emerged earlier than those torts in which

---

[1] U.S. Restatement of Law of Torts, § 907.

[2] *Per* HOLT, C.J., *Ashby* v. *White* (1703), 2 Ld. Raym. 938, at p. 955.

[3] The recovery of possession in ejectment and detinue was more proprietary than delictual. See Pollock, *The Law of Torts*, 9th Edn., p. 184.

[4] Sixpence, *Feize* v. *Thompson* (1808), 1 Taunt. 121; one shilling, *Sapwell* v. *Bas*, [1910] 2 K.B. 486; cf. five guineas, *Constantine* v. *Imperial Hotels, Ltd.*, [1944] 1 K.B. 693 criticized *infra*, p. 23.

[5] E.g. *Sykes* v. *Midland Bank Executor and Trustee Co., Ltd.*, [1971] 1 Q.B. 113, cf. the award of £1 in *Boaks* v. *Associated Newspapers* (1967), 111 Sol. Jo. 703.

damage is the gist of the action, and thus at a time when it was the wrongfulness of the defendant's conduct and the desire to prevent retaliation which prompted the law's intervention.[1] As a poor generalization it may be said that they all involve a direct interference with the personal or proprietary security of the plaintiff. The following are generally held to fall within the category: trespass to person, goods or land, defamation,[2] malicious prosecution, interference with contract, and interference with intangible interests such as trade marks, or copyright.

(ii) *Loss to the plaintiff must be neither proved nor presumed* When suing for a tort actionable *per se*, the plaintiff may, of course, offer proof of actual loss, and for such loss he will recover substantial damages. But even if he is unable to prove actual loss, the plaintiff's award is not necessarily restricted to nominal damages, for he will receive substantial damages for any loss which the court presumes to flow from the tort. Damages for torts actionable *per se* are said to be "at large", that is to say the court, taking all the relevant circumstances into account, will reach an intuitive assessment of the loss which it considers the plaintiff has sustained. Thus in cases of libel, the jury awards a sum to compensate the loss to the plaintiff's reputation which it presumes he has sustained as a result of the defamatory statement. Only where the court considers that the plaintiff has suffered no loss, will it award him nominal damages. Cases are infrequent, but *Constantine* v. *Imperial Hotels, Ltd.*[3] is an example. The plaintiff, the famous West Indian cricketer, had been refused accommodation at the defendant's hotel. He successfully alleged that the defendants were in breach of the duty which they owed as innkeepers to receive and lodge travellers: an old tort, actionable *per se*. Because he had shown no actual loss, the plaintiff recovered only nominal damages. But the decision has been rightly criticized on the ground that damages were "at large" and the court should have presumed some loss to the plaintiff, if only as a result of his unjustifiable humiliation and distress.[4]

(b) Breach of contract

A case for nominal damages arises on a breach of contract where loss to the plaintiff is neither proved nor presumed. Breach of contract is similar to torts actionable *per se* in that, to establish a cause of action, the plaintiff need not show actual loss. It is different from those torts

---

[1] See Fleming, *Introduction to the Law of Torts*, pp. 22–23.
[2] But as regards slander only those four categories which are actionable *per se*.
[3] [1944] K.B. 693.
[4] *Street*, p. 16.

in that, in general, the courts do not presume any loss to flow from the breach. This may be explained by the fact that a contract usually involves a transaction for pecuniary advantage and the breach of it is therefore likely to produce only pecuniary loss. There are, however, exceptional situations in which damages are "at large". The nature of certain types of contract is such that breach will result in a loss of reputation rather than a definite pecuniary loss. Judical authority sanctioned substantial compensation on this basis in three situations:

    (i) where the defendant was in breach of a promise to marry,[1] but the action has since been abolished by statute.[2]

    (ii) where a banker dishonoured a trading customer's cheque.[3]

    (iii) where an artist or author was prevented from appearing in an engagement,[4] or from publishing his works.[5]

If the plaintiff cannot prove actual loss, and fails to bring his case within these three exceptional categories, he will be restricted to an award of nominal damages.[6]

3   The functions of nominal damages

Traditionally, two practical functions are claimed for an award of nominal damages:[7] it may serve as a declaration of a legal right, or as a justification for an order on costs.

(a)   Declaration of legal right

As has already been mentioned,[8] at one time an award of nominal damages was the only means a court of law had of recording a verdict for the plaintiff whose right had been infringed, but who had sustained no actual loss. Given this fact, nominal damages were more than useful —they were necessary.[9] Today, the courts have more effective remedies at their disposal to perform this function, in particular the injunction,[10]

---

[1] *Smith* v. *Woodfine* (1857), 1 C.B. N.S. 660.
[2] Law Reform (Miscellaneous Provisions) Act 1970, s. 1.
[3] *Rolin* v. *Steward* (1854), 14 C.B. 595; *Wilson* v. *United Counties Bank*, [1920] A.C. 102, cf. where the customer is not a trader, the loss is not presumed: *Gibbons* v. *Westminster Bank*, [1939] 2 K.B. 882.
[4] *Herbert Clayton and Jack Waller, Ltd.* v. *Oliver*, [1930] A.C. 209.
[5] *Joseph* v. *National Magazine Co.*, [1959] Ch. 14.
[6] *Groom* v. *Crocker*, [1939] 1 K.B. 194.
[7] McGregor, §§ 297–299.
[8] *Supra*, p. 22.
[9] *Pindar* v. *Wadsworth* (1802), 2 East 154: commoner successfully brings action on case for injury done to common although his own loss was minimal. "If a commoner could not maintain an action for injury of this sort, a mere wrong-doer might by repeated torts in course of time establish evidence of a right of common." *Per* GROSE, J., at p. 162.
[10] See Keeton & Sheridan, *Equity*, Chap. 17.

and the ever-expanding declaratory judgment.[1] Yet there is one situation in which an award of nominal damages would appear still to be expedient. At the commencement of an action, the plaintiff (or his counsel) may feel that he has some hope of obtaining substantial damages, but that his chance of succeeding is not very great. He would be unduly prejudiced if he were forced to choose between applying for a declaration of right (thereby waiving his claim for substantial damages) and pursuing his claim for substantial damages with the risk that if he failed to make out his case, he would be deprived of a verdict, and also costs. Nominal damages seem, therefore, to be justified where the plaintiff has established a cause of action and *bona fide* has sought substantial compensation, though without success.

(b) Justification for an order on costs

"A mere peg on which to hang costs"[2] is the classic description of the alleged second function of nominal damages. Even though the plaintiff is unable to prove actual loss, he may wish to force the action to a successful conclusion so that he may recover his costs from the defendant. It may however be doubted whether the value of this function survives closer examination. Costs are at the discretion of the court.[3] In general they will be awarded to the "successful" plaintiff,[4] but the court may not regard the plaintiff who obtains nominal damages as "successful". As DEVLIN, J. has remarked[5]

> "I do not think that a plaintiff who recovers nominal damages ought necessarily to be regarded in the ordinary sense of the word as a 'successful' plaintiff. In certain cases he may be, e.g. where part of the object of the action is to establish a legal right, wholly irrespective of whether any substantial remedy is obtained."

An honest endeavour to establish or confirm a legal right may be rewarded by an order on costs, but such a favourable conclusion will not be reached if the plaintiff has prolonged his cause merely to recover costs. It is therefore evident that an order on costs cannot stand as an independent justification for nominal damages. Costs will be awarded only if, and to the extent that, nominal damages serves its primary function, namely as a declaration of a legal right. In short, an order on costs results from rather than accounts for nominal damages.

---

[1] See Zamir, *The Declaratory Judgment.*
[2] *Per* MAULE, J., *Beaumont* v. *Greathead* (1846), 2 C.B. 494, at p. 499.
[3] Supreme Court of Judicature (Consolidation) Act 1925, s. 50.
[4] *Cooper* v. *Whittingham* (1880), 15 Ch. D. 501.
[5] *Anglo-Cyprian Trade Agencies* v. *Paphos Wine Industries*, [1951] 1 All E.R. 873, at p. 874.

III CONTEMPTUOUS DAMAGES

1 General

Where damages are "at large", and the plaintiff has suffered no loss,
he may be awarded a derisory sum, usually a halfpenny.[1] This is
generally referred to as "contemptuous damages". The award indicates
that though the plaintiff is strictly entitled to a verdict, not only has he
suffered no loss, but in the opinion of the court he ought not to have
brought an action at all: he has won the case on a technical point, but
the moral victory lies with the defendant. The use of the terms "moral"
and "technical" begs many questions. Perhaps it would be exaggerated
to see this appeal to a "morality" above the law as a potential threat to
a man's expectation that his legal rights will be protected by the law.[2]
But the fact that a plaintiff, entitled only to contemptuous damages, will
invariably be deprived of costs,[3] and, in exceptional cases, may even
have to pay those of the defendant,[4] emphasizes the crucial impact that
this award has on the plaintiff's rights. It also suggests that clearer
directions as to the incidence and limits of contemptuous damages
would be desirable.

2 Scope of the award

Indeed, judicial discussion of the topic is scanty. The following
principles, drawn from the authorities, leave many questions as to the
scope of the award unanswered.

(a) In practice, contemptuous damages are awarded only by juries.[5]

---

[1] The minimum legal tender, thus formerly a farthing. In *Marsham* v. *Buller*
(1618), 2 Roll. Rep. 21, the jury awarded half a farthing. Counsel for the defendant claimed there was no such coin. DODERIDGE, J. replied: "Vestre purse est
plein, mes si vous estes al Oxon vous aves un draught de beer pur half a farthing."
[2] "A law which actually exists, is a law, though we happen to dislike it . . ."
Austin, *Province of Jurisprudence Determined*, p. 184; see also Hart, *Positivism
and the Separation of Law and Morals* (1958), 71 Harv. L.R. 593.
[3] *Martin* v. *Benson*, [1927] 1 K.B. 771. In prolonged defamation cases, the
costs may be exceptionally heavy. Thus in *Dering* v. *Uris*, the plaintiff was
awarded ½d. damages, but had to pay all his own costs and those of the defendant after he had rejected the payment into court of 40s. His total loss was
about £20,000. (1964), *Times*, 7 May.
[4] *Per* PHILLIMORE, J. *Red Man's Syndicate* v. *Associated Newspapers, Ltd.*
(1910), 26 T.L.R. 394, at p. 395.
[5] A dubious exception is *Gamble* v. *Sales* (1920), 36 T.L.R. 427. DARLING, J.
in a breach of promise to marry case awarded ¼d. where, because of the state
of the defendant's health, he considered that "marriages of this kind" were to
be discouraged and that the plaintiff had lost "nothing of value."

In modern times, they have therefore had their most frequent application in actions for defamation.[1]

(b) In directing the jury, the trial judge should not suggest that only a token sum should be awarded.[2] It is always a question for the jury, taking the plaintiff's own conduct into account, what amount of compensation is appropriate, and the court should be slow to interfere with its verdict.[3]

(c) The court may, however, interfere if it is evident that the jury's verdict was a compromise: that is, they preferred not to reach a definite conclusion on the defendant's liability, and so to find for the plaintiff, but to award him only contemptuous damages.[4]

(d) The court may, apart from this, only interfere if it considers that the amount assessed was so small that twelve reasonable jurors could not have reached it.[5]

3 The compensatory principle

Although for the sake of convenience the award of contemptuous damages has been included in a chapter concerned with non-compensatory damages, it should be noted that it can be regarded simply as an application of the fundamental principle of compensation. The derisory sum is, in the eyes of the jury, the amount appropriate to compensate the plaintiff. Since he has won his case, he is entitled to an award of damages, but the value of his success is next to nothing.

IV EXEMPLARY DAMAGES

Undoubtedly the class of damages which is most clearly based on a non-compensatory principle is that of exemplary damages.[6] The

---

[1] In *Armytage* v. *Haley* (1843), 4 Q.B. 917, at p. 918 LORD DENHAM, C.J. considered the award inappropriate to negligence; and if the tort involves a loss of liberty contemptuous damages will not be awarded: *Pike* v. *Waldrum and Steam Navigation Co.*, [1952] 1 Lloyd's Rep. 431, at p. 455.

[2] *English and Scottish Co-operative Properties Mortgage and Investment Society, Ltd.* v. *Odhams Press*, [1940] 1 K.B. 440.

[3] *Kelly* v. *Sherlock* (1866), L.R. 1 Q.B. 686.

[4] *Per* BLACKBURN, J., *Kelly* v. *Sherlock, ibid.*, at pp. 697–698; *Falvey* v. *Stanford* (1874), L.R. 10 Q.B. 54.

[5] *English and Scottish Co-operative Properties Mortgage and Investment Society, Ltd.* v. *Odhams Press*, [1940] 1 K.B. 440.

[6] The expression is to be preferred to the alternatives "punitive" or "vindictive" damages; *per* LORD HAILSHAM, L.C., *Cassell & Co., Ltd.* v. *Broome*, [1972] A.C. 1027, at p. 1073.

explicit object of the award is to punish and deter the defendant.
Where his wrong has been committed "with the utmost degree of
malice or vindictively, arrogantly or high-handedly",[1] then, within the
limits laid down by LORD DEVLIN in *Rookes* v. *Barnard*,[2] damages in
excess of the sum required to compensate the plaintiff may be awarded.
An understanding of the historical development of the subject is
essential.

1   Historical development

(a)   Origins of award

The early confusion between compensation and punishment has
already been described.[3]   Large awards of damages in a civil process
were regularly employed to punish or deter wrongful conduct.[4]   In the
eighteenth century, exemplary damages were used to defend the liberty
of the subject against arbitrary or unconstitutional government activities.

In *Huckle* v. *Money*[5]

> P was held for six hours by a King's Messenger on suspicion of having
> printed the North Briton.   He suffered no physical injury and very
> little pecuniary loss, but in an action for false imprisonment, he was
> awarded £300 by the jury.   The Court of Common Pleas refused to
> interfere.

PRATT, C.J. was vehement in his defence of the award: the jury

> "saw a magistrate . . . exercising arbitrary power, violating Magna
> Carta, and attempting to destroy the liberty of the kingdom, . . . they
> heard the King's Counsel, and saw the solicitor of the Treasury
> endeavouring to support and maintain the legality of the warrant in a
> tyrannical and severe manner.   These are the ideas which struck the
> jury on the trial; and I think they have done right in giving exemplary
> damages."[6]

The ambit of the award was subsequently expanded to include other
cases of wanton interference with the plaintiff's rights: seduction,[7]

---

[1] Per TAYLOR, J., *Uren* v. *John Fairfax & Sons Pty., Ltd.* (1966), 117 C.L.R.
118, at p. 129.
[2] [1964] A.C. 1129, at pp. 1220–1239.
[3] *Supra*, pp. 4–5.
[4] Especially in the Star Chamber with the object of suppressing duelling:
see Holdsworth, *H.E.L.*, vol. 5, pp. 209–212.
[5] (1763), 2 Wils. 205.
[6] *Ibid.*, at p. 207.
[7] *Tullidge* v. *Wade* (1769), 3 Wils. 18, at p. 19.

assault[1] and trespass to land.   A colourful and typical illustration of the last head occurred in *Merest v. Harvey*.[2]

> D, inebriated, entered P's land, demanding to be allowed to join P's shooting party.   P declined to invite him.   D became incensed, hurled abusive language, fired several shots at birds on P's estate, and threatened in his capacity as magistrate to commit P.   It was held that the jury's award of £500 was not excessive.

GIBBS, C.J. commented:

> "I wish to know in a case where a man disregards every principle which actuates the conduct of a gentleman, what is to restrain him except large damages?"[3]

(b) Doctrine doubted

In the present century, doubts began to be expressed as to the scope and function of exemplary damages.[4]   In two important cases, the courts showed themselves unwilling to extend the boundaries of the award to actions in contract[5] or for adultery.[6]   Yet in others, judges continued to exploit the doctrine.[7]   Further doubt was engendered by the confusion between "exemplary" and "aggravated" damages.[8]   For a long time, the common law had recognized that actual loss to the plaintiff might be aggravated by the defendant's aggressive or malicious conduct on the ground that it injured the plaintiff's pride or dignity.   The law would, in short, compensate the plaintiff for his justifiable humiliation.[9] To the extent that damages are awarded on this basis they are, of course, compensatory and not punitive.   But since both exemplary and aggravated damages are dependent on the defendant's conduct,[10] the line between them is sometimes difficult to draw, and a reading of

---

[1] *Loudon v. Ryder*, [1953] 2 Q.B. 202.
[2] (1814), 5 Taunt. 442.
[3] *Ibid.*, at p. 443.
[4] See, e.g. Willis (1909), 22 Harv. L.R. 419.
[5] *Addis v. Gramophone Co.*, [1909] A.C. 488.   The anomalous exception was breach of promise of marriage but the action has now been abolished (*supra*, n. 2, p. 24).
[6] *Butterworth v. Butterworth and Englefield*, [1920] P. 126.   This action too has been abolished: Law Reform (Miscellaneous Provisions) Act 1970, s. 4.
[7] It was applied by analogy to trespass to goods (*Owen and Smith v. Reo Motors* (1934), 151 L.T. 274) and breach of copyright (*Williams v. Settle*, [1960] 1 W.L.R. 1072).
[8] Prior to 1964 there was an "extraordinary confusion of terminology reflecting differences in thinking and principle": *per* LORD HAILSHAM, L.C. *Cassell & Co., Ltd. v. Broome*, [1972] A.C. 1027, at p. 1069.
[9] For a full account of this head of damages see *infra*, pp. 237–238.
[10] Aggravated damages are awarded for the plaintiff's *reaction* to the defendant's conduct, but to determine whether or not this reaction was justifiable the court must, of course, consider the nature of the conduct.

the early cases does not clearly reveal which was the subject of the award.[1]

(c)   Rookes v. Barnard

It was against this background that in *Rookes* v. *Barnard*[2] LORD DEVLIN, with the concurrence of other members of the House of Lords, re-examined the whole doctrine of exemplary damages. In general the doctrine was objectionable in that it confused the civil and criminal functions of the law,[3] thereby depriving the defendant of the protection bestowed on him by the criminal law.[4] Many of the previous decisions apparently authorizing the award of exemplary damages could be construed as cases of aggravated damages.[5] Nevertheless the doctrine could not be totally renounced "without a complete disregard of precedent, and indeed of statute."[6] There were three cases alone in which, in accordance with authority and policy, the award of exemplary damages might be justified: (1) where government servants had been guilty of "oppressive, arbitrary or unconstitutional action"; (2) where "the defendant's conduct had been calculated by him to make a profit for himself which may well exceed the compensation payable to the plaintiff"; and (3) where such an award was sanctioned by statute.[7] Further, where exemplary damages are awarded, three considerations were to be borne in mind:[8] (1) the plaintiff cannot recover exemplary damages unless he was the victim of punishable behaviour; (2) restraint is to be exercised, for an award of exemplary damages can be used as a weapon both for and against liberty; (3) the means of the parties, while irrelevant in the assessment of compensation, are relevant to the award of exemplary damages.

(d)   Reception of Rookes v. Barnard

Until the remarkable decision of the Court of Appeal in *Broome* v. *Cassell & Co., Ltd.*,[9] the principles propounded by LORD DEVLIN were of course accepted in the English cases, though only one case has come to light in which the plaintiff actually succeeded in recovering exemp-

---

[1] See, e.g. *Williams* v. *Settle, supra,* where the award was expressed to be by way of exemplary damages but seems to have been based on injury to the plaintiff's feelings and his sense of family dignity and pride"; *per* SELLERS, L.J. at p. 1082.
[2] [1964] A.C. 1129, at pp. 1220–1239.
[3] *Ibid.*, at p. 1221.
[4] *Ibid.*, at p. 1230.
[5] The House of Lords only expressly overruled one decision: *Loudon* v. *Ryder*, [1953] 2 Q.B. 202.
[6] [1964] A.C. 1129, at p. 1226.
[7] *Ibid.*, at pp. 1226–1227.
[8] *Ibid.*, at pp. 1227–1228.
[9] [1971] 2 Q.B. 354.

lary damages.[1] But in the Commonwealth jurisdictions, its reception has been mixed. The High Court of Australia expressly refused to follow it,[2] and the Privy Council on appeal held that in a matter such as this uniformity in the common law jurisdictions was not to be prized too highly, and that each system should decide for itself whether to accept the doctrine.[3] New Zealand appears to have followed Lord Devlin,[4] but Canada, after a brief flirtation,[5] seems now to have divorced itself from his view.[6] Exemplary damages are still allowed in the majority of American jurisdictions,[7] but a recent decision of the Supreme Court[8] may have undermined the practice at least in cases of libel. Back in England, the matter was brought to a head by the challenge to LORD DEVLIN in *Cassell & Co., Ltd.* v. *Broome*.[9]

> D1 wrote and D2 published a book purporting to give an authoritative account of a wartime disaster in which 11 ships were sunk. Passages in the book represented that P, as commander of the convoy escort, bore a share of the responsibility. The evidence revealed that D1 and D2 had been aware from an early stage that P regarded the material as defamatory. They nevertheless proceeded to publish it with only minor modifications. The trial judge directed the jury that they should award exemplary damages only if the case fell within the second of LORD DEVLIN's categories, and if they wished on this basis to award exemplary damages they should be assessed independently of compensatory damages. The jury awarded £15,000 compensatory and £25,000 exemplary damages against both D1 and D2. The Court of Appeal upheld the award on the alternative grounds: (1) the award of exemplary damages was not limited to LORD DEVLIN's three categories—*Rookes* v. *Barnard* had been decided *per incuriam*[10] (2) even if *Rookes* v. *Barnard* was binding on them, the case came within LORD DEVLIN's second category. The further appeal to the House of

---

[1] *McReady* v. *Raum* (1970), *Times*, 24 October.
[2] *Uren* v. *John Fairfax & Sons Pty., Ltd.* (1966), 117 C.L.R. 118; *Australian Consolidated Press* v. *Uren* (1966), 117 C.L.R. 185.
[3] *Australian Consolidated Press* v. *Uren*, [1969] 1 A.C. 590.
[4] *Greville* v. *Wiseman*, [1967] N.Z.L.R. 795.
[5] E.g. *Schuster* v. *Martin* (1965), 50 D.L.R. (2d) 176.
[6] E.g. *McKinnon* v. *Woolworth* (1968), 70 D.L.R. (2d) 280; according to another decision, no distinction should be drawn between "aggravated" and "exemplary" damages, *S.* v. *Mundy* (1970), 9 D.L.R. (3d) 446.
[7] Prosser, *Torts*, 4th Edn., p. 11.
[8] *Rosenbloom* v. *Metromedia*, 403 U.S. 29 (1971).
[9] [1972] A.C. 1027 affirming [1971] 2 Q.B. 354 though it "may well be the most hostile affirmation of a Court of Appeal decision in our history." Stone (1972), 35 M.L.R. 449, at p. 451.
[10] The Court of Appeal reached this conclusion on the grounds (a) that in 1964 the House of Lords was still bound by its own previous decisions in *Hulton & Co., Ltd.* v. *Jones*, [1910] A.C. 20 and *Ley* v. *Hamilton* (1935), 153 L.T. 384 which had approved awards of exemplary damages; (b) LORD DEVLIN's three categories were "illogical, arbitrary and restrictive"; (c) the law had been changed without prior discussion with counsel of the categories. The reasoning

Lords was dismissed on this latter ground,[1] but their Lordships (with VISCOUNT DILHORNE dissenting) firmly rejected the first ground on which the Court of Appeal had decided the case.

The result is that LORD DEVLIN's principles have survived the challenge, though perhaps not entirely unscathed. The task now is to consider in greater detail the scope and merits of these principles as seen in the light of the reappraisal in *Cassell* v. *Broome*.

2 General principle[2]

The fundamental principle emerging from both *Rookes* v. *Barnard*[3] and *Cassell & Co., Ltd.* v. *Broome*[4] is that in general exemplary damages should not be awarded; the object of a damages award is to compensate the plaintiff. In order to assess the merits of this principle, it is first necessary to discover what objects an exemplary award is supposed to pursue. Like other forms of punishment, it may be said that the award has a threefold purpose: to punish, deter and prevent. The defendant has committed a wrong in an unconscionable manner and for this he should be made to suffer by punishment. At the same time this should both deter him from repeating his conduct, and deter others from acting in a similar way. Lastly, it is preventive in two senses: it should prevent the plaintiff from resorting to self-help, and it should prevent the defendant from deriving a profit from the commission of a tort, where the material benefit he procures exceeds the compensation payable to the plaintiff.[5]

There would appear to be three fundamental objections to damages in civil actions being used to attain these ends.

(i) At the heart of our legal system there is a primary distinction between civil and criminal law. Some overlap is inevitable: every award of damages will, to a certain extent, punish the defendant. But if a penal sanction is inflicted as an end in itself, then the defendant's

---

was denounced by the House of Lords: the decision in *Rookes* v. *Barnard* was not inconsistent with the two cases cited, and (b) and (c) were not sufficient grounds on which the Court of Appeal might refuse to follow a House of Lords decision. On this aspect of the case, see McGregor (1971), 34 M.L.R. 520 and Stone (1972), 35 M.L.R. 449.

[1] The appeal against the trial judge's direction and the actual amount awarded was also dismissed, though on narrower majorities. On these aspects, see *infra*, pp. 37–38.

[2] The subject has provoked much academic discussion. See, especially: Street, pp. 33–36, Morris (1931), 44 Harv. L.R. 1173, Fridman (1970), 48 C.B.R. 373, Stone (1972), 46 A.L.J. 311.

[3] [1964] A.C. 1129.

[4] [1972] A.C. 1027.

[5] This last function was specifically retained by LORD DEVLIN, *infra*, p. 35.

conduct should, in principle, constitute a criminal offence.[1] The maxim *nulla poena sine lege* may have become a "democratic platitude",[2] but it contains a truth few would wish to deny.[3] As Dicey once wrote, "a man may with us be punished for a breach of law, but he can be punished for nothing else."[4]

(ii) If the law punishes a man in the civil courts, it deprives him of the protection it grants him in the criminal courts.[5] While not an exhaustive analysis, the following may give some idea of the advantages which the defendant will gain in criminal proceedings: (A) a heavier burden of proof for the prosecution to discharge; (B) favourable rules of evidence;[6] (C) the absence of an appeal from acquittal; (D) the fact that the judge and not the jury determines the severity of the sentence.

(iii) There is no reason why the plaintiff, rather than the State, should benefit from the sanction imposed upon the defendant.[7] In truth, that the plaintiff gets a windfall in these cases is symptomatic of the erstwhile confusion between exemplary and aggravated damages.

To counter these objections, other arguments have been advanced. It is suggested, for example, that the alleged clear distinction between civil and criminal law is unrealistic: (A) it is a legitimate aim of an award of damages to deter[8] or to enforce certain standards of conduct;[9] (B) the criminal law has power to compensate the victim;[10] (C) by its adherence to liability based on fault the law of torts is already committed to an admonitory function.[11] But though the fact stated in (B) shows there to be a case where an object of the civil law is pursued in the criminal courts, this does not, by itself, justify the converse situation: punishment administered in the civil courts. It must be reiterated that greater protection is provided for the defendant in the criminal courts. It would further seem that both (A) and (C) are refuted by

---

[1] *Cassell & Co., Ltd.* v. *Broome, supra, per* LORD REID at p. 1087, *per* LORD MORRIS at p. 1100.
[2] Williams, *Criminal Law: The General Part*, 2nd Edn., p. 576.
[3] Williams, *ibid.*, at p. 575; Hall, *Principles of Criminal Law*, 2nd Edn., p. 27.
[4] *Law of the Constitution*, 10th Edn., p. 202.
[5] *Cassell & Co., Ltd.* v. *Broome, supra, per* LORD REID at p. 1087, *per* LORD MORRIS at p. 1100, *per* LORD DIPLOCK at p. 1127, *per* LORD KILBRANDON at p. 1135.
[6] E.g. under the Criminal Evidence Act 1898, evidence as to the bad character of the accused is generally inadmissible.
[7] *Per* LORD MORRIS, *Cassell & Co., Ltd.* v. *Broome, supra*, at p. 1100.
[8] Morris, n. 2, p. 32, *supra*.
[9] Fridman, n. 2, p. 32, *supra* and see LORD WILBERFORCE in *Cassell & Co., Ltd.* v. *Broome, supra*, at p. 1114.
[10] E.g. under the Criminal Justice Act 1972, s. 1, and the Theft Act 1968, s. 28(1).
[11] Morris, n. 2, p. 32, *supra*.

modern trends in the law of torts: the move away from liability based on fault to that based on risk, and the complementary principle of loss-distribution.[1]

Finally it may be argued that there are special grounds for allowing the award of exemplary damages generally in actions for defamation.[2] It is in this area that the scope of the criminal law is particularly limited, in contrast to its obvious concern with the intentional infliction of physical harm, and, in certain circumstances, economic loss. There is, moreover, the problem of establishing what is meant by "compensation" for injury to reputation.[3] The distinction between exemplary and aggravated damages, though clear in theory, will not always be easy to apply in practice.[4] It may be conceded that there is a stronger case for the admission of exemplary damages in this area than in any other, but it may be doubted whether the arguments advanced are sufficient to override the objections listed above. If it is felt that there is need for greater deterrence, then consideration might be given to an extension of the criminal law to cover, for example, statements made with the intention of flagrantly destroying or harming a man's reputation.

3   The exceptions

There were, according to LORD DEVLIN, "certain categories of cases in which an award of exemplary damages can serve a useful purpose in vindicating the strength of the law."[5] These same categories have been criticized as being illogical and inconsistent.[6] It remains to examine the scope of the exceptions and the merits of the criticism.

(a)   "Oppressive, arbitrary or unconstitutional actions by servants of the government"

It is apparent from the opinions expressed in *Cassell* v. *Broome*[7] that this first exception is to be widely construed:

---

[1] "Indemnity insurance has inevitably drained off whatever direct admonitory effect might once have attached to an adverse judgment." Fleming, *Introduction to the Law of Torts*, p. 14. See also Williams, 4 Current Legal Problems 137.

[2] E.g. *per* LORD WILBERFORCE, *Cassell & Co., Ltd.* v. *Broome*, [1972] A.C. 1027, at p. 1119.

[3] Cf. *infra*, p. 231.

[4] See, e.g. *Fielding* v. *Variety Incorporated*, [1967] 2 Q.B. 841, and *infra*, p. 238.

[5] [1964] A.C. 1129, at p. 1226.

[6] See, especially, LORD DENNING, M.R. in *Broome* v. *Cassell & Co., Ltd.*, [1971] 2 Q.B. 354, at p. 381 and TAYLOR, J. in *Uren* v. *John Fairfax & Sons, Ltd.* (1966), 117 C.L.R. 118, 130–136.

[7] [1972] A.C. 1027.

"It would embrace all persons purporting to exercise powers of government, central or local, conferred upon them by statute or at common law by virtue of the official status or employment which they held."[1]

Even thus extended, the rule would seem difficult to justify in terms of principle. There is force in the argument that the matter should depend upon conduct rather than status,[2] and that today the courts have more sophisticated weapons to do battle than the rather blunt instrument of exemplary damages.[3] However, it represents a typical manifestation of the judiciary's sensitivity to the abuse of power by the executive and as such is deeply embedded in the common law.[4]

(b) "The defendant's conduct has been calculated by him to make a profit for himself which may well exceed the compensation payable to the plaintiff"

Again, LORD DEVLIN'S original formulation of the second exception has been broadened by subsequent interpretation. Of course, it is not sufficient that the tort is committed in the course of some general profit-making enterprise.[5] Nevertheless the cases immediately following *Rookes* v. *Barnard* tended to stress the requirement that the defendant must have in mind a "specific profit" accruing directly from the tort.[6] Others have tended to concentrate on LORD DEVLIN'S use of the word "calculate" to argue that there must be positive evidence of the defendant having made some form of arithmetical calculation of the profit to be made from the tort and of the damages and costs to which he would make himself liable. This was, indeed, the main ground of appeal in *Cassell* v. *Broome* itself. But the House of Lords, confirming the Court of Appeal on this point, found no difficulty in holding that the case did come within the second exception. There was the clearest evidence, particularly from the appearance of the dust cover on the book, that the defendants in the knowledge that they might be defaming the plaintiff, were nevertheless prepared to sell the book on its sensational interpretation.[7] The specific words used by Lord Devlin were regarded as illustrative, rather than exhaustive, of the general principle.[8] Calculation in a strict sense is unnecessary.

---

[1] *Per* LORD DIPLOCK, *ibid.*, at p. 1130, and to the same effect LORD HAILSHAM, L.C. at p. 1078 and LORD REID at p. 1088.
[2] *Per* VISCOUNT DILHORNE, *ibid.*, at p. 1108.
[3] *Per* LORD DIPLOCK, *ibid.*, at p. 1130.
[4] See the eighteenth-century constitutional cases, *supra*, p. 28, and more particularly, *Ashby* v. *White* (1703), 2 Ld. Raym. 938, *per* HOLT, C.J. at p. 956.
[5] *McCarey* v. *Associated Newspapers, Ltd.*, [1965] 2 Q.B. 86.
[6] *Broadway Approvals* v. *Odhams Press* (*No.* 2), [1965] 2 All E.R. 523; *Mafo* v. *Adams*, [1970] 1 Q.B. 548.
[7] *Per* LORD HAILSHAM, L.C., [1972] A.C. 1027, at pp. 1058–1059.
[8] *Per* LORD HAILSHAM, L.C., *ibid.*, at p. 1078; *per* LORD DIPLOCK, *ibid.*, at p. 1129.

"The situation contemplated is where someone faces up to the possibility of having to pay damages for doing something which may be held to have been wrong but where nevertheless he deliberately carries out his plan because he thinks that it will work out satisfactorily for him. He is prepared to hurt somebody because he thinks that he may well gain by so doing even allowing for the risk that he may be made to pay damages."[1]

This exception may be justified on either of two policy grounds.

(i) *Unjust enrichment* The narrower view is not directly based on punitive considerations. It is that the victim of a tort should be able to recover any benefit which the tortfeasor has acquired through the commission of the tort.[2] The ordinary restitutionary remedy does not extend to cases where the plaintiff has not sustained an equivalent loss,[3] and an exemplary damages award might conveniently fill the gap. On this view the award should be limited to the amount (if any) of the defendant's gain.

(ii) *Deterrence* There was more support in *Cassell* v. *Broome* for a broader view based on deterrence. Although it may not in general be a proper object of the law of torts to deter, nevertheless its principles must not be framed in such a way as positively to encourage the tortfeasor. He must be shown that tort does not pay.[4] On this view, the award need not be limited to the defendant's gain, actual or prospective.[5]

(c)   Statutory authority[6]

There is only one instance of a statute expressly authorizing the award of exemplary damages. Section 13(2) of the Reserve and Auxiliary Forces (Protection of Civil Interests) Act 1953 provides that in an action for conversion falling within the statute the court may take into account the defendant's conduct and award, if it thinks fit, exemplary damages. The object of the Act was to provide for the protection of the civil interests of persons who are called up for service in the Reserve or Auxiliary Forces. As a matter of policy, it was presumably thought that to protect them against wanton interference, deterrence in the civil courts was a more expedient weapon than the creation of a

---

[1] *Per* LORD MORRIS, *ibid.*, at p. 1094, and to similar effect LORD HAILSHAM, L.C. at p. 1079 and LORD DIPLOCK at p. 1130.
[2] McGregor (1971) 34 M.L.R. 520, at pp. 525–526, cf. LORD DIPLOCK in *Cassell & Co., Ltd.* v. *Broome, supra,* at p. 1130.
[3] See Goff & Jones, *Law of Restitution*, Chap. 33.
[4] *Cassell & Co., Ltd.* v. *Broome*, [1972] A.C. 1027, *per* LORD HAILSHAM, L.C. at p. 1079, *per* LORD WILBERFORCE at p. 1119, *per* LORD DIPLOCK at p. 1130, *per* LORD KILBRANDON at p. 1133.
[5] *Per* LORD DIPLOCK, *ibid.*, at p. 1130.
[6] For the possibility of an award in a survival action see *infra*, pp. 113–117.

new criminal offence.[1] A more doubtful case is section 17(3) of the
Copyright Act 1956. This provides that the court may have regard to
"the flagrancy of the infringement, and any benefit shown to have
accrued to the defendant by reason of the infringement" and if it is

> "satisfied that effective relief would not otherwise be available to the
> plaintiff, the court, in assessing damages for the infringement, shall
> have power to award such additional damages by virtue of this sub-
> section as the court may consider appropriate in the circumstances."

On the authority of the provision, as well as on common law principles,
exemplary damages were awarded in *Williams* v. *Settle*.[2] However a
reading of the sub-section, in particular the words "effective relief
would not otherwise be available to the plaintiff" strongly suggests that
Parliament had in mind aggravated rather than exemplary damages.[3]

4 Rules applicable to cases within exceptions

(a) Joint tortfeasors

It seems clear that the need to impose a penal sanction against one of
two joint tortfeasors should not affect the measure awarded against the
other. The House of Lords has now held that where damages are to
be awarded against more than one defendant in the same action in
respect of the same loss,

> "only one sum can be awarded . . . and this sum must represent the
> highest *common* factor, that is, the *lowest* sum for which any of the
> defendants can be held liable on this score."[4]

As a consequence, the plaintiff may recover more if he elects to sue the
most guilty tortfeasor on his own.

(b) Judge and jury

In general, today, it is only in actions for defamation that juries sit
in civil cases. Where they do, the usual rule applies that it is for the

---

[1] In *Cassell & Co., Ltd.* v. *Broome, supra*, at p. 1133, LORD KILBRANDON
expressed the view that this provision envisaged the award of *aggravated* rather
than *exemplary* damages. But this was as part of the general proposition that
as a result of the pre-1964 confusion between exemplary and aggravated damages
all references to "exemplary" should be construed as referring to "aggravated"
damages.
[2] [1960] 2 All E.R. 806.
[3] It was so held by UNGOED-THOMAS, J. in *Beloff* v. *Pressdram, Ltd.*, [1973]
1 All E.R. 241, at pp. 265–266.
[4] *Per* LORD HAILSHAM, L.C., *Cassell & Co., Ltd.* v. *Broome*, [1972] A.C. 1027,
at p. 1063.

judge to determine questions of law and for the jury to decide questions of fact. Applied to the award of exemplary damages this means that it is for the judge first to rule whether evidence exists which entitles a jury to find facts bringing the case within one of exceptions, and then for the jury to reach a verdict on the facts as to whether an award of exemplary damages is justified, and if so, for how much.[1] The amount assessed can be set aside only if it is so large (or small) that twelve reasonable jurors could not have arrived at the figure.[2]

(c) Quantum

There is very little to offer in the way of guidance as to the amount that should be awarded. The basic principle is that the figure should reflect the gravity of the defendant's offence.[3] It would seem inappropriate, however, to rely on the amounts payable by way of fines for analogous criminal offences. A fine does not always accurately reflect the gravity of an offence.[4] Among his "considerations" Lord Devlin suggested that awards should be "restrained" and that the court is entitled to take into account the means of either plaintiff or defendant.[5] Most important of all, before awarding a separate sum by way of exemplary damages, the jury or court should first be satisfied that the defendant is not sufficiently punished by the amount of compensatory damages that he will have to pay.[6]

V DAMAGES AGREED BY CONTRACT

1 Introduction

The parties to a contract may have made special provision for damages payable on breach, and the plaintiff may then seek to recover (or the defendant to restrict the award to) the agreed sum, rather than the actual loss. The situation can arise in three different ways: the parties may agree that in case of breach (i) the party in default will pay

---

[1] *Per* LORD HAILSHAM, L.C., *Cassell & Co., Ltd.* v. *Broome, ibid.*, at pp. 1081–1082.

[2] In *Cassell & Co., Ltd.* v. *Broome, supra*, it was decided by a majority of four to three that £25,000 exemplary damages (in addition to £15,000 compensatory damages) was not beyond that which twelve reasonable men could have awarded.

[3] See WIDGERY, J.'s direction to the jury in *Manson* v. *Associated Newspapers*, [1965] 1 W.L.R. 1038, at pp. 1045–1046.

[4] White, [1965] C.L.J. 209.

[5] *Supra*, p. 30.

[6] *Per* LORD DEVLIN, *Rookes* v. *Barnard*, [1964] A.C. 1129, at p. 1228 unanimously confirmed in *Cassell & Co., Ltd.* v. *Broome*, [1972] A.C. 1027, at pp. 1062, 1089, 1096, 1104, 1118, 1121–1122, 1134.

the other £x,[1] (ii) the plaintiff must prove actual loss, but his compensation will be limited to £x,[2] (iii) the party in default will forfeit £x already given to the other by way of deposit or in part payment.[3]

With regard to exemplary damages, the discussion revolved around a conflict between the view that damages should only compensate the plaintiff, and the view that, in the appropriate case, damages may serve a deterrent or punitive purpose. This section is characterized by a similar conflict. At one extreme is the principle that damages should be restricted to compensating the plaintiff for the loss he has sustained as a result of the breach of contract. At the other extreme is the principle of freedom of contract which requires that the parties should be free to determine for themselves the consequence of a breach. An unqualified adherence to either of these principles would be impossible: on the one hand, it would be impracticable, expensive and detrimental to commerce if the plaintiff in an action for breach of contract had, in every case, to rely on a court's assessment of his loss; on the other hand, the court could hardly stand by in cases of real exploitation, where the stipulated sum was designed to intimidate the promisor into performance rather than to compensate the promisee for his expected loss.

"If you agree to build a house in a year, and agreed that if you did not build the house for £50, you were to pay a million of money as a penalty, the extravagance of that would at once be apparent."[4]

English law has, therefore, reached a position midway between the two extremes by holding that, in general, the claim for the agreed sum will be enforced only if it is a reasonable pre-estimate of the loss likely to occur on breach.

2 Historical development

The history of this subject is a chronicle of the pendulum of judicial opinion gently swinging between the extremes of freedom of contract and paternalistic interference with unconscionable bargains. In the medieval period, the penal bond was a favourite mode of enforcing a contractual obligation.[5] D would promise to pay P £x on a certain day, but if he performed his obligation before that day, the bond would be void. The sum agreed upon was generally a very high figure, and was intended as a security for performance, not as an assessment of compensation. Although such bonds were upheld by the common law

---

[1] *Infra*, pp. 41–51.
[2] *Infra*, pp. 51–52.
[3] *Infra*, pp. 52–56.
[4] *Per* LORD HALSBURY, L.C., *Clydebank Engineering and Shipbuilding Co.* v. *Don Jose Ramos Yzquierdo y Castaneda*, [1905] A.C. 6, at p. 10.
[5] See, in general, Simpson (1966), 82 L.Q.R. 392.

courts, equity began to restrain the promisee from bringing an action upon them.[1] The cry was "equity suffers not advantage to be taken of a penalty or forfeiture where compensation can be made."[2] It was subsequently echoed in the common law courts,[3] and finally confirmed by a statute in 1697[4] which provided that if the promisor was in default of the obligation on which the bond was conditioned, judgment could be entered for the penal sum, but that the action would be stayed on payment of damages assessed by the jury.

It was the essence of a penal bond that the primary obligation was to pay the agreed sum; the contractual obligation was only the event on which the conditional defeasance operated. The law had considered this a usurious device and had effectively disposed of it. Would it reach the same conclusion where the contractual obligation was the primary obligation, and the agreed sum was expressed to be payable on breach of that obligation? The answer was uncertain in the eighteenth century.[5] In *Astley* v. *Weldon* (1801),[6] it was clearly laid down that the courts would not allow the promisee to recover a penalty, even in cases where it was not the primary obligation. If the loss resulting from the breach would be invariably less than the stipulated sum, or if the latter was "very enormous or excessive",[7] then it was a penalty and unenforceable. The contract under consideration was one of employment: the parties agreed that "either of them neglecting to perform that agreement should pay to the other £200". This was held to be a penalty. The clause covered a number of obligations of varying degrees of importance. For example, the plaintiff had promised to pay the defendant's travelling expenses which amounted to £1 11s. 6d. Clearly £200 would be an excessive payment for the breach of this obligation. The implication behind the judgments was that only if the sum could be regarded as a genuine pre-estimate of the loss likely to occur, could it be treated as "liquidated damages" and thus recoverable.

In this way the courts finally reached a compromise between the two conflicting principles described above: the parties were free to deter-

---

[1] See Yale, *Introduction to Lord Nottingham's Chancery Cases*, 79 Selden Society, pp. 7–30.

[2] Francis' *Maxims of Equity* (1728) cited by Simpson, *loc. cit.*, at p. 418; but where the assessment of compensation was thought impossible, equity would not grant relief: *Tall* v. *Ryland* (1670), 1 Cas. in Ch. 183.

[3] E.g. *King* v. *Atkins* (1670), 1 Sid. 442.

[4] 8 & 9 Will III, c. 11, s. 8.

[5] In *Lowe* v. *Peers* (1768), 4 Burr. 2225, LORD MANSFIELD said that the court would grant relief against a penalty, but not where the covenant was to pay liquidated damages. Yet, *semble*, his "penalty" referred to cases where the promise to pay the agreed sum was the primary obligation.

[6] (1801), 2 Bos. & P. 346.

[7] *Per* LORD ELDON, *ibid.*, at p. 351.

mine the quantum of damages payable on breach, but, to be recoverable, the sum must bear a reasonable proportion to the loss likely to result from such a breach. The modern applications of this rule must now be considered.

3   Liquidated damages and penalties

In the ordinary case where a sum of money is expressed to be payable on the breach of one or more obligations, the crucial question is whether such sum is to be regarded as "liquidated damages" or as a "penalty". In the former case, the plaintiff can recover the sum, irrespective of his actual loss, while in the latter, he may recover only so much as will compensate him for his actual loss.[1] The classic exposition of the distinction was given by Lord Dunedin in *Dunlop Pneumatic Tyre Co., Ltd.* v. *New Garage & Motor Co., Ltd.*[2] This may usefully serve as a framework for most of the discussion.

(a)   General

"The essence of a penalty is a payment of money stipulated as *in terrorem* of the offending party; the essence of liquidated damages is a genuine covenanted pre-estimate of damage."[3]

This requires little comment. The notion that a party may be punished for failing to perform his contractual obligations is repugnant to a system of law which subscribes to a general compensatory principle of damages. Exemplary damages are not recoverable for breach of contract.[4] Consistently English law regards the punitive element in no more favourable a light when it is the subject of a contractual agreement. "*Caveat promisor*" is not a reliable precept in this context.

(b)   Intention of the parties

"The question whether a sum stipulated is penalty or liquidated damages is a question of construction to be decided upon the terms and inherent circumstances of each particular contract, judged of as at the time of the making of the contract . . ."[5]

It is significant that Lord Dunedin refrained from making any reference to the intention of the parties, this in marked contrast to some judicial

---

[1] For a more detailed account of the effect of a decision as to whether an agreed sum is liquidated damages or a penalty, see *infra*, pp. 50–51.
[2] [1915] A.C. 79, at pp. 86–88.
[3] *Ibid.*, at p. 86.
[4] *Addis* v. *Gramophone Co., Ltd.*, [1909] A.C. 488.
[5] [1915] A.C. 79, at pp. 86–87.

statements in the nineteenth century. For example, LOPES, L.J. in *Law v. Redditch Local Board* had said:

> "The distinction between penalties and liquidated damages depends on the intention of the parties to be gathered from the whole of the contract. If the intention is to secure performance of the contract by the imposition of a fine or penalty, then the sum specified is a penalty; but if . . . the intention is to assess the damages for breach of the contract, it is liquidated damages."[1]

The view held by some modern writers[2] that this still represents the law may be doubted. The subjective approach can be regarded as a dying tribute to the freedom of contract theory. In reality, the courts are concerned not with the honesty of the parties' intentions, but with whether the sum was a reasonable pre-estimate of compensation.[3] Where a sum is unconscionable or grossly disproportionate to the anticipated loss, it is unlikely that the court will allow the plaintiff to recover the sum, even if it is found as a fact that the parties honestly intended it as compensation. The test is therefore an objective one: given all the circumstances of the case, at the time of the agreement, was the stipulated sum a reasonable pre-estimate of the loss likely to occur on breach?

(c) Words used

> "Though the parties to a contract who use the words 'penalty' or 'liquidated damages' may *prima facie* be supposed to mean what they say, yet the expression used is not conclusive. The court must find out whether the payment stipulated is in truth a penalty or liquidated damages."[4]

This undisputed rule adds further weight to the argument in favour of the objective test. On numerous occasions the courts have disregarded the use of "by way of liquidated damages" or similar expressions, and held the sum to be a penalty.[5] More surprising, perhaps, is the frequency with which they have regarded as liquidated damages a sum expressed to be "a penalty".[6] Some judges have suggested that the

---

[1] [1892] 1 Q.B. 127, at p. 132; see also *Palmer v. Temple* (1839), 9 Ad. & El. 508, *per* DENMAN, C.J. at p. 520; and *Pye v. British Automobile Commercial Syndicate, Ltd.*, [1906] 1 K.B. 425, *per* BIGHAM, J. at pp. 428–429.

[2] E.g. Cheshire & Fifoot, *Law of Contract*, 8th Edn., p. 602.

[3] *Williston on Contract*, §778; *Corbin on Contract*, §1059.

[4] [1915] A.C. 79, 86.

[5] E.g. *Kemble v. Farren* (1829), 6 Bing. 141; *Public Works Commissioner v. Hills*, [1906] A.C. 368. In hire-purchase contracts the phrase "by way of agreed compensation" has frequently been ignored, e.g. *Bridge v. Campbell Discount Co., Ltd.*, [1962] A.C. 600; *Cooden Engineering Co., Ltd. v. Stanford*, [1953] 1 Q.B. 86.

[6] E.g. *Diestal v. Stevenson*, [1906] 2 K.B. 345; *Alder v. Moore*, [1961] 2 Q.B. 57; *Robert Stewart Ltd. v. Carapanayoti, Ltd.*, [1962] 1 All E.R. 418.

words used raise a presumption in favour of the category expressed.[1] Even if this is technically correct, it would seem to be of no great importance. It is a rare case where terminology has tipped the scales in either direction.

(d) Varied stipulations

"There is a presumption (but no more) that it is a penalty when 'a single lump sum is made payable by way of compensation, on the occurrence of one or more or all of several events, some of which may occasion serious and others but trifling damage.'"[2]

At one time the rule was that wherever the contract contained more than one obligation, and a single large sum was made payable for the breach of any one of them, the sum was necessarily a penalty. The case of *Astley* v. *Weldon*,[3] described above,[4] illustrated the rule in application. But this was too dogmatic: it followed that in almost all cases of multiple contractual obligations, the agreed sum was irrecoverable. The judicial pendulum had swung too violently away from freedom of contract. The movement was checked when in the *Dunlop* case[5] the House of Lords held that where a single sum was stipulated for the breach of one or more of several obligations, it was a *presumption*, not a *rule of law*, that the sum was a penalty. There are circumstances where the presumption may be rebutted and the sum regarded as liquidated damages. These will now be examined.

(i) The loss likely to arise from the breach of some or all of the obligations may be uncertain or difficult to assess. The parties are, therefore, entitled to speculate on a sum, which may, in the end, prove to be unrealistic. So long as the speculation is a reasonable one, the sum will be liquidated damages. It is only where "you can clearly see that the loss on one particular breach could never amount to the stipulated sum, (that) you may come to the conclusion that the sum is penalty."[6] In the *Dunlop* case,

Ds agreed not to tamper with the markings on Ps' tyres, nor to sell the tyres below the listed price, nor to persons whose supplies Ps had decided to suspend, nor to exhibit or export them without Ps' consent. £5 was made payable for every tyre "sold or offered" in breach of the

---

[1] The words of LORD DUNEDIN quoted at the beginning of the paragraph imply this. Other statements to the same effect are: *Willson* v. *Love*, [1896] 1 Q.B. 626, *per* LORD ESHER, M.R., at p. 630; *Alder* v. *Moore*, [1961] 2 Q.B. 57, *per* DEVLIN, L.J., at p. 75.

[2] [1915] A.C. 79, at p. 87, quoting LORD WATSON in *Lord Elphinston* v. *Monkland Iron & Coal* (1886), 11 App. Cas. 332, at p. 342.

[3] (1801), 2 Bos. & P. 346.

[4] *Supra*, p. 40.

[5] [1915] A.C. 79.

[6] *Per* LORD DUNEDIN, *ibid.*, at p. 89.

agreement. There were many ways in which tyres could be "sold or offered" in breach of the agreement, but the loss likely to result from any such breach was difficult to assess. £5 was considered a reasonable speculation.

(ii) On a true construction of the agreement it may appear that the sum was made payable for the breach of a single obligation or (which amounts to the same) of a number of similar obligations. It is impossible to define what amounts to a "single obligation". If D promises not to sell a tyre or a tube below a certain price, it would be pedantic to suggest that there were two obligations: one not to sell a tyre, and the other not to sell a tube. The court must therefore look at the substance of the agreement and determine whether the sum was payable on the breach of obligations which were truly different in nature or effect. The agreed sum of £5 in the *Dunlop* case was payable on what was, in effect, the breach of a single obligation: not to sell tyres contrary to the terms of the agreement.[1] This may be contrasted with the decision in *Ford Motor Co. (England), Ltd. v. Armstrong*.[2] The defendant, a car dealer, covenanted not to sell cars below a certain price, or to certain persons, or to exhibit them without the plaintiff's consent. The agreement was, therefore, very similar to that in the *Dunlop* case; but, whereas in the latter the sum was payable for every tyre "sold or offered", in *Ford Motor v. Armstrong* it was payable "for every breach" of the agreement. This meant that, unlike the *Dunlop* case, the sum covered the term not to exhibit: this term was different, both in its object and importance, from the stipulations regarding the sale of cars. Hence the presumption that the sum was a penalty was not rebutted.

(iii) Even if the sum is construed to apply to the breach of different obligations, it may still be valid as liquidated damages if it is an attempt to "average out" the loss likely to be suffered from the breach of all the obligations. In formulating the proposition, LORD PARKER[3] gave the following illustration: if the breach of one term would result in the probable loss of £5 to £15, and the breach of another term £2 to £12, a sum of £8 covering both breaches would be reasonable. It is implicit in this illustration that, first, there must be some uncertainty as to what loss will be sustained, and, secondly, the difference between the losses likely to arise from the several breaches must not be great. Clearly, if one breach was likely to produce a loss of £10, and another

---

[1] *Per* LORD ATKINSON, *ibid.*, at p. 92.
[2] (1915), 31 T.L.R. 267.
[3] [1915] A.C. 79, at p. 99; see also SCRUTTON, L.J. in *English Hop Growers* v. *Dering*, [1928] 2 K.B. 174, at p. 182.

a loss of £100, the parties could not agree on a sum of £55 to apply to both.

(e) Debt

"It will be held to be a penalty if the breach consists only in not paying a sum of money, and the sum stipulated is a sum greater than the sum which ought to have been paid."[1]

Thus D, for good consideration, promises to pay P £100 by a certain date. He also agrees that, if he fails to pay the sum by that date, he will pay P, "as compensation", £150. The latter sum is to be held a penalty. At first sight, this may appear an obvious and sound principle; the sum of £150 may operate *in terrorem* of the promisor. But further consideration will reveal that this need not be the case; that the rule is, in fact, a harsh one. P in reliance on the prompt payment of the debt, may have committed himself to further financial undertakings or advances of capital. If so, the figure of £150 may be no more than an attempt to predict the amount required to compensate P for D's failure to pay the debt on time. It is fallacious to assume that a sum in excess of the debt must necessarily be penal.[2]

Further the rule is governed by doubtful authority. It has never been the *ratio* of an English decision.[3] It is true that there are several instances of *obiter dicta* in support of the rule,[4] but these statements are based on suspect arguments. First, reliance is placed on the common law rule that substantial damages (apart from interest) cannot generally be recovered for the non-payment of a debt,[5] but this principle is itself dubious, and has been weakened by recent judicial trends.[6] Secondly, it can be regarded as "a survival of the time when equity reformed unconscionable bargains merely because they were unconscionable."[7] But this generalization cannot be upheld today. If, and insofar as, the sum is disproportionate to the contractual debt, then it will be treated as a penalty under the rule to be considered in (vi). If the sum is a reasonable pre-estimate of the loss likely to be sustained on non-payment, then it should be recoverable as liquidated damages.

---

[1] [1915] A.C. 79, at p. 87.
[2] Of course, if the sum payable is the amount of the loan plus interest, this will not be a penalty.
[3] Cf. U.S.A. *Kothe* v. *R. C. Taylor Trust*, 280 U.S. 224 (1929).
[4] E.g. *Astley* v. *Weldon* (1801), 2 Bos. & P. 346, *per* CHAMBRE, J., at p. 354; *Thompson* v. *Hudson* (1869), L.R. 4 H.L. 1, *per* LORD WESTBURY, at p. 30; *Law* v. *Redditch Local Board*, [1892] 1 Q.B. 127, *per* LORD ESHER, M.R., at p. 130.
[5] *Per* LORD DUNEDIN, [1915] A.C. 79, at p. 87.
[6] *Muhammad Issael Sheikh Ahmad* v. *Ali*, [1947] A.C. 414; *Trans Trust S.P.R.L.* v. *Danubian Trading Co.*, [1952] 2 Q.B. 297. See *infra*, p. 306.
[7] *Per* LORD DUNEDIN, [1915] A.C. 79, at p. 87.

(f) **Proportion**

"It will be held to be a penalty if the sum stipulated for is extravagant and unconscionable in amount in comparison with the greatest loss that could conceivably be proved to have followed from the breach."[1]

This is, perhaps, the most important rule relating to liquidated damages and penalties, and the one with which the court will often have the greatest difficulty. The court must attempt to put itself into the position of the parties at the time of the making of the contract, and, viewing the nature of the agreement and all its terms, determine whether the sum stipulated was a reasonable pre-estimate of the loss likely to result from breach. Accurate assessment of future loss, as will be seen in another context,[2] is a formidable task, but as LORD DUNEDIN pointed out in the *Dunlop* case,[3]

"It is no obstacle to the sum stipulated being a genuine pre-estimate of damage, that the consequences of the breach are such as to make precise pre-estimation almost an impossibility. On the contrary, that is just the situation when it is probable that pre-estimated damage was the true bargain between the parties."

In the last resort, the question whether a sum is unconscionable or not will depend on the nature of the contract. To demonstrate this it is proposed to examine three classes of contract which have been the subject of judicial attention in this respect: agreements in which time is of the essence, "restrictive" agreements, and hire-purchase agreements. The first two fall into a simple pattern and may be disposed of briefly. The third has given rise to considerable difficulties and is worthy of a more detailed discussion.

(i) *Agreements in which time is of the essence*   In contracts falling into this category,[4] a provision is often inserted to the effect that, if the contractual obligation is not performed within the specified time, an agreed sum of damages will be payable. The clause may take either of two forms: the sum may be payable whatever the extent of the breach (e.g. D agrees that if he exceeds the period of time stipulated for the work, he will pay P £x); or it may be graduated according to the extent of the breach (e.g. D agrees that if he exceeds the period of time stipulated for the work, he will pay P £x for every day (or week) of delay). The first case is likely to be treated as a penalty: the same sum is payable whether the delay is substantial or trivial, and thus it is unlikely to be regarded as a reasonable pre-estimate of the loss

---

[1] *Ibid.*
[2] See the discussion of "future uncertainties", *infra*, pp. 82–85.
[3] [1915] A.C. 78, at pp. 87–88.
[4] Charterparties and building contracts are frequent examples.

occurring on breach.[1] If, however, the case falls within the second class it will generally be regarded as liquidated damages: the parties, by making the sum proportionate to the extent of the breach, have indicated an attempt to pre-estimate loss.[2]

(ii) *"Restrictive" agreements* In the nineteenth century an agreed damages clause was frequently added to covenants not to practise a trade within a certain period of time, or within a certain area.[3] In modern times, its popularity has been transposed to covenants restricting the sale or resale of goods, generally the instruments of price-maintenance agreements: P supplies goods to D, who agrees not to resell them below a certain price or to certain persons without P's consent. A sum of £*x* is made payable for every article sold or resold in breach of the agreement. How is the court to determine whether £*x* is a reasonable sum? These contracts pose special problems in the assessment of damages, for the breach by D of his agreement may have far-reaching effects on the whole structure of P's trade. As SANKEY, L.J. has said:[4] "the damage is really the undermining of the market, and the undermining of the existence of the plaintiff company." In consequence, the courts have been loth to interfere with the stipulated sum on the ground that it is out of all proportion to the anticipated loss.[5]

(iii) *Hire-purchase agreements* Nowhere has the conflict between freedom of contract and interference with unconscionable bargains been more turbulent than in the domain of hire-purchase. Most hire-purchase agreements contain a "minimum-payment" clause, that is to say a clause under which the hirer promises that on the occurrence of any

---

[1] E.g. *Public Works Commissioner* v. *Hills*, [1906] A.C. 368. The South African Government commissioned the building of a railway within a specified time. The contractors deposited £50,000 with the Government, which sum was forfeitable if they exceeded the specified time limit, whatever the extent of the delay. The provision was held to be a penalty.

[2] Demurrage clauses (agreements for a sum payable on the detention of a ship beyond the number of days allowed for loading and unloading) are good illustrations: they are invariably treated as liquidated damages clauses. See *Chandris* v. *Isbrandtsen-Moller*, [1951] 1 K.B. 240, at p. 249, and *Suisse Atlantique Société d'Armement Maritime S.A.* v. *N.V. Rotterdamsche Kolen Centrale*, [1967] 1 A.C. 361.

[3] E.g. *Sainter* v. *Ferguson* (1849), 7 C.B. 716; *Reynolds* v. *Bridge* (1856), 6 E. & B. 528.

[4] *English Hop Growers* v. *Dering*, [1928] 2 K.B. 174, at pp. 188–189. See also *Imperial Tobacco Co. (of Great Britain and Ireland)* v. *Parslay*, [1936] 2 All E.R. 515, at p. 519.

[5] Cf. where the sum is payable on the breach of different kinds of obligation, *Ford Motor Co. (England), Ltd.* v. *Armstrong*, (1915), 31 T.L.R. 267, *supra*, p. 44. This area of the law is now governed by the Resale Prices Act 1964. See generally Lever, *The Law of Restrictive Practices and Resale Price Maintenance*.

of a number of events, he will return the goods hired to the owner
(generally a finance company) and, in addition, pay a sum which, together with payments already made or due, will equal a certain proportion of the hire-purchase price. The events on the occurrence of
which this sum is payable invariably include any breach by the hirer
of his agreement. (They may also include events which do not constitute breaches of contract, e.g. the lawful termination of the contract
by the hirer. This situation will be considered at the end of the present
chapter.) The sum is generally expressed to be payable by way of
agreed compensation for the depreciation of the goods which are the
subject of the agreement. The task of the court, therefore, is to determine whether, in all the circumstances of the case, the sum payable is
a reasonable pre-estimate of the loss that the owner is likely to sustain
through depreciation of the goods.[1]

In *Bridge* v. *Campbell Discount*[2] the hirer agreed to pay a sum which,
together with payments already made or due (by way of deposit or
instalments) would equal two-thirds of the hire-purchase price. The
House of Lords was of the opinion that this was a penalty. Naturally,
the longer the article remained in the hirer's possession, the more would
its value depreciate. Yet the clause operated in such a way that the
sum payable would decrease as the period of hire continued and more
instalment payments were made.

> "It is a sliding scale of compensation, but a scale that slides in the
> wrong direction. . . . The fact that this anomalous result is deliberately
> produced by the formula employed suggests, I think, that the real pur-
> pose of this clause is not to provide compensation for depreciation at all
> but to afford the owners a substantial guarantee against the loss of their
> hiring contract."[3]

Moreover, the sum was made proportionate not to the market value of
the goods but to the hire-purchase price. The latter included a considerable interest element which was in no way relevant to the calculation of loss through depreciation.[4] The deficit of one-third of the
hire-purchase price which the owners would not recover would be, in
most cases, more than offset by the realizable value of the article when
restored to their possession. Indeed, if the hirer committed his breach
within the first six months of the agreement, the owner's profit would
far exceed any loss through depreciation. LORD RADCLIFFE doubted
whether the owner "could ever validly protect himself on the scale of

---

[1] N.B. Most hire-purchase contracts are now governed by the Hire Purchase
Act 1965. See *infra*, n. 5, p. 49.
[2] [1962] A.C. 600.
[3] *Per* LORD RADCLIFFE, *ibid.*, at p. 623.
[4] *Ibid.*, at p. 625.

two-thirds that is envisaged here, without much more elaborate provisions for adjustment according to the circumstances in which the claim
falls due."[1]

In *Phonographic Equipment* (1958), *Ltd.* v. *Muslu*,[2] the clause took a
slightly different form. The proportion of the sum payable to the hire-
purchase price was to increase by 5 per cent for every month during
which the hirer retained possession of the goods, from a minimum of
50 per cent. to a maximum of 75 per cent. Thus if the hirer were in
breach during the first month, he would pay 50 per cent.; if during the
second month, 55 per cent. and so on. Certainly there is evidence here
of an attempt to make the "scale of compensation" slide in the right
direction, and the Court of Appeal held the sum to be liquidated
damages. But the correctness of the decision may be questioned in the
light of subsequent case-law.[3] The increase in compensation for
depreciation would continue only up to the fifth month of the hiring,
when the maximum of 75 per cent. would be reached. After that time,
the sum payable would decrease, as under the clause in *Bridge's* case.[4]

These cases validly illustrate the court's approach to the question of
proportion, but it must be observed that most hire-purchase agreements are now governed by the Hire-Purchase Act 1965,[5] section 28(1)
of which provides, in effect, that a minimum payment clause stipulating
for the payment of a sum exceeding one-half of the hire-purchase price
is to be regarded as a penalty.[6] No doubt this will serve as a useful
guide in the characterization of minimum payment clauses in contracts
not falling within the statute.

(g) Effect

We must, finally, consider the legal consequences of a sum held to
be liquidated damages or a penalty.

---

[1] *Ibid.* See also *Landom Trust* v. *Hurrell*, [1955] 1 All E.R. 839. In considering a similar clause, DENNING, L.J. remarked that the sum was inserted
by the finance companies "by rule of thumb, without regard to the make of car,
its age, the market conditions or anything of the kind. It is the same for all",
ibid., at p. 841.
[2] [1961] 3 All E.R. 626.
[3] VEALE, J. in *E.P. Finance* v. *Dooley*, [1964] 1 All E.R. 527 held an identical
clause to be a penalty on the ground that *Muslu* had been impliedly overruled
by *Bridge* v. *Campbell Discount Co., Ltd.*, [1962] A.C. 600. The latter proposition was doubted in *Lombank, Ltd.* v. *Excell*, [1964] 1 Q.B. 415 in which the
Court of Appeal contented itself with the conclusion that the legal effect of
these clauses depends on the facts and circumstances in each particular case.
See on this case-law: Ziegel, [1964] C.L.J. 117.
[4] [1962] A.C. 600.
[5] S. 2(3): all h.p. agreements in which the total hire-purchase price is between
£30 and £2,000.
[6] Even if the sum is 50 per cent. or less, the court still has power to substitute
an ordinary compensatory award for the agreed sum if such sum exceeds the
owner's actual loss: s. 28(2).

(i) *Sum held to be liquidated damages* On the breach of an obligation governed by a liquidated damages clause, the plaintiff is entitled to recover the stipulated sum without proof of actual loss. This is so even in the rare case of his actual loss exceeding the agreed amount.[1] Nor may he substitute for liquidated damages another remedy, legal or equitable, such as an injunction.[2] But the plaintiff may, of course, claim unliquidated damages, or another remedy, for the breach of an obligation which is not governed by the liquidated damages clause. This is always a question of construction. In *Aktieselskabet Reidar* v. *Arcos, Ltd.*,[3]

> A demurrage clause provided for the payment of £25 every day beyond the specified time that the charterers would spend loading the ship. The loading exceeded the specified period and demurrage became payable. But the delay also meant that the charterers were unable to fulfil their obligation to load a full cargo, which constituted a separate breach, giving rise to a separate and independent loss. It was held that they were entitled to unliquidated damages for this additional loss. The demurrage clause governed loss accruing only from detention of the vessel.

(ii) *Sum held to be a penalty* If the sum is regarded as a penalty, the plaintiff will recover his actual loss, as determined by the ordinary rules of quantification.[4] Some doubt has, however, arisen concerning the situation where the plaintiff's actual loss exceeds the amount stated in the penal clause. The possibility is not as remote as it might seem. A sum may be regarded as penal on the ground that it is payable on the breach of a number of obligations of varying importance. The plaintiff's actual loss may have resulted from the breach of the most important obligation. In such a case the position seems to be that, (A) if the plaintiff sues for the recovery of a sum which is held to be a penalty, he may recover no more than the stipulated sum;[5] but that (B) if he sues simply for breach of contract, and does not rely on the penal clause, he may recover compensation for his actual loss, however great.[6] That the extent of the plaintiff's recovery should depend on his form of pleading is clearly unsatisfactory. It is respectfully suggested that in all cases the plaintiff may recover full compensation for

---

[1] *Diestal* v. *Stevenson*, [1906] 2 K.B. 345.
[2] *Carnes* v. *Nesbitt* (1862), 7 H. & N. 778.
[3] [1927] 1 K.B. 352.
[4] See *infra*, Chaps. 8–9.
[5] "Beyond the penalty you shall not go; within it, you are to give the party any compensation which he can prove himself entitled to", *per* LORD ELLENBOROUGH, *Wilbeam* v. *Ashton* (1807), 1 Camp. 78.
[6] *Wall* v. *Rederiaktiebolaget Luggude*, [1915] 3 K.B. 66, approved by the House of Lords in *Watts, Watts & Co., Ltd.* v. *Mitsui & Co., Ltd.*, [1971] A.C. 227.

his actual loss. The proposition stated in (A) would seem to be a survival of the old common law action of debt,[1] and should have no application to the modern law of contract. The result would, of course, be different if the clause were construed not as a penalty (or liquidated damages) but as a limitation clause. In this case, as we shall see in the next section, the promisee's remedy would be limited to the agreed amount.

4 Limitation clauses

The object of an agreed damages clause may be to limit the amount which the plaintiff can recover on breach, rather than attempt to pre-estimate the loss likely to result. Thus D sells goods to P, warranting them free from defects, but limiting his liability for the breach of such warranty to £10 per item. The clause is different from a liquidated damages clause in the following respects.

(i) It cannot be avoided on the ground that it is unconscionable or disproportionate to actual loss. The law of penalties does not apply.[2]

(ii) It is to be classed as a form of exception clause, and its validity is therefore dependent on the law governing such contractual terms.[3]

(iii) The plaintiff must prove actual loss. But he can do so only up to the maximum stipulated in the clause. In no circumstances can he recover a greater amount.

It is always a question of construction whether a given clause is a limitation clause on the one hand, or a penalty or liquidated damages provision on the other. In most cases the words used will prove conclusive, but ambiguous expressions are not unknown. The court will then have to determine from the surrounding circumstances whether the sum was intended as a pre-estimate of loss, or whether it was intended to limit the promisor's liability. In the *Suisse Atlantique* case,[4]

A charterparty fixed certain periods of time for the loading and discharging of cargo. If the cargo was longer delayed, the charterers were to pay demurrage at $1,000 per day. The House of Lords unanimously construed this as liquidated damages provision.

---

[1] The penal bond was, of course, enforceable at common law, and set a maximum limit to the sum recoverable by the promisee.

[2] The contention that a limitation clause may be held to be penal in that its pre-estimate of loss was too small to be reasonable was rejected by the House of Lords in *Suisse Atlantique Societe d'Armements Maritime S.A.* v. *N.V. Rotterdamsche Kolen Centrale*, [1967] 1 A.C. 361. See, especially, LORD UPJOHN, at p. 421.

[3] *Suisse Atlantique* case, *ibid.*, per VISCOUNT DILHORNE, at p. 395, per LORD UPJOHN, at p. 421.

[4] [1967] 1 A.C. 361.

LORD WILBERFORCE said:

> "The form of clause is, of course, not decisive, nor is there any rule
> of law which requires that demurrage clauses should be construed as
> clauses of liquidated damages; but it is the fact that the clause is
> expressed as one agreeing a figure, and not as imposing a limit; and as
> a matter of commercial opinion and practice demurrage clauses are
> normally regarded as liquidated damage clauses."[1]

Another illustration is provided by *Cellulose Acetate Silk Co., Ltd.* v.
Widnes Foundry (1925), *Ltd.*[2]

> Ds agreed to erect and deliver an acetone recovery plant within 18
> weeks and to pay £20 to Ps for every week of delay. The wording of
> the clause may have suggested that the parties intended this to be
> liquidated damages but the fact that Ps' loss was likely to be (and in
> the event was) much greater than £20 per week prompted the House
> of Lords to construe it as a limitation clause.

5   Forfeiture of deposits and part payments

(a)   General principle

Instead of requiring that a party in breach should pay an agreed sum
as compensation, the contract may make provision for an advance payment, by way of deposit or part payment, which will be forfeited if the
depositor or purchaser should fail to perform his contract. Where
there is no express provision as to forfeiture it is generally inferred
that on non-performance a deposit will be forfeited,[3] but that a part
payment will be recoverable.[4]

It will be appreciated that those differences that exist between cases
of forfeiture of part payments and the payment of agreed damages on
breach are differences of form rather than of substance. They are,
that in forfeiture (1) the money is paid or payable *before* breach; and
(2) the plaintiff who seeks recovery of his deposit or part payments is
the party in breach of contract (whereas in a liquidated damages case,
the plaintiff is the victim of the breach). Both devices share the important common feature that they may operate *in terrorem* of the party
performing his obligations. Hence it might legitimately have been
assumed that cases of forfeiture were as vulnerable to equitable intervention as cases of penalties. Yet, as will be seen, the courts have been
remarkably slow to grant relief in cases of forfeiture. The reasons for

---

[1] *Ibid.*, at p. 436. See also VISCOUNT DILHORNE, at p. 395 and LORD UPJOHN,
at p. 421.
[2] [1933] A.C. 20.
[3] *Howe* v. *Smith* (1884), 27 Ch.D. 89.
[4] *Mayson* v. *Clouet*, [1924] A.C. 980.

this reticence are hard to discern. Those offered seem to be in the nature more of excuses than explanations. Thus it is said:

(i) "Here it is the contract-breaker who is the plaintiff and is trying to undo a situation which is blessed by the maxim that possession is nine-tenths of the law."[1] Doubtless it is a policy of the law that wrongdoers should not be heard to complain—*ex turpi non oritur actio.* But this policy should not be applied uncritically. The wrong must be considered relative to the circumstances of the case. Further it may be doubted whether the maxim that possession is nine-tenths of the law, even if it may be supported in other contexts, has any value here.

(ii) The courts "are much readier to find that one who has put out hard cash and who was professing to estimate a future loss really intended to do so than one who has merely promised to pay."[2] This would seem to be unrealistic: it is rarely the depositor/purchaser who decides how large the deposit shall be, or attempts to pre-estimate loss. In almost every case it is the depositee/vendor who lays down the terms of the agreement.[3]

(iii) "In practice, the law as to penalties has not been applied to deposits because they usually bear a reasonable proportion to the inconvenience likely to be suffered by the vendor."[4] In practice, this would certainly seem to be true, but, of course, it does not follow from the fact that the forfeiture of a deposit (or part payment) is generally a reasonable attempt to compensate the depositee/vendor for his loss, that it will be reasonable in all circumstances. There is no reason in principle, it is submitted, why the courts should not in all cases of forfeiture examine the circumstances and determine whether or not the sum forfeited is unconscionable in relation to the anticipated loss. We must now examine in greater detail the courts' treatment of forfeiture clauses.

(b) At common law

At common law, the simple rule prevails that where the contracting parties have agreed that a sum deposited is to be forfeited on breach of contract, the party in default may in no circumstances recover the money.[5]

---

[1] McGregor, §378.
[2] *Ibid.*
[3] In contracts for the sale of land, the standard form contains a stipulation for the deposit of 10 per cent. of the purchase price.
[4] Treitel, p. 826.
[5] The best judicial discussion of the position at common law is to be found in *Stockloser* v. *Johnson*, [1954] 1 Q.B. 476.

(c) In equity

In equity, the judicial attitude has undergone some transformation, and the position today is far from clear. One proposition can stand unchallenged: where a contract provides for payment by instalments, and on default of any payment for the forfeiture of instalments already paid, equity may relieve against forfeiture if the contract has not been rescinded and the purchaser is able and willing to perform: in other words, if the remedy of specific performance is available.[1] The problem is whether equity will extend its jurisdiction to cases where specific performance is unavailable: will it relieve the purchaser against forfeiture of his deposit or part payments on the ground that the sum forfeitable is unconscionable in relation to the vendor's apprehended loss?

The earlier cases do not seem to countenance the possibility.[2] Other cases, without denying the possibility, have refused relief on the ground that the sum forfeited was not unconscionable.[3] In *Steedman* v. *Drinkle*,[4] however, relief was granted.

> Under a contract for the sale of land between the vendor P and the purchaser D, D had paid a deposit of $1,000 and had agreed to pay the balance of the purchase price by instalments.   It was stipulated that time was of the essence, and if D defaulted in payment of the instalments, P was free to rescind the contract and retain "as liquidated damages" the payments already made.   D defaulted in payment, but before P had rescinded the contract, D successfully claimed recovery of the payments he had already made, even though specific performance was unavailable.[5] "The stipulation in question was one for a penalty."[6]

In effect, the modern law of relief against forfeiture has turned on the interpretation of this decision. In *Stockloser* v. *Johnson*,[7] the majority of the Court of Appeal considered that *Steedman* v. *Drinkle* had established a general doctrine of relief against forfeiture analogous

---

[1] *Re Dagenham (Thames) Dock Co., Ex parte Hulse* (1873), 8 Ch. App. 1022; *Kilmer* v. *British Columbia Orchard Lands, Ltd.*, [1913] A.C. 319.
[2] *Palmer* v. *Temple* (1839), 9 Ad. & El. 508; *Howe* v. *Smith* (1884), 27 Ch. D. 89.
[3] *Pye* v. *British Automobile Commercial Syndicate, Ltd.*, [1906] 1 K.B. 425; *Mussen* v. *Van Diemen's Land Co.*, [1938] Ch. 253.
[4] [1916] 1 A.C. 275.
[5] There was no implied agreement to extend the time for payment; nor was there anything in the conduct of the vendor which amounted to a waiver of the right to treat time as of the essence: *per* LORD HALDANE, *ibid.*, at p. 280.
[6] *Ibid.*, at p. 279.
[7] [1954] 1 Q.B. 476.

to that of relief against penalties. For the doctrine to apply, propounded DENNING, L.J.,

"two things are necessary: first, the forfeiture clause must be of a penal nature, in this sense, that the sum forfeited must be out of all proportion to the damage, and, secondly, it must be unconscionable for the seller to retain the money."[1]

Clearly the first condition is the test that is applied to the ordinary case of agreed damages: it is to be determined in the circumstances existing at the time of the agreement. The second condition is a necessary addition for those cases in which the sum of money is already in the hands of the victim of the breach: the court must also test for unconscionability at the time of the suit. This may be illustrated by the facts in *Stockloser* v. *Johnson*[2] itself.

P sold to D certain plant and machinery. D agreed that if he were to default by a period of 28 days in his instalment payments P would be entitled to rescind the contract, recover possession and retain the instalments already paid. It was clear that the forfeiture clause was of a penal nature: the amount forfeitable might far exceed P's loss, e.g. if D defaulted after having paid 75 per cent. or more of the purchase price. But D failed to satisfy the second condition. By the time he claimed relief, he had already received substantial royalties from the use of the plant. In the circumstances of the case, it was held not unconscionable for P to retain the instalments already paid, which amounted to less than 40 per cent. of the total purchase price.[3]

Those who thought that, by this majority opinion, the law had been put on a sound footing were to be disappointed. ROMER, L.J., in the same case, took a narrower view of the decision in *Steedman* v. *Drinkle*.[4] He felt that it only illustrated the rule that relief could be granted before rescission where the purchaser was able and willing to perform his contractual obligations.[5]

"In my judgment," he continued, "the decision cannot be regarded as satisfactory authority for the view that an equity exists in a purchaser, as against a vendor who has validly rescinded the agreement by reason

---

[1] *Ibid.*, at p. 490. See to the same effect SOMERVELL, L.J., at p. 484.
[2] [1954] 1 Q.B. 476.
[3] "The buyer seems to have gambled on the royalties being higher than they were. He thought that they would go a long way to enable him to pay the instalments; but owing to bad weather they turned out to be smaller than he had hoped and he could not find the additional amount necessary to pay the instalments. The judge summarized the position neatly when he said that the purchaser 'is in the position of a gambler who has lost his stake and is now saying that it is for the court of equity to get it back for him.'": *per* DENNING, L.J., *ibid.*, at p. 492.
[4] [1916] 1 A.C. 275.
[5] [1954] 1 Q.B. 476, at pp. 500–501. FARWELL, J. in *Mussen* v. *Van Diemen's Land Co.*, [1938] Ch. 253 had reached a similar conclusion.

of the purchaser's default, to recover instalments of purchase-money
which the vendor is contractually entitled to retain."¹

This view was adopted by SACHS, J. in *Galbraith* v. *Mitchenhall
Estates, Ltd.*² The learned judge, in the latter case, regarded the propositions enunciated by the majority in *Stockloser* v. *Johnson* as *obiter*,
in that, on the facts, the plaintiff was not entitled to relief.³ Moreover
he considered that ROMER, L.J.'s view had been supported by the
Court of Appeal in *Campbell Discount Co., Ltd.* v. *Bridge.*⁴ He therefore concluded that the narrower interpretation of *Steedman* v. *Drinkle*
had been approved by the greater weight of authority, and he would
not dissent from it.⁵

It is, however, cautiously submitted that, for the following reasons,
the broader approach of DENNING and SOMERVELL, L.J. in *Stockloser* v.
Johnson is to be preferred.

(i) The broader view is more consistent with the general principles
of damages as well as of equitable relief. The narrower view
gives rise to an unnecessary and harsh distinction between the
forfeiture of sums already paid, and the promise to pay agreed
damages.

(ii) It is far from clear that the Court of Appeal in *Campbell Discount
Co., Ltd.* v. *Bridge*⁶ in fact lent its support to ROMER, L.J.'s view.
HOLROYD PEARCE, L.J. referred to the conflict of opinions, but
did not commit himself to either.⁷ HARMAN, L.J. was, in general,
opposed to the extension of equitable relief where it amounted
to an interference with contractual agreements, but made no
reference to *Stockloser* v. *Johnson.*⁸ DAVIES, L.J. merely con-
curred.⁹

(iii) ROMER, L.J.'s interpretation of *Steedman* v. *Drinkle* is hard to
reconcile with the judgment of the court in that case. LORD
HALDANE, L.C. seems to have regarded the facts that the seller
had not rescinded and that the buyer was able and willing to
perform as immaterial in granting relief.

6 Money payable on events other than breach

Damages, within the ordinary meaning of the term, are payable only

---

¹ [1954] 1 Q.B. 476, at p. 501.
² [1965] 2 Q.B. 473.
³ *Ibid.*, at p. 483.
⁴ [1961] 1 Q.B. 445. The decision was reversed by the House of Lords on a
ground not affecting the issue, [1962] A.C. 600.
⁵ [1965] 2 Q.B. 473, at p. 484.
⁶ [1961] 1 Q.B. 445.
⁷ *Ibid.*, at p. 457.
⁸ *Ibid.*, at pp. 458–459.
⁹ *Ibid.*, at p. 459.

on the breach of an obligation, contractual or delictual.[1] The last situation to be considered in this chapter is, strictly speaking, not a case of damages at all: the contracting parties agree that on the occurrence of some event which does not constitute a breach of contract, one party shall pay to the other a certain sum of money. The reason why it is necessary in this context to consider the legal effect of such an agreement is that, in certain contracts, it has been employed as a substitute for damages. Thus in *Bridge* v. *Campbell Discount Co., Ltd.*[2]

> The hirer was given the right to terminate the agreement by notice. Another clause stipulated that if the agreement was for any reason terminated before the vehicle became the hirer's property, he must pay to the owners by way of "agreed compensation for depreciation" a sum, which, together with instalments already paid, would equal two-thirds of the h.p. price. The hirer voluntarily terminated and returned the vehicle.[3] The owners claimed the sum payable under the minimum-payment clause.

Now, if the sum had been payable only on breach of contract, the court would simply have to decide whether the stipulation was for liquidated damages or whether it was a penalty, on the principles already discussed. But since the money was payable on an event other than breach, it can be (and was) argued that the law of penalties does not apply, because the sum is not damages: it becomes due on the voluntary exercise of a right to terminate the contract. The practical objection to this logical argument is that it facilitates the complete evasion of the law of penalties: the promisee simply makes the sum payable on a number of events, one of which does not constitute a breach of contract. Clearly the law is here faced with a serious dilemma: should it tread the path of logic or of justice?

(a) The logical approach

At first, it was content to adopt the logical view. In *Elsey & Co., Ltd.* v. *Hyde*,[4] and in a number of subsequent decisions,[5] the court concluded that the sum, however extravagant, was recoverable. It could not be regarded as a penalty because it was payable on the hirer's own election to determine, and not on a breach of contract.

---

[1] *Supra*, p. 1.
[2] [1962] A.C. 600.
[3] But the House of Lords held that, on the facts, the hirer did not exercise his lawful right to terminate the contract. His conduct constituted a breach. See *infra*, p. 58.
[4] (1926), Jones & Proudfoot, *Notes on Hire Purchase Law*, 2nd Edn., p. 107.
[5] E.g. *Associated Distributors* v. *Hall*, [1938] 2 K.B. 83; *Re Apex Supply Co., Ltd.*, [1942] Ch. 108.

(b) The practical approach

As many were quick to discern there is a paradox implicit in this logical approach. Because he is protected by the law of penalties, a person who breaks his contract is in a better position than one who voluntarily terminates his contract. This consideration has led LORD DENNING to the extreme view, expressed in *Bridge* v. *Campbell Discount Co., Ltd.*[1] that "the courts have power to grant relief against the penal sum contained in this 'minimum-payment' clause, no matter for what reason the hiring is terminated."[2] No other judicial statement has gone to this length, and it is unlikely to be followed.[3] Although the intervention of the Legislature has shown that this particular area of hire-purchase law required urgent attention, LORD DENNING'S proposition would seem to carry such a wide import as to have far-reaching effects on a great variety of contractual situations, not so peculiarly appropriate for this treatment.

(c) The compromise solution

In *Bridge*'s case, the House of Lords held (Viscount Simonds dissenting) that on the facts the hirer had not exercised his option to determine, but had committed a breach of the agreement. On that basis, the sum payable was held to be a penalty.[4] But the House was divided equally on the question whether relief could have been granted if the hirer had lawfully terminated the contract. LORD MORTON[5] and VISCOUNT SIMONDS[6] remained faithful to the logical view that the law of penalties could not apply to a sum which was payable at the option of one of the parties. The opposing view was urged by LORD DENNING on the wide ground quoted above,[7] and by LORD DEVLIN on the narrower ground that the minimum-payment clause could not be valid for one purpose (lawful termination of contract) and invalid for another (breach of contract).[8] LORD RADCLIFFE reserved his opinion.[9] The compromise which the law has reached may be stated thus: where a sum is payable on the occurrence of a number of events, some of which involve a breach of contract, and others which do not, the question whether the law of penalties can be applied to the stipulated sum

---

[1] [1962] A.C. 600.
[2] *Ibid.*, at p. 631.
[3] In *United Dominions Trust* v. *Ennis*, [1968] 1 Q.B. 58, HARMAN and SALMON, L.JJ. (*obiter*) discredited this view, but LORD DENNING, M.R. adhered to his earlier statement.
[4] See *supra*, p. 48.
[5] [1962] A.C. 600, at p. 615.
[6] *Ibid.*, at p. 613.
[7] *Ibid.*, at p. 631.
[8] *Ibid.*, at p. 634.
[9] *Ibid.*, at p. 625.

depends on the event which in fact occurs. If the right to the stipulated sum arises on an event which constitutes a breach, the law of penalties does apply.[1] If the event does not constitute a breach, the sum will always be recoverable, however unconscionable.[2]

---

[1] *United Dominions Trust* v. *Ennis, supra.*

[2] With regard to hire-purchase agreements governed by the statute, the Hire-Purchase Act 1965, provides that the hirer may terminate the agreement at any time, but on so doing will be liable to pay a sum which, together with payments already made or due, is equal to 50 per cent. of the hire-purchase price, or any lesser amount specified in the agreement: s. 27(1) and s. 28(1). Even this is subject to the residuary power in the court to order the payment of a lesser sum to compensate the owner for his actual loss: s. 28(2).

CHAPTER THREE

Doctrines Limiting the Compensation Principle

I CAUSATION AND REMOTENESS

1 Introduction

The area covered by the first two doctrines which limit the extent of the plaintiff's recovery is one of the most complex and difficult in the law of obligations. There are several reasons for this: causal problems provoke philosophical discussion; verbal formulae are used to draw distinctions which are at most questions of degree; there is no uniformity as to what are the problems which the various theories are attempting to solve. Above all, there is no neat and universally accepted conceptual framework for the subject. It straddles the distinction between "liability" and "compensation". As a consequence it has received extensive treatment in the standard textbooks on tort and contract.[1] An equally extensive coverage in a book devoted to the principles of damages is not thought necessary. Here the aim will be, first to distinguish between the various issues which are dealt with under the broad heads of causation and remoteness, and, then, to give a brief account of the principles governing such of those issues as are relevant to the quantification process.

(a) Causation and remoteness

Most would agree[2] that a distinction can be drawn between two groups of problems. The first called variously "causation", "condition", "cause in fact", "scientific cause" determines whether as a matter of *fact* the harm was caused by the event or conduct in question. The answer is generally to be sought in the *sine qua non* test or its

---

[1] In addition, there is, of course, a vast amount of specialist literature. A useful bibliography is set out in Honoré, 11 I.E.C.L., Chap. 7. See in particular, Hart & Honoré, *Causation in the Law*, Becht and Miller, *The Test of Factual Causation*, and McGregor, Chap. 6.

[2] Honoré, *supra*, pp. 7–106.

exceptions. The second, generally referred to as "remoteness', or "legal cause" determines whether as a matter of *policy*, recovery of the harm sustained should, in law, be excluded. In English law, the answer is usually sought in the "foreseeability" test or its variants.

(b) Liability and damages

To distinguish between those aspects of causation and remoteness which relate to liability and damages respectively, it is necessary to revert to the classification formulated in Chapter One.[1] It will be recalled that the various questions to be determined by the court were subsumed under four heads—(i) breach, (ii) injury, (iii) loss, (iv) compensation. To establish liability the plaintiff must satisfy the requirements of (i) and (ii), whereas (iii) and (iv) belong to the law of damages. It will be appreciated that for the purpose of delimiting questions of damages from questions of liability, the crucial distinction is between "injury", the *physical* impairment of the plaintiff's person or property which is the immediate result of the unlawful activity, and "loss", the pecuniary or non-pecuniary consequence of the "injury" for which the plaintiff claims compensation.[2] In cases where this distinction can be clearly drawn, that is where the defendant inflicts some physical injury to the plaintiff's person or property, adjudication on the causation and remoteness issues are divided into two stages. To establish *liability* for the consequences of the injury, the plaintiff must prove that the injury sustained was caused by the tort or breach of contract *and* that it was not too remote a consequence. As regards *damages*, he will recover for such losses as resulted from, and were not too remote a consequence of, the injury for which on the above test the defendant is admittedly liable. The same principles of causation determine the link between breach and injury and between injury and loss, but, as will be demonstrated,[3] the "foreseeability" doctrine while applied as the criterion for remoteness to *injuries*, and therefore liability, is not regarded as the proper mode of limiting compensation for losses, and therefore is not, at least in this context, germane to the law of damages. In cases of pure economic injury, on the other hand, there is no physical injury to the plaintiff's person or property and the same distinction between liability and damages cannot be drawn. The result is that the same principles of causation and remoteness (usually the "foreseeability" doctrine) must satisfy the requirements of both: in short they

---

[1] *Supra*, pp. 1–2.
[2] The distinction has been explained by LORD REID in *Baker* v. *Willoughby*, [1970] A.C. 467, at p. 492 and EVELEIGH, J. in *Wieland* v. *Cyril Lord Carpets*, [1969] 3 All E.R. 1006, at pp. 1009–1010.
[3] *Infra*, p. 69.

determine both the existence and the extent of the defendant's liability. This contrast between cases of physical injury and pure economic injury may be illustrated.

> *Physical injury*   P a pedestrian sustains an injury to his leg as the result of a collision between two vehicles, driven by D and E respectively. He incurs certain medical expenses and experiences pain. To establish a cause of action against D, P must show that the injury to his leg was (1) caused by, and (2) a foreseeable consequence of, D's tort. He will recover damages for the expenses and the pain and suffering if he shows that these losses resulted from, and were not too remote a consequence of, the injury to the leg, but he need not show that they were a "foreseeable" consequence of the injury.

> *Economic injury*   D, an engineer, in breach of contract, fails to deliver to P a special piece of machinery which P is to use in the manufacture of certain products. P may recover damages from D for such profits as were within the contemplation of the parties at the time of the contract as liable (or not unlikely) to result from the breach.

(c)   Tort and contract

In substance, tort and contract are governed by the same principles of *causation*. As regards *remoteness*, there are important differences, both theoretical and practical. There is a theoretical divergence in the formulation of the two doctrines. In tort, the question is whether the harm was reasonably foreseeable as *at the time of the tort*.[1] In contract, the test is applied against the background of circumstances existing not at the time of the breach but *at the time of the making of the contract*.[2] It would further appear that there is a difference in the degree of likelihood required. The defendant attempting to prove that the harm sustained was too remote has a harder task in tort.[3] The practical difference follows from the distinction drawn in the last paragraph. Most cases of breach of contract involve no physical injury and the principle of foreseeability established in *Hadley* v. *Baxendale*[4] is habitually employed as part of the quantification process.

2   Causation

(a)   Sine qua non test

Whether one is concerned with the relationship between the breach and the injury or the injury and the loss, whether in tort or in contract, the basic principle is the same: the *sine qua non* test. The plaintiff

---

[1] *The Wagon Mound*, [1961] A.C. 388.
[2] *Hadley* v. *Baxendale* (1854), 9 Exch. 341.
[3] *Koufos* v. *Czarnikow*, [1969] 1 A.C. 350, *infra*, p. 75.
[4] *Supra*.

must show that the breach or injury played a necessary part in the chain of events leading up to the plaintiff's loss. An alternative formulation is that the loss would not have occurred but for the breach or the injury. In *Tickner* v. *Glen Line*[1]

> P was suffering from an indirect hernia before he sustained a small direct hernia in an accident. One operation cured both hernias. Ds were held not liable for the accident but *obiter* DEVLIN, J. observed that even if they had been liable, damages would only have been nominal. P would in any case have had to undergo an operation to cure the earlier hernia. The injury inflicted by Ds was not the *sine qua non* of the loss.

(b) Combining causes

In the ordinary case where the plaintiff can base his claim on the defendant's breach alone, subject to the other limiting doctrines, he may recover from the defendant compensation for his whole loss. But what if the injury inflicted by the defendant would not have produced the loss sustained by the plaintiff were it not combined with another legally relevant event, that is one for which a third person is liable? If the loss resulting is divisible, the damages will be apportioned between the two defendants. Thus in *James* v. *Woodall Duckham Construction*[2]

> P was injured in an accident for which D1 was liable. As a result he suffered from a nervous disorder which, according to medical opinion, would cease only when his claim against D1 would be settled. Through the negligence of his solicitor D2, proceedings against D1 were delayed for three years. It was held that D1 was liable for the losses sustained up to the time when P's claim should have been brought, and D2 was liable for the subsequent losses.

Where, however, the harm is indivisible, that is, it is impossible to say what element of the plaintiff's loss was caused by each defendant, each defendant is liable for the whole,[3] though there is some authority for holding that each should be liable for only a proportionate part of the harm.[4]

(c) Concurrent sufficient causes

The case where two or more injuries combined to produce the loss

---

[1] [1958] 1 Lloyd's Rep. 468.
[2] [1969] 2 All E.R. 794.
[3] *Sadler* v. *Great Western Rail Co.*, [1895] 2 Q.B. 688. But the plaintiff cannot, of course, recover more than his loss, and the defendant held liable may recover contribution from the other tortfeasors.
[4] Per STABLE, J., *Bank View Mills, Ltd.* v. *Nelson Corporation*, [1942] 2 All E.R. 477, at p. 483, reversed on other grounds, [1943] 1 K.B. 337; *Pride of Derby* v. *British Celanese*, [1952] 1 All E.R. 1326, affirmed on other grounds, [1953] Ch. 149.

must be carefully distinguished from that where each was sufficient without the other to produce the harm, that is, where each was a *sine qua non* of the loss. For example

> P loses business profits when he is physically injured by D1. At the same time, the firm's machinery is damaged by D2.

Both D1 and D2 will argue that the injury for which he was responsible was not a *sine qua non* of the lost profits; the loss would in any event have resulted from the other's tort. It is obvious that the law cannot rest content with such a result, however logical, and it is well established that in such circumstances D1 or D2 may be held liable for the whole.[1] Where the injury for which the defendant is liable is concurrent with one for which no legal liability can be imposed (for example, if, in the hypothetical case, D2 was able to absolve himself from liability), the same considerations may not apply. The plaintiff would, quite independently of D1's tort, have lost his profits, and it is at least arguable that D1 is not liable for the loss.[2]

(d) Successive causes[3]

These difficulties become more acute when loss results from successive or overlapping causes. The problems were beautifully illustrated by the recent House of Lords case of *Baker* v. *Willoughby*[4]

> P sustained an injury to his leg when he was hit by D1's vehicle. Before P's claim against D was heard, he was shot in the same leg by D2 during an armed robbery. The leg had to be amputated. D2 was manifestly a man of straw and was not sued. The question thus arose as to the extent of D1's liability.

It might be helpful to describe the problem in a diagrammatic form.

The graph represents P's assets, pecuniary and non-pecuniary. At x he is injured by D1 and at y by D2. l is the position he would have been in if no injury had been inflicted, m if he had been injured only by D1, and n his actual position after the injury inflicted by D2. a represents his losses between the two accidents, $a + b$ the losses he would have sustained if he had been injured by D1 alone, and c the additional losses resulting from the injury inflicted by D2. Two propositions may go unchallenged. First, D1 alone is liable for a;[5] the injury inflicted

---

[1] *Crossley & Sons, Ltd.* v. *Lightowler* (1867), 2 Ch. App. 478. Here also the *Pride of Derby* decision, *supra* is some authority for apportionment. See also n. 3, p. 63, *supra*.

[2] An inference from *Carslogie S.S.* v. *Royal Norwegian Government*, [1952] A.C. 292; but *contra*, Honoré 11 I.E.C.L. 7–140.

[3] Street, pp. 168–179; McGregor & Strachan (1970), 33 M.L.R. 378.

[4] [1970] A.C. 467.

[5] This was implicit throughout *Baker* v. *Willoughby*, *supra*, and indeed was, on the C.A.'s view, the only loss for which P could recover compensation from D1.

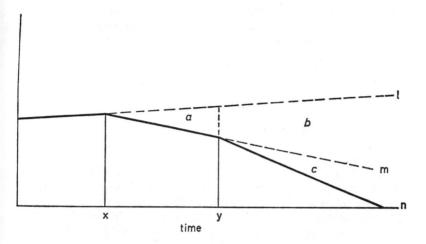

by D2 was not a cause of that loss. Secondly, D2 alone is liable for
c.[1] D2's actions were a *sine qua non* of this loss. D1's actions were not.
But who is liable for *b*? On strictly *causal* notions, it would seem that
there is a somewhat stronger case for imposing liability on D2.[2] Neither
of the two injuries inflicted was a *sine qua non* of *b* but D2 is alone
responsible for *c*, and at least for causal purposes, it seems more natural
to treat *b* and *c* together: combined, they constitute P's continuing and
future loss. The consequences of D1's breach, it may be said,[3] have
been "swallowed up" or "overtaken" by D2's breach. Yet there would
appear to be far stronger arguments based on temporal notions for
imposing liability on D1. Once P's cause of action against D1 has
accrued, he may recover an indemnity from D1 for the consequences
of his injury. The extent of D1's liability may be reduced only if
evidence is produced of a subsequent event which diminished the loss
(e.g. an unexpected recovery or an early death).[4] P's loss is not
diminished by the mere fact that another person may be liable: the
case may be treated as if the two injuries were concurrent causes.[5]
Moreover, there is a strong body of opinion that D2 should in no

---

[1] In *Baker* v. *Willoughby*, *supra*, D1 was not liable for the additional losses
caused by D2's tort, and it was clear from their Lordships' opinions that D2
would have been so liable.
[2] Cf. Strachan (1970), 33 M.L.R. 378, at p. 394.
[3] See the judgments of the C.A. in *Baker* v. *Willoughby*, [1970] A.C. 467,
especially WILLMER, L.J., at p. 480.
[4] *Per* LORD PEARSON, *Baker* v. *Willoughby*, *ibid.*, at p. 496; Honoré 11 I.E.C.L.
7–137 *et seq.*; and on the evidence which may be admitted see *supra*, pp. 16–
18.
[5] *Per* LORD REID, *Baker* v. *Willoughby*, *supra*, at p. 494.

event be liable for *b* since he takes his victim as he finds him, with his assets already reduced to the extent of *m*.[1] These arguments have proved decisive in English[2] courts both in personal injury[3] and in property injury[4] cases. D1 has been held liable for *a* + *b*, D2 only for *c*.

What if one of the successive injuries is the result of a natural event, that is one for which no legal liability can be imposed? Let it be assumed, first, that the injury at *x* was caused by a natural event. The defendant responsible for the injury at *y* is liable only for *c*[5] since P without the intervention of a legal wrong would in any event have lost *a* + *b*. Where the defendant's breach precedes the natural event (which thus occurs at *y*), the result is not so obvious. If the *Baker* v. *Willoughby* solution is applied D will still be liable for *b*, while if the alternative view is taken he will be liable only for *a*. English law appears to favour the latter solution.[6] It is submitted that this is the preferable approach. The *sine qua non* doctrine is applied. P would, irrespective of D's interference, in any event have sustained the loss and it is not the task of the law of tort or contract to shift the burden of naturally occurring losses on to another.

(e) Conclusions

Certain generalizations may be drawn from the principles formulated in the preceding paragraphs. Where a loss results from a natural event and a single unlawful act, and both are sufficient causes, in general the *sine qua non* test will determine liability. Where, on the other hand, the sufficient causes of a loss involve two or more unlawful acts, the test can no longer cope with the problems. The reason for this distinction seems clear. An injured party should not be worse off because more than one party has inflicted an injury upon him. The task of the law is then to allocate responsibility equitably between those in breach. But as regards injuries inflicted without legal responsibility, there is no legitimate reason why the law should shift the burden from

---

[1] *Performance Cars* v. *Abraham*, [1962] 1 Q.B. 33; *Baker* v. *Willoughby*, *supra*, *per* LORD REID, at p. 493, *per* LORD PEARSON, at p. 495.

[2] But not apparently in Canada (*Stene* v. *Evans* (1958), 14 D.L.R. (2d) 73) or Australia (*Leschke* v. *Jeffs* (1955), 49 Q.J.P.R. 138).

[3] *Baker* v. *Willoughby*, *supra*.

[4] *The Haversham Grange*, [1905] P. 307; *Performance Cars* v. *Abraham*, *supra*; but cf. *The Victoria* (1926), 24 Ll.L. Rep. 219 and *per* LORD NORMAND (*obiter*), *Carslogie S.S.* v. *Royal Norwegian Government*, [1952] A.C. 292, at pp. 306–311.

[5] *Crookall* v. *Vickers Armstrong*, [1955] 2 All E.R. 12 but the onus of proving that *b* was caused by an earlier disability is on the defendant and it is not an easy one to shift: *Dupey* v. *Maltby Strick Lines*, [1955] 2 Lloyd's Rep. 645. The problem arises particularly in cases of industrial disease: see, e.g. *McGhee* v. *National Coal Board*, [1972] 3 All E.R. 1008.

[6] *Carslogie S.S.* v. *Royal Norwegian Government*, *supra*.

the injured party to another. If the injured party would in any event have sustained those losses, he alone should bear them.

3 Remoteness in tort

(a) Distinguished from causation

That the injury for which the defendant was liable was a cause of the loss is a necessary but not a sufficient condition for the plaintiff's recovery. It is obvious that not all causes which satisfy the *sine qua non* test will entail legal responsibility. To give but one of many possible illustrations, in *Quinn v. Burch Brothers.*[1]

> P, an independent sub-contractor, was carrying out building work for Ds. P asked Ds for a step-ladder but they did not supply one. In order to continue work, P made use of a trestle which, as he knew, was not suitable for the purpose. The trestle slipped and P was injured.

Obviously, the defendant's failure to provide a suitable ladder was a *sine qua non* of the accident but for the purposes of legal responsibility it was clearly felt by the Court of Appeal that there was much greater causative potency in the plaintiff's decision to use the trestle. The defendant's breach, it was said, was "the occasion which brought about this conduct of the plaintiff but in no way caused it."[2] In the well-known words of LORD WRIGHT,

> "the law cannot take account of everything that follows a wrongful act; it regards some subsequent matters as outside the scope of its selection. . . . In the varied web of affairs, the law must abstract some consequences as relevant, not perhaps on grounds of pure logic but simply for practical reasons."[3]

A line has to be drawn somewhere so that the burden of liability will not crush those who have to pay the bill.[4] The law has devised several methods of doing this.[5] Perhaps it might be more accurate to say that the law has formulated several expressions to mark the division between relevant and irrelevant causal concepts. Some of these concentrate on the causal potential of the original events: thus, cause and condition; *causa causans* and *causa sine qua non*; effective and ineffective cause. Others focus on the consequences and inquire whether it was, foreseeable as resulting from, the natural and probable result of, the direct

---

[1] [1966] 2 Q.B. 370.
[2] *Ibid.*, *per* SELLERS, L.J., at p. 390.
[3] *Liesbosch Dredger* v. *S.S. Edison*, [1933] A.C. 449, at p. 460.
[4] Fleming, *Law of Torts*, 4th Edn., p. 178.
[5] See especially Honoré, 11 I.E.C.L. 7–45 *et seq.*

and immediate consequence of, within the risk created by, the original event. A third group purports to determine whether an intervening event severed the chain of causation or was a *novus actus interveniens*.

(b)   General application of remoteness doctrine

There is no essential difference between these various formulations, and on one view the matter is one for the application of common sense rather than legal propositions.[1] The court is confronted with a situation in which the plaintiff seeks compensation for harm resulting from some unusual occurrence, and it must decide whether this departure from the normal chain of events was so marked that in justice the defendant should not pay for the consequences. Where this departure results from an intervening act of the plaintiff himself, the court is likely to inquire whether he acted reasonably in the circumstances.[2] Where the act of a third party combines with the tort, the court is less likely to impose liability on the defendant for the consequent harm if the act was deliberate,[3] negligent[4] or unforeseeable.[5] As regards the intervention of natural phenomena, it is difficult to add anything to the proposition that in order to escape liability, the defendant must show that it was unusual or unexpected.[6]

(c)   Significance and scope of foreseeability test

In *The Wagon Mound* (*No.* 1),[7] a decision of crucial importance on the orthodox view,[8] the Privy Council insisted that in negligence

"the essential factor in determining liability is whether the damage is of such a kind as the reasonable man should have foreseen,"[9]

thus purporting to displace the rule which had prevailed since 1921 that liability should extend to all the "direct consequences" of the tort.[10] Although perhaps not theoretically binding on them, the

---

[1] E.g. *per* DENNING, L.J., *Jones* v. *Livox Quarries*, [1952] 2 Q.B. 608, at p. 616. The view has been elevated into a general theory of causation: Hart & Honoré, *Causation in the Law*, especially Chap. 2.

[2] E.g. *Haynes* v. *Harwood*, [1935] 1 K.B. 146; *Marcroft* v. *Scruttons*, [1954] 1 Lloyd's Rep. 395; *McKew* v. *Holland and Hannen and Cubitts*, [1969] 3 All E.R. 1621.

[3] E.g. *Weld-Blundell* v. *Stephens*, [1920] A.C. 956.

[4] E.g. *S.S. Singleton Abbey* v. *S.S. Paludina*, [1927] A.C. 16.

[5] E.g. *Ruoff* v. *Long & Co.*, [1916] 1 K.B. 148.

[6] E.g. *Thurogood* v. *Van den Berghs and Jurgens*, [1951] 2 K.B. 537.

[7] [1961] A.C. 388.

[8] For the immense literature on the subject see the references cited in Dias, [1962] C.L.J. 178, n. 3 and [1967] C.L.J. 63, n. 4.

[9] *Per* VISCOUNT SIMONDS, [1961] A.C. 388, at p. 426.

[10] *Re Polemis and Furness, Withy & Co.*, [1921] 3 K.B. 560.

English courts have followed the ruling,[1] and it seems that they will apply the principle generally throughout the law of torts.[2] It is of course possible to argue that the shift from "directness" to "foreseeability" is of little practical consequence;[3] but it should be regarded as significant in two different respects. In the first place, and on a more theoretical level, it contains an overt recognition that a moral judgment is involved.[4] Secondly—and for the purposes of this book this is extremely important—its role has been limited, in some circumstances at least, to determining the existence of liability rather than the quantum of compensation. In other words, it has been applied to limit the *kind* of harm recoverable but not the *extent* of that harm. To appreciate the scope of the foreseeability test, in tort today, three different areas of liability must be considered.

(i) *Physical injury* The first such area is that where the defendant's tortious conduct inflicts a physical injury on the plaintiff's person or property. Here the plaintiff must show that the *type* of injury inflicted was a reasonably foreseeable consequence of the tort, but he need not show that the *losses* consequent on that injury were equally foreseeable. As one judge has recently said,

> "in determining liability for . . . possible consequences (of an injury), it is not necessary to show that each was within the foreseeable extent or foreseeable scope of the original injury in the same way that the possibility of injury must be foreseen when determining whether or not the defendant's conduct gives a claim in negligence."[5]

In other words, at least where the defendant's conduct inflicts a physical injury on the plaintiff it may be said that the *Wagon Mound* principle forms part of the law of liability but not part of the law of damages.[6] The proposition can be illustrated by reference to the well-known case of *Smith* v. *Leech Brain*.[7]

> As a result of Ds' negligence P's lip was burnt by a piece of molten metal. The burn produced a cancerous growth in the tissues of the lip which already had a malignant condition. P died from the cancer some three years after the accident. But for the burn, cancer might never have developed. P's widow succeeded in an action both under

---

[1] Clearly accepted by the House of Lords in *Hughes* v. *Lord Advocate*, [1963] A.C. 837.
[2] The principle was applied to the tort of nuisance in *The Wagon Mound (No. 2)*, [1967] 1 A.C. 617.
[3] Salmond, *Torts*, 15th Edn., p. 734.
[4] Honoré, 11 I.E.C.L. 7–59.
[5] Per EVELEIGH, J., *Wieland* v. *Cyril Lord Carpets*, [1969] 3 All E.R. 1006, at pp. 1009–1010.
[6] Cf. Street, *Law of Torts*, 5th Edn., p. 144.
[7] [1962] 2 Q.B. 405.

the Law Reform Act 1934 and the Fatal Accidents Acts 1846 to 1959, despite the fact that death was not reasonably foreseeable as resulting from the accident.

Liability was established by proving that the injury (the burn) was a foreseeable consequence of the defendant's negligence. The consequence of that injury, death, was part of the law of *damages* and was not governed by the foreseeability doctrine.

(ii) *Pure economic injury*   Where no physical injury intervenes, the distinction between "liability" and "damages" can no longer be clearly drawn, and the scope of the foreseeability test is uncertain. On the one hand, in the as yet undeveloped area of liability in negligence for pure economic loss, it appears that the foreseeability test when applied as a test of remoteness is satisfied when *any* pure economic injury is foreseeable.[1]   On the other hand, in torts such as passing off and the infringement of patents, judges have for some time committed themselves to the view that the plaintiff may recover damages only for such losses as were the natural and probable consequences of the defendant's unlawful act,[2] and this is usually regarded as the ancestor of the modern foreseeability rule.

(iii) *Intentional torts*   There is a general principle that intended consequences can never be too remote.[3]   But this does not dispose of the problem for intentional torts, for though the defendant may intend to inflict harm on the plaintiff he may not have intended to inflict the particular losses actually sustained. The question thus arises whether foreseeability determines the extent of liability in such circumstances. In *Doyle* v. *Olby*[4] LORD DENNING, M.R. said:

> "the defendant is bound to make reparation for all the actual damages directly flowing from the fraudulent inducement. . . .   All such damages can be recovered: and it does not lie in the mouth of the fraudulent person to say that they could not reasonably have been foreseen."[5]

Of course, these remarks may refer only to the tort of deceit, but, assuming it can be applied generally to intentional torts the dictum admits of two possible constructions. In the first place, it may be

---

[1] See LORD DENNING, M.R. in *Spartan Steel* v. *Martin*, [1972] 3 W.L.R. 502, at p. 508 and *Morrison S.S. Co., Ltd.*, v. *S.S. Greystoke Castle*, [1947] A.C. 265.
[2] *Per* LORD MACNAGHTEN, *United Horse-Shoe and Nail Co., Ltd.* v. *Stewart* (1888), 13 App. Cas. 401, at p. 416; *per* SWINFEN EADY, L.J., *Spalding* v. *Gamage, A. W., Ltd.* (1918), 35 R.P.C. 101, at p. 117.
[3] Cf. LORD LINDLEY in *Quinn* v. *Leatham*, [1901] A.C. 495, at p. 537.
[4] [1969] 2 Q.B. 158.
[5] *Ibid.*, at p. 167.   The attitude of the other judges in the case was ambiguous: WINN, L.J. conceded (at p. 168) that a consequence would not "necessarily" be too remote because it was not contemplated; SACHS, L.J. clearly envisaged

interpreted *narrowly*. If the emphasis is on "directly flowing from" instead of "reasonably foreseeable", then it would seem merely to substitute one formulation of the remoteness doctrine for another. Losses may be held too remote, but the foreseeability doctrine should not provide the test. On a *broader* interpretation, the dictum may be regarded as dispensing altogether with remoteness as a limit to liability. It is submitted that the former construction should be preferred. It cannot be that the defendant is to be liable for all the consequences which result from his intentional act. For example,

> D fraudulently induces P to buy a business, the liabilities of which, contrary to his representations, exceed its assets. On leaving his new office, P falls down the stairs and injures himself.

Clearly, the defendant's fraud was a *causa sine qua non* of the fall, but it would indeed be harsh to impose on him liability for the consequences. The reluctance to apply the doctrine of remoteness was understandable in the context of the facts in *Doyle* v. *Olby*.[1]

> P was induced to buy a business on Ds' fraudulent misrepresentation, *inter alia*, that all the business was done over the counter, whereas one member of the firm had acted as travelling sales representative. P could not afford to employ a traveller and consequently sustained a considerable loss of profits.

While obviously keen to award the plaintiff compensation for this loss, the Court of Appeal must have felt themselves inhibited from so doing by the decision in *Liesbosch, Dredger* v. *Edison S.S.*[2] There the House of Lords had denied recovery for those losses which had resulted from the plaintiff's impecuniosity. But it does not follow from this case that any claim for a loss to which the plaintiff's own financial problems had contributed must automatically be denied. Questions of remoteness are invariably questions of degree, and whether the test is formulated in terms of "directness" or "reasonable foreseeability" it lay within the power of court to hold that such a consequence was not too remote. It was not a sufficient reason for abandoning the remoteness doctrine altogether.

4 Remoteness in contract

The doctrine of remoteness plays a more significant role in the law of damages than its counterpart in tort for two reasons. First breaches of contract most frequently give rise to purely economic injury, and as

---

some test of remoteness (at p. 171) but did not indicate any criterion on which it should be judged. See also Treitel (1969), 32 M.L.R. 552.

[1] [1969] 2 Q.B. 158.
[2] [1933] A.C. 449.

has been explained[1] where physical injury does not intervene it is impossible to draw a clear line between questions of liability and questions of quantification. Secondly, in contract the doctrine of remoteness not only prevents the award of certain losses which were too remote but in some cases actually prescribes the amount which the plaintiff may recover, that is to say, that though a plaintiff may be debarred from recovering compensation for the actual loss which he sustained on the ground that it was too remote, he may nevertheless recover damages for such notional losses as would not have been too remote.[2]

In this chapter the task will be to examine the general principle of remoteness emanating from the so-called rule in *Hadley* v. *Baxendale*.[3] In Chapters Eight and Nine, it will be seen how the doctrine is applied to the quantification process.

(a) *Hadley v. Baxendale* formulation

The first[4] deliberate formulation of general principles was embodied in the judgment of the Court of Exchequer[5] in *Hadley* v. *Baxendale*.

> Ps delivered a broken millshaft to Ds, carriers, to convey to its makers as a model for a replacement. Ps had no spare shaft, but Ds were told only[6] that the article was a broken millshaft, and that Ps were owners of the mill in question. Ds were late in delivering the shaft. The jury awarded a sum for the loss of profits while the mill remained idle. On appeal, a new trial was ordered.

The judgment of ALDERSON, B. has been quoted and analysed in so many succeeding cases that it is desirable to reproduce a lengthy passage from it.[7]

(A) "where two parties have made a contract which one of them has broken, the damage which the other party ought to receive in respect

---

[1] *Supra*, p. 61.

[2] *Infra*, p. 319.

[3] (1854), 9 Exch. 341.

[4] For the history of contract damages prior to the decision see Washington (1931), 47 L.Q.R. 345, (1932), 48 L.Q.R. 90.

[5] "A more extensive and accurate knowledge of decisions in our law books, and a more acute power of analysing and discussing them, and . . . a longer acquaintance with the exigencies of commerce and the business of life, never combined to assist at the formation of any decision," *per* POLLOCK, C.B., *Wilson* v. *Newport Dock* (1866), L.R. 1 Exch. 177, at p. 189.

[6] It is incorrectly stated in the headnote to the case at 9 Exch. 341 that Ds' clerk was told that the mill was stopped and that the shaft must be delivered immediately. If that had been the case, then Ds would have known of the special circumstances, sufficient to make them liable. See ASQUITH, L.J. in *Victoria Laundry (Windsor), Ltd.* v. *Newman Industries, Ltd.*, [1949] 2 K.B. 528, at p. 537.

[7] (1854), 9 Exch. 341, at pp. 354–355.

of such breach of contract should be such as may fairly and reasonably be considered either"

(I) "arising naturally, i.e., according to usual course of things, from such breach of contract itself, or"

(II) "such as may reasonably be supposed to have been in the contemplation of both parties, at the time they made the contract, as the probable result of the breach of it."

(B) "If the special circumstances under which the contract was actually made were communicated by the plaintiffs to the defendants, and thus known to both parties, the damages resulting from the breach of such a contract, which they would reasonably contemplate, would be the amount of injury which would ordinarily follow from a breach of contract under these special circumstances so known and communicated. But, on the other hand, if these special circumstances were wholly unknown to the party breaking the contract, he, at the most, could only be supposed to have had in his contemplation the amount of the injury which would arise generally and in the great multitude of cases not affected by any special circumstances, from such a breach of contract."

(C) "For, had the special circumstances been known, the parties might have specially provided for the breach of contract by special terms as to the damages in that case. . . ."

In the instant case, on the one hand, loss of profits was not a loss "arising naturally" from the delay in delivering a piece of machinery. On the other hand, the special circumstances of the case, that the mill would remain idle until a replacement was obtained, were not communicated to the defendants.

(b) Single rule of reasonable contemplation

The so-called rule (or rules) in *Hadley* v. *Baxendale* is expressed in (A). The first question which is said to arise is whether the sentence embodies one or two rules. In several early cases it was made the subject of a lively dispute. On one view,[1] a distinction was to be drawn between losses "arising naturally from the breach" (AI) which, to be recoverable, did not require the contemplation of the parties, and "special losses" which required the contemplation actual or implied of the parties (AII). The alternative view had it that AI like AII depended on the contemplation of the parties "for damages which may reasonably be supposed to have been contemplated by the contracting parties, are damages which naturally arise from a breach of contract."[2]

---

[1] See, e.g. LORD ESHER, M.R. in *Hammond & Co.* v. *Bussey* (1888), 20 Q.B.D. 79, at pp. 88–89.
[2] *Per* CROMPTON, J., *Smeed* v. *Foord* (1859), 1 E. & E. 602, at p. 616.

The dispute is surely without real significance as it can make no difference in result which view is taken.[1]   Nevertheless, with occasional dissenters,[2] the dominant opinion today prefers the second view if only for the sake of neatness.   This follows on the restatement of the rule(s) in *Victoria Laundry (Windsor), Ltd.* v. *Newman Industries, Ltd.*,[3] in which the Court of Appeal proposed a single rule based on "reasonable foreseeability".[4]   After the criticism of this expression by the House of Lords in *Koufos* v. *Czarnikow*,[5] it now seems preferable to refer to "reasonable contemplation", but whatever formulation is employed, the single-rule view is still favoured.[6]   It may be said that the rule, based as it is on the contemplation of the parties (actual or implied) contains aspects both objective and subjective.   As regards the "ordinary, natural" losses within AI, the test is a wholly objective one: what the ordinary person entering into such a contract would expect to result. AII, on the other hand, contains elements both subjective and objective: it is *subjective* in the sense that it depends on special circumstances known to both parties; it is *objective* in that actual contemplation is not required—it need only "reasonably be supposed to have been in the contemplation of the parties."

(c) Degree of likelihood required

The use of the word "naturally" in AI and "probable" in AII[7] raises a question as to the required degree of likelihood that the contemplated loss might result from the breach.   Given that the two words "naturally" and "probable" are intended as equivalents, and given that the court adopts the notional standard of what the parties would have contemplated if they had considered the possibilities of breach, how probable must the loss claimed in fact have been?   There has been a plethora of answers to this question.

In *R. and H. Hall, Ltd.* v. *W. H. Pim (Junior) & Co., Ltd.*,[8] VISCOUNT DUNEDIN said, "it is enough . . . that there is an even chance of its

---

[1] See, e.g. LORD UPJOHN in *Koufos* v. *Czarnikow*, [1969] 1 A.C. 350, at p. 421.
[2] E.g. DIPLOCK, L.J. in *Robophone Facilities* v. *Blank*, [1966] 1 W.L.R. 1428, at p. 1448. See also the observations of DEVLIN, J. in *Biggin & Co.* v. *Permanite*, [1951] 1 K.B. 422, at p. 436.
[3] [1949] 2 K.B. 528.
[4] *Ibid.*, at p. 529.
[5] [1969] 1 A.C. 350, *infra*, p. 75.
[6] *Ibid.*, *per* LORD REID, at p. 382, *per* LORD MORRIS, at p. 395, *per* LORD UPJOHN, at p. 421.
[7] In *Koufos* v. *Czarnikow*, *supra*, at p. 410, LORD HODSON considered that the word "probable" covered both parts of the rule, but it is difficult to see how, on construction, this is possible.
[8] (1928), 33 Com. Cas. 324.

happening"[1] while LORD SHAW's concern was whether it was "not likely to occur".[2]

In *Monarch S.S. Co.* v. *Karlshamns Oljefabriker*,[3] the various expressions used were: what "could reasonably have been foreseen,[4] "grave risk",[5] "serious possibility",[6] and "real danger".[6]

The Court of Appeal in restating the law in the *Victoria Laundry* case approved the latter two formulations and added: "for short, we have used the word 'liable' to result. Possibly the colloquialism 'on the cards' indicates the shade of meaning with some approach to accuracy".[7]

One might legitimately have imagined that by this time the barrel of linguistic devices had run dry, that the matter was very much one for the discretion of the trial judge, benefiting as he could from the fluidity of judicial expression. But in *Koufos* v. *Czarnikow*[8] the question was raised again before the House of Lords.

Ps chartered Ds' ship to carry sugar to Basrah. Owing to a deviation of the ship, delivery of the sugar was delayed for nine days during which time the market price had fallen by £1 7s 3d. per ton. It was held that Ps were entitled to the loss in the market on the ground that Ds should have contemplated that Ps would wish to sell the sugar at market price on arrival and would therefore sustain a loss should the ship be delayed and the market price fall.

One point on which their Lordships were unanimous was the relationship of *Hadley* v. *Baxendale* rules in contract to the *Wagon Mound*[9] rule in tort. The expression employed by the Court of Appeal in the *Victoria Laundry* case ("reasonably foreseeable as liable to result"[10]) seemed on the face of it to accord with that laid down for tort ("of such a kind as the reasonable man should have foreseen").[11] The House considered, however, that the degree of probability should be higher in contract than in tort.[12] In tort the defendant should be liable for slight but foreseeable risks. Thus, concluded LORD REID,[13] a

---

[1] *Ibid.*, at p. 330.
[2] *Ibid.*, at p. 336.
[3] [1949] A.C. 196.
[4] *Ibid.*, *per* LORD PORTER, at p. 214.
[5] *Ibid.*, *per* LORD MORTON, at p. 235.
[6] *Ibid.*, *per* LORD DU PARCQ, at pp. 233, 234.
[7] *Per* ASQUITH, L.J., [1949] 2 K.B. 528, at p. 540.
[8] [1969] 1 A.C. 350.
[9] [1961] A.C. 388, *supra*, p. 68.
[10] [1949] 2 K.B. 528, at p. 539.
[11] *Wagon Mound (No. 1)*, *supra*, at p. 426.
[12] [1969] 1 A.C. 350, *per* LORD REID, at pp. 385–386; *per* LORD HODSON, at p. 411; *per* LORD PEARCE, at pp. 413–414; *per* LORD UPJOHN, at pp. 422–423.
[13] *Ibid.*, at p. 386.

tortfeasor would have been liable for the stoppage of the mill in *Hadley* v. *Baxendale*.[1] But in contract this would be too harsh. How, then, to characterize the degree of probability required? The hapless student is confronted with yet more verbiage:

> (i) LORD REID required a "very substantial degree of probability" or an event which was "not unlikely"[2]
>
> (ii) LORD MORRIS did not have much faith in any one word or phrase[3] but seemed content with "liable to result or at least not unlikely to result".[4]
>
> (iii) LORD HODSON too favoured "liable to result"[5] although it had been rejected by LORD REID.[6]
>
> (iv) LORD PEARCE preferred "serious possibility" or "real danger" which he equated with the ambiguous words "liable to result".[7]
>
> (v) LORD UPJOHN agreed with LORD PEARCE.[8]

These attempts to achieve some sort of certainty in this field are, it is suggested, fruitless. It is impossible to translate the linguistic devices used into more specific criteria. It is a question rather of appreciating the general sentiments expressed by their Lordships, and more particularly the contrast drawn between contract and tort.

(d) Scope of "reasonable contemplation"

It is now necessary to examine in greater detail the meaning and scope of "reasonable contemplation". Several questions arise: (i) must the parties provide for the recovery of the loss by a contractual term? (ii) what is the significance of the existence or absence of communication of the special circumstances? (iii) what is the relationship between actual and imputed knowledge? (iv) by what standards does the court determine what it is reasonable for the parties to contemplate? These will be considered in turn.

(i) *The consensus theory*   If the judgment of ALDERSON, B. is revisited,[9] it will be seen that in C he refers to the possibility that the parties *might* have provided for liability in the special circumstances by express terms. Some judges have fastened on to this dictum and concluded

---

[1] (1854), 9 Exch. 341.
[2] [1969] 1 A.C. 350, at p. 388. This view was adopted by MEGAW, J. in *Allan Peters* v. *Brocks Alarms*, [1968] 1 Lloyd's Rep. 387. See also DONALDSON, J. in *Aruna Mills* v. *Dhanrajmal Gobindram*, [1968] 1 Q.B. 655.
[3] [1969] 1 A.C. 350, at p. 397.
[4] *Ibid.*, at p. 406.
[5] *Ibid.*, at pp. 410–411.
[6] *Ibid.*, at p. 389.
[7] *Ibid.*, at p. 415.
[8] *Ibid.*, at p. 425.
[9] *Supra*, p. 73.

that liability for losses beyond those "arising naturally" (AI) is dependent on the existence of an implied term in the contract to that effect.[1] Of course, from one point of view it may be said that this is an argument without essence: implied terms are simply devices used by the law to found liability in certain circumstances[2] and to insist on their use here is merely to create an unnecessary fiction. Yet the point may not be altogether without significance. In the heyday of the "*consensus*" theory of contract, the view was commonly held that to make a person liable for special losses he must consciously accept the risk of such special liability.

> "The knowledge must be brought home to the party sought to be charged, under such circumstances that he must know that the person he contracts with reasonably believes that he accepts the contract with the special condition attached to it."[3]

However, a careful reading of passage C in ALDERSON, B.'s judgment reveals clearly that the notion of a contractual term was employed only as a reason for imposing liability where *actual* knowledge as to the special circumstances existed. If, and to the extent that, knowledge is imputed, then the requirement of acceptance of risk can at most be a fiction. Further, the requirement can operate effectively only if a clear line is drawn between AI liability (ordinary losses) and AII liability (special losses), and as has been shown[4] this distinction is no longer favoured. Against the background of these facts, it is now clear that the courts have abandoned the *consensus* theory.[5]

(ii) *Significance of communication*   In passage B quoted from *Hadley* v. *Baxendale*[6] ALDERSON, B. illustrated the principle of AII with the hypothesis of an actual communication of special circumstances by the plaintiff to the defendants. Two questions arise from this: (i) is communication *necessary* to impose liability? (ii) is communication *sufficient* to impose liability? The answer to (i) is necessarily linked with the attitude to the *consensus* theory described in the last paragraph. If the distinction between AI and AII is drawn, then it may be argued that for the purposes of liability under AII the "special circumstances" must

---

[1] See, e.g. WILLES, J. in *British Columbia, etc., Saw Mill Co.* v. *Nettleship* (1868), L.R. 3 C.P. 499, at p. 509 and in *Horne* v. *Midland Rail Co.* (1872), L.R. 7 C.P. 583, at p. 591, adopted in SALTER, J. in *Patrick* v. *Russo-British Grain Export*, [1927] 2 K.B. 535, at p. 540.
[2] Treitel, p. 166. Cf. the doctrine of frustration, *ibid.*, at pp. 779–780.
[3] *Per* WILLES, J., *Nettleship*'s case, *supra*, at p. 509.
[4] *Supra*, p. 74.
[5] *Victoria Laundry* case, [1949] 2 K.B. 528, at p. 540; *Koufos* v. *Czarnikow*, [1969] 1 A.C. 350, at pp. 421–422.
[6] (1854), 9 Exch. 341, *supra*, p. 73.

be brought to the attention of the defendant.[1] If, on the other hand, in accordance with the prevailing opinion, there is but one rule based on "reasonable contemplation", then to insist on communication would make the law both impracticable and rigid.   The answer to (ii) would seem to be that in general communication before or at the time of the contract (though not after)[2] will be sufficient to impose liability.   There are dicta against this view but these are from cases in which the now defunct *consensus* theory was relied on.[3]   At the last resort it is a question of fact, taking into account all the circumstances of the case, including the form and context of the communication, whether it was sufficient for the defendant reasonably to contemplate the loss as resulting from the breach.[4]

(iii) *Actual and implied knowledge*   In some cases, the court will reach its decision on the basis of the imputed knowledge of the parties at the time of the contract; in others, the parties may wish to go further and adduce evidence of actual knowledge.   The latter course will usually be taken by a plaintiff who fears that the objective test of implied knowledge will operate to limit the losses for which he claims compensation. He will attempt to show that the defendant possessed some knowledge which encompassed the particular losses which he pleads. But the subjective test may also be invoked by a *defendant* who seeks to persuade the court to take into account certain consequences of the breach which proved profitable to the plaintiff, in order that the damages might be reduced.[5]   In such circumstances it will be for the plaintiff to argue that such consequences were too remote.

(iv) *Standard of reasonable businessman*   Where argument is confined to the objective text of imputed knowledge, then the standard to be applied is generally said to be that of the "reasonable businessman."[6] It would seem that this is intended to refer to the knowledge of the reasonable businessman engaged in the trade of the party in question. This test, though it has not found expression in the judgments, is,

---

[1] Thus, e.g. DIPLOCK, L.J. in *Robophone Facilities* v. *Blank*, [1966] 1 W.L.R. 1428, at pp. 1447–1448.

[2] *Per* BRETT, L.J. in *Hydraulic Engineering* v. *McHaffie* (1878), 4 Q.B.D. 670, at p. 676 which must be taken as superseding the contrary view expressed by BRAMWELL, B. in *Gee* v. *Lancs. and Yorkshire Rail Co.* (1860), 6 H. & N. 211, at p. 218.

[3] *British Columbia, etc., Saw Mill Co.* v. *Nettleship* (1868), L.R. 3 C.P. 499.

[4] E.g. *Candy* v. *Midland Rail Co.* (1878), 38 L.T. 226.

[5] *Per* DEVLIN, J., *Biggin & Co.* v. *Permanite*, [1951] 1 K.B. 422, at p. 436. See e.g. *Joyner* v. *Weeks*, [1891] 2 Q.B. 31 (though the point was decided on grounds of causation rather than remoteness) and *infra*, pp. 370–375.

[6] *Per* LORD WRIGHT in *Monarch S.S.* v. *Karlhamns Oljefabriker*, [1949] A.C. 196, at p. 222, *per* LORD MORRIS in *Koufos* v. *Czarnikow*, [1969] 1 A.C. 350, at p. 400.

nevertheless, reflected in the decisions. Thus, whereas a merchant who sells goods may reasonably contemplate that his purchaser will resell goods, and thus be liable for the loss of profit on the subsale,[1] a carrier of goods will in general not be expected to contemplate this consequence, and thus will not be liable for an equivalent loss.[2] Where evidence of actual knowledge is laid before the court, then naturally, the extent of the defendant's liability will be commensurable with the extent of his knowledge. In *Foaminol Laboratories* v. *British Artid Plastics*[3]

> Ds agreed to provide Ps with containers for a new cosmetic which Ps were about to put on the market. Ds knew that the product was a new one and that money would be spent on advertising the product, but they did not know that Ps had also secured the co-operation of a number of editresses of female magazines who were to introduce the product to their readers. Ds failed to deliver the containers. They were held liable for *inter alia* the ordinary advertising expenses which had been wasted but not for the arrangement with the editresses as their knowledge of Ps' campaign did not extend to this.

II   CERTAINTY

1   Introduction

One of the most problematical aspects of the assessment process is the speculation which is necessarily involved. The court must attempt to predict what would have happened to the plaintiff if the tort or breach of contract had not occurred. In addition, if compensation for future losses is claimed, some estimate of what will happen to the plaintiff must be made. In this section it will be seen how the law deals with the inevitable uncertainties involved. On the one hand, it excludes from its consideration some losses which it regards as wholly "speculative". On the other hand, it prescribes the method for qualifying compensation for those losses which, though uncertain, may nevertheless be made the subject of an award.

2   Analogous doctrines

So described, the doctrine of certainty must be distinguished from other doctrines which perform similar but not identical functions.

---

[1] E.g. *R. & H. Hall, Ltd.* v. *W. H. Pim (Junior) & Co., Ltd.* (1928), 33 Com. Cas. 324.
[2] *The Arpad*, [1934] P. 189. The distinction between seller and carrier is brought out by the C.A. in the *Victoria Laundry* case, [1949] 2 K.B. 528, at p. 537.
[3] [1941] 2 All E.R. 393.

(a) Establishing a cause of action

To establish a cause of action the plaintiff must prove on *the balance of probabilities* the existence of a number of facts required by the law as a condition for the type of liability in question.   Even though it may be uncertain whether or not the facts grounding liability did exist, the court must decide one way or the other.   If, on the balance of probabilities, it is more likely that the alleged facts existed, then for the purposes of establishing liability, it is proved that they did exist.[1]   But the law of damages, since it is concerned with measuring the degree of loss, is more flexible: it can and must evaluate the chance of an uncertain loss accruing.   Once the cause of action has been established, the plaintiff may recover a sum representing the chance of securing an uncertain, even improbable, benefit, provided only that the chance was more than "entirely speculative".[2]

(b) Causation and remoteness

Judges sometimes confuse questions of certainty with questions of remoteness.   It is perhaps another illustration of the almost instinctive recourse to the remoteness doctrine as providing the solution to so many of the problems arising in the law of damages.   In *The Bodlewell*[3]

> P ship was damaged by D ship.   At the time P ship was engaged on a series of unprofitable voyages the object of which was to establish for her a foothold in the trade.   Her owners claimed damages for the contingency that she would have made a profit once she had established herself.   BARGRAVE DEANE, J. held that the loss was too "remote".

With respect, the problem was one of certainty.   It could not be said that the chance of earning a profit was unforeseeable, or that it was not effectively caused by the defendant's tort.   The question was whether the chance was so small that it should be ignored.   These issues must be separately determined.[4]   Conversely what are properly questions of causation or remoteness may be mistaken for questions of certainty.   The doctrine of certainty deals with future or hypothetical events.   If, by the time of the trial, a loss has actually materialized it can hardly fail for lack of certainty, though it may still fail to satisfy the requirements of causation or remoteness.   It is beside the point to argue that if events had turned out differently the loss might never have occurred.

---

[1] *Per* LORD REID, *Davies* v. *Taylor*, [1972] 3 All E.R. 836, at p. 838; and see *Sykes* v. *Midland Bank Executor and Trustee Co.*, [1971] 1 Q.B. 113, *infra*, p. 81.
[2] *Davies* v. *Taylor*, *supra*.
[3] [1907] P. 286.
[4] See, e.g. *Hall* v. *Meyrick*, [1957] 2 Q.B. 455, *per* ASHWORTH, J. at pp. 469–471. His decision was reversed by the Court of Appeal but on other grounds.

The point emerged clearly in *Sykes* v. *Midland Bank Executor and Trustee Co.*[1]

> Ps, a firm of architects, entered into an underlease with the approval of their solicitors Ds. Ps were under the mistaken impression that under the terms of the lease, the superior landlords could not reasonably withhold consent to their subletting the premises. They were unable to sublet and sued Ds for negligently failing to explain to them the true effect of the terms of the lease.

The plaintiffs failed on the ground that they could not show that the loss sustained (payment of an excessive rent) was caused by the defendants' breach, that is, they had not discharged the onus of proving that if they had been properly advised they would not have entered into the lease at the same rent. The ingenious argument formulated by plaintiffs' counsel that in any case the court should, on the principles of certainty, evaluate the chance of their not having entered the underlease on the same terms was rejected. The loss had already occurred; it was no longer uncertain. If it was caused by the defendants' breach, they were liable for it. If, on the balance of probabilities, they did not cause it, it is futile for the plaintiffs to argue that there had always been a possibility that they might have caused it.

(c) Proof

Finally the doctrine must be distinguished from that which compels the plaintiff to prove his losses with the required standard of exactness. The standard will vary according to the type of loss pleaded. Reference has already been made[2] to the distinction between special damages, which must be proved exactly, and general damages which need not. But within this distinction there are further variations. For example, while both non-pecuniary and future pecuniary losses are treated as general damages, it is clear that more is required by way of proof of the latter than of the former. It is impossible to provide more in the way of generalization. As BOWEN, L.J. said in *Ratcliffe* v. *Evans*[3]

> "In all actions . . . on the case where the damage actually done is the gist of the action, the character of the acts themselves which produce the damage, and the circumstances under which these acts are done, must regulate the degree of certainty and particularity with which the damage done ought to be stated and proved. As much certainty and particularity must be insisted on . . . as is reasonable, having regard to

---

[1] [1971] 1 Q.B. 113.
[2] *Supra*, pp. 3–4.
[3] [1892] 2 Q.B. 524, at pp. 532–533.

the circumstances and to the nature of the acts themselves by which the damage is done."

Some indication of the degree of proof required for each category of loss will be given subsequently in this work as the various heads of damages are described.

3 Principles of the doctrine of certainty

The doctrine of certainty may be divided into four principles.

(a) Difficulty of assessment no bar to recovery

It has always been clear that compensation for certain types of loss must in their nature be speculative. No one could be dogmatic about the sum assessed for the loss of a non-pecuniary asset. The fact that precise pecuniary estimation was impossible was not regarded as an obstacle to recovery.[1] Where, however, the plaintiff claimed damages for some form of commercial loss, especially loss of profits, a different sentiment prevailed. The courts were for some time reluctant to award damages for "general loss of business" on the grounds that the losses were impossible to quantify.[2] This was particularly hard on those enterprises (e.g. fishing) whose receipts were necessarily uncertain.[3] Some judges were prepared to assert as a general rule that "in actions for breach of contract the damages must be such as are capable of being appreciated or estimated".[4] But by the end of the nineteenth century, the reluctance to award damages in these circumstances had been largely overcome. A decision which was clearly influential in this respect was *Simpson* v. *London and North Western Rail Co.*[5]

> P, a manufacturer, regularly attended agricultural shows to put on display samples of his goods and attract custom. Ds failed to deliver the samples in time for a show. P recovered from Ds damages for loss of custom. The objection that the lost profits were impossible to quantify was repudiated: "a sufficient answer is that it must be assumed that the plaintiff would make some profit."[6]

---

[1] Cf. *supra*, p. 20.
[2] E.g. *The Columbus* (1849), 3 Wm. Rob. 158. This must be distinguished from the objection that the plaintiff is unable to provide sufficient proof of the loss (e.g. *Watson* v. *Gray* (1900), 16 T.L.R. 308) which is still good law. See *infra*, pp. 292–293.
[3] E.g. *Hall* v. *Ross* (1813), 1 Dow 201.
[4] Per POLLOCK, C.B., *Hamlin* v. *Great Northern Rail Co.* (1856), 1 H. & N. 408, at p. 411.
[5] (1876), 1 Q.B.D. 274. See also *Marcus* v. *Myers and Davis* (1895), 11 T.L.R. 327.
[6] Per FIELD, J. (1876), 1 Q.B.D. 274, at p. 278.

The consequence was that, a plaintiff might recover damages for such loss of earnings as commission[1] and gratuities.[2] The principle was expressed in the most forceful terms in *Chaplin* v. *Hicks*:[3] "the fact that the damages cannot be assessed with certainty does not relieve the wrongdoer. . . ."

(b) No recovery for entirely speculative chances

There are some losses which depend on so many contingencies that the chance of the plaintiff sustaining them is very small. Compensation for such losses is in general not recoverable. The classic instance was postulated by ERLE, C.J. in *Priestley* v. *Maclean*:[4]

> "Supposing a lady to have been injured and disfigured in a railway accident, she could not say that she ought to recover damages because she was prevented from going to a ball, at which she might have met a rich husband."

Prior to the decision in *Chaplin* v. *Hicks*[5] the rule was rigorously applied, sometimes with harsh results.[6] But that case established a new trend.

> P entered for a beauty competition organized by D, a theatrical manager. 50 of the entrants were to be selected for interview, and 12 of these were to be offered theatrical engagements. P was selected as one of the 50 for interview but through D's breach she was not informed in time and was thus deprived of the opportunity of securing an engagement. The Court of Appeal held that P's chance of winning an engagement was not too speculative and she should recover substantial damages for the loss.

Although the rule that a chance may be too small to permit recovery was explicitly restated in that case,[7] examples of its application since are rare.[8] The court can generally account for even small contingencies on the principle next to be discussed.

(c) Contingent losses to be quantified according to the likelihood of the loss occurring

Assuming a loss is contingent or speculative how are the damages to be quantified? The answer can at least be inferred from the judgments

---

[1] *Trollope & Sons* v. *Martyn*, [1934] 2 K.B. 436.
[2] *Manubens* v. *Leon*, [1919] 1 K.B. 208.
[3] *Per* VAUGHAN WILLIAMS, L.J., [1911] 2 K.B. 786, at p. 792.
[4] (1860), 2 F. & F. 288, at p. 289.
[5] *Supra.*
[6] E.g. *Sapwell* v. *Bass*, [1910] 2 K.B. 486 (D failed to supply a stallion to serve P's mare. P was not allowed to recover for the chance of acquiring a valuable foal).
[7] *Per* FARWELL, L.J., [1911] 2 K.B. 786, at p. 798.
[8] But see, e.g. *Davies* v. *Taylor*, [1972] 3 All E.R. 836.

in *Chaplin* v. *Hicks*.[1] Although the members of the Court of Appeal were not prepared to commit themselves on the amount to be awarded (it was a jury trial) they clearly regarded as significant the fact that the plaintiff had approximately a one in four chance of winning a prize. The principle then emerges that the damages should be quantified according to the chance of the loss occurring.[2] Thus the average of the benefits which would have been earned if the plaintiff had won should be divided by four. The process is well illustrated by *Barry* v. *British Transport Commission*.[3]

> For three weeks before he was injured P was working as a member of a gang and earning at the special rate of £14 per week. Before that he had earned an average of £7 per week. The evidence suggested that there was a bare probability (no more) that he would have become a permanent member of the gang if he had not been injured. He was awarded damages at about 60 per cent. of the special rate of earnings.

The corollary to the method by which chances are quantified is that deductions are to be made for the small chance that probable losses might not occur. Thus account is often taken of the possibility that a seriously disabled plaintiff may die earlier, or may recover more rapidly, than anticipated.[4] A deduction is also to be made for the possibility that the anticipated future losses might have been sustained even if there had been no tort or breach of contract. Thus earnings might have been affected by unemployment, illness, redundancy or strikes.[5] A disabled vessel might in any case have been prevented by the outbreak of war or the hazards of the sea from earning its profit in the performance of a charterparty.[6] The amount to be deducted for these contingencies will vary according to the nature of the risk.[7]

(d) Special rule for claims in contract

A somewhat illiberal rule prevails in cases of breach of contract. If the extent of a contractual benefit lost as a result of the breach would have depended on the exercise of a discretion by the defendant himself, it is to be assumed, for the purpose of assessing the value of the lost benefit that he would have exercised his discretion in a manner most favourable to himself and least favourable to the plaintiff.[8] The most

---

[1] *Supra.*
[2] *Davies* v. *Taylor, supra*, at pp. 838, 845 and 847.
[3] [1954] 1 Lloyd's Rep. 372.
[4] *Winkworth* v. *Hubbard*, [1960] 1 Lloyd's Rep. 150 and *infra*, p. 188.
[5] *Per* JAMES, L.J., *Phillips* v. *London and South Western Rail Co.* (1879), 5 Q.B.D. 78, at pp. 81–82 and *infra*, p. 187.
[6] *The Star of India* (1876), 1 P.D. 466.
[7] See *infra*, n. 5, p. 187.
[8] *Cockburn* v. *Alexander* (1818), 6 C.B. 791 and the authorities cited *infra*, pp. 310–312.

typical instance arises in employment contracts. A plaintiff suing for wrongful dismissal is limited to the wages he would have earned during the period of notice for lawful termination required under the contract.[1] The law assumes that the defendant would have exercised his right lawfully to terminate the contract at the first possible opportunity. This rule is fully analysed (and criticized) in a subsequent chapter.[2]

III MITIGATION

1 Introduction and policy

The object of the doctrine of mitigation is to relieve the defendant from liability for those consequences of the injury which the plaintiff avoided or might reasonably have avoided. The classic formulation is that of VISCOUNT HALDANE, L.C. in *British Westinghouse Electric and Manufacturing Co., Ltd.* v. *Underground Electric Rail Co. of London, Ltd.*[3] Having stated the basic compensatory principle, he continued:

"but this first principle is qualified by a second, which imposes on a plaintiff the duty of taking all reasonable steps to mitigate the loss consequent on the breach, and debars him from claiming any part of the damage which is due to his neglect to take such steps."

Though stated in the context of a case on breach of contract, the doctrine applies equally to compensation in tort.[4] The policy considerations are the same for both. In the first place, it is a necessary corollary to the compensatory principle. The defendant is to compensate the plaintiff only for losses actually sustained. If through his own reasonable efforts the plaintiff has reduced his losses, then the defendant's liability will be limited to such losses. It would be injust both to this "reasonable" plaintiff and to the defendant if the "unreasonable" plaintiff who does not attempt to minimize his loss should receive more. Secondly, the doctrine may be attributed to a desire on the part of the law to discourage activities which are economically wasteful and encourage the careful husbanding of resources.[5] It is one method of reducing the overall cost to society of legally compensatable injuries.

---

[1] *British Guiana Credit* v. *Da Silva*, [1965] 1 W.L.R. 248, *infra*, p. 312.
[2] *Infra*, pp. 309–314.
[3] [1912] A.C. 673, at p. 689.
[4] The doctrine has been expounded most often in cases of contract. It has always been implicit in tort awards but not received such explicit recognition. See, however, *Darbishire* v. *Warren*, [1963] 1 W.L.R. 1067, *per* HARMAN, L.J., at p. 1071, *per* PEARSON, L.J., at p. 1075, *per* PENNYCUICK, J., at p. 1078 and *Bellingham* v. *Dhillon*, [1973] 1 All E.R. 20.
[5] McCormick, p. 127; Williston, *Contract*, 3rd Edn., § 1302.

2 **Mitigation distinguished from other doctrines**

"Mitigation" as the term will be used throughout this section refers to the standard of conduct required of the plaintiff in relation to the losses incurred as a result of the defendant's tort or breach of contract. As will be illustrated,[1] the doctrine not only stands on its own as an independent principle, but is also enmeshed in many rules of quantification. However, it must first be distinguished from certain doctrines with which it has no, or at the most very little, connection.

(a) **Extenuating circumstances in certain tort actions**

In some of the torts which protect a plaintiff's intangible interests (defamation, false imprisonment, malicious prosecution) a defendant's liability may be reduced either by his own honourable or morally justifiable conduct or else by the plaintiff's own improper motive or bad reputation. In such cases, the set of extenuating circumstances are often said to "mitigate" the damages. In fact, this is but one way of ascertaining how much the plaintiff has actually "lost" as a consequence of the defendant's tort. It is unconnected with the doctrine to be analysed in this section, and will be discussed in the context of the particular torts in question.[2]

(b) **Contributory negligence**[3]

In actions for tort,[4] and probably also for breach of contract,[5] a plaintiff's damages may be reduced (wholly or partly) on the ground that his own negligent conduct caused (wholly or partly) the *injury*. The doctrine of mitigation, on the other hand, is concerned with the plaintiff's responsibility for the *losses* resulting from that injury. It is evident that the distinction already drawn[6] between *injury* and *loss* again provides the key.[7] Thus where a motor cyclist's injuries are aggravated by his failure to wear a crash helmet, his damages may

---

[1] *Infra*, pp. 90–92.
[2] *Infra*, p. 236.
[3] Williams, *Joint Torts and Contributory Negligence*, ch 11.
[4] *Infra*, Chap. 11, pp. 103–107.
[5] *Quinn* v. *Burch Bros.*, [1966] 2 Q.B. 370, affirmed on different grounds by the C.A. (*ibid.*).
[6] *Supra*, p. 1.
[7] The distinction drawn by Street, p. 27, that in contributory negligence the event occurs before the wrong would seem to be inaccurate. In many cases the plaintiff's act will follow the defendant's *tortious act* but will precede his *injury* (see, e.g. *Harvey* v. *Road Haulage Executive*, [1952] 1 K.B. 120). The distinction drawn in the text was expressly recognized in the U.S. case *Yazoo* v. *Fields* 195 So. 489 (1940). In contrast, Williams, *op. cit.*, regards the duty to mitigate as merely a "species" of the "broad doctrine" of contributory negligence. It may be conceded that hard cases will exist where the line is difficult to draw (the same problem arises regarding the distinction between remoteness

properly be reduced on the ground of contributory negligence.[1] But where he fails to alleviate his losses by refusing to undergo an operation, then mitigation will be the appropriate defence.[2] In general the legal consequences of the two defences are similar: both serve to apportion losses between plaintiff and defendant. The differences that do exist are minor and technical.[3]

(c) Set-off in contract

Where P sues D for D's breach of contract and P is himself in breach, as a result of which D sustains a loss, then the amount of D's loss may be set-off against D's liability. In such circumstances it may be said that P's breach goes in "mitigation" of his award. The question of the nature and operation of this set-off is properly a question of civil procedure rather than of damages and will not be considered here.[4]

(d) Deduction for compensating advantages

A distinction which is more difficult to make in theory, but which will be valuable for the purposes of exposition may be said to exist between the questions (i) whether a reduction is to be made on account of the plaintiff having sustained a loss which he could reasonably have avoided; and (ii) whether a deduction is to be made for a compensating advantage which the plaintiff enjoyed as a result of the breach (for example, if he received a benefit under an insurance policy). In truth, there is a major overlap between the two. While many (though not all) cases of compensating advantage result from the plaintiff's own efforts and therefore might legitimately be regarded as "mitigating" the loss, all cases of mitigation may loosely be described as giving rise to "compensating advantages". The difference between the subject-matter of this and the next section of this chapter lies, therefore, not so much in the factual situation involved as in the legal problem arising therefrom. With "mitigation" the court is concerned with the standard of conduct required of the plaintiff: did he do what was reasonable to keep his losses to a minimum? In other words, should he have created for himself a "compensating advantage"? In the next section, the problem

---

and measure in tort) but this does not seem a sufficient reason for abandoning a distinction which has existed throughout the history of the law of damages (thus giving rise to different sets of subrules) and which assists greatly in clarifying the principles involved.

[1] *O'Connell* v. *Jackson*, [1972] 1 Q.B. 270.
[2] *McAuley* v. *London Transport Executive*, [1957] 2 Lloyd's Rep. 500.
[3] These are very fully discussed in Williams, *op. cit.*, pp. 283–287 and Street, pp. 37–39.
[4] For an account of the rules involved see Rules of the Supreme Court, Ord. 18, r. 17.

to be considered is, given that a compensating advantage was in fact enjoyed by the plaintiff, should the court take it into account in quantifying the plaintiff's loss.   The inquiry there turns on the relationship between the compensating advantages and the tort or breach of contract giving rise to the plaintiff's loss.

3 Principle of mitigation

The basic rule of mitigation is a simple one: a plaintiff may not recover for those losses which he should reasonably have avoided.   In contract, *Payzu, Ltd.* v. *Saunders*[1] provides a good example.

> Ds contracted to deliver goods to Ps in instalments.   Ds, wrongly assuming that Ps could not pay for the goods, refused to deliver the second and subsequent instalments unless Ps would pay cash on receipt.   Ps refused this offer and sued Ds for breach.   It was held that though Ds were in breach by refusing to deliver, Ps should have alleviated their loss by accepting Ds' offer of delivery for ready cash. They were therefore not entitled to compensation for the "avoidable loss", the consequences of non-delivery of goods viz. the difference between the contract price and the market price of the goods at the date of breach.

In tort an analogy is provided by *McAuley* v. *London Transport Executive*.[2]

> P was injured in an accident for which Ds were liable.   He was advised by his doctor, but refused, to have an operation which would, if successful, have restored him to his previous earning capacity.   The court held that his refusal was unreasonable and rejected his claim for continued loss of earnings.

It follows that where the court rejects a claim for losses which it considered "avoidable", it will award instead damages representing such loss as the plaintiff would have sustained if he had acted reasonably in mitigation.   Thus in *Payzu, Ltd.* v. *Saunders*,[1] the plaintiff recovered compensation for the pecuniary disadvantage of paying cash immediately on delivery, i.e. loss of the period of credit available under the original contractual terms; and in *McAuley* v. *London Transport Executive*,[2] the plaintiff recovered for his loss of earnings up to the time when he would have recovered if he had undergone the operation.

A second corollary to the basic principle allows the plaintiff to recover expenses incurred in reasonable efforts to mitigate his losses.   In *Holden* v. *Bostock*[3]

---

[1] [1919] 2 K.B. 581.
[2] [1957] 2 Lloyd's Rep. 500.
[3] (1902), 18 T.L.R. 317.

Ds sold to Ps sugar for brewing beer. The sugar contained arsenic and had to be destroyed. In order to prevent or minimize any loss of business, Ps indicated in advertisements that they had changed their brewing methods. Ps were awarded, *inter alia*, the cost of the advertisements.

Two points arising under these general principles require more detailed examination.

(a) Duty to mitigate

It would be a mistake to take literally the dictum of VISCOUNT HALDANE, L.C. in the *British Westinghouse* case[1] that the plaintiff is under a "duty" to mitigate. This is, strictly speaking inaccurate: no other person can enforce against the plaintiff a legal obligation to mitigate his loss. The only sanction is that his damages will be reduced.[2] It is a "duty" or "obligation" owed to himself.[3] The point is, of course, only a verbal one.

(b) Standard of reasonableness

The standard required of the plaintiff is that "which a reasonable and prudent person might in the ordinary conduct of business properly have taken".[4] Whether the plaintiff has acted reasonably or not is a question of fact for the trial judge, taking into account all the circumstances of the particular case.[5] The onus is on the defendant to show that what the plaintiff did or failed to do was unreasonable.[6] The court should not be over-eager to discharge the defendant's burden:

"It is often easy after an emergency has passed to criticize the steps which have been taken to meet it, but such criticism does not come well from those who have themselves created the emergency. . . . (The plaintiff) will not be held disentitled to recover the cost of such measures merely because the party in breach can suggest that other measures less burdensome to him might have been taken."[7]

The standards imposed vary according to the nature of the loss and

---

[1] [1912] A.C. 673, at pp. 689, *supra*, p. 85.
[2] See PEARSON, L.J. in *Darbishire* v. *Warren*, [1963] 1 W.L.R. 1067, at p. 1075.
[3] *Per* MACKINNON, J., *Wallems Rederij* v. *Muller*, [1927] 2 K.B. 99, at pp. 104–105. See also BURCH, J. in *Rock* v. *Vandive*, 189, P. 157 (1920) on the application of Hohfeld's *Fundamental Legal Conceptions* to the question.
[4] *Per* VISCOUNT HALDANE, L.C., *British Westinghouse* case, [1912] A.C. 673, at p. 690.
[5] *Payzu, Ltd.* v. *Saunders*, [1919] 2 K.B. 581, *per* BANKES, L.J. at p. 588, *per* SCRUTTON, L.J., at p. 589.
[6] *Yetton* v. *Eastwoods Froy*, [1967] 1 W.L.R. 104, at p. 115.
[7] *Per* LORD MACMILLAN, *Banco de Portugal* v. *Waterlow & Sons, Ltd.*, [1932] A.C. 452, at p. 506.

will emerge alongside the detailed rules of assessment. Yet some provisional impression may be gleaned from the following examples.

(I) P need not take action which will put his commercial reputation at risk,[1] or which will cause loss to innocent third persons.[2]

(II) Where seeking an alternative to D's performance, P should, in general, get the best rates available in the market,[3] but need not travel great distances in order to find his market.[4]

(III) In cases of wrongful dismissal, P should not aim too high in seeking alternative employment,[5] but the court will not, as a rule, expect him to take a post of a much lower status,[6] especially if it is with the same employer who dismissed him.[7]

(IV) Where D makes to P an offer of alternative, though less valuable, performance, P should ascertain the exact nature of the offer, rather than dismiss it out of hand.[8] Whether or not it will then be reasonable for P to accept the offer will depend on such factors as: the "personal relationship" between P and D,[9] the nature and extent of D's breach,[10] the terms of the offer having regard to P's business methods and his financial position[11]—his impecuniosity may be a sufficient ground to make refusal reasonable.[12]

(V) Where a professional adviser fails to exercise sufficient care over his client's affairs, the client will not be expected to take his chance in suing a third party to remedy the defect, or to have insured against the possibility of loss.[13]

4 Principle applied in ordinary rules for quantification

The doctrine of mitigation has a twofold function. On the one hand it can be employed in its own right independently of the rules of quantification, as a plea, available to the defendant, for reducing

---

[1] *James Finlay & Co.* v. *Kwik Hoo Tong*, [1929] 1 K.B. 400.
[2] *Banco de Portugal* v. *Waterlow, supra.*
[3] *Watson Norie* v. *Shaw* (1967), 111 Sol. Jo. 117.
[4] *Lesters Leather & Skin Co.* v. *Home and Overseas Brokers* (1948), 64 T.L.R. 569: "I cannot say that the buyers are bound to go hunting the globe . . ." *Per* Lord Goddard, C.J.
[5] *Dunk* v. *Waller*, [1970] 2 Q.B. 163.
[6] *Yetton* v. *Eastwoods Froy*, [1967] 1 W.L.R. 104, cf. *Barnes* v. *Port of London Authority*, [1957] 1 Lloyd's Rep. 486.
[7] *Shindler* v. *Northern Raincoat*, [1960] 2 All E.R. 239.
[8] *Houndsditch Warehouse Co., Ltd.* v. *Waltex, Ltd.*, [1944] K.B. 579.
[9] *Yetton* v. *Eastwoods Froy, supra.*
[10] *Shindler* v. *Northern Raincoat, supra.*
[11] *Payzu, Ltd.* v. *Saunders Co., Ltd.*, [1919] 2 K.B. 581.
[12] *Clippens Oil Co., Ltd.* v. *Edinburgh and District Water Trustees*, [1907] A.C. 291, cf. on *remoteness* the *Liesbosch* case, [1933] A.C. 449, *supra*, p. 71.
[13] *Pilkington* v. *Wood*, [1953] Ch. 770.

damages. On the other hand, it is, on a surprisingly large scale, latent in many rules of quantification. Transition from the former to the latter category may be regarded as an historical development:[1] in well-litigated areas the requirement of mitigation became so self-evident that it became integrated with the rules of quantification, and lost its separate identity. This occurred, for example, when the "market" rules were embodied in the Sale of Goods Act 1893.[2] In other cases, as in contracts for the performance of a service, the requirement of mitigation was not so instinctive, and consequently the doctrine remained distinct. The rules of quantification which are founded on the principle of mitigation will be examined in detail later, but a brief indication of the types of rules in question may be given here.

(a) Out of pocket expenses

In any action for tort or breach of contract, the plaintiff may claim as special damages incidental or out of pocket expenses. Thus in a personal injury case, a plaintiff's living expenses may be increased,[3] while in fatal accident cases funeral expenses are generally incurred.[4] The defendant's breach of contract may result in the plaintiff being liable to a third party. He may have paid out not only a sum by way of compensation but also made himself liable for legal costs.[5] These items of expenditure will, in general, be recoverable if the outlay was "reasonably necessary" and if the amount involved was "reasonable" in the circumstances. If, however, the expense was excessive or should have been avoided, the plaintiff's award will be to that extent reduced.

(b) Restoration cost

Where the tort or breach of contract has resulted in a physical injury to the plaintiff's person or property then he may, in general, be awarded a sum to compensate for the money spent in his own efforts to restore himself or his property to the *status quo ante*. In personal injury cases he may recover his medical expenses;[6] in property injury cases he may recover the cost of repairs.[7] A similar measure may be applied for breach of covenant in a lease to repair.[8] Again the doctrine of

---

[1] McGregor, §§ 216–217.
[2] *Infra*, pp. 324 and 326.
[3] *Infra*, pp. 173–175.
[4] *Infra*, pp. 264–265.
[5] *Infra*, pp. 360–362.
[6] *Infra*, pp. 173–175.
[7] *Infra*, pp. 132–135.
[8] *Infra*, pp. 338–339.

mitigation will indicate in what circumstances such efforts at restoration are to be expected, and whether the amount spent was reasonable.

(c) Cost of substitute

Where the due performance of a contract or the absence of tortious conduct would have conferred on the plaintiff a profit (potential or actual), he may not, in many cases, recover from the defendant the gross profits that would have been made if the defendant had properly performed his obligation. He is generally expected to mitigate his loss by finding for himself in the market a substitute profit-earner.[1] Where such a "duty" exists, compensation will be limited to the cost of the substitute (in the case of tort) or the difference between the contract price and the cost of the substitute (in the case of contract) plus the net difference in profit-earning potential between the *status quo ante* and the situation resulting from substitution.

5   Application of doctrine to special situations in contract

(a) Anticipatory breach

The plaintiff need take no steps in mitigation before the defendant is in breach of his contract. In the ordinary case the defendant is not in breach until the date of performance has passed. But where he repudiates before that date—a so-called "anticipatory breach"—the plaintiff is given an option whether or not to accept the breach. If he refuses to accept, the contract subsists until at least the date for performance, and the ordinary rules apply. If, however, he accepts the repudiation, the contract comes to an end at that time and the plaintiff must take such steps in mitigation of his loss as are reasonable, without waiting for the date of performance.[2]

(b) Action for agreed sum

An action in debt for an agreed sum is not of course an action for damages and strictly speaking does not come within the scope of this book. But it is worth adding that, at least on existing authority,[3] the ordinary doctrine of mitigation appears not to apply to such an action.[4] Consequently, if the defendant repudiates the plaintiff may ignore the

---

[1] *Infra*, pp. 322–324.
[2] *Melachrino* v. *Nickoll and Knight*, [1920] 1 K.B. 693. See also *Garnac Grain* v. *Faure and Fairclough*, [1968] A.C. 1130 and *Novick* v. *Benjamin*, [1972] 2 S.A.L.R. 842.
[3] Cf. Treitel, pp. 833–834.
[4] And see *Mount* v. *Oldham Corpn.*, [1973] 1 All E.R. 26.

repudiation, perform his side of the bargain and sue for the contract price. In *White and Carter* v. *McGregor*[1]

> Ps, advertising agents, agreed to advertise Ds' garage business on litter bins. The display was to last for three years but Ds repudiated before performance had begun. Ps ignored the repudiation, prepared the advertisements and claimed the agreed price. The House of Lords held by a majority that they could succeed.

Whether or not the plaintiffs' action in this case was justifiable, the principle as stated can hardly be absolute. An expert is instructed by his employer to travel to Hongkong and make a report there. The employer repudiates before the expert has set off. The latter can hardly ignore the repudiation, proceed to Hongkong, carry out his duties and claim the appropriate payment.[2] But whether the principle is limited by the requirement that the plaintiff has to show some legitimate interest in completing performance[3] or by some variations on the doctrine of mitigation is as yet far from clear.[4]

IV DEDUCTION FOR COMPENSATING ADVANTAGES

1 General

The plaintiff's losses consequent on the defendant's tort or breach of contract are reduced wholly or in part by a compensating advantage. He might save on expenses which would not have been incurred if he had not been injured: a disabled person who must spend the rest of his life in a nursing home must necessarily save on certain living expenses. He might by his own, or by another's, efforts find a substitute to that which has been lost. The loss might be indemnified by insurance, private or public. In all these cases the question arises whether the value of the benefit is to be deducted from the plaintiff's award. If the compensatory principle is to be rigorously applied, a deduction should be made: the plaintiff is to be compensated only for such losses as he has actually sustained. If he has found relief in some other source, he will not require such a complete indemnity from the defendant. But the law has never taken such a clear stand, and it has refrained from formulating any general principle. Attitudes and rules have varied according to the nature of the benefit and the nature of the

---

[1] [1962] A.C. 413.
[2] *Ibid., per* LORD REID, at p. 428, *per* LORD MORTON, at p. 432, *per* LORD KEITH, at p. 442.
[3] *Ibid., per* LORD REID, at p. 431. See also MEGARRY, J. in *Hounslow London Borough Council* v. *Twickenham Garden Developments*, [1971] Ch. 233, at pp. 252–253.
[4] Tabachnik, 25 Current Legal Problems 149.

plaintiff's injury. As a result, it has been found convenient to consider the rules in detail in their appropriate context in subsequent
parts of the book,[1] and to offer here only the broadest of generalizations.

2 Criteria

It is possible to enumerate with confidence only a few criteria for
determining whether or not a deduction is to be made for a compensating advantage and these affect only a minority of cases.

(a) Causation

For a compensating advantage to be relevant at all it must be clear
that it accrued as a consequence of the harm inflicted on the plaintiff.
A windfall on the premium bonds or the football pools must, of course,
be ignored.   But once the *sine qua non* test of causation has been
satisfied, further generalization is difficult.   Some decisions have
expressly been based on the distinction between those cases where the
injury was the *causa causans* of the benefit and those where it was only
the *causa qua non* of the benefit[2] but they are difficult to rationalize and
more often than not disguise policy decisions.

(b) Mitigation

If the advantage accrued from an act of mitigation which the plaintiff
himself undertook, then in accordance with the principles discussed in
the previous section a deduction must be made.[3]   The problem still
exists for those advantages which do not result from the plaintiff discharging his "duty" to mitigate.

(c) Statute

There are certain statutory provisions which expressly determine
whether or not a benefit is to be deducted.[4]   The great majority of
benefits are, however, governed only by common law principles.

(d) Purpose

Perhaps the most satisfactory general criterion is whether it was the
"purpose" of the benefit to indemnify the plaintiff in which case a
deduction ought to be made, or rather to provide him with a benefit in

---

[1] *Infra*, pp. 107–115 (tax); pp. 134, 151–154 (property injuries); pp. 218–
230 (personal injuries); pp. 274–278 (economic injuries); pp. 370–375 (contract).
[2] *Infra*, p. 225.
[3] See further *supra*, p. 88.
[4] E.g. Law Reform (Personal Injuries) Act 1948, s. 2(1), *infra*, p. 224, and Fatal
Accidents Act 1959, s. 2, *infra*, p. 277.

addition to anything he may recover by way of common law damages.[1]
But the instruments conferring the advantage on the plaintiff are rarely
explicit on the point, and clear inferences are not always easy to draw.

(e) Policy

At the last resort, the court must resort to policy considerations. Is
it "fair" that the plaintiff should accumulate both the damages and
the benefit? The answer to this question will vary according to the
nature of the plaintiff's loss, and, more particularly, the source of the
compensating advantage, and must therefore be postponed until the
various categories of benefits have been described in some detail.

---

[1] *Infra*, p. 228.

CHAPTER FOUR

General Factors Relevant in the Assessment of Damages

In the first chapter, the general principles for assessing compensation were described. The *prima facie* figure derived from an application of such principles may have to be modified in the light of certain other factors present.

I INTEREST

1 Introduction

There will be an inevitable delay between the time when the plaintiff incurred his loss and the date when he obtained judgment for damages. If it is assumed that the defendant should have indemnified the plaintiff at the moment of the loss, it is clear that delay in payment will exacerbate the loss. In the nineteenth century LORD HERSCHELL, L.C. stated the general principle,

> "that when money is owing from one party to another and that other is driven to have recourse to legal proceedings in order to recover the amount due from him, the party who is wrongfully withholding that money from the other ought not in justice to benefit by having that money in his possession and enjoying the use of it, when the money ought to be in the possession of the other party who is entitled to its use."[1]

Today the emphasis appears to be more on the plaintiff's deprivation than on the defendant's unjust enrichment.[2] If so, it follows that even though the plaintiff himself is responsible for the delay in payment, he should nevertheless be entitled to the interest—he has been kept out of his money.[3] Three questions arise for consideration:

---

[1] *London, Chatham and Dover Rail Co.* v. *South Eastern Rail Co.*, [1893] A.C. 429, at p. 437.

[2] E.g. BRANDON, J. in *The Mecca*, [1968] P. 665, at p. 674; but see also *Jefford* v. *Gee*, [1970] 2 Q.B. 130, *infra*, pp. 101–102.

[3] *May* v. *Basset & Sons* (1970), 114 Sol. Jo. 269.

(i) in what circumstances will a defendant be liable to pay interest?
(ii) for what period of time will it be awarded?
(iii) at what rate will it be fixed?

2 Liability for interest

(a) At common law

For centuries the courts were extremely reluctant to supplement damages awards with interest. To exact payment for the use of money savoured of usury.[1] Challenges to the traditional objection arose only through the advance of commerce in the seventeenth and eighteenth centuries. But though judges regretted the inhibition[2] the position remained that interest would be awarded only where the defendant had expressly agreed to pay it, or such a promise could be inferred either from the terms of the contract (for example, where there was a provision for payment on a certain day as in promissory notes and bills of exchange), or from the conduct of the parties or from commercial custom.[3]

(b) In Admiralty

The Court of Admiralty diverged significantly from the common law on this question.[4] In the early cases, interest was awarded not so much for being deprived of the use of money but rather as a form of substantial damages: in cases of total loss of ships, it was regarded as one method of compensating for loss of profits where no evidence of particular profits lost was available.[5] In other cases, however, the discretion to award interest was exercised more freely. Where a ship was merely damaged interest supplemented an award for the cost of repairs;[6] and it was given even in cases of personal injury and death which were tried in the Admiralty court.[7]

(c) Legislation

During the nineteenth century the defects of the common law were only partially remedied. Legislation permitted the award of interest

---

[1] For an admirable account of the historical development of interest see McCormick, § 51. See also *infra*, pp. 304–305.
[2] E.g. *Arnott* v. *Redfern* (1826), 3 Bing. 353, *per* BEST, C.J. at p. 359; *London, Chatham and Dover Rail Co.* v. *South Eastern Rail Co., supra, per* LORD HERSCHELL, L.C., at p. 437, *per* LORD WATSON, at p. 442, *per* LORD SHAND, at pp. 443–444.
[3] *Per* LORD ELLENBOROUGH, *De Havilland* v. *Bowerbank* (1807), 1 Camp. 50.
[4] See *The Northumbria* (1869), L.R. 3 A. & E. 6.
[5] E.g. *The Amalia* (1863), 1 Moore P.C. (N.S.) 471; and *infra*, pp. 125–126.
[6] E.g. *The Napier Star*, [1933] P. 136.
[7] *The Aizkarai Mendi*, [1938] P. 263.

only in exceptional cases.[1]   In 1934 the Law Revision Committee recommended[2] that a general discretion to award interest should be conferred on the courts.   As a consequence section 3(1) of the Law Reform (Miscellaneous Provisions) Act 1934 provided that,

> "In any proceedings tried in any court of record for the recovery of any debt or damages, the court may, if it thinks fit, order that there shall be included in the sum for which judgment is given interest at such rate as it thinks fit on the whole or any part of the debt or damages for the whole or any part of the period between the date when the cause of action arose and the date of judgment:
>
> Provided that nothing in this section—
>> (a) shall authorise the giving of interest upon interest;
>> *or* (b) shall apply in relation to any debt upon which interest is payable as of right whether by virtue of any agreement or otherwise;
>> *or* (c) shall affect the damages recoverable for the dishonour of a bill of exchange."

Three exclusions from the statutory power deserve special mention.

(i) It does not affect interest payable for any period of time after the date of judgment.   Interest on judgment debts is governed by section 17 of the Judgments Act 1838.[3]   It is not part of the damages award and does not, therefore, arise for discussion here.[4]

(ii) Compound interest is excluded.   This is a relic from the days when interest was regarded as necessarily usurious.   It is consistent with some early Chancery cases which held void clauses seeking to impose compound interest on debtors who defaulted in payment.[5]

(iii) The provision does not apply to cases in which interest is payable as of right.   Theoretically, the result is that the Act complements rather than replaces the common law.   In practice, however, there is little indication that the courts wish to revert to the old and confusing authorities which laid down the conditions on which interest might be awarded.

Apart from these few exclusions, everything is left to the discretion of the court including, of course, whether or not interest is to be awarded at all.   A search among the post-1934 cases as to when this

---

[1] The most important were (a) negotiable instruments (Bills of Exchange Act 1882), (b) contracts in writing on debts payable at a certain time, or oral contracts with notice in writing that interest will be claimed (Civil Procedure Act 1833), (c) conversion or trespass to goods (*ibid.*), (d) judgment debts (Judgments Act 1838).

[2] Second Interim Report Cmd. 4546.

[3] This may be amended by the Lord Chancellor under s. 44 of the Administration of Justice Act 1970.

[4] For an account of this see e.g. Halsbury, *Laws of England*, vol. 22, pp. 782–783.

[5] E.g. *Lord Ossulston* v. *Lord Yarmouth* (1707), 2 Salk 449.

discretion will be exercised reveals little. The most helpful generalization may be found in the report of the Law Revision Committee whose recommendations were implemented by the 1934 Act. It was said[1]

"in practically every case a judgment against the defendant means that he should have admitted the claim when it was made and have paid the appropriate sum as damages."

In such circumstances, the full rate of interest is to be awarded from the date when the cause of action accrued. Where, on the other hand, in the opinion of the court, it was reasonable to dispute the claim, it may decide not to award interest at all.[2]

If these be the principles on which the discretion to award interest should be exercised, it is far from clear that they have been applied in practice. There seems to have been a tendency to award interest only where the defendant was in some way responsible for the delay in paying compensation.[3] As regards claims for personal injuries and death, this was particularly evident,[4] and, following the recommendations of the Winn Committee on Personal Injuries Litigation[5] section 22 of the Administration of Justice Act 1969 radically changed the position. In personal injury and fatal accident cases, the court is now *required* to award interest unless it is satisfied that there are "special reasons" why it should not do so. The effect is to shift the burden as to whether the court should award interest from the plaintiff to the defendant. The Act does not alter the principles which the court should apply in awarding interest: it simply makes it obligatory for the court to apply those principles.[6]

3 Rate of interest

An aversion to usury was discernible in the long-surviving tradition that interest at over four per cent. should not be awarded.[7] But it is now recognized that the rate must reflect the current commercial value of money.

There have been divergent views on how this principle is to be implemented. In Admiralty regard has been had to "commercial lending and borrowing rates" during the period for which interest is payable.[8] In the Commercial Court it seems that the prescribed rate is generally

---

[1] Cmd. 4546 (1934), para. 8.
[2] E.g. *Le Mura* v. *Victoria Insurance Co.*, [1971] Qd.R. 198.
[3] Walker (1970), 112 N.L.J. 308.
[4] See Law Commission Working Paper No. 41, para. 251.
[5] Cmnd. 3691 (1968), paras. 324–325.
[6] *Per* LORD DENNING, M.R., *Jefford* v. *Gee*, [1970] 2 Q.B. 130, at p. 143.
[7] E.g. *The Kong Magnus*, [1891] P. 223, and see the observations of KARMINSKI J. in *The Abadesa* (*No.* 2), [1968] P. 656, at pp. 663–664.
[8] *The Abadesa, supra*; *The Mecca*, [1968] P. 665.

at one per-cent above the prevailing bank rate.[1] But recently, for the award of interest under section 22 of the 1969 Act, the Court of Appeal has laid down[2] that ordinarily it should take the mean or average rate obtainable on the short-term investment account during the relevant period,[3] and it is likely that this method will be extended to cases not falling within those statutory provisions.[4] Of course, the rate is at the discretion of the court and it may be varied in cases where either party was responsible for gross delay.[5]

4 Period of time for which interest is payable

The court's next duty is to select the period of time for which interest is payable. As has been seen,[6] the period in question must end at the date of judgment.[7] The difficulty arises in determining the time from which it must run. The question turns on what is regarded as the theoretical basis for the award of interest. On one view, the plaintiff is being compensated for being kept out of his money. He has been deprived of the use of his money from the moment that he incurred his loss, and accordingly interest should be payable as from that date. On a second view, the emphasis should be more on the defendant "wrongfully withholding" the plaintiff's money, and if this is right interest should run only from the time when the defendant ought reasonably to have settled the plaintiff's claim. It has already been suggested that under modern conditions the first approach seems preferable:[8] the second carries implications of punitive considerations. It remains to see how the courts have approached the problem.

(a) Maritime collisions

In Admiralty, the first view seems on the whole to have been preferred. Thus in an action for damage to a ship interest was awarded

---

[1] *F.M.C. (Meat)* v. *Fairhold Cold Stores*, [1971] 2 Lloyd's Rep. 221; cf. *Applegate* v. *Moss*, [1971] 1 Q.B. 406.

[2] *Jefford* v. *Gee, supra.*

[3] The rates are fixed from time to time by the Lord Chancellor. So far they have been: from 1 October, 1965, 5 per cent.; from 1 September, 1966, $5\frac{1}{2}$ per cent.; from 1 March, 1968, 6 per cent.; from 1 March, 1969, $6\frac{1}{2}$ per cent.; from 1 March, 1970, 7 per cent.; from 1 April, 1971, $7\frac{1}{2}$ per cent. Having selected the period for which interest is payable (*infra*), the court takes the average of the appropriate rates above: see *The Funabashi*, [1972] 2 All E.R. 181.

[4] It has been applied in Admiralty; *The Funabashi, ibid.*

[5] *Jefford* v. *Gee, supra,* at p. 151; and see *Kemp* v. *Tolland*, [1956] 2 Lloyd's Rep. 681 (interest reduced from 5 per cent. to 4 per cent.).

[6] *Supra*, p. 98.

[7] This may be the date of an appeal judgment, but if so the court must take into account any interest payable on the first judgment debt: *Cook* v. *Kier*, [1970] 2 All E.R. 513.

[8] It has been adopted generally in the U.S.A.: see Restatement on Tort, § 913.

from the date when the plaintiffs actually paid for the repairs[1]; while in cases of total destruction it ran from the date of the loss.[2] In a case of personal injuries and death, on the other hand, the court selected the Registrar's report on damages as the appropriate time,[3] a decision which seems more consistent with the second view.

(b) Awards under s. 3 of the 1934 Act

Again in cases where the court has exercised its discretion under section 3 of the Law Reform Act 1934, the first approach has been adopted. For example, in an action for wrongful dismissal, interest was awarded from the date of dismissal.[4]

(c) Awards under s. 22 of the 1969 Act[5]

In *Jefford* v. *Gee*[6] the Court of Appeal issued a series of directions[7] as to the method of awarding interest on personal injury and fatal accident awards under section 22 of the Administration of Justice Act 1969.

(i) *Special damages* The principle to be applied here is clearly that of the first approach. Interest is to be awarded from the date of the loss. In the case of medical expenses, this will be when they are paid. As regards loss of wages, theoretically these should be calculated on each week's loss from that week to the date of trial. An alternative and simpler method is to add up the loss every six months, and award interest for each such period to the date of the trial.[8] In the end, the Court of Appeal felt that in the ordinary case such calculations would be too detailed. Interest, they suggested, should instead be dealt with on broad lines. Rather than award *full* interest from the *exact* date of the

---

[1] *The Hebe* (1847), 2 Wm. Rob. 530.
[2] *The Northumbria* (1869), L.R. 3 A. & E. 6. If the ship carried cargo interest was payable on the probable value of the ship at the end of the voyage from that date. The reason for choosing this later date was that here interest was a method of compensating for lost profits and this had already been allowed for in the award for freight from the date of the collision to the anticipated arrival in the port of ultimate destination: *ibid.*, at p. 12.
[3] *The Aizkairi Mendi*, [1938] P. 263.
[4] *Bold* v. *Brough, Nicholson and Hall*, [1963] 3 All E.R. 849.
[5] Walker (1970), 112 N.L.J. 308.
[6] [1970] 2 Q.B. 130.
[7] The judgment of the C.A. was described by FISHER, J. in *Waite* v. *Redpath Dorman Long*, [1971] 1 Q.B. 294, at p. 297 as "unusual". Not only was everything said on the 1969 Act completely *obiter* (the decision itself was made under the 1934 Act), but also "the court appears not so much to be stating the law as to be giving administrative directions".
[8] This was the recommendation of the Winn Committee Cmnd. 3691 (1968), para. 325.

loss, interest at *half* the normal rate[1] should be awarded from the time of the accident.

(ii) *Damages for lost future earnings*   No interest should be awarded as *ex hypothesi* the loss has not yet occurred.   On the contrary the court must allow for the fact that the plaintiff is receiving his indemnity in advance of the anticipated loss.[2]

(iii) *Damages for pain and suffering and lost amenities*   In dealing with these heads of damages, the Court of Appeal seems disconcertingly to shift from the first to the second approach.   Consistently with the rule on special damages, the starting point is the date of the loss.   But since it is difficult to select particular times for the incidence of non-pecuniary losses, the criterion is abandoned and is replaced by a test dictated by the second approach.   Interest becomes payable not from the time of the loss but "from the time when the defendant ought to have paid . . . but did not".[3]   In some cases this will be the date of letter before the action, but at the latest it should be the date when the writ was served. The rule may be criticized both on theoretical and on practical grounds. Theoretically it is inconsistent with the period of time selected for special damages.   It seems also to be inconsistent with the rule that no interest should be awarded for future pecuniary loss.   In most cases, a substantial allowance is made for *future* pain and suffering and loss of amenities.   Yet no effort is made in *Jefford* v. *Gee* to distinguish between past and future non-pecuniary losses.   As for practical considerations, the Court of Appeal clearly intended that the rule should "stimulate the plaintiff's advisers to issue and serve the writ without delay".[4]   It may be questioned, however, whether this is as desirable a consequence as the Court of Appeal seems to have assumed.   It will often force the plaintiff's legal advisers to issue proceedings at an early date which will increase the costs and prejudice the chances of a negotiated settlement.[5]

(iv) *Fatal Accidents Acts*   Here also the second approach seems to have been preferred.   Interest is to be awarded from the date of service of the writ, since this will allow a reasonable time for investigating the claim.   The criticisms made of the rule on non-pecuniary losses apply also here.

(v) *Loss of expectation of life in survival actions*   Interest on an award for loss of expectation of life in a survival action should run from the date

---

[1] See *supra*, pp. 99–100.
[2] *Infra*, p. 189.
[3] [1970] 2 Q.B. 130, at p. 147.
[4] *Ibid.*
[5] Walker, *supra*, at p. 310 and see the editorial at (1970), 120 N.L.J. 307.

of the service of the writ.   It will be argued below[1] that claims for non-pecuniary losses should not survive the death of the accident victim. If, however, the artificial premise that the estate has sustained a non-pecuniary loss is accepted, it would seem right to treat it for the purposes of interest, as analogous to other non-pecuniary losses.

II   REDUCTION FOR CONTRIBUTORY NEGLIGENCE[2]

1   General

At common law, contributory negligence was a complete defence to tortious actions.   This clearly led to injustice when the plaintiff was only partially responsible for his injuries.   A principle of apportionment was introduced by section 1(1) of the Law Reform (Contributory Negligence) Act 1945 which provided that

> "Where any person suffers damage as a result partly of his own fault and partly of the fault of any other person or persons, a claim in respect of that damage shall not be defeated by reason of the fault of the person suffering the damage, but the damages recoverable in respect thereof shall be reduced to such extent as the court thinks just and equitable having regard to the claimant's share in the responsibility for the damage."

Several problems arise on the construction of this provision.   Most raise the issue of liability and are comprehensively treated in the standard textbooks on tort.[3]   One problem which is relevant to the law of damages concerns the method of apportionment once there has been a finding of contributory negligence: in short, how does the court determine the extent to which damages should be reduced?

2   Criteria for apportionment

Different views are held as to how the statutory provision should be interpreted.

(a)   Question of fact

One popular view is that the question is solely one of fact.[4]   The use of the words "just and equitable" is regarded as conferring an almost

---

[1] Pp. 118–119.

[2] Payne (1955), 18 M.L.R. 344; Redmond (1957), 31 A.L.J. 520.

[3] On the question whether the provision applies in actions for breach of contract see Williams, *Joint Torts and Contributory Negligence*, § 80, and the standard texts on contract.

[4] E.g. GERRARD, J. in *Connor* v. *Port of Liverpool Stevedoring*, [1953] 2 Lloyd's Rep. 604, and see McGregor, § 92.

absolute discretion on the court of first instance. In the words of one eminent judge

> "It is a question, not of principle or of positive findings of fact or law, but of proportion, of balance and relative emphasis, and of weighing different considerations. It involves an individual choice or discretion. . . ."[1]

Consequently, on this view, an appellate court should interfere with a trial judge's apportionment only in exceptional circumstances. These might exist where a judge has failed to take into account or has misapprehended a factor vitally relevant to the issue.[2] But, it may be objected that this construction takes no account of the statutory injunction to have "regard to the claimant's share in the responsibility for the damage." A legal norm must limit the exercise of the court's power of apportionment. The nature of the test will then depend on the meaning of the words just quoted.

(b) Causal potency

There are some who find it significant that for the purposes of the 1945 Act resort is had to the plaintiff's share in the *responsibility* for the damage, whereas under section 1(1) of the Maritime Conventions Act 1911, the loss is apportioned "to the degree in which each vessel is at fault."[3] The contention is that the court should have regard to the causal potency of the plaintiff's act rather than on the degree of his fault or negligence.[4] The test is whether the plaintiff's conduct "contributed more (or less) immediately to the accident. . . ."[5] This is, however, open to the obvious and insuperable objection that logically there are no degrees of causation.[6] Any attempt to determine the amount by which damages are to be reduced *solely* on the basis of causative notions is doomed to failure.[7]

---

[1] LORD WRIGHT in *"British Fame" (Owners)* v. *"MacGregor" (Owners)*, [1943] A.C. 197, at p. 201. The decision was on s. 1(1) of the Maritime Conventions Act 1911 but in this respect at least the principles to be applied are the same: see, e.g. *National Coal Board* v. *England*, [1954] A.C. 403 and *The Miraflores and The Abadesa*, [1966] P. 18 affirmed, [1967] 1 A.C. 826.

[2] Per VISCOUNT SIMON, L.C., *The MacGregor, supra*, at p. 199 and see, e.g. *Stapley* v. *Gypsum Mines*, [1953] A.C. 663, and *Williams* v. *Sykes*, [1955] 3 All E.R. 225.

[3] See *Smith* v. *Bray* (1939), 56 T.L.R. 200 on the similar provision in the Law Reform (Married Women and Tortfeasors) Act 1935, s. 6.

[4] *Collins* v. *Herts. County Council*, [1947] K.B. 598.

[5] Per LORD REID, *Stapley* v. *Gypsum Mines, supra*, at p. 682.

[6] Cf. *supra*, pp. 67–68.

[7] Per DENNING, L.J., *Davies* v. *Swan Motor*, [1949] 2 K.B. 291, at p. 326, *per* LORD PEARSON, *The Miraflores, and The Abadesa*, [1967] 1 A.C. 826, at p. 845.

(c) Comparative blameworthiness

The natural tendency is to turn from causation terminology to notions of fault or blameworthiness. On the third view, the court distributes responsibility according to the relative blameworthiness or comparative negligence of the parties.[1] But this principle as a complete criterion is also subject to difficulties. In the first place, it can hardly function efficaciously in situations where the defendant is strictly liable, that is, liable independently of any fault (e.g. under the Factories Acts). To apply the "comparative blameworthiness" test here would in many cases defeat the object of the strict liability.[2] To meet this objection and to dispense with the notion of pure *moral* culpability it has been suggested that the test should be reformulated as the extent to which the conduct of the plaintiff departs from the norm attained by the reasonable man.[3] It may, however, be doubted whether the character of the plaintiff's conduct can be judged in isolation from the nature of the defendant's liability. The court must, it is submitted, inquire of *both* parties (1) what standard of conduct is imposed on them by law; (2) how far short of the standard did the conduct of each party fall.[4] The second objection to the "comparative blameworthiness" test is that it fails to take account of causative factors. Now it may be, as indicated above, that logically causation cannot be apportioned but clearly a judgment on the plaintiff's conduct must involve some consideration of the causative relationship between the conduct and the harm resulting.[5] The plaintiff's conduct might have been more "culpable", in the sense that it involved a greater departure from the standard reasonably to be expected of him, but *causally* it might not have been so influential in producing the harm. It is for this reason that the courts tend to stress that regard should be had both to comparative blameworthiness and to causative potency.[6] The court should consider not only the degree of the plaintiff's negligence but also the degree to which that negligence caused the harm suffered.[7] A good illustration is provided by *The Marinar*.[8]

---

[1] *Dorrington* v. *Griff Fender*, [1953] 1 All E.R. 1177; *The Miraflores, supra*.

[2] *Per* SACHS, L.J., *Mullard* v. *Ben Line Steamers*, [1970] 1 W.L.R. 1414, at p. 1418.

[3] *Payne, supra,* n. 2, p. 103 adopted by the High Court of Australia in *Pennington* v. *Norris* (1956), 96 C.L.R. 10.

[4] See e.g. *Quintas* v. *National Smelting Co.*, [1961] 1 All E.R. 630 and *Leach* v. *Standard Telephones*, [1966] 2 All E.R. 523.

[5] Cf. Hart and Honoré, *Causation in the Law*, pp. 214–215.

[6] *Per* DENNING, L.J., *Davies* v. *Swan Motor, supra*, at p. 326; *per* LORD TUCKER, *National Coal Board* v. *England*, [1954] A.C. 403, at p. 427; *per* LORD PEARCE, *The Miraflores, supra*, at p. 845.

[7] Hart and Honoré, *loc. cit.*

[8] [1968] 2 Lloyd's Rep. 165.

P ship and D ship collided in the fog. In the Admiralty court the judge and his assessors found that (1) D's speed was too high and her master had not constantly attended to the radar; (2) P had taken an improper course. It was held that the "blameworthiness' of D was double that of P (implying an apportionment of $\frac{2}{3}/\frac{1}{3}$) but that the "causative potency" of P's fault was greater than the "causative potency" of any of D's faults. Liability was apportioned $\frac{3}{5}$ against D and $\frac{2}{5}$ against P.

(d) Conclusion

It is evident that no one test can provide the complete solution. Regard should be had to all three principles. Even then, it is, of course, impossible to derive an arithmetical formula from a verbal proposition, and the exact amount of reduction will at the last resort depend on the judge's instinct and experience of other cases.[1]

3 Rationale of apportionment

Apportionment, though of recent vintage in the common law world, has been widely accepted as the fairest method of distributing the burden of accidents between the tortfeasor and the negligent plaintiff.[2] It is difficult to justify the doctrine on purely causal grounds—the plaintiff should recover no compensation for that part of the harm which resulted from his own culpable conduct—because it is generally impossible to say that any part of the harm was wholly caused by the act of the plaintiff or defendant. More acceptable is the moral justification that the plaintiff should bear responsibility for the consequences of his own faults or the deterrence argument that on grounds of expediency a sanction should be directed against those who fail to take adequate care of themselves. There are some who argue that this rationalization is consistent more with nineteenth century laissez-faire ideas than with the realities of modern industrial society.[3] Even however if the traditional rationale is admitted, it is far from clear that apportionment in its existing form is the appropriate method of satisfying its dictates. As Professor Atiyah has shown,[4] as a punitive measure against the plaintiff is it notoriously capricious in its effect, for the amount of the sanction (i.e. the extent of loss uncompensated) will be assessed not merely according to the degree of the plaintiff's fault but also on the amount of harm actually sustained—the greater the harm, the more severe the

---

[1] A representative selection of typical apportionments is set out in Clerk & Lindsell, § 1000.
[2] See in general Honoré, 11 I.E.C.L. 7–144 *et seq.*
[3] Atiyah, pp. 153–154; Tunc, *La Sécurité Routière*, pp. 34–38. Under the National Insurance scheme, industrial injury benefits are not reduced on the ground of contributory negligence.
[4] *Op. cit.*, at p. 152.

sanction—and on the degree of the defendant's fault—the less culpable the defendant's conduct, the more severe the sanction.

III TAXATION[1]

1 General

The plaintiff may recover as part of his award compensation for the loss of profits or earnings which, if they had been secured, would have been liable to tax. Damages for lost earnings in an action for personal injuries or wrongful dismissal provide the most obvious examples. Now if the compensatory principle is to prevail it may seem obvious that the plaintiff's remedy should be limited to compensation for his net earnings, that is for his gross earnings less tax since that is what he would have received if the contract had been performed or the tort had not been committed. Strangely, until 1955 it was almost universally held in the common law jurisdictions that tax considerations should be ignored.[2] But in that year, in the now famous case of *British Transport Commission* v. *Gourley*,[3] the House of Lords held that to be consistent with the compensatory principle an award of damages in a personal injuries action for loss of earnings (past or future) must take into account the tax which the plaintiff would have paid if he had not been injured. The principle has since been applied to actions under the Fatal Accidents Acts,[4] for wrongful dismissal,[5] for trespass and conversion,[6] for libel[7] and to awards of compensation for compulsory purchase orders.[8] Most but not all jurisdictions have accepted it.[9]

---

[1] The literature on this subject is vast. See, in particular Street, pp. 88–104; Whiteman & Wheatcroft, *Income Tax and Surtax*, Chap. 20; Simon, *Taxes* 3rd Edn. C4. §§ 413–417; Jolowicz, [1960] C.L.J. 86; Bale (1966), 44 C.B.R. 66; Dworkin, [1967] B.T.R. 315, 373.

[2] England: *Billingham* v. *Hughes*, [1949] 1 K.B. 643. Australia: *Davies* v. *Adelaide Chemical (No. 2)*, [1947] S.A.S.R. 67. Canada: *Fine* v. *Toronto Transportation Commission*, [1946] 1 D.L.R. 221. New Zealand: *Union S.S. Co. of New Zealand, Ltd.* v. *Ramstad*, [1950] N.Z.L.R. 716. Scotland: *Blackwood* v. *Andre*, 1947 S.C. 333, cf. *M'Daid* v. *Clyde Navigation Trustees*, 1946 S.C. 462. In the U.S.A. only a few jurisdictions were prepared to take tax considerations into account: see 63 A.L.R.2d. 1398.

[3] [1956] A.C. 185. The ruling had been anticipated by an unreported decision of LORD GODDARD, C.J. in a Fatal Accident action: *Zinovieff* v. *British Transport Commission* (1954), *Times*, 1 April.

[4] *Zinovieff* v. *British Transport Commission, ibid.* The principle has also been applied to *increase* an award where the interest to be earned on investment of the lump sum award would be taxable in the hands of the plaintiff: *Taylor* v. *O'Connor*, [1971] A.C. 115. On this, see *infra*, p. 271.

[5] *Beach* v. *Reed Corrugated Cases*, [1956] 2 All E.R. 652.

[6] *Hall* v. *Pearlberg*, [1956] 1 All E.R. 297.

[7] *Rubber Improvement, Ltd.* v. *Daily Telegraph*, [1964] A.C. 234.

[8] *West Suffolk County Council* v. *Rought*, [1957] A.C. 403.

[9] *Gourley* has been followed in New Zealand (*Smith* v. *Wellington Woollen Manufacturing Co., Ltd.*, [1956] N.Z.L.R. 491), and Australia (*Hamlyn* v.

2   Conditions for application of *Gourley* principle

There are three conditions which must be satisfied if the court is to reduce damages in accordance with the principles:

(i) if there had been no tort or breach of contract tax would have been paid on the item for the loss of which compensation is claimed;

(ii) the damages awarded are not themselves subject to tax;

(iii) there is no legislative provision to the contrary.

(a)   Loss of taxable revenue

It must first be clear that the item for the loss of which compensation is payable would, if actually earned, have been liable to tax.[1]   There have been different attempts to limit the scope of the doctrine on the ground that the particular benefit lost was not itself taxable.

(i) In the first place, it is disputed whether an award for expenditure incurred as opposed to loss of profits comes within the ambit of the rule. In *Sykes* v. *Midland Bank*[2]

> As a result of the negligence of their solicitor D, the P firm paid a higher rent for the premises it occupied than it should have done.   The partners of the firm recovered damages for this increased expenditure. PAULL, J. refused to make a deduction for the saving of tax since "tax is not payable on rent although the amount payable for rent is a factor which is included when the profits of a firm are assessed."[3]

It does not follow in all cases that increased expenditure will reduce profits,[4] but where, as in *Sykes*, it would clearly have done so, there seems to be no adequate ground for distinguishing between damages for increased expenditure and for lost profits.[5]   In both cases there is a saving of tax and had the plaintiffs in *Sykes* claimed loss of profits as an item of damages *Gourley* would have applied.   PAULL, J.'s approach was not followed, rightly, it is submitted, in *Rosenberg & Son, Ltd.* v. *Manchester Corporation.*[6]   The Lands Tribunal there held that in awarding compensation for the expenses of removal on the compulsory acquisition of leasehold property, allowance was to be made for the tax

---

Hann, [1967] S.A.S.R. 387), but not in Canada (*R.* v. *Jennings* (1966), 57 D.L.R.(2d) 644.   See generally Dworkin, *supra,* n. 1, p. 107.

[1] This may of course raise problems of tax law (e.g. whether a receipt is income or capital).   Such matters lie outside the scope of this book.

[2] [1969] 2 Q.B. 518, reversed on another ground [1971] 1 Q.B. 113.

[3] [1969] 2 Q.B. 518, at p. 537.

[4] It depends on how the profits are computed.   See *infra*, pp. 352–354.

[5] Note [1969] B.T.R. 334.

[6] (1971), 23 P. & C.R. 68.

saving. There was no difference in principle between a reduction in tax liability resulting from increased expenditure and one resulting from diminished profits.

(ii) In *Herring* v. *British Transport Commission*,[1] DONOVAN, J. suggested that the rule did not apply to compensation for a benefit which was not itself taxable but which would have been included in the accounts of the plaintiff's business the profits of which would have been taxed. Again, it seems artificial to distinguish between the loss of a complete profitable enterprise and the loss of only part of a profitable enterprise. DONOVAN, J.'s suggested limitation was rejected by PHILLIMORE, J. in *McGhie & Sons* v. *British Transport Commission*.[2]

(iii) A third suggestion is that the rule should not apply where the benefit for the loss of which compensation is payable is taxable but not against the plaintiff himself.[3] This will occur, for example, where the plaintiff is a married woman who is living with her husband and whose earnings are taxed not separately but on her husband. It has been said[4] that in such circumstances the incidence of tax should be ignored because "her real loss can only be measured by her gross earnings." But this would seem to be over-technical. If, for tax purposes, the income of husband and wife were taxed jointly, it would be unreal to treat them as separate for the purposes of the *Gourley* principle.

(b) Award of damages not taxable

For the *Gourley* principle to apply it is, of course, essential that the amount of damages should not itself be subject to tax—the plaintiff would otherwise be taxed twice. It might have been thought that compensation payable for the loss of a taxable benefit would necessarily itself be taxable. It has indeed been recognized that for the purposes of income tax compensation for the loss of trading receipts retains the characteristics of the lost receipts.[5] Damages for wrongful dismissal were formerly not taxable,[6] but now, if the sum awarded in this action exceeds £5000, it is taxable under the special provisions relating to "golden handshakes".[7] Theoretically, awards under £5000 may be subject

---

[1] [1958] T.R. 401.
[2] [1963] 1 Q.B. 125.
[3] There was a hint of this approach in *Sykes* v. *Midland Bank, supra*, at p. 537, where PAULL, J. stressed that though the increased rent would affect the profits of the *firm*, the relevant tax was payable by the individual *partners* on the income they drew from the business.
[4] Kemp & Kemp, Vol. 1, pp. 64–66.
[5] E.g. *Wiseburgh* v. *Domville*, [1956] 1 All E.R. 754 and see Whiteman & Wheatcroft, *op. cit.*, § 7–17 *et seq.*
[6] *Beach* v. *Reed Corrugated Cases*, [1956] 2 All E.R. 652.
[7] Income and Corporation Taxes Act 1970, ss. 187–188 replacing Finance Act 1960 ss. 37–38. In *Parsons* v. *B.N.M. Laboratories*, [1964] 1 Q.B. 95 it

to capital gains tax;[1] but hitherto the Inland Revenue appears not to have put the matter to the test.[2]   With the possible exception of a trader claiming for lost profits,[3] it seems generally agreed that an award for personal injuries is not taxable.[4]   Awards of interest in Admiralty[5] and under the Law Reform (Miscellaneous Provisions) Act 1934[6] have been held liable to income tax, but it has recently been enacted that this should not apply in actions for personal injury or death.[7]   Liability under a foreign fiscal system will be sufficient to exclude the *Gourley* rule,[8] but in this as in other cases there is some conflict of opinion as to which of the two parties bears the onus of proving that the award will be taxed. On one view,[9] it lies on the plaintiff for he generally must prove his loss. The better view, however, would seem to be that it lies on the party who seeks to invoke the *Gourley* rule:[10] it is for the plaintiff to prove his loss of earnings, and for the defendant to establish the ground, if any, on which the prima facie sum should be reduced.

(c) No contrary legislation

Even though the first two conditions may be satisfied, it may yet be decided that in accordance with the legislature's express or implied intention, damages are not to be reduced.   Where statute provides that a certain award is not to be taxed, it is a reasonable inference that it intended the recipient to benefit, and if *Gourley* is applied the exemption will go to relieve the defendant and not the plaintiff.   The reasoning has been applied to section 19 of the Finance Act 1971 which exempts from income tax awards of interest in actions for personal injury and death.[11]

---

was held (reversing the Master's decision) that to oust *Gourley* it was not sufficient that the award was one of a class of payments to which these provisions applied.   It must *itself* attract tax and therefore must exceed £5000.

[1] See Whiteman & Wheatcroft, *op. cit.*, § 15–12, and more generally Wheatcroft, *Capital Gains Taxes*, § 6–31 *et seq.* and McGregor, §§ 427–432.

[2] Whiteman & Wheatcroft, *loc. cit.*

[3] *Ibid.*, § 20–05.

[4] This was conceded by counsel in *British Transport Commission* v. *Gourley*, [1956] A.C. 185 and has not been questioned since.

[5] *The Norseman*, [1957] p. 224.

[6] *Riches* v. *Westminster Bank*, [1947] A.C. 390.

[7] Finance Act 1971, s. 49.   Nevertheless, it has been held that *Gourley* does not apply: *Mason* v. *Harman*, [1972] R.T.R. 1, *infra*.

[8] *Praet* v. *Poland*, [1962] 1 Lloyd's Rep. 566.

[9] *Per* CARTER, Q.C. Official Referee, *Hall & Co.* v. *Pearlberg*, [1956] 1 W.L.R. 244, at p. 247.   *Per* LORD MORTON, *West Suffolk County Council* v. *Rought*, [1957] A.C. 403, at p. 413.

[10] This appears to be the effect of *Re Associated Portland Cement*, [1966] Ch. 308.

[11] *Mason* v. *Harman*, [1972] R.T.R. 1.

3 Assessment of damages when *Gourley* applies

The court must attempt to estimate what tax would have been paid on the benefits for the loss of which compensation is payable.[1] Naturally, accuracy is hardly attainable: in the *Gourley* case it was stressed that assessment must be made on broad lines.[2] As regards future losses, it can be nothing more than speculation but the court is to assume that the incidence of tax will be that prevailing at the date of judgment.[3] Consideration will have to be given to all the various factors which may affect tax liability including reliefs for dependants and for other purposes, contributing family and other private income.[4] The court should even take into account the possibility that the plaintiff would have employed tax-avoiding devices to mitigate his liability.[5] These issues are, of course, determined in the absence of Inland Revenue representation; and in the case of foreign tax considerations the court will have to rely on expert advice.[6]

4 Assessment when *Gourley* does not apply

Where *Gourley* does not apply, because, for example, the awards of damages will be taxable in the hands of the plaintiff, the obvious and general principle is that assessment should be unaffected by tax considerations. There have been two attempts to diverge from this position.

(a) Increase of damages award

The first and more dubious instance occurred in a salvage case, *The Telemachus*.[7] The award of compensation to the master and crew of the salving ship was admittedly taxable. WILLMER, J. held that nevertheless *Gourley* should apply, as it were, in reverse. The damages should be *increased* by a sum equal to the tax liability of the salvers, thus in effect shifting the tax burden to those responsible for the salvage emergency. The avowed purpose of this strange decision was the "encouragement to mariners to perform services of a salvage nature"[8] but the decision can hardly survive the objection that the learned judge was thereby overreaching the intention of Parliament by transferring

---

[1] See, generally, *Lyndale Fashion Manufacturers* v. *Rich*, [1973] 1 All E.R. 33.
[2] [1956] A.C. 185, *per* EARL JOWITT, at p. 203, *per* LORD GODDARD, at p. 207, *per* LORD REID, at p. 215.
[3] *Ibid.*, *per* LORD GODDARD, at p. 209. *Semble* budget proposals, not yet implemented, may be considered: *Daniel* v. *Jones*, [1961] 3 All E.R. 24.
[4] See, e.g. *Beach* v. *Reed Corrugated Cases*, [1956] 2 All E.R. 652.
[5] *Ibid.*, *per* PILCHER, J., at p. 658.
[6] See *Praet* v. *Poland*, [1962] 1 Lloyd's Rep. 566.
[7] [1957] P. 47.
[8] *Ibid.*, *per* WILLMER, J. at p. 50.

the burden of tax liability from the party on whom it was imposed to another.[1]   It was on this ground that PILCHER, J. in *The Makedonia*[2] criticized and refused to follow the decision.[3]

(b)   Accounting for tax at both ends

A more appealing departure featured in the Scottish case of *Stewart* v. *Glentaggart*[4]

> In an action for wrongful dismissal P claimed £9680 lost earnings.   An award of this sum would be taxable under the "golden handshake" provisions.[5]   It was held that since there might be a significant difference between the tax that would have been paid on the earnings (if there had been no breach) and the tax that would be payable on the damages award, the incidence of tax liability should be accounted for. P's true loss should be ascertained by taking his net lost income (i.e. after deducting for tax in accordance with *Gourley*) and then estimating the sum which would leave P with this amount when the tax on the award of damages in his hands has been paid.

This is the most ambitious method of ascertaining the plaintiff's real loss, but the price to be paid for the logically more satisfying solution is probably too high.   The objections to the measure were most lucidly expressed by PEARSON, L.J. in *Parsons* v. *B.N.M. Laboratories*:[6]   it would increase the length and expense of trials; the data for assessing the tax on the award of damages might not be available for some considerable time after the breach; the Inland Revenue would not be a party to the action and if they wished to challenge a decision they would have to go to a higher court; it would in effect thwart the legislature's intentions by modifying the tax burden expressly imposed by it.   This criticism of the *Stewart* approach was strictly *obiter* but it may safely be assumed that the method favoured by the Scottish court will not be followed.

5   Assessment when *Gourley* partially applies

The final problem arises where only a proportion of the award in the plaintiff's hands will be taxed.   Such is the case, most significantly, under the "golden handshake" provisions, for the first £5000 are

---

[1] Hall (1957), 73 L.Q.R. 212, at p. 220.
[2] [1958] 1 Q.B. 365, at p. 379.
[3] His reasoning was cited with approval by PEARSON, L.J. in *Parsons* v. *B.N.M.*, *Laboratories, Ltd.*, [1964] 1 Q.B. 95, at pp. 138–139.
[4] 1963 S.L.T. 119.
[5] *Supra*, p. 109 and *infra*, p. 113.
[6] *Supra*, at pp. 138–139.   See also MOCCATTA, J. in *Praet* v. *Poland*, [1962] 1 Lloyd's Rep. 566, at pp. 595–596.

exempted from tax.[1] Where an award exceeds £5000, should *Gourley* apply to the first £5000? The question arose for decision in *Bold* v. *Brough, Nicholson and Hall*.[2] PHILLIMORE, J. held that *Gourley* did apply to the first £5000 as if only that sum had been awarded. In other words he treated the £5000 as the lower slice in the lost earnings and deducted from it the income tax that would have been paid if the income had been earned.

6 Critique

The *Gourley* decision gave rise to immediate controversy among both academics and practitioners,[3] and the Law Reform Committee which in 1958 was asked to examine the matter was unable to agree on the merits of the rule.[4] A majority favoured retention of the rule,[5] a view which has been endorsed by the Scottish Law Reform Committee[6] and more recently the Law Commission.[7]

The primary argument in favour of reducing damages to reflect taxation considerations is that based on the compensatory principle. It received ample expression in the *Gourley* case itself. In the words of LORD GODDARD, if the plaintiff

> "is disabled by an accident from earning his salary, I cannot see on what principle of justice the defendants should be called upon to pay him more than he would have received if he had remained able to carry out his duties. . . . Damages which have to be paid for personal injuries are not punitive, still less are they a reward. They are simply compensation."[8]

The arguments directed against the rule can be considered under five heards.

(a) Punitive

The least reputable argument is that the "wrongdoer" should not benefit from the plaintiff's liability to tax. This may be summarily dismissed as based on punitive considerations.[9]

---

[1] Income and Corporation Taxes Act 1970, s. 188(3) re-enacting Finance Act 1960, s. 38(3).
[2] [1963] 3 All E.R. 849.
[3] Baxter (1956), 19 M.L.R. 65; Hall (1957), 73 L.Q.R. 212; Stevenson and Orr, [1956] B.T.R. 3.
[4] Seventh Report, Cmnd. 501.
[5] Of the minority who recommended that *Gourley* be repealed, three members thought that tax considerations should be excluded altogether while three proposed that awards should be taxable in the hands of the plaintiff.
[6] Sixth Report, Cmnd. 635 (1959).
[7] Working Paper No. 41, paras. 131–137.
[8] [1956] A.C. 187, at pp. 207–208. See also EARL JOWITT, at p. 197, and LORD REID, at p. 212.
[9] See, further, *infra*, p. 225.

(b) *Res inter alios acta*

It is sometimes said that the relationship between the plaintiff and the Inland Revenue is *vis-à-vis* the defendant *"res inter alios acta"*, "completely collateral" or "too remote". Objections in these forms have been raised against all instances of deduction for compensating advantages. But as will be seen[1] causal criteria are of little assistance in this area and more often than not disguise what are basically policy decisions.

(c) "The paradox"

A criticism which was prominent in the years immediately following the *Gourley* decision was that the rule contained a paradox. For the purposes of tax law, the award of damages in the hands of the plaintiff is regarded as capital, and yet with the object of reducing the damages to accord with the plaintiff's notional tax liability, the court treats the loss as income.[2] This argument is, in truth, a technical one.[3] It seems simply to reflect, first the truism that consonant with the principles at present prevailing in common law jurisdictions losses of income must be capitalized in order that a lump sum be awarded,[4] and secondly the fact that tax law does not recognize as a general principle that compensation necessarily retains the characteristics of the loss which it replaces.[5]

(d) Policy of loss-distribution

It tends sometimes to be forgotten that where a plaintiff is prevented by a tort or breach of contract from earning benefits which would have been taxed not only he but also the Inland Revenue sustains a loss. Where *Gourley* applies, this loss goes uncompensated. Where, however, the award of damages in the hands of the plaintiff is taxed, that loss is shifted from the Inland Revenue to the defendant who must compensate the plaintiff to the extent of his "gross" loss. The question whether the defendant (and the loss-distributing sources which lie behind him) should indemnify the Inland Revenue (and therefore the taxpayer) raises issues of a fundamentally political nature,[6] but it is at the very least arguable that the proper loss distribution is not achieved by the *Gourley* rule.[7]

---

[1] *Infra*, pp. 225–226.
[2] Jolowicz, [1959] C.L.J. 86.
[3] McGregor 11 I.E.C.L. 9–138.   See also Street, pp. 89–91 and Bale (1966), 44 C.B.R. 66, at pp. 70–72.
[4] The problem would, presumably, not exist if a system of periodical payments were to be introduced: McGregor, *supra*, n. 3.
[5] *Supra*, p. 109.
[6] Cf. *infra*, pp. 229–230.
[7] Hall (1957), 73 L.Q.R. 212.

(e) Impracticability

Perhaps the most forceful objection to the rule is based on the impracticability of its application. Tax problems of some complexity must be solved by judges and practitioners not usually expert in this field. The Inland Revenue is not represented in the proceedings and if it wishes to challenge a ruling it must take it to a higher court. More problematic still is the amount of speculation involved: the tax exemptions and allowances, the other sources of income, the tax avoidance schemes. It is submitted that in circumstances where the award of damages is not taxable in the hands of the plaintiff, the *Gourley* approach is an evil but a necessary evil. It seems preferable to have a solution, albeit a complex one, which adheres to the compensatory principle than to run the risk of gross over-compensation. But in the light of the objections discussed in this and the last paragraph there is a very strong case for introducing legislation which would impose taxation on all awards.

IV SURVIVAL OF ACTIONS

1 General

At common law, in general no action in tort could survive the death of either the tortfeasor or the injured party: *actio personalis moritur cum persona.* Claims for breach of contract, on the other hand, were exempt from the rule. The difference between the two causes of action was abolished by the Law Reform (Miscellaneous Provisions) Act 1934[1] which provided that all actions save those for defamation, seduction and adultery[2] could survive death either against, or for the benefit of, the deceased's estate. The question to be considered here is the extent to which the death of either party will affect the measure of damages.

2 Death of wrongdoer

The death of the wrongdoer cannot affect the existence or extent of the plaintiff's loss, and, unless a strictly punitive view is taken, it should not alter the amount which the plaintiff is entitled to recover. This is indeed the position in English law, and, perhaps unjustifiably,[3] the principle holds good even for exemplary damages.[4]

---

[1] S. 1(2).
[2] The action for damages for adultery has since been abolished by Law Reform (Miscellaneous Provisions) Act 1970, s. 5.
[3] See *infra*, p. 118.
[4] The Act prescribes no exception to the rule that the full measure may be awarded against the estate. Cf. LORD KILBRANDON in *Cassell & Co., Ltd.* v. *Broome,* [1972] A.C. 1027, at p. 1133.

3 Death of injured party

(a) Survival action and Fatal Accident Acts action

A survival action brought for the benefit of the injured party's estate must be carefully distinguished from an action brought by his dependants in their own right. The latter arises under the Fatal Accidents Acts, and, broadly speaking, the measure of damages is the loss which the dependants themselves sustain as a result of the death.[1] In a survival action the party claiming compensation is the estate of the deceased person (more particularly its representatives). The cause of action is founded not on the death but on a right which had vested in the injured party before his death.[2] It is in addition to and not in derogation of any right under the Fatal Accidents Acts,[3] though as will be seen,[4] the award under one action, actual or prospective, is taken into account in assessing compensation for the other.[5]

(b) General principle governing measure

The general principle is that the estate may recover damages for all losses which the victim had sustained before his death and for which he would have recovered compensation if he had survived to pursue his action. One consequence is that the damages may have to be reduced on account of his contributory negligence[6] or his receipt of a National Insurance benefit.[7] Another is that while damages may be awarded for all losses, pecuniary and non-pecuniary, accruing up to the time of death,[8] no compensation is recoverable for those losses which would have accrued only if the injured party had not died (e.g. future loss of earnings or loss of amenities). There is no direct authority for this last proposition,[9] but it is fully accepted in practice,[10] and, moreover, is but a simple application of the principle that the court should take

---

[1] *Infra*, pp. 264–278.
[2] The action survives even where death is instantaneous: *Morgan* v. *Scoulding*, [1938] 1 K.B. 786.
[3] Law Reform Act 1934, s. 1(5).
[4] *Infra*, pp. 276–277.
[5] *Davies* v. *Powell Duffryn Collieries, Ltd.*, [1942] A.C. 601.
[6] Law Reform (Contributory Negligence) Act 1945, s. 1(4).
[7] Law Reform (Personal Injuries) Act 1948, s. 2(1). However other compensatory advantages (e.g. life insurance benefits: *Harris* v. *Brights Asphalt Contractors*, [1953] 1 Q.B. 617, at p. 634) are to be ignored: Law Reform (Miscellaneous Provisions) Act 1934, s. 1(2)(c).
[8] *Rose* v. *Ford*, [1937] A.C. 826. The case is also authority for the proposition that loss of expectation of life, as an item of damages, is to be regarded as accruing at the date of the injury; cf. *infra*, p. 201.
[9] But it must follow from the rule in *Oliver* v. *Ashman*, [1962] 2 Q.B. 210 that a living plaintiff is not entitled to damages for his loss of earnings during the "lost years": *infra*, pp. 184–187.
[10] Clerk & Lindsell, § 419, n. 25.

account of events occurring between the date of injury and the date of trial which go to mitigate the losses incurred.[1] Death of the injured party has *eo tanto* reduced his losses.

(c) Exceptions to general principle

There are three exceptions to the general principle.

(i) *Funeral expenses* In general no distinction is drawn between cases where death results from the injury or event for which the defendant is liable and causes where it is in no way connected with the defendant's conduct. But there is one exception to this: in the former case, the estate may recover damages for funeral expenses.[2] This also constitutes an exception to the general principle above for it is an item which would not, of course, have been recoverable by the injured party himself. There is, moreover, a further difficulty: the estate would in any case have incurred the expenses. The only loss, therefore, is the liability to pay them at the date of the earlier death.

(ii) *Exemplary damages* The Law Reform Act of 1934[3] expressly provides that an award of exemplary damages shall not survive for the benefit of the estate.[4]

(iii) *Mitigation* The representatives of the estate just like the injured party himself must be under a duty to mitigate the loss. But what is to be regarded as a reasonable step in mitigation may vary as between the representatives and the injured party. As a consequence the measure of damages awarded to the estate may in some circumstances differ from that which would have been awarded to the injured party if he had lived. This would seem to be the explanation for the decision in *Otter* v. *Church, Adams, Tathem & Co.*[5]

> D's, solicitors, negligently advised P that he had an absolute interest in certain property. In fact he had an entailed interest. Had he appreciated this, he could have barred the entail. He died without discovering the mistake and the entailed property did not pass to his estate.

Clearly if he had discovered the mistake during his lifetime, P could have mitigated the loss by disentailing, and he would have been entitled only to nominal damages. After the death it was too late, and

---

[1] *Supra*, pp. 16–18.
[2] Law Reform Act 1934, s. 1(2)(c).
[3] S. 1(2)(a).
[4] For a criticism of this rule see *infra*, p. 118.
[5] [1953] Ch. 280.

there was nothing the representatives could do to mitigate the loss of the entailed property. They were thus entitled to full compensation for this loss.

(d) Critique

It is not difficult to ascertain the true rationale of survival actions. Though a man's death may curtail those losses which were *personal* to himself, it should not affect *property* losses, since his estate steps into his shoes as far as his assets and liabilities are concerned, and stands to gain or lose as he would have gained or lost.[1] The exclusion of the actions in defamation, seduction and adultery from the 1934 Act indicates that the draftsmen were to some extent influenced by these considerations. Unfortunately, they concentrated on a few causes of action which protected primarily personal interests rather than on personal losses themselves. As a result major anomalies have emerged.

(i) *Exemplary damages* The rule that an award of exemplary damages may survive *against* the estate of a deceased tortfeasor but may not survive *to benefit* the estate of the deceased injured party is thoroughly illogical. If the object of an exemplary damages award is to punish the tortfeasor, it should make no difference that the injured party has died, but it should make a difference that the tortfeasor himself has died. It is difficult to see what purpose is served by punishing the estate of the tortfeasor. The sins of the father are indeed visited on his sons.

(ii) *Non-pecuniary losses* The only possible justification for the rule in *Rose* v. *Ford*[2] allowing damages for non-pecuniary losses to survive for the benefit of the estate is the objective conceptual notion that a man's estate is the extension not only of his proprietary assets but also of his personality, and that therefore, any "personal" loss is a loss not only to himself but also to his estate.[3] But this would seem to be wholly artificial. It runs counter to the notion that the object of compensation is to restore to the plaintiff as far as possible what he has lost.[4] It cannot be said that a man's estate loses a leg, life or happiness. What the estate loses are the pecuniary advantages consequent on the existence of that leg, life, etc. and these losses are covered by the heads of pecuniary damages. The estate may, then, get a windfall. *Andrews* v. *Freeborough*[5] provides a good illustration.

---

[1] The distinction is well brought out in some of the old cases on breach of promise to marry. See especially *Finlay* v. *Chirney* (1888), 20 Q.B.D. 494.

[2] [1937] A.C. 826.

[3] Cf. *infra*, pp. 195 and 214.

[4] Cf. *infra*, pp. 215–218.

[5] [1967] 1 Q.B. 1.

P, a girl aged 8, sustained a severe brain injury as a result of D's negligence. She became unconscious immediately and died a year later without regaining consciousness. The representative of P's estate was awarded *inter alia* £2000 for P's loss of amenities and £500 for her loss of expectation of life. The award was upheld, somewhat reluctantly, by the Court of Appeal.

WINN, L.J. said:

"It is a somewhat strange form of compensation which is neither received by the person entitled to be compensated nor even awarded to him or her in his or her own right. Money can do little to ease the path of a departed soul."[1]

The attempt to defend the rule on the ground that since the dependants may not in their own right claim for non-pecuniary loss[2] this will serve as some form of substitute[3] must surely fail. The existence of one anomaly can hardly justify the creation of another. It is submitted that the rule in *Rose* v. *Ford* should be abrogated by legislation: compensation for non-pecuniary losses should not survive for the benefit of the estate.[4]

---

[1] *Ibid.*, at p. 26.
[2] *Infra*, pp. 272–274.
[3] *Per* PEARSON, L.J., *Oliver* v. *Ashman*, [1962] 2 Q.B. 210, at p. 243.
[4] This is the position in some other common law (notably Canadian) jurisdictions. See McGregor, 11 I.E.C.L. 9–202

CHAPTER FIVE

Injuries to Property Rights

I INTRODUCTION

1 Scope and classification

In this chapter the principles for assessing damages for injuries to a person's interest in property will be considered. The types of property which may injuriously be affected will be divided into the traditional categories of chattels and land. The common law has from the beginning attributed considerable significance to the distinction between real and personal property.[1] The development of remedies for the tortious interference with property rights has been conducted along independent but parallel channels. It is therefore convenient to consider under separate sections the rules governing damages for injuries to chattels and to land, although, as will be seen, there is a certain similarity of approach.

Property may be injured in three different ways.

(a) Destruction

The plaintiff's property may be destroyed by the defendant's tort. This category of injury, however, hardly applies to land. It is just conceivable that land may be swallowed up in an earthquake or washed away by a flood, but it is extremely unlikely that the situation will be such as to give rise to an action in tort. Discussion of damages for the destruction of land has therefore been omitted. As regards chattels, what constitutes "destruction" is a matter of degree. For the purpose of assessing damages, the courts include under this head not only cases of "total destruction" where the property has disappeared or completely disintegrated, but also cases of "constructive total loss" where, although parts of the property remain intact, it is nevertheless in such a condition

---

[1] Lawson, *Introduction to the Law of Property*, pp. 18–19.

as to make repair impracticable or uneconomic—in popular terms it is a "write-off".[1]

(b) Damage

The second category of injury arises where the impairment of the plaintiff's property falls short of destruction: it has been merely damaged.

(c) Misappropriation

Finally the defendant may have misappropriated the plaintiff's property. As regards land, this will generally take the form of wrongful occupation. With regard to chattels, it occurs where the defendant acts in a way inconsistent with the plaintiff's rights over the thing. Where the plaintiff is permanently deprived of his property, one might legitimately assume that the measure of damages should entirely conform with the principles applied where the property has been destroyed. In practice, as will appear, such conformity is generally achieved, but the courts tend to treat the two cases quite separately. In part, this results from the fact that special actions (e.g. conversion and detinue) must be brought for misappropriation; in part, from the fact that in cases of misappropriation deprivation may not be permanent, and it is sought to apply general principles to misappropriation whether the deprivation is permanent or temporary. The objection might be made that damages should reflect the nature of the plaintiff's loss rather than the cause of action. But it seems that English law has not yet reached the stage when general principles governing remedies for injuries are allowed to precede the formulation of specific actions in tort[2] and it has therefore been found convenient to follow the practice established by the courts and to treat the two cases separately. Parallels and contrasts will, however, be drawn where appropriate.

2 The concept of value

In this branch of the law of damages, many of the courts' pronouncements press into service the concept of "the value of the plaintiff's property". For example, in cases of destruction or misappropriation it is generally said that the plaintiff is entitled to the value of his property at the time of the tort. So ambiguous is the term "value", so many problems does the courts' reliance on it create, that it is thought desirable to begin with some general observations.[3]

---

[1] See further, *infra*, pp. 132–133.
[2] Winfield (1922), 22 Col.L.R. 1.
[3] For an outstanding and extensive analysis of these problems see Bonbright, *Valuation of Property*, Chaps. 1–14.

(a) Use of concept

The law of damages is but one of several areas of the law in which property must be "valued". In each area the "valuation" serves a different purpose. In the law of taxation, for example, it determines the extent to which the assets of taxpayer are taxable.[1] In the law of insurance it measures the extent of an insured person's interest.[2] In the law of damages it is used as a means of indemnifying the plaintiff for the injuries his property has sustained. It follows that "value" as a legal concept has no single ascertainable meaning. It is one of those abstract legal words which varies in its import according to its context and its purpose within that context.[3] By itself it offers no guidance as to how the "valuation" should be accomplished. To state, as courts frequently do in damages cases, that the plaintiff is entitled to "the value of his property" is not to conclude the inquiry as to the assessment of compensation but to commence it. The statement by itself is no more than a convenient way of expressing the conclusion that the defendant must give to the plaintiff such a sum of money as will compensate him for the injury to his property. "Value" is, in fact, a harmless but dispensable linguistic vehicle for providing a link between the admission that the defendant is liable for the injuries which he has caused and the principles for assessing the compensation to which the plaintiff is entitled. We must, not, therefore be content with an alleged principle of quantification which is laid down in terms of "value".[4] We must pursue the inquiry further and attempt to ascertain what principle of compensation is in fact being applied.

(b) Various meanings of value

It follows that when the courts adopt the "value formula", they are impliedly adopting one or other of a series of methods of assessment, and the choice of the particular method will vary according to the requirements of the case. At this stage it is proposed to give a broad outline of the most important methods of assessing compensation which are implicit in the use of the ambiguous "value" concept. A more detailed analysis will be provided at appropriate places in the text.

(i) *Selling price* "Value" is perhaps most frequently used to denote the price which the property would fetch if it were offered for sale in

---

[1] E.g. for estate duty under s. 1 of the Finance Act 1894.
[2] E.g. under s. 27 of the Marine Insurance Act 1906.
[3] Hart (1954), 70 L.Q.R. 37; Ross (1957), 70 Harv. L.R. 812.
[4] Recently the Law Reform Committee (18th Report Cmnd. 4774, 1971) has revealed a mistrust of principles of assessment formulated in terms of "value": *ibid.*, para. 91.

ordinary market conditions. "The worth of a thing is the price it will bring."[1]

(ii) *Buying price* A similar though not necessarily identical measure is the price which the plaintiff would have to pay to purchase an equivalent article in ordinary market conditions. "By market value ... is meant the price at which the article before damage, or a comparable article, could be purchased."[2] This figure may differ significantly from (i) where, for example, the plaintiff may acquire an article at wholesale price, but be able to sell it at retail price.

(iii) *Cost of adaptation* If the plaintiff is unable to get an exactly equivalent article on the market, the court may award him such a sum as will be required to purchase the nearest appropriate equivalent and to adapt it for his own particular purpose. In a Scottish case concerning the destruction of a hopper digger barge, the pursuers recovered "the price which the pursuers would have had to pay for a barge and the cost which they would have had to incur in making it suitable as a hopper digger barge".[3]

(iv) *Cost of manufacture* In extreme cases, the plaintiff may be awarded the sum required for the manufacture or reconstruction of the thing.[4]

(v) *Special value to the owner* All of the above measures are based on objective market conditions. If, in the light of the uniqueness of the property or of a special use to which it is put by its owner, the court considers that the figures arrived at by such measures do not represent the "real loss" to the plaintiff, then it might fix a special, subjective value on the thing. "In considering the commercial value of a yacht ... the element of sentiment and predilection ... is a matter that has to be borne in mind."[5]

(vi) *Capitalized potential* The last and perhaps most complex meaning which "value" might bear includes not only the exchange or purchasing value of a thing, but also a dynamic element: the potential of the thing to earn profits for its owner. The plaintiff may then be said to recover "the value of the (thing) ... as a going concern".[6]

---

[1] *Per* DR. LUSHINGTON, *The Clyde* (1856), Sw. 23, at p. 25.

[2] *Per* PENNYCUICK, J., *Darbishire* v. *Warren*, [1963] 1 W.L.R. 1067, at p. 1078.

[3] *Per* LORD HUNTER, *Clyde Navigation Trustees* v. *Bowring S.S.* (1929), 34 Ll.L. Rep. 319, at p. 320.

[4] E.g. *Harbutt's Plasticine* v. *Wayne Tank and Pump Co., Ltd.*, [1970] 1 Q.B. 447.

[5] *Per* LANGTON, J., *Piper* v. *Darling* (1940), 67 Ll.L. Rep. 419, at p. 423.

[6] *Per* LORD WRIGHT, *Liesbosch Dredger* v. *Edison S.S.*, [1933] A.C. 449, at p. 464.

II DESTRUCTION OF CHATTELS

1 Introduction

The first class of injury to be considered is that in which the defendant's tort destroys the plaintiff's chattel.[1] As has already been indicated for the purposes of ascertaining the principles of compensation the courts include under this head cases of "damage beyond repair" or "constructive total loss".[2]

In this and in the following section on damage to chattels, the great majority of cases formulating principles of compensation has been concerned with the damage to, or destruction of, ships. It has on several occasions been reiterated that no special rules apply in the Court of Admiralty, that for the purposes of assessing damages a vessel may be treated like any other chattel.[3] In general this is no doubt true, but it should be noted that if, as will be suggested, the court has some discretion as to which of several *methods* of quantification it may adopt, the factors to be taken into account in deciding which method to adopt will vary according to the subject-matter of the action.[4] The economic considerations involved in the loss of an Atlantic liner can hardly be equated with those which are affected by the destruction of a favourite china vase.

2 General principle

The general principle to be applied to this as to other categories of injury is, of course, the general compensatory principle of *restitutio in integrum*. "It is not questioned," said LORD WRIGHT in the definitive case of *Liesbosch Dredger* v. *S.S. Edison*[5]

> "that when a vessel is lost by collision due to the sole negligence of the wrongdoing vessel the owners of the former vessel are entitled to what is called *restitutio in integrum*, which means that they should recover such a sum as will replace them, as far as can be done . . . in the same position as if the loss had not been inflicted on them. . . ."

What then has been "lost" as a result of the tort? To what extent is the plaintiff's situation different from what it would have been if the tort had not been committed? The plaintiff's *basic* loss is the deprivation of

---

[1] As to the nature of the plaintiff's interest in the chattel see, in relation to misappropriation, *infra*, pp. 154–155.

[2] See further, *infra*, pp. 132–133.

[3] E.g. *per* BOWEN, L.J., *The Argentino* (1888), 13 P.D. 191, at p. 201; *per* DEVLIN, L.J., *The Hebridean Coast*, [1961] A.C. 545, at p. 562.

[4] See, e.g. *Pomphrey* v. *Cuthbertson*, 1951 S.C. 147.

[5] [1933] A.C. 449, at p. 459.

the thing itself, to which may be added as *consequential* losses all the disadvantages accrued and accruing to him through not having the thing in his possession. In the course of its history, the Court of Admiralty has approached the problem of quantifying compensation for these losses in two different ways. In the nineteenth century, it considered separately the basic loss and the various consequential losses and arithmetically arrived at a total figure. Following the *Liesbosch* decision[1] a more flexible approach was propounded. The specific losses would not be quantified separately. Their cumulative effect would be "taken into account" in assessing "the value of the thing as a going concern" (the sixth meaning of value, *supra*). In fact, as will be seen, one of the most popular methods of assessing "the value" is to adopt in essence the former arithmetical approach. It will therefore be necessary to consider in detail both approaches.

3 The arithmetical approach

The underlying theme of this approach was to gather together all the items of loss which could be assessed with certainty and simply add them together. Generally the method would proceed by the following steps.[2]

(a) Basic loss

The plaintiff's basic loss (deprivation of the ship itself) would be calculated by reference to its "market value".[3] By "market value" was meant the *selling price* (meaning (i), *supra*), the price the ship would have fetched in ordinary market conditions.[4] To ascertain this sum, the court would rely mainly on the opinions of "competent persons who knew the ship shortly previous to the time it was lost" or, alternatively, of "persons conversant with shipping and the transfers thereof" who had not been acquainted with the particular vessel.[5] After much dispute, it was held that the "value" was to be ascertained as at the date of the collision.[6]

(b) Interest

To the sum thus assessed interest would be added as representing the loss of the capital invested in the vessel by the owner. The amount

---

[1] [1933] A.C. 449.
[2] For a very detailed account see Roscoe, *Measure of Damages in Actions of Maritime Collisions*, 3rd Edn.
[3] *The Clyde* (1856), Sw. 23.
[4] *Ibid.*, at p. 25.
[5] *The Ironmaster* (1859), Sw. 441, at p. 443.
[6] *The Philadelphia*, [1917] P. 101, in contrast to earlier decisions (e.g. *The Kate*, [1899] P. 165; *The Racine*, [1906] P. 273) where the "value" was assessed

on which the interest (generally 4 per cent.) would be calculated varied according to whether or not the ship was engaged on a profit-making enterprise. If it was, interest would be awarded on the market value of the vessel plus the value of the freight, payable from the date when the freight would have been paid: the end of the voyage.[1] If it was not engaged on a profit-making voyage, the interest on the market value of the ship was payable from the date of the collision.[2] The reason advanced for the distinction was that if the owner recovered for the loss of freight he was *pro tanto* obtaining a return on his capital, and interest should be payable only when that return ceased. If he could recover no loss of freight, interest should be payable as from the loss of the capital investment—the time of destruction.[3]

(c) Profits

Loss of freight or profits was only gradually recognized as a legitimate item of damages. To begin with, the owner could recover only the profits accruing from the voyage on which the ship was engaged at the time of its loss.[4] In time this was extended to profits to be earned from all charterparties existing at the time of collision.[5] Claims for the loss of general future profits, in particular for a trawler's loss of fishing, were, however, dogmatically excluded.[6]

(d) Expenses

In addition, though there is little authority on the subject, the plaintiff could undoubtedly recover out-of-pocket expenses resulting from the collision; for example, the transport of cargo or crew, postage and telegraph expenses.

(e) Deductions

From the total of these items certain deductions might be made. If an award was made for the loss of freight, then a sum representing the expenses the shipowner would have had to pay to earn that freight

---

as it would have been at the end of the voyage. The earlier rule was designed to allow for depreciation in the "value" of the ship where the owner recovered for loss of freight. The same result was more satisfactorily achieved in *The Philadelphia* by assessing the "value" at the time of the loss, and deducting from the award for loss of freight a sum for contingencies and "wear and tear".

[1] *The Northumbria* (1869), L.R. 3 A. & E. 6.
[2] *Straker* v. *Hartland* (1864), 2 Hem. & M. 570.
[3] Per PHILLIMORE, P., *The Northumbria, supra,* at p. 12.
[4] *The Betsey Caines* (1826), 2 Hag. Adm. 28.
[5] *The Racine,* [1906] P. 273; *The Philadelphia,* [1917] P. 101.
[6] *The City of Rome* (1887), 8 Asp. M.L.C. 542, n.; *The Anselma de Larringa* (1913), 39 T.L.R. 587, cf. the Scottish case *Main* v. *Leask,* 1910 S.L.T. 365.

would be deducted.[1] Where recovery was allowed for future losses, deductions would also be made for wear and tear and other possible contingencies to which a trading vessel was subject.[2]

4 The *Liesbosch* approach

The pursuit of perfect precision implicit in the rules stated above could achieve but limited success. The vessel might have no available market. It might not earn profits. The owner might have a replacement ready to use in such emergencies. The arithmetical approach hardly catered for such circumstances. Further the relationship between the "market value" and "loss of profits" was insufficiently scrutinized. The price that a vessel might fetch in the market could not always be ascertained in the abstract: that is independently of its profit-earning capacity. If such an element were to be taken into account in assessing "market value" would not the owner be over-compensated if he were to recover, in addition, a sum for the loss of future profits? Finally, it was far from certain that Admiralty practice as expressed in these "rules-of-thumb" was always the appropriate method of assessing damages for the destruction of chattels other than ships.

In *Liesbosch Dredger* v. *S.S. Edison*,[3] LORD WRIGHT, giving the leading opinion in the House of Lords, re-examined the whole question of damages for the destruction of chattels. Since many types of chattels were owned and employed in many varied ways, it was "impossible to lay down any universal formula" for the measure of damages.[4] The basic measure was indeed the "value" of the chattel at the time and place of loss, but in calculating the "value", the arithmetical approach was discredited.[5] The "value" was not the "market value" but the "value" of the chattel to its owner "as a going concern".[6] Thus in quantifying the award, the court should not simply take the "market value" and add to it the future profits which had been lost, but should arrive at "a capitalized value of the (chattel) as a profit-earning machine".[7]

The essence of this approach (which had been first formulated by GORELL BARNES, J. in an earlier case)[8] is, therefore, a shift in the concept of "value" from selling price (meaning (i)) to *capitalized potential* (meaning (vi)). The principle being thus formulated, much greater

---

[1] *The Philadelphia*, [1917] P. 101.
[2] *Ibid.*
[3] [1933] A.C. 449.
[4] *Ibid.*, at p. 465.
[5] *Ibid.*, at pp. 462–463.
[6] *Ibid.*, at p. 464.
[7] *Ibid.*, at p. 464.
[8] *The Harmonides*, [1903] P. 1.

freedom is conferred on the court. In reaching an overall estimate of "value" it is not bound to accede to any strict arithmetical *rule*. Instead it has at its disposal a number of *methods*, the choice between which will depend on the nature of the chattel, its employment at the time of the loss and subsequent circumstances. "The dominant rule of law is the principle of *restitutio in integrum,* and subsidiary rules can only be justified if they give effect to that rule."[1] It remains to consider what methods are available and what considerations may determine their application.

(a) Cost of replacement methods (value meanings (ii)–(iv))

The most usual methods today of assessing the "value" of a chattel at the time of its destruction are those based on the cost of finding a reasonable replacement. This is the most direct application of the *restitutio in integrum* doctrine. It is awarding the plaintiff such a sum as will enable him to put himself in the position he was in before the commission of the tort. Where a chattel of the identical kind to that destroyed is available for purchase in the ordinary market, the plaintiff will recover the price to be paid for this purchase.[2] Where the substitute article has to be adapted to serve the plaintiff's particular purpose, he may recover the expenses of such work,[3] and also for the loss of user or of profits during any delay before the replacement is ready for use,[4] or alternatively for the hire of a substitute during that period.[5] If nothing less than specific replacement will adequately compensate the plaintiff's loss, then even though an approximate replacement is available on the market, it would seem in principle that he has the right to demand the cost of manufacturing an exact equivalent to the chattel destroyed.[6] Where, on the other hand, specific replacement is deemed unreasonable, the plaintiff may recover the purchase-price of another chattel, which reasonably meets his needs, and which is in a similar condition to that which was destroyed.[7]

(b) Market value method (value meaning (i))

As an alternative to the replacement methods the court may base the award on the "market value" (i.e. selling price) of the chattel at the

---

[1] Per Lord Wright, *Liesbosch Dredger* v. *S.S. Edison,* [1933] A.C. 449, at p. 463.

[2] *Moore* v. *D.E.R., Ltd.,* [1971] 3 All E.R. 517.

[3] *Clyde Navigation Trustees* v. *Bowring Steamship* (1929), 34 Ll.L. Rep. 319; *Jones* v. *Port of London Authority,* [1954] 1 Lloyd's Rep. 489.

[4] *Jones* v. *Port of London Authority, ibid.*

[5] *Moore* v. *D.E.R., Ltd.,* [1971] 3 All E.R. 517.

[6] Per Devlin, J., *Jones* v. *Port of London Authority, supra,* at p. 490.

[7] *Uctkos* v. *Mazzetta,* [1956] 1 Lloyd's Rep. 209.

time of loss, plus a sum for loss of profits or for loss of use. Little attempt has been made in the case-law to rationalize the choice of this method in preference to the cost of replacement method. The key consideration, it is suggested, is *restitutio in integrum*. Whereas the application of the cost of replacement method will put the plaintiff in the position he would have been in if the chattel had *remained in his possession*, by recovering the "market value" the plaintiff is being indemnified on the basis that he would have *sold* his chattel. The distinction then would seem to turn on the nature of the plaintiff's holding of the chattel: if for him the use and possession of the thing is of greater importance, the cost of replacement method should be invoked; if, on the other hand, he possesses the thing more as a capital investment intending eventually to profit by its sale, then the "market value" method would seem more appropriate. This argument will be considered again in relation to misappropriation.[1]

If the "market value" method is chosen, how will it be applied? In general the court is likely to be guided by the arithmetical method discussed above, but with two important qualifications, resulting from the *Liesbosch* decision. First, the court must be wary of duplicating the profit element.

> "The value of prospective freights cannot simply be added to the market value but ought to be taken into account in order to ascertain the total value for the purpose of assessing the damage, since if it is merely added to the market value of a free ship, the owner will be getting *pro tanto* his damages twice over."[2]

This may be illustrated by contrasting two decisions. In *The Llanover*,[3] the "market value" of a ship lost during the Second World War already reflected the great profit-earning potential of the vessel and the plaintiffs could not recover under a separate head for loss of trading profits. In *The Fortunity*,[4] where the vessel destroyed was one of a fleet of motor cruisers which the plaintiffs hired out on the Broads, the award included not only the "market value" but also for the loss of profits for one season. In that case, the evidence revealed that though the selling price of a motor cruiser would to a certain extent be governed by the profits it would be expected to make, yet it would not take account of the very heavy bookings which had already been made for the vessel for the season immediately following its destruction. Secondly, since in *The Liesbosch* it was emphasized that profits should be taken into account in assessing "value" rather than by simply adding to the "market value",

---

[1] *Infra*, at p. 145.
[2] *Per* LORD WRIGHT, *Liesbosch Dredger* v. *S.S. Edison*, [1933] A.C. 449, at p. 464.
[3] [1947] P. 80.
[4] [1960] 2 All E.R. 64.

it would seem to follow that the requirement that specific contractual engagements must be proved has now been abandoned. An award may be made for future profits generally, provided that they satisfy the rules as to certainty.[1] Where the chattel is not a profit-earner, then, though there is no direct authority on the point, the plaintiff should recover for loss of use in addition to the "market value".[2] The principles for assessing loss of use have been evolved under the head of damage to chattels and a full discussion may be found in that context.[3]

(c) Special value (value meaning (v))

Where a chattel has a "value" peculiar to itself or to its owner or where its owner employs it for a special or unusual purpose, in general the cost of replacement method will be applied. If, however, the court considers that in the circumstances the purchase of a replacement was unadvisable or unreasonable or impossible (a unique article, a work of art, an heirloom, cannot by its nature be replaced), it may determine on a sum which in no way reflects objective commercial criteria but which seeks to express the "real subjective value" of the chattel to its owner. An assessment thus envisaged will be based on such factors as the original cost of the chattel, the length of time the plaintiff had it in his possession, the extent of deterioration, the amount spent on repairs, the uses to which the chattel is put, and even the intangible features of "sentiment" and "predilection".[4] In *The Harmonides*[5] the court regarded the "market value" of a ship assessed by the Registrar at £18,000 as inadequate in the light of the special business of the vessel as an Atlantic liner, and varied the award to £31,000.

5 Expenses and constructive total loss

Finally it must be noted that whichever of the above methods is adopted by the courts, the plaintiff may, in addition, recover for all reasonable out-of-pocket expenses which were made necessary through the loss of his chattel. This head of damages is of greatest significance in cases of constructive total loss. Here, it will be recalled, the chattel is severely damaged rather than totally destroyed. In such cases, it will normally be reasonable for the plaintiff to incur expenses in ascertaining whether or not the wreck was to be regarded as beyond reasonable repair. Such expenses, including those for the raising and

---

[1] *The Fortunity, ibid.* and *supra*, pp. 82–84.
[2] *Per* SCRUTTON, L.J., *obiter*, in *The Edison*, [1932] P. 52, at p. 61.
[3] *Infra*, pp. 135–140.
[4] *Piper* v. *Darling* (1940), 67 Ll.L. Rep. 419.
[5] [1903] P. 1.

transport of the wreck may, provided they are reasonable, legitimately be charged to the defendant's account.[1] One final difference is worth mentioning: the scrap value of the wreck should be deducted from the sum available.[2]

III   DAMAGE TO CHATTELS

1   General principle

The principles governing compensation for the destruction of chattels contained, it might be said, aspects both conceptual and functional. *Conceptually*, they identified the plaintiff's loss with the "value" of the destroyed article. *Functionally*, they sought to put the plaintiff in the position he would have been in if the tort had not been committed. Where the chattel is merely damaged the analogous dual aspect is clear. *Conceptually*, the plaintiff has lost the difference between the "value" of the goods in their undamaged condition and their "value" after they have sustained injury. A few cases have referred to this aspect of the general principle.[3] Happily the great majority of English decisions content themselves with exploring the *functional* aspect:

> "The basic measure of damage ... is restitution. In the case of injury to a chattel, it may happen that restitution can be effected either by repair of the existing article or by the purchase of a comparable article. ... In such a case the measure of damage is restitution by whichever method it would be reasonable for the owner of the chattel to adopt in the particular circumstances."[4]

Thus, where a chattel is damaged, there are two possible modes of assessment: (1) if the chattel is in such a condition that it is reasonable to repair it, the basic measure is the cost of such repairs; (2) if the injury is so severe that it is not reasonable to repair it, the case will be treated as one of contructive total loss, in which case the rules relating to the destruction of a chattel will apply. The principles governing (2) have already been discussed. Here attention will be confined to (1).

Since the use of the concept "value" has been abandoned in this area, the courts must qualify independently basic and consequential losses. We may begin with the former.

---

[1] *Jackson* v. *Dowre Boat Co.*, [1957] 2 Lloyd's Rep. 134.
[2] *Griffin & Co., Ltd.* v. *De-la-Haye and De-la-Haye Contractors*, [1968] 2 Lloyd's Rep. 253.
[3] E.g. *Hughes* v. *Quentin* (1838), 8 C. & P. 703; *Darbishire* v. *Warren*, [1963] 1 W.L.R. 1067.
[4] *Per* PENNYCUICK, J., *Darbishire* v. *Warren, ibid.*, at p. 1078.

2 Basic loss: cost of repairs

The basic loss is invariably measured by estimating the cost necessary to restore the article to its condition before the injury. Several points under this principle require elaboration.

(a) It must be reasonable to repair

In determining whether or not it was reasonable to repair the chattel, the court will look first to the cost of repairs. If this cost exceeds the "value" of the article (by which presumably is meant the purchase price of an equivalent article on the market), the presumption is that repair was unreasonable.[1] This presumption may be rebutted by the existence of special circumstances. There has been no comprehensive account of when such special circumstances might exist, but a few instances may be given.

In *Algeiba* v. *Australind*[2]

> The cost of repairing the P ship exceeded her value when sold. But her owners discharged the onus of proving that repairs were reasonable by showing (1) at the time of the accident it was difficult to find a substitute vessel, and (2) the P ship was of "special value" to its owners as it was unusually well equipped for the particular work which they were undertaking.

The question as to whether sentimental value may constitute "special circumstances" turns on an interpretation of the decision in *O'Grady* v. *Westminster Scaffolding*[3]

> P's car "Hortensia", a 1938 M.G. and his pride and joy, was damaged in accident for which D was liable. P spent £253 on repairs and £207 in hiring substitutes during repairs. The pre-accident "market value" of "Hortensia" was £180–£200. EDMUND DAVIES, J. held that in the circumstances P had acted reasonably and awarded him the full cost of repairs.[4] In coming to his decision, he was "mindful of his (P's) obvious attachment to the vehicle",[5] but he also referred to the difficulty of obtaining a similar vehicle on the open market.[6]

---

[1] *Italian State Railways* v. *Minnehaha* (1921), 6 Ll.L. Rep. 12; *Darbishire* v. *Warren, supra*. In calculating the "value" of the article, the court must take into account the scrap value of the wreck, since the proceeds therefrom will contribute to the cost of a replacement: *The Minnehaha, supra*, at p. 13.

[2] (1921), 8 Ll.L. Rep. 210.

[3] [1962] 2 Lloyd's Rep. 238.

[4] His delay in commencing repairs was, however, regarded as unreasonable and a sum was deducted from the award for the hiring expenses.

[5] [1962] 2 Lloyd's Rep. 238, at p. 239.

[6] *Ibid.*, at p. 240.

O'Grady was considered in *Darbishire* v. *Warren*[1] in which the Court of Appeal rejected a claim for the cost of repairing a second-hand shooting brake where such cost substantially exceeded the pre-accident "value" of the car. The plaintiff was awarded a sum representing the "market value" of the vehicle on the ground that he should have treated it as a constructive total loss. In distinguishing *O'Grady*, their Lordships laid greater emphasis on the uniqueness and irreplaceability of "Hortensia" than on the sentimental attachment of its owner.[2] It is indeed difficult clearly to extract the subjective element in "uniqueness" and "irreplaceability" but it is submitted that, despite the problems of quantification, recognition of a non-pecuniary element in the award is both proper and desirable.

(b) Repairs must be necessary

For the plaintiff to recover the full cost of repairs he must show that the need for repairs arose from the accident for which the defendant was liable.[3] Further the repairs for which the defendant must account must be necessary to restore the chattel to its former condition. If the repairs were merely expedient for the better functioning of the chattel they cannot be charged to the defendant's account.[4] Both of these principles are but applications of the general principles of causation which have already been examined.[5]

(c) Cost of repairs must be reasonable

Even if the repairs were necessary, the plaintiff will recover the cost only if it was reasonable. If the court considers that the plaintiff was charged an excessive amount, then, as in *The Pactolus*,[6] it is entitled to reduce the award to what is the "ordinary and accustomed rate" for the job.[7]

(d) Cost of repairs may include overhead charges

The normal measure is for labour and materials. This is always the case where a chattel is sent to an independent contractor for repairs. Where, however, the plaintiffs themselves provide facilities for repairs the question arises whether they can demand that the defendant contribute to the expense of maintaining such facilities. In *London*

---

[1] [1963] 1 W.L.R. 1067.
[2] *Ibid.*, at pp. 1072, 1077–1078, 1079.
[3] *The Haversham Grange*, [1905] P. 307; *Organic Research Chemicals* v. *Ricketts*, [1961] C.L.Y. 2346.
[4] *The Pactolus* (1856), Sw. 173.
[5] *Supra*, pp. 62–67.
[6] *Supra*.
[7] *Ibid.*, *per* DR. LUSHINGTON, at pp. 175–176.

Transport Executive v. *Foy Morgan*[1] the claim succeeded, but the decision should be interpreted in the light of *London Transport Executive* v. *Court*[2] in which it was held that the plaintiffs could not recover for those overhead expenses which they would in any case have incurred. In other words, for overheads to be recoverable, the repairs must have given rise to some exceptional expenses.

(e) Repairs make chattel more valuable than before injury

The execution of repairs may make the chattel more valuable than it was before it was injured. Clearly it would be unreasonable in many cases to restore the article to its exact physical condition at the time of the accident, warts and all.[3] Yet in principle it does not follow that the plaintiff should thereby benefit and still recover the full cost of repairs. To be consistent with the general compensatory principle a sum should be deducted from the plaintiff's award for the consequent increase in the "value" of his article. Such is the position in the United States of America.[4] In England, it has been held[5] that no deduction should be made from the award. The argument advanced is that if a deduction were made it would be in effect to force the plaintiff to invest his money in the modernizing of his chattel which might be inconvenient and unwanted.[6] The difficult choice lies between an almost certain overcompensation of the plaintiff and the possibility of compelling the plaintiff to invest capital in his chattel against his will. It is submitted with some hesitation that the American solution is to be preferred. Not only is it more consistent with the *restitutio in integrum* doctrine (there is just a hint of the "punitive" approach in the prevailing English rule)[7] but it would also deter the plaintiff from executing unnecessary repairs at the expense of the defendant. In short, the defendant should bear the risk of complete but not excessive compensation.

(f) Chattel only partially repaired

In the converse situation where the injured article has been only partially repaired, the general compensatory principle is without doubt applied. The plaintiff will recover in addition to the cost of partial

---

[1] [1955] C.L.Y. 743.

[2] [1954] C.L.Y. 888.

[3] In contrast to a game of cricket in which a lost ball must be replaced by one in as worn a condition as its predecessor.

[4] E.g. *Broadie* v. *Randall*, 32 A.L.R. 708 (1923); *Cato* v. *Silling*, 73 S.E.2d. 731 (1952).

[5] *The Gazelle* (1844), 2 Wm. Rob 279; *The Pactolus* (1856), Sw. 173; and in relation to damage to land, *Harbutt's Plasticine* v. *Wayne Tank*, [1970] 1 Q.B. 447, *infra*, p. 165.

[6] Per WIDGERY, L.J., *Harbutt's Plasticine* case, *ibid.*, at p. 473.

[7] The courts seem ready to stress that the "wrongdoer" should not escape the burden created by his wrong.

repairs a sum representing the difference in "value" (generally the selling price) between the condition of the chattel at the time of the accident and its partially repaired condition.[1]

(g) Repairs not yet executed

The fact that at the time of the action repairs have not yet been executed creates no special difficulty. It will be recalled that the cost of repairs is only a convenient way of expressing the plaintiff's basic loss. There is thus no magic in the repairs having been executed. The estimated cost of repairs is, in principle, an equally valid measure,[2] and this remains true even if the repairs are never carried out.[3] The only qualification that needs to be added is that the plaintiff must not benefit from any rise in the cost of repairs through his delay in having them executed.[4] The cost of repairs should be estimated at the time when it was reasonable to execute them. This is to apply the ordinary rule of mitigation of loss.

3 Consequential losses

To put the plaintiff in the position he would have been in but for the tort involves not only compensating him for the *static* element in his loss, the impairment of the quality of his article, but also for a *dynamic* element, the loss of use of the article during the period of repairs. Provided that his claim does not fall foul of the principles of causation, remoteness or mitigation, the "party who has suffered injury is clearly entitled to an adequate compensation for any loss he may sustain for the detention of his (chattel) during the period which is necessary for the completion of repairs."[5] Three methods are available for three different factual situations: where, during the period for repairs, the plaintiff has (i) lost the use of a profit-earning chattel; (ii) hired a substitute chattel; (iii) lost the use of a non-profit-earning chattel. These will be considered in turn.

(a) Profit-earning chattels

(i) *General principle* Where a chattel customarily earns profits for its owner, the normal measure for the loss of its use during repairs is, naturally, the profits it would have earned but for its detention.[6]

---

[1] *The Georgiana* v. *The Anglican* (1872), 21 W.R. 280.

[2] *The Kingsway*, [1918] P. 344.

[3] *The Glenfinlas*, [1918] P. 363, n.; *The London Corporation*, [1935] P. 70.

[4] But it may be reasonable to await the approval of insurers: *Martindale* v. *Duncan* (1973), 117 Sol. Jo. 168.

[5] *Per* Dr. Lushington, *The Gazelle* (1844), 2 Wm. Rob. 279, at p. 283.

[6] For statements to this effect see, especially *The Argentino*, *per* Bowen, L.J. (1888), 13 P.D. 191, 201 and *per* Lord Herschell (1889), 14 App. Cas. 519, at p. 523.

Damages for loss of profits may be awarded either as special or as general damages.

(ii) *Special damages* To plead special damages the plaintiff must offer proof of some current or future contractual engagement from which he was bound to withdraw as a result of detention for repairs.[1] An award under this head will, of course, exclude an award of general damages for the loss of use during the same period.[2] In considering a claim for special damages, the court must be certain that the alleged loss of specific profits was real and not notional. The contractual engagement may, for example, eventually be completed albeit much later than anticipated.[3] The injured chattel may be one of a "team" which undertakes a series of commissions in rotation, in which case detention for repairs will result not in the loss of specific profits for one such commission, but in the chattel losing its "place in the queue".[4] In this and in the previous example the measure of damages is for the delay in the performance of the contract, and the plaintiff must fall back on general damages.

(iii) *General damages* Where no special damages are pleaded, the court must attempt to assess the profits which would have been earned if the chattel had not been detained. In simple cases, the court can merely multiply the number of days lost through repairs by the average daily profits. This was possible in, for example, *The Risoluto*,[5] where a fishing vessel was incapacitated for part of the season. But the presence of complicating factors might make the solution more elusive. If the chattel would, even if not injured, have been unemployed for a certain period of time, that period of time must be deducted from the number of days for which the plaintiff can claim for loss of profits.[6] Further, where there are great disparities in trading profits over short periods of time, the court may have a singularly difficult task in determining what average profit should be the basis of the calculation. Such a situation arose in *The Soya*.[7]

> At the time of the collision, Ps' ship was about to earn £*x* per day on a charterparty. After 20 days repairs she was able to complete this engagement. Owing to exceptional trading conditions, she was able to follow the engagement with further charterparties but at average

---

[1] *The Argentino*, *supra*.
[2] *The Pacific Concord*, [1961] 1 All E.R. 106.
[3] *The Soya*, [1956] 2 All E.R. 393. See also *S.S. Strathfillen* v. *S.S. Ikala*, [1929] A.C. 196 where the plaintiffs were subject to an annual quota of possible trade. After the completion of repairs the plaintiffs were still able to discharge their quota.
[4] *The Black Prince* (1862), Lush. 568.
[5] (1883), 8 P.D. 109.
[6] *The Black Prince*, *supra*; *S.S. Strathfillen* v. *S.S. Ikala*, *supra*.
[7] [1956] 1 W.L.R. 714.

profits of £6*x* per day. Ps claimed damages of 20 × £6*x* on the ground
that if performance of the first charterparty had not been delayed Ps
would have benefited from the higher profits prevailing at the time.
The Court of Appeal held that the lost profits should be assessed on the
basis of the rates prevailing *at the time of the collision*, and awarded
20 × £*x*.

It is submitted that the decision is an incorrect application of the
doctrine of certainty. The court clearly regarded the loss of £120*x* as
subject to too many contingencies; there was insufficient proof of loss
on this scale.[1] But it does not follow that the award must thereby
be reduced to the lowest possible figure. The plaintiffs should be compensated for the lost chance of earning at the higher rate. The basis
of assessment, therefore, should have been some figure on the scale
between £*x* per day and £6*x* per day.[2]

(iv) *Deductions* The plaintiff is under a duty to mitigate his loss.[3]
Thus from the award for loss of profits will be deducted a sum representing those profits which he actually did make or should have made
during the period for which he claims compensation. For example in
The Star of India[4]

> As a result of the collision for which Ds were responsible, Ps had to
> withdraw from a charterparty worth 55*s*. per ton. But they were able
> to secure another charterparty worth 45*s*. per ton. Ps were thus en-
> titled to the difference between profits at 55*s*. per ton and profits at 45*s*.
> per ton.

But for the deduction to be made, it must be clear that the profits
actually earned were in mitigation of the plaintiffs' loss. There must
be an adequate causal link between the accident for which the defendants are liable and the earning of the substitute profit. No deduction
will have to be made if the plaintiffs can show that even if the accident
had not occurred they would still have earned the profit. In *The
World Beauty*[5]

> P ship was engaged on charterparty A until September 1958. In
> August 1957 she was prospectively engaged on charterparty B from
> not earlier than August 1958 and not later than October 1958. In April
> 1958 P ship was damaged in a collision for which Ds were liable. A
> substitute vessel Q was engaged to complete charterparty A, but on the
> day that Q was available, the repairs on P were completed. It was then

---

[1] *Ibid., per* LORD EVERSHED, M.R., at p. 720.
[2] Cf. *supra*, pp. 83–84.
[3] *Supra*, pp. 85–90.
[4] (1876), 1 P.D. 466.
[5] [1970] P. 144.

arranged that P should commence on charterparty B 100 days earlier than had originally been agreed. In assessing damages for loss of the use of P ship, the court took account of the profits accruing from the completion of charterparty A by Q ship. But the profit earned on charterparty B was not to be deducted, since it would have been earned quite independently of the accident. The only gain acquired under charterparty B to be taken into account was the advancement of the profits by 100 days.

Deductions will also be made for the saving of expenses which would have been incurred if the chattel had been profitably employed.[1] This may include the saving on depreciation through wear and tear.[2] Finally, a deduction should be made for the ordinary risks and contingencies involved in the employment of the particular class of profit-earning chattels.[3]

(b)   Temporary replacement by another chattel

(i) *General principle*   Whether the plaintiff has lost the use of a profit-earning (*supra*) or of a non-profit-earning (*infra*) chattel, one way of mitigating his loss is to hire a substitute while the injured article is being repaired. It follows by a simple application of the *restitutio in integrum* doctrine that if the substitute faithfully carries out what the injured chattel would have done if available, the measure of damages will be the cost of hiring the substitute[4] It is, in general, recoverable from the time of the injury until the injured chattel is ready to resume its duties.[5] But deductions will be made if the plaintiff unreasonably delays in effecting the repairs.[6] Moreover the replacement hired and the cost of hiring must be reasonable.

In *Watson Norie* v. *Shaw*[7]

> P hired, at £40 per week, a vehicle of similar character to that which had been injured by Ds. Ds produced evidence that with reasonable diligence P could have acquired an equivalent for £25 per week. P's award was limited to the lower rate.

(ii) *Source of replacement*   The plaintiff may, however, have incurred no cost in providing a replacement since either (1) he may himself

---

[1] *The Gazelle* (1844), 2 Wm. Rob. 279.
[2] *The Star of India, supra*; but this will of course only apply where the depreciation through use would have been greater than if the chattel remained idle.
[3] *Professor Gruvel* v. *Barry Graving Dock* (1926), 25 Ll.L. Rep. 434.
[4] *The Greta Holme*, [1897] A.C. 596; *The Hebridean Coast*, [1961] A.C. 545; and see *The World Beauty, supra*.
[5] *Pomphrey* v. *Cuthbertson*, 1951 S.C. 147.
[6] *O'Grady* v. *Westminster Scaffolding*, [1962] 1 Lloyd's Rep. 238; cf. *Martindale* v. *Duncan* (1973), 117 Sol. Jo. 168.
[7] (1967), 111 Sol. Jo. 117.

have had a reserve chattel available for such emergencies or (2) he may have distributed the load among other chattels employed by him for the same or similar purposes. These two situations must be carefully distinguished.

In the first, the plaintiff is in fact availing himself of a substitute although the chattel is provided from his own resources. He is, in the language of Admiralty law, "chartering additional tonnage". The cost of providing the substitute is clearly recoverable, as special damages.[1] A convenient mode of calculating the award on this basis is to assess the notional hire of a substitute: what would it have cost the plaintiff to have hired a substitute from an external source.[2]

If, however, as in the second hypothesis, it cannot be shown that the plaintiffs had provided any effective substitute, that is, had not put any of their other chattels to *additional* employment, the notional cost of hiring a substitute will not be the appropriate measure. Instead, the plaintiff must fall back on general damages for the loss of use[3] under section (a) *supra* if he has lost any profits, or under section (c) *infra* if he has lost no profits.

(c) Non profit-earning chattels

If the chattel is not a profit-earner and the plaintiff has not hired a substitute, the problem of measuring the plaintiff's loss of the use of the chattel becomes more acute. There is little *tangible* pecuniary loss with which the courts can grapple.[4] This elusiveness led the courts at first to reject any general claim for loss of use. But there can be no doubt that however elusive the loss may be it is a real one. If a man invests a capital sum in the purchase of, for example, a motor car, he expects as a return on his investment not only possession of the thing bought but also continual use of it. What he loses, therefore, as a result of its detention is a small percentage of its capital "value". The principle of recovery for the loss of use was finally recognized by the House of Lords in *The Greta Holme*.[5]

Although the doctrine was accepted in 1897, the courts have been reluctant to commit themselves to precise methods of quantification. In *The Greta Holme*,[6] the House of Lords contented itself with the suggestion that general damages for loss of use must be "reasonably

---

[1] *The Greta Holme, supra*; *The Mediana*, [1900] A.C. 113.
[2] *Per* LORD MERRIMAN, P., *The Hebridean Coast*, [1961] A.C. 545, at p. 549. See also *per* LORD BRAMPTON, *The Mediana*, [1900] A.C. 113, at p. 123.
[3] *The Hebridean Coast, supra*.
[4] There are, of course, the expenses incurred during detention, but these do not really go to the loss of use of the chattel.
[5] [1897] A.C. 596.
[6] *Supra*.

assessed".[1] The speeches in *The Mediana*[2] were equally vague: for example, "the jury might give whatever they thought would be the proper equivalent for the unlawful withdrawal of the subject-matter."[3] As recently as 1969, a judge was still speaking of "judicial guesswork" in this context.[4] Nevertheless two modes of assessing the loss have been formulated.

(i) *Standing charge cost*   The first is based on the cost of maintaining and operating the chattel.[5] The alleged justification for this measure is that the cost represents the "value" of the chattel to its owner.[6] It is, however, difficult to trace the connection between the money spent on a thing and the benefit to be derived from its use. Indeed, as has been observed judicially,[7] the measure puts "a premium upon in-efficiency." The higher the cost, the greater the damages. Yet it has been applied as "a reasonably stable basis for calculation and one which is as fair to both sides as can be devised."[8]

(ii) *Interest on capital and depreciation*   Another method was formu-lated by the House of Lords in *Admiralty Commissioners* v. *S.S. Chekiang*.[9] The plaintiff has lost part of the "return" on the capital invested in the purchase of the damaged article. He should therefore recover interest on the capital value of the chattel at the time of the injury. The capital value is assessed as the original cost less deprecia-tion. This measure seems to come closer to the plaintiff's real loss, and has the additional merit of being more flexible, for the court is able to vary the percentage for depreciation and for interest.[10] The objection to the measure is that it may draw unjustifiable distinctions according to the age and the amount of depreciation.[11] Some chattels depreciate quicker than others. Is it to be assumed that the older the vehicle the less valuable the use?

4 Expenses

Finally, for the sake of completeness it is worth observing that the

---

[1] *Per* LORD WATSON, *supra*, at p. 604.
[2] [1900] A.C. 113.
[3] *Per* LORD HALSBURY, *ibid.*, at p. 118.
[4] GEOFFREY LANE, J. in *Birmingham Corporation* v. *Sowsbery*, [1970] R.T.R. 84, at p. 86.
[5] *The Marpessa*, [1907] A.C. 241.
[6] *Per* LORD LOREBURN, *ibid.*, at pp. 244–245.
[7] *Per* GEOFFREY LANE, J., *Birmingham Corporation* v. *Sowsbery*, *supra*, at pp. 86–87.
[8] *Ibid.*, at p. 87.
[9] [1926] A.C. 637. See also *The Susquehanna*, [1926] A.C. 655.
[10] *Per* LORD SUMNER, *Admiralty Commissioners* v. *S.S. Chekiang*, *supra*, at p. 647. See also *The Hebridean Coast*, [1961] A.C. 545 and on interest generally *supra*, pp. 96–103.
[11] *Per* GEOFFREY LANE, J., *Birmingham Corporation* v. *Sowsbery*, *supra*, at p. 87.

plaintiff may recover in addition to damages for his basic loss—the cost of repairs—and for consequential losses—damages for loss of use— all reasonable out-of-pocket expenses which necessarily arise from the tort.

IV MISAPPROPRIATION OF CHATTELS

1 Introduction

The third category of injury to personal property for which damages might be awarded is misappropriation. Here the plaintiff is to be compensated for the economic loss which he sustains from having been deprived, either temporarily or permanently, of his goods. One might legitimately have assumed that to apply the basic compensatory principle of *restitutio in integrum* to this class of injury would cause no undue difficulty. If the plaintiff were permanently deprived of his property, then the position would be the same as if his chattel had been destroyed, and, presumably, the same principles of compensation should apply. If, on the other hand, the deprivation was only temporary, the plaintiff would, in essence, recover only for the loss of use of the thing during the period of wrongful detention. The principles governing compensation for the loss of use during detention for repairs after the chattel has been damaged would seem to provide the necessary guidance for quantifying this particular loss. What need then for special rules governing the assessment of damages for misappropriation? In pure theory it is hard to find an adequate answer to this question. In the practice of the courts, the cumulative influence of three different factors has made the independent development of principles almost inevitable. These three factors may be considered in turn.

(a) Different remedies

Compensation for damage to or destruction of chattels could be awarded on the commission of a number of torts (e.g. negligence, trespass, nuisance and certain torts of strict liability) but the principles governing quantification remained the same. In the present topic, however, the availability of different forms of action, especially the plaintiff's power to elect to sue either in detinue, a quasi-proprietary action,[1] or in conversion,[2] a purely tortious action, has tended to distort the principles of assessment. It may indeed seem unreasonable that

---

[1] See the analysis of DIPLOCK, L.J. in *General and Finance Facilities* v. *Cooks Cars*, [1963] 1 W.L.R. 644, at pp. 648–657 and generally Kiralfy (1948), 12 M.L.R. 426.

[2] The other actions which may be brought for misappropriation are trespass, wrongful or excessive distress, and replevin.

the measure of the plaintiff's loss should depend on the form of action which is brought.[1] In *The Mediana*,[2] LORD HALSBURY, L.C. had occasion to observe that "whatever be the form of action, the principle of assessing damages must be the same in all courts and for all forms of what I may call the unlawful detention of another man's property."

(b) Different subject-matter

In theory the types of property which may be the subject-matter of a misappropriation action are identical to those which may be damaged or destroyed. In practice, as is apparent from the cases discussed above, the principles for the assessment of compensation for damage to or destruction of chattels have for the most part been developed in respect of ships. Misappropriation cases have, in contrast, dealt with a wide variety of chattels, many of which are capable of rapid and substantial fluctuations in "value". This has given rise to special problems of time in assessing the plaintiff's loss.[3] It will, however, be suggested that the courts' approach to these problems is on the whole an unhappy one, that a more attractive alternative approach is available which would at once provide a fairer solution and at the same time accord with the principles governing the damage and destruction cases.[4]

(c) Preoccupation with "value" concept

The preoccupation of the courts with the concept of "value" in this area is even more pronounced than in the destruction cases, and with more harmful results. Many judges and textbook writers, for example, have been content to express the basic rule of quantification in terms of the "value" of the thing appropriated. As will be shown, in many cases this is clearly not the principle to be applied, and the constant reiteration of the "value" rule has tended to obscure the operation of the general compensatory doctrine of *restitutio in integrum*. As was said in a recent decision in the High Court of Australia:[5]

"the principle . . . that the injured party should receive compensation in a sum which, so far as money can do so, will put him in the same position as he would have been if . . . the tort had not been com-

---

[1] The Law Reform Committee in its 18th Report, Cmnd. 4774 (1971) has recommended that the remedies for trespass to goods, conversion and detinue should be replaced by a new tort of "unlawful interference with chattels": *ibid.*, paras. 16–28.

[2] [1900] A.C. 113, at p. 118.

[3] *Infra*, pp. 146–150.

[4] *Infra*, p. 147.

[5] *Per* TAYLOR and OWEN, JJ., *Butler* v. *Egg and Egg Pulp Marketing Board* (1966), 114 C.L.R. 185, at p. 191. See also 18th Report of the Law Reform Committee, *supra*, n. 1, at para. 91.

mitted . . . is as much applicable to actions of conversion as it is to the case of other actionable wrongs . . . (T)he statement which appears so often in the books that the general rule is that the plaintiff . . . is entitled to recover the full value of the goods converted . . . should not be allowed to obscure the broad principle that damages are awarded by way of compensation."

In the light of the complexities described above, it is thought desirable to approach the problems of quantification for the misappropriation of chattels from basic principles. To this end, the modes of assessment will be divided, as for other types of injury, between basic and consequential losses. Further, no primary distinction will be drawn according to the various forms of action which may be brought in English law. Any divergence from the general rules applying to all categories of claim will be considered as and when it arises.

2   Basic loss

(a)   General

It has constantly been reiterated by both judges[1] and writers[2] that the normal measure of damages for the misappropriation of a chattel is its "value". As a general principle, this formula is unhelpful and misleading. First, it fails to distinguish between two fundamentally different situations: where the defendant has returned the chattel to the plaintiff, and where he has not. In the former case, the plaintiff should clearly not recover the full "value" of the thing. Secondly, it fails to take account of the nature of the plaintiff's interest in the chattel. If he has only a limited interest in the property, again he will not be entitled to full "value". Thirdly, it is by itself ambiguous. As was demonstrated in the introduction to this chapter, the use of the concept "value" conceals a variety of different approaches.

The "value" formula dates from a time when the assessment of damages was a task for the jury,[3] and when no principles for exact quantification existed. When principles came to be formulated, the court could rely only on the general doctrine of *restitutio in integrum*.[4] Without doubt, to say that the plaintiff was entitled to "the value of the thing converted" was a convenient and shorter way of expressing that he was entitled to be put in the position that he would have been in had he not been deprived of his chattel. But whereas the former is a

---

[1] As illustrative of numerous statements, see, e.g. *per* LORD ROCHE in *Caxton Publishing Co., Ltd.* v. *Sutherland Publishing Co., Ltd.*, [1939] A.C. 178, at p. 192.
[2] E.g. McGregor, §987.
[3] E.g. *Fisher* v. *Prince* (1762), 3 Burr. 1363; *Finch* v. *Blount* (1836), 7 C. & P. 478 and see generally Matthews (1921), 35 Harv. L.R. 15.
[4] E.g. *Chinery* v. *Viall* (1860), 5 H. & N. 288.

mere verbal *description* on the plaintiff's loss, the latter serves also as a *guide* as to how that loss is to be measured. The chief defect of the "value" formula is that it often disguises the fact that the *restitutio in integrum* doctrine does or should lie as the basis of any rule governing the assessment of damages. It is suggested that there is a strong case for abandoning the general principle incorporating the "value" formula.

We may now consider the various methods of assessing the basic loss. As indicated above, the measure of damages will depend, at the outset on (1) the extent of the plaintiff's interest in the property and (2) whether the deprivation has been permanent or temporary, i.e. whether the chattel has been redelivered to its rightful possessor. We may begin with those cases where the plaintiff is absolutely entitled and the chattel has not been redelivered.

(b) Market value methods (value meaning (i) and (ii))

Where there is a market available for the chattel of which the plaintiff has been permanently deprived, it is generally said that he is entitled to its "market value".[1] But the phrase "market value" is ambiguous: it might refer to the selling price, the price which the article would fetch in the ordinary market, or the buying price, the price at which an equivalent article could be bought. The distinction has never been rationalized in English law[2] but is certainly applied by the courts. Two cases may be contrasted to illustrate this.

In *France* v. *Gaudet* [3]

P bought champagne at Ds' wharf at 14s. per dozen bottles. Ds converted the merchandise. P recovered the price at which he would have sold the champagne, viz. 24s. per dozen bottles.[4]

In *Hall* v. *Barclay*[5]

Ds erected and tested certain equipment belonging to Ps. After dismantling the machinery they retained possession and subsequently converted it. Ps were entitled to the price for which similar machinery could be purchased on the market.[6]

---

[1] *Hall, Ltd.* v. *Barclay*, [1937] 3 All E.R. 620.
[2] Cf. Street, pp. 198–199.
[3] (1871), L.R. 6 Q.B. 199.
[4] 24s. per dozen was in fact the price at which the plaintiff had agreed to sell the wine to a third party, but, in the light of subsequent cases (e.g. *The Arpad*, [1934] P. 189) it seems preferable to regard the subcontract price merely as evidence of the selling price in the general market. See, generally, *infra*, pp. 333–335.
[5] [1937] 3 All E.R. 620.
[6] In fact, there was no available market and the plaintiffs were thus entitled to the cost of replacement (*infra*). The principle stated in the test is, however, unaffected.

Whether the buying or the selling price is taken as the "market value" is seldom made clear in the reported cases but it is submitted that the distinction, as illustrated in the cases above, can be justified according to the *restitutio in integrum* doctrine.[1] If the plaintiff held the property in order to sell it at some future date, as in *France* v. *Gaudet*, then to restore the plaintiff to the position he would have been in but for the tort involves awarding him the price at which he would have sold the article. If, however, it was the plaintiff's intention to retain possession of the chattel for his own benefit, as in *Hall* v. *Barclay*, then to restore him to that position involves giving him a sum of money which will enable him to purchase an equivalent article in the market.

(c) Methods other than market value (value meanings (iii)–(v))

The "market value" methods may be inapplicable for either of two reasons: (1) there may be no available market for the chattel in question; (2) the plaintiff may claim that recovery of the "market value" will not adequately compensate him for his own personal loss. For example, the loving master of a faithful dog may not be satisfied that the "market value" of the particular breed of dog is adequate compensation. There is a surprising lack of case-law in England covering these areas but there would seem to be no good reason why the principles applicable to destruction cases[2] should not be appropriate here. By way of analogy, then, the methods may be formulated as follows.

(i) *Adaptation cost* If an exactly equivalent article is not available for purchase, the plaintiff may recover the cost of purchasing a similar article and of adapting it for his own particular purpose.

(ii) *Reproduction cost* Failing this, the plaintiff may recover the cost of manufacturing a suitable substitute. But for this method to be applicable, the plaintiff must show that he intended actually to use and benefit from the article which is to be reproduced—otherwise the reproduction cost will not be a true measure of his loss.[3]

(iii) *Special value* If none of the objective economic criteria is appropriate, the court will have to fall back on a subjective test: it must award a sum which will express "the real or fair value" of the chattel to its owner. English authority for this method is slight.[4] In *Caxton Publishing Co., Ltd.* v. *Sutherland Publishing Co., Ltd.*[5] the defendants

---

[1] See also on destruction cases, *supra*, p. 129.
[2] *Supra*, pp. 127–131.
[3] *Hall* v. *Barclay*, [1937] 3 All E.R. 620, at p. 626.
[4] It is more widely used in the U.S.A.: see McCormick, §45.
[5] [1939] A.C. 178.

converted some written material in which the plaintiffs had the copyright interest by publishing it along with other materials as part of a book. It could not be said that there was a "market value" for these sheets of paper since there was no machinery for selling them independently of the book of which they formed a part. As LORD PORTER admitted, "the value is not necessarily the price for which the owner could sell the article. . . . It is the value known or unknown which has to be paid, and that value is not necessarily the price which the owner could have obtained or would have taken."[1] In the event, however, the court could rely on a tangible economic criterion: the book, into which the offending pages had been bound, had a selling price; the damages for the conversion of the pages could therefore be assessed by taking a proportionate part of the book's selling price. Where there is no such convenient touchstone available, the court will have to base its assessment on such factors as the original cost of the chattel, the length of time in the owner's possession, the extent of deterioration, and the uses to which the article is put. Whether or not the plaintiff may recover anything for his sentimental attachment to the thing is as problematic here as where his chattel was destroyed.[2] There is no English authority in the misappropriation cases, but in the United States of America such a claim is generally rejected.[3] It is, however, submitted that there is no reason in principle why it should not be allowed. Injury to one's justifiable sentiment and attachment falls into the same category as *solatium*[4] and should legitimately be the object of compensation, provided it is sufficiently proved.

(d) Time

One of the most perplexing aspects of the assessment of damages for the misappropriation of chattels is the problem of the extent to which the quantum of the award should be affected by fluctuations in the "market value" of the converted article. The difficulties in this area of law have, it is thought, been caused by the simultaneous operation of two distinct factors: the preoccupation with the concept of "value", and the availability of two different forms of action (conversion and detinue). It is intended first to deal with the general problem of fluctuations in "value", and then to consider the appropriate solution as applicable to cases of conversion and detinue.

---

[1] *Ibid.*, at p. 203.
[2] In *Piper* v. *Darling* (1940), 67 Ll.L. Rep. 419 where the plaintiff's yacht was destroyed one of the factors apparently taken into account was "sentiment and predilection". See also the cases discussed on pp. 132–133 in relation to damage to chattels.
[3] See the cases cited in Annotation 12 A.L.R. 2d 7.
[4] *Infra*, pp. 272–274, and see *Jarvis* v. *Swan Tours, Ltd.*, [1973] 1 All E.R. 71.

(i) *General* When, as a gloss on the *restitutio in integrum* principle, the "value of the thing" formula was propounded as the measure of damages for the misappropriation of a chattel, it was only natural that the question should arise as to when that value should be assessed. A chattel may have been worth £x when appropriated by the defendant and £2x at the date of judgment. To which sum was the plaintiff entitled? If, however, we ignore the value formula and return to the basic *restitutio in integrum* principle, it will be seen that the problem can be expressed in a different form. The task of compensation according to this principle is to put the plaintiff in the position he would have been in but for the tort. This task is accomplished, in general, by awarding him (a) for his *basic loss*, a pecuniary equivalent of what he has lost *at the time of the tort* and (b) for his *consequential losses*, a pecuniary equivalent of all losses (subject to the doctrines of remoteness, certainty and mitigation) suffered as a result of and subsequent in time to the commission of the tort. The basic loss should therefore be calculated as at the time of the commission of the tort, whereas consequential losses should be assessed as and when they arise up to the moment of judgment.

If, therefore, fluctuations in the "market value" of his chattel constitute a loss to the plaintiff resulting from the defendant's tort he may on this account recover a sum as *consequential loss*. To what extent, then, may an increase in the "market value" of a chattel constitute a consequential loss? It will do so where, by being deprived of possession of his article, the plaintiff has lost the opportunity of procuring a pecuniary advantage from the higher "value" of the thing. Thus, if the "market value" of the chattel has risen from £x at the time of conversion to £2x at the time of judgment, the plaintiff may show that as a result of the tort he has lost the opportunity of selling the chattel at a higher price, and thereby making a profit of £x. But it must be observed that damages for loss of an opportunity will rarely represent the profit that would have been made if the opportunity had been taken. The court, taking into account all the circumstances of the case (including, for example, whether the plaintiff was a trader or not) and how the reasonable man would have reacted to the prevailing market conditions, must assess the likelihood of the plaintiff having gained a pecuniary advantage from the continued possession of the thing. A percentage based on this likelihood is then taken of the contingent loss claimed by the plaintiff.[1]

We may now consider the torts of conversion and detinue in the light of this approach.

---

[1] The principle follows from the doctrine of certainty, *supra*, pp. 83–84. For a discussion of a similar problem in cases of pure economic injury, see *infra*, p. 253.

(ii) *Conversion* Conversion may be defined as a "dealing with goods in a manner inconsistent with the right of the true owner."[1] It is "a single wrongful act and the cause of action accrues at the date of the conversion."[2] In the light of principles elaborated above, it follows that the basic loss (generally ascertained by the "market value" methods) should be assessed at the time of the wrongful dealing with the chattel. The "value" of the chattel at the date of judgment is relevant only as evidence of consequential pecuniary loss for which the defendant may be liable. The great majority of cases are consistent with this approach. In the nineteenth century, it was constantly reiterated that the proper measure was the "value" of the article at the time of conversion.[3] The apparent exceptions may be interpreted as conceding that compensation for consequential loss resulting from an increase in "value" might be recovered rather than as deciding that the assessment of basic loss must be shifted from the time of the tort to the time of judgment.[4]

At first glance the decision in *Sachs* v. *Miklos*[5] might seem to be contrary to the proposed principle. Indeed, it was first interpreted as indicating that the value of the goods should be assessed as in detinue at the time of the judgment.[6] For that view, reliance was placed on a dictum of LORD GODDARD, C.J., who, purporting to follow the decision in *Rosenthal* v. *Alderton*,[7] observed that "the measure of damages is the same in conversion as in detinue where the facts are only that the defendant has the goods in his possession and could hand them over but would not."[8] But as commentators later pointed out,[9] this was to misconstrue the effect of *Rosenthal* v. *Alderton*, for the Court of Appeal in that case simply affirmed that where the plaintiff sues in *detinue*, the measure of damages should not be affected by the fact that the defendant's conduct might also constitute the tort of conversion.[10] Moreover the *dictum* must be read in the light of the rest of the judgment, and this, it is submitted, is perfectly in accord with the proposed

---

[1] Per ATKIN, J., *Lancashire and Yorkshire Rail Co.* v. *MacNicoll* (1918), 88 L.J.K.B. 601, at p. 605.

[2] Per DIPLOCK, L.J., *General and Finance Facilities* v. *Cooks Cars*, [1963] 1 W.L.R. 644, at p. 648.

[3] E.g. *Mercer* v. *Jones* (1813), 3 Camp. 477; *Falk* v. *Fletcher* (1865), 18 C.B.N.S. 403.

[4] See, especially, *Greening* v. *Wilkinson* (1825), 1 C. & P. 625 where ABBOTT, C.J. refers to the plaintiff's loss of "a good opportunity of selling the goods if they had not been detained." *Ibid.*, at p. 626.

[5] [1948] 2 K.B. 23.

[6] See, e.g., *Beaman* v. *A.R.T.S.*, [1948] 2 All E.R. 89, at p. 93 and *Munro* v. *Willmot*, [1949] 1 K.B. 295.

[7] [1946] K.B. 374.

[8] [1948] 2 K.B. 23, at pp. 38–39.

[9] Elliott (1951), 9 N.I.L.Q. 157; DIPLOCK, L.J. in *General and Finance Facilities* v. *Cooks Cars*, [1963] 1 W.L.R. 644, at p. 649.

[10] [1946] K.B. 374.

principle. In 1943 the goods in question had been wrongfully sold by the defendants for £15. At the time of judgment they were worth £115. What LORD GODDARD, C.J. held was not that the "value" of the goods at the time of the judgment should be taken as the measure, but that in assessing damages for conversion, account should be taken of all of the plaintiff's losses which resulted from the defendant's wrongful act, including that arising from the increase in "value".[1] The case was remitted to the court of first instance to determine whether as a matter of fact the loss claimed through the increase in "value" was a direct consequence of the defendant's tort, or whether it resulted from the plaintiff's own failure to mitigate the damage. It seems clear that the plaintiff was entitled to the £15 as basic loss, whereas it was left to the lower court to determine whether or not he was entitled to any consequential loss, and if so, for how much. Support for this interpretation of *Sachs* v. *Miklos* may be drawn from DIPLOCK, L.J.'s judgment in *General and Finance Facilities* v. *Cooks Cars*[2] in which he asserted that the measure of damages in conversion was "generally the value of the chattel at the date of the conversion together with any consequential damage flowing from the conversion and not too remote to be recoverable in law."

(iii) *Detinue* There is and always was an important difference between the torts of conversion and detinue. The former is a personal action for damages and it is constituted by a single act. Detinue, on the other hand, is a continuing cause of action based on the wrongful detention of the plaintiff's property. In this action the plaintiff claims restitution of his chattel or its "value" plus damages for detention. It is of the utmost importance to appreciate that the alternative payment of "value" is not, strictly speaking, damages at all: it is a restitutionary remedy for a wrong which continues up to the time of the judgment. It therefore follows that the chattel must be "valued" at the date when the defendant is bound to restore to the plaintiff either the chattel or its "value": the date of the verdict.[3] What, then, if the "value" of the article has fallen between the date of the defendant's first default and the date of judgment? The answer, as might be anticipated from the analogous solution in conversion, is that the plaintiff may recover any losses resulting from fluctuations in "value" as consequential damages.[4]

---

[1] "The question is what is the plaintiff's loss, what damage he has suffered, by the wrongful act of the defendants," *per* LORD GODDARD, C.J., *loc. cit.*, at p. 39.
[2] *Supra*, at p. 649.
[3] *Rosenthal* v. *Alderton*, [1946] K.B. 374. See also *per* DIPLOCK, L.J., *General and Finance Facilities* v. *Cooks Cars*, [1963] 1 W.L.R. 644, at p. 649.
[4] *Williams* v. *Archer* (1847), 5 C.B. 318; *Rosenthal* v. *Alderton, supra.*

(iv) *Conversion or detinue?* This section on "time" may be concluded by reconsidering the substantive difference between the remedies in conversion and detinue. Certainly it is clear that the time at which the *basic loss* is assessed is different. But then, as has been seen, in each tort compensation for the basic loss may be supplemented by allowing damages for consequential losses. Where such consequential losses are claimed in respect of fluctuations in the "market value", the plaintiff is in effect claiming for the loss of an opportunity to sell the chattel at the higher or highest "value". Since the measure for the loss of an opportunity will rarely be equal to the profit that would have been made if the opportunity had been taken, the plaintiff in claiming for consequential losses will rarely be able to recover the full amount of rises or falls in the "value" of the chattel.[1] It is therefore to his advantage to elect between conversion or detinue. This may be illustrated:

(a) *Rise in value* from £2x at the time of appropriation to £3x at the date of judgment. In *detinue*, plaintiff may recover £3x. In *conversion*, plaintiff may recover £2x + such a proportion of the rise in "value" (£x) as represents the likelihood of his having sold the chattel at a price higher than £2x.

(b) *Fall in value* from £2x at the time of appropriation to £x at the date of judgment. In *conversion*, plaintiff may recover £2x. In *detinue*, plaintiff may recover £x + such a proportion of the fall in "value" (£x) as represents the likelihood of his having sold the chattel at a price higher than £x.

In English law, the plaintiff may elect between remedies.[2] It might be argued that this is to impose too great a burden on the defendant. The latter must himself wholly bear the risk of any fluctuations in the "value" of the chattel he has appropriated irrespective of whether or not the plaintiff would have benefited from such fluctuations. It would seem, therefore, to be more consistent with the *restitutio in integrum* doctrine if the plaintiff were restricted to one possible remedy, which would take account of the possibilities of his having obtained a pecuniary advantage from fluctuations in "value". To this end a case might be made out for abolishing the action in detinue insofar as it allows the plaintiff to recover the "value" of his property at the date of judgment.[3]

---

[1] Cf. the opinion of the Law Reform Committee, Cmmd. 4774 (1971), para. 88.

[2] *Rosenthal* v. *Alderton, supra*, at p. 379.

[3] See the 18th Report of the Law Reform Committee, *supra*, para. 93.

(e) Defendant improves chattel[1]

We pass to the situation in which an increase in "value" results not from market fluctuations but from the defendant's own act and his own expense. For example, during the period of wrongful detention he may have the chattel repaired. Is the plaintiff entitled to damages assessed on the basis of the condition of the chattel before improvement, or on the basis of its fully improved condition?

(i) *General principle* A simple application of the *restitutio in integrum* doctrine provides a simple answer. If the plaintiff is to be put in the position he would have been in but for the tort, the basic loss for which he must be compensated is the loss of the chattel in its unimproved condition. On this view a plaintiff would be entitled to the "value" of the chattel in its unimproved condition or—which comes to the same thing—a sum representing the expenses incurred by the defendant is to be deducted from the present "value" of the chattel. The principle may be illustrated by *Munro v. Willmott*.[2]

> P deposited his car with D. With the object of getting a good price for the unlawful sale of the car, D spent £85 on repairs and renovations. LYNSKEY, J. held that though D was liable for the "value" of the car, which he assessed at £120,[3] allowance had to be made for the amount D had spent on improvements. P was thus awarded £120−85 = £35.

The vast majority of the decided cases on this subject deal with the situation prevalent in the nineteenth century of the defendant wrongfully severing minerals beneath the plaintiff's land.[4] Clearly the minerals are worth more at the pit head than in their unsevered condiction, the defendant having incurred the expense of severing them and bringing them to the surface. Although there were important exceptions, to be discussed below, the general principle applied that the plaintiff would be allowed as compensation the "market value" of the minerals in their original unsevered condition, or, which produces the same result, from the "market value" of the minerals at the pit mouth was to be deducted a sum representing the cost of severing and raising.[5]

---

[1] There appears to be no authority dealing with the situation where a third party improves the chattel, but the Law Reform Committee, *supra*, at para. 89 recommends that it should be treated as if the improvements were effected by the defendant.

[2] [1949] 1 K.B. 295.

[3] Purporting to follow *Sachs v. Miklos*, [1948] 2 K.B. 23, he assumed the measure of damages in conversion and detinue to be the same and the "value" was assessed as at the date of judgment. But see *supra*, p. 148.

[4] For a full account of the case-law see McGregor, §§996–1004 and Gordon (1955), 71 L.Q.R. 346.

[5] *Livingstone v. Raywards Coal Co.* (1880), 5 App. Cas. 25 among many others.

The principle seems clear and its application simple, but two subsidiary problems require discussion, the first arising from the case-law, the second from a theoretical standpoint.

(ii) *Punitive aspects*   To the general principle of deduction as applied to the case of wrongful severing, the authorities furnish an important exception: the defendant will receive no allowance for severing the the minerals where his appropriation of them was fraudulent or wilful.[1] There are two possible justifications for this exception: first, it may be a principle of the law of accession that where one person knowingly makes physical additions to the chattel of another without the latter's consent, the whole becomes the property of the owner of the original chattel.   This will be discussed under the next head.   The alternative justification is based on an assumption that the law of torts may serve a punitive function. The sanction imposed on the defendant should increase in proportion to his knowledge of the wrongdoing.[2] But this, as has been seen, is wholly inconsistent with the general compensatory principle in damages, and today, exemplary damages may be awarded only within the narrow limits laid down in *Rookes* v. *Barnard*.[3]

(iii) *Detinue and the law of accession*   One learned author has attempted to show that adherence to the principle of deduction as stated above leads to disturbing anomalies.[4]   He argues that according to the law of accession, when A without the consent or encouragement of B improves B's property, the accession becomes part of B's original property and A acquires no rights to compensation.   If A has converted the property several anomalies ensue: (a) if, instead of bringing an action for damages, B retakes the property, he is entitled to do so without incurring any obligations to A for the improvements—by deducting the cost of improvements from an award of damages the law seems to be encouraging either self-help or the converter's disposing of the property as quickly as possible; (b) it follows that, strictly speaking, no deduction should be made from an award of "value" in *detinue* since this is not an award of damages but an order for the payment of the equivalent "value" of the chattel at the time of judgment as an alternative to specific restitution;[5] (c) if the converter has conveyed the chattel

---

[1] *Jegon* v. *Vivian* (1871), 6 Ch. App. 742.   Originally, the proposition was also true where the defendant was merely *negligent*: *Wood* v. *Morewood* (1841), 3 Q.B. 440n.

[2] McGregor, §1001, attempts to rationalize the exception by treating it as a case of exemplary damages; and see LORD DIPLOCK in *Cassell & Co., Ltd.* v. *Broome*, [1972] A.C. 1027, at p. 1129.

[3] [1964] A.C. 1129, as confirmed by *Cassell & Co., Ltd.* v. *Broome*.

[4] Gordon, *supra*.

[5] The point is not made by Gordon, *loc. cit.*, but follows indubitably from anomaly (a).

to a third party, the third party if held liable to the owner must pay the improved "value" of the article. The converter may then have to indemnify the purchaser for his loss, namely for the full, improved "value". If the converter is made liable through this circuitous method he will thus be accountable for a greater sum than if a direct action were brought against him.

It is clear that there is here a potential conflict between two principles of law: the doctrine of *restitutio in integrum* and the doctrine of *accession*. There are situations, on the one hand, in which if the doctrine of accession is to be consistently applied, the plaintiff will recover damages in excess of the compensatory measure to which he would otherwise be entitled and, on the other hand, if *restitutio in integrum* is to prevail the law of accession will be circumscribed. There would appear to be three possible solutions to this conflict.

Neither doctrine to prevail A compromise solution might be urged on the assumption that the doctrine of accession only applies where the act of the converter in adding to the original property was clearly wrongful; that is to say, where A improves property which he knows belongs to B, he should receive no allowance for the improvement, but if he is ignorant of the fact that it belongs to B, a deduction should be made from B's award of damages. There is some authority for the proposition that the doctrine of accession should be so restricted,[1] and it would go some way to explain the exception referred to above relating to the wrongful severing of minerals. But there are strong objections to this compromise: any distinction between "innocent" and "clearly wrongful" conversion is not only a difficult one to draw in practice, but it also conflicts with the principle that outside the narrow area of exemplary damages, the measure of the plaintiff's loss should not depend on the defendant's state of mind.

The doctrine of accession to prevail This axiomatic reasoning militates also against the suggestion that the doctrine of accession should apply to all cases of improvements to converted chattels, and that in no case should an allowance be made for the defendant's efforts. Moreover so to hold would involve reversing a considerable body of case-law.

The doctrine of restitutio in integrum to prevail The remaining possible solution is that the doctrine of *restitutio in integrum* should prevail over the law of accession. Certainly the existing case-law seems to favour this approach.[2] What then of the anomalies described above?

---

[1] *Per* Lord Eldon, L.C., *Lupton* v. *White* (1808), 15 Ves. 432, at pp. 437 and 442; *per* Lord Moulton, *Sandeman & Sons* v. *Tyzack and Branfoot S.S. Co., Ltd.*, [1913] A.C. 680, at p. 695.
[2] See the authorities cited in Gordon, *supra*. The Law Reform Committee (18th Report, Cmnd. 4774, 1971) also recommends this solution (para. 89).

The third (c) is most easily disposed of. The third party purchaser should be allowed to set off against the plaintiff the improvements in "value" resulting from the converter's efforts, in which case the converter would be liable to indemnify only to the extent of the original "value".[1] The problem arising from the second (b) is not peculiar to the situation where the converter improves the article. It is the result of the essentially proprietary nature of the detinue action, and will persist so long as English law retains this dual system of recovery.[2] The first anomaly (a) does not appear to be a serious one. Self-help or recaption is not a remedy *within* the law of tort. The law of damages must pursue an object of pure compensation, and should not be affected by the fact that a party who does not need a remedy at law will be better off. It would be surprising if in practice this did encourage self-help.

(f) Limited interest in chattel

Insistence on the dogmatic formula that the measure of damages for the misappropriation of property is the "value of the thing" has tended to obscure yet another aspect of this branch of the law: the situation in which the plaintiff or defendant has a limited interest in the property. There are several possibilities which must be considered.

(i) *Plaintiff has limited interest, defendant has no interest* The situation where the plaintiff has a limited interest and the defendant has no interest in the chattel itself gives rise to two possibilities.

(A) At the time of the conversion, the plaintiff had possession but not ownership. It is a well-settled rule that he is entitled to the full "value" of the thing, unaffected by the interest of the third party owner.[3] This accords with the policy of putting the plaintiff in the position he would have been in but for the tort. But the relationship of the claim to that of the third party with the remaining interest in the property remains somewhat obscure. Certainly he must account to the third party to the extent of that person's interest in the property.[4] But it seems that he may recover full "value" even if the defendant has returned the chattel to the owner out of possession.[5] Is it to be assumed that the plaintiff may recover the full "value" only if the third party

---

[1] The Law Reform Committee has recommended that this should be the law: *ibid.*

[2] Cf. the proposals of the Law Reform Committee, *ibid.*, paras. 93–96.

[3] *The Winkfield*, [1902] P. 42. The action was brought in the negligence but the rule clearly applies to misappropriation: *Swire* v. *Leach* (1865), 18 C.B.N.S. 479.

[4] *Per* COLLINS, M.R., *The Winkfield, supra*, at pp. 60–61.

[5] *Wilson* v. *Lombank*, [1963] 1 All E.R. 740.

makes no objection? There is no authority on the point, and, worse still, there is no machinery for joining the third party to the proceedings.

(B) At the time of the conversion, the plaintiff had ownership but not possession. The extent of his recovery against the tortfeasor is disputed. It has been argued that since he has only a limited pecuniary interest, as opposed to actual possession, the award of damages should not put him in a better position, and he should recover only to the extent of his interest.[1] Others suggest that the absence of possession should make no difference and that he should be entitled to full "value".[2] The Law Reform Committee, with the intention of clarifying this area of the law, has recommended[3] that a plaintiff with a limited interest may *prima facie* recover only to the extent of that interest, but he will be treated as a full owner if he has the authority of those with the remaining interests. He will be presumed to have such authority if at the time of the tort he was in possession or had a right to immediate possession.

(ii) *Plaintiff and defendant both have interests* Where the defendant has the remaining interest in the property he will not be liable for the full "value". The plaintiff may recover only to the extent of his interest, or, to put it another way, from the compensation awarded for basic loss must be deducted a sum representing the interest of the defendant in the thing.[4] The difficulties generally arise in determining the existence and extent of the defendant's interest. The answer must invariably be sought in the law governing the transaction which is the subject-matter of the action.

Pledge/Lien Where P deposits the property with D as security for a loan from D to P, and D wrongfully sells the property, then if the contract is regarded as a *lien* the wrongful sale will terminate the agreement and P will be entitled to immediate possession. Consequently, D will have no interest for which a deduction must be made from P's award.[5] If, however, it is a case of *pledge*, the wrongful sale will not terminate the agreement. D's interest in the property will remain intact, and a sum representing the amount of the unpaid debt will be deducted from P's award.[6]

Illegal distress/excessive distress Where P is indebted to D, the latter may in certain circumstances distrain goods in P's possession.[7] If the

---

[1] Clerk & Lindsell, §1166; Salmond, p. 755. Both rely on *Bloxam* v. *Hubbard* (1804), 5 East 407.

[2] Winfield & Jolowicz, p. 496; McGregor, §1015 (denying that *Bloxam* v. *Hubbard* is authority to the contrary).

[3] *Supra*, paras. 73–75.

[4] E.g. *Donald* v. *Suckling* (1866), L.R. 1 Q.B. 585; *Whiteley* v. *Hilt*, [1918] 2 K.B. 808.

[5] *Mulliner* v. *Florence* (1878), 3 Q.B.D. 484.

[6] *Johnson* v. *Stear* (1863), 15 C.B.N.S. 330; *Donald* v. *Suckling*, *supra*.

[7] See Halsbury, *Laws of England*, vol. 12, p. 87.

distress is wrongful, P will have an action in damages for the misappropriation of his goods. But a distinction is drawn between cases of *illegal* distress, where the act was wrongful from the beginning, and *excessive* distress where, although a lawful right to distrain existed, P took more goods than was reasonably necessary to satisfy the debt. In the former case, D has no interest in the property and P will be entitled to the full "value".[1] In the latter case, he has an interest which is not defeated by the fact that he has taken more than he was entitled to, and the amount of money due from P to D will be deducted from P's award.[2]

Hire-Purchase contracts   Where D, the hirer under a hire-purchase contract (with the owner P) in breach of that agreement assigns the goods to E, it might have been thought that the extent of P's remedy against D or E for the misappropriation would depend on the construction of the hire-purchase contract. If on the wrongful assignment P was entitled to terminate the agreement and enter into possession, no interest would remain in D (or E) and P would recover the full "value" of the chattel.[3] If, however, on construction, the agreement was not terminated P would recover only to the extent of his interest in the chattel, viz. the amount of hire and purchase money remaining unpaid.[4] But in *Wickham Holdings* v. *Brooke House Motors*[5] the Court of Appeal held that as a *matter of law* P could recover against E no more than his "real loss" which was his limited interest in the property. The ostensible difficulty with this conclusion is that it defeats P's lawful right to terminate the agreement which, if conceded, renders P full owner and thus entitled to full "value". It may be that the decision can be construed as a radical reappraisal of the property rights within a hire-agreement: each payment includes a capital element which is part of the purchase-price, thus conferring on the hirer a proprietary interest in the chattel indefeasible by the exercise of the right to terminate under the contract. But this would indeed be a startling innovation and there is little in the language of the judgments to justify such a conclusion. It seems safer to justify the decision on the narrower ground that an assignment in breach of contract is nevertheless effective to transfer the assignor's interest to the assignee.[6]

(iii) *Detinue*   Is the measure different if the plaintiff, with the limited interest, sues in detinue rather than conversion? The case-law is uncertain. In *Wickham Holdings* v. *Brooke House Motors*[7] the claim

---

[1] *Keen* v. *Priest* (1859), 4 H. & N. 236.
[2] *Fell* v. *Whittaker* (1871), L.R. 7 Q.B. 120.
[3] *United Dominions Trust* v. *Parkway Motors*, [1955] 2 All E.R. 557 but see n. 5, *infra*.
[4] *Belsize Motor Supply* v. *Cox*, [1914] 1 K.B. 244.
[5] [1967] 1 All E.R. 117, expressly overruling *United Dominions Trust* v. *Parkway Motors, supra*.
[6] Goode, *Hire-Purchase Law and Practice* (2nd edn.), p. 586.
[7] *Supra*.

was made in both conversion and detinue, but in their judgments the members of the Court of Appeal seemed to ignore the possibility of any distinction between the two causes of action. Yet in *Astley Industrial Trust* v. *Miller*[1] CHAPMAN, J. regarded the award of only the limited interest in the earlier case as appropriate to conversion but not to detinue. In his view, the plaintiff was entitled in detinue either to specific recovery of the thing or its "value". The crux of the matter seems to be whether or not the plaintiff's limited interest is sufficient to entitle him to an order of specific restitution. If it is, because, for example, he was in actual possession at the time of the tort, he may recover in the alternative the full "value". But if the defendant's or another's interest is such as to prevent an order for specific restitution, the plaintiff will be restricted to his limited interest in the thing.[2] If the distinction seems unjustifiable, it would seem to be inevitable so long as the remedy in detinue for "value" is retained as an alternative to specific recovery.

(g) Redelivery of property

(i) *General* It is obvious that the "value of the goods" rule cannot apply where the defendant has redelivered the property to the plaintiff. Although redelivery will not bar any of the actions for the misappropriation of goods, it is clear that to the extent that it restores the plaintiff to his position before the tort, his basic loss is *pro tanto* reduced.[3] The plaintiff then seeks to recover compensation only for the temporary deprivation of his chattel: to recover substantial damages he must therefore show that he has sustained some consequential losses.[4]

(ii) *Trespass to goods* It is here that the measure of damages for trespass to goods can be considered within the framework of the general principles of compensation for misappropriation. If the trespass results in damage to the plaintiff's goods, the award will be assessed on the principles already discussed.[5] Independently of the loss caused by any such damage, the plaintiff may claim compensation for the temporary deprivation of his chattel. The mode of quantification will be exactly as if the plaintiff had sued in conversion and the defendant had redelivered the chattel: substantial damages only for consequential losses.[6]

(iii) *Replevin* It is convenient also to consider under this head the claim for replevin. Where goods are taken out of the plaintiff's pos-

---

[1] [1968] 2 All E.R. 36, at p. 44.
[2] Guest, *Law of Hire Purchase*, §522.
[3] *Williams* v. *Archer* (1847), 5 C.B. 318.
[4] See *infra*, pp. 159–162.
[5] *Supra*, pp. 131–141.
[6] *Owen and Smith* v. *Reo Motors (Britain), Ltd.* (1934), 151 L.T. 274.

session, he may, under the action of replevin, obtain their immediate return, subject to an adjudication as to whether he has a right to remain in possession. If the plaintiff succeeds in the ensuing action he will be entitled also to an award of damages. The measure of the award will be assessed as in other cases of misappropriation where the property has been redelivered subject to this one exception, that in replevin redelivery has been effected at the instance of and at expense to the plaintiff. He may, therefore, in addition to any damages for consequential losses, recover a sum for legal and other expenses involved in replevying the goods.[1]

(iv) *What constitutes redelivery* Generally the defendant will offer and the plaintiff will accept redelivery at some time before judgment is entered, but there are other and less obvious acts which, for the purposes of assessing damages, will constitute "redelivery". The return of an equivalent article will suffice.

In *Solloway* v. *McLaughlin*[2]

> P deposited shares with his stockbrokers Ds. Ds fraudulently sold some of them. When, some time later, P intimated that he wished to close his account with Ds, Ds bought the same number of shares in the same company but at a price lower than that at which they had sold. It was held that the return of the equivalent though not identical shares mitigated P's loss.

A "notional redelivery" may also be sufficient. In *Hiort* v. *London and North Western Rail Co.*[3]

> Ps deposited goods with Ds on the understanding that Ds were to deliver them in accordance with the instructions that Ps would give them. Ds delivered the goods to X without, but in anticipation of, Ps' order. The delivery order was in fact received by Ds a few days later. X was unable to pay for the goods. Although the delivery constituted a conversion, it was clear that Ps' loss did not result from the tort. They would have sustained the same loss if no tort had been committed. One member of the Court of Appeal, however, preferred to base his decision not on causation but on the fact that the predelivery was the "equivalent to a return of the goods."[4]

The same ground has been used as a mitigation of loss where the defendant used some of the proceeds of his conversion to satisfy the plaintiff's debt to a third party.[5]

---

[1] *Smith* v. *Enright* (1893), 63 L.J.Q.B. 220.
[2] [1938] A.C. 247.
[3] (1879), 4 Ex.D. 188.
[4] *Per* BRAMWELL, L.J., *ibid.*, at p. 196.
[5] *Plevin* v. *Henshall* (1833), 10 Bing. 24; *A. L. Underwood, Ltd.* v. *Bank of Liverpool*, [1924] 1 K.B. 775.

(v) *Fluctuations in value of thing redelivered*   If redelivery is offered by
the defendant in satisfaction of the basic loss, *prima facie* the chattel
to be returned will have the same "value" as at the time of conversion.
If there has been a depreciation in its value resulting from detention
the defendant is liable for that loss.[1]   In *Solloway* v. *McLaughlin*,[2] on
the facts as set out above, the Privy Council held that the defendant
stockbrokers were liable for the difference in the "value" of the shares
between their conversion and redelivery.   But, it is submitted, this
was to misconceive the nature of the plaintiff's loss.   The full decline
in "value" should only be awarded, if it can be shown that if no tort
had been committed, the plaintiff would have sold the shares at the
highest value.   If this cannot be proved, then the plaintiff has lost
not the decline in "value" but the *opportunity* of selling the shares at a
price higher than that which they would have fetched at the time of
redelivery.   For this loss the plaintiff should have been awarded a
proportion of (but not the whole of) the difference in "value" as a
consequential loss.[3]

If, on the other hand, the "value" of the thing returned has risen
since the time of misappropriation, the benefit will simply accrue to
the plaintiff now restored to possession, without any allowance being
made to the defendant.   A possible exception may exist where the improvement in "value" was the result of the defendant's own efforts.
This has already been considered.[4]

3   Consequential losses

(a)   Introduction

Losses resulting from the misappropriation of goods have, as with
most other classes of injury, been divided into *static/basic* elements and
dynamic/consequential elements.   In the present context the latter
assume a particular significance since in certain cases of misappropriation (for example, where the goods have been redelivered) they represent the only substantive losses.   The situation under consideration is
manifestly similar to that in which the plaintiff claims consequential
losses resulting from the detention of his chattel for repairs.[5]   In
principle one might anticipate a uniform approach.   In practice, the
rules for the assessment of damages have been developed along independent channels.   As has been suggested,[6] one of the chief reasons for

---

[1] *Hall & Co.* v. *Pearlberg*, [1956] 1 All E.R. 297.
[2] *Supra.*
[3] See *supra*, p. 147.
[4] *Supra*, pp. 151–154.
[5] *Supra*, pp. 135–140.
[6] *Supra*, p. 142.

the divergence lies in the type of chattel which tends to form the subject-matter of litigation. Principles for compensation where the plaintiff's chattel is damaged have, in the great majority of cases, been developed in cases concerning *functional* chattels (e.g. ships, motor vehicles). Misappropriation cases, on the other hand, have generally involved *merchantable* chattels. Two significant consequences follow from this distinction: first, chattels in the former category tend to *earn* profits, while those in the latter category tend to be the *objects* of profit-making transactions; secondly, damages for the mere detention of the chattel will in the former case be based on loss of *use*, but in the latter on loss of *possession*. It seems inevitable that the mode of assessment will vary to a certain extent to accord with the nature of the property, but care must be taken that such divergence does not in any way conflict with the general principles that underlie all modes of assessment.

(b) Loss of profits

This last submission is well illustrated by the authorities on the recovery of lost profits. It will be recalled that where a profit-earning chattel is detained for repairs, the plaintiff may recover the profits which but for the detention the chattel would have earned.[1] Frequently such recovery was based on evidence of contractual engagements to which the plaintiff was, at the time of the tort, already committed.[2] Damages for loss of general profits have been awarded in misappropriation cases.[3] But there is apparent authority for the view that in ordinary circumstances claims for profits to be earned on specific contracts should not be allowed. The crucial decision is *The Arpad*[4]

> Ps bought wheat from Ds at 36s. per quarter and resold it at 36s. 6d. per quarter. Ds failed to deliver some 47 tons. Ps had already paid Ds for the wheat, and thus claimed damages both in conversion and in contract for the loss of the wheat at the rate of 36s. 6d. per quarter. It was held that both in contract[5] and in tort Ps were entitled only to the market value of the wheat at the time of non-delivery *viz.* 23s. 6d. per quarter.

The decision has traditionally been seen as an application of the doctrine of remoteness,[6] but it seems to accord more easily with the doctrine of mitigation. The principle is well established in actions for breach of contract[7] (and the same principle must apply in tort) that a

---

[1] *Supra*, p. 135.
[2] E.g. *The Argentino* (1888), 13 P.D. 191.
[3] *France* v. *Gaudet* (1871), L.R. 6 Q.B. 199; *Re Simms, Ex parte Trustee*, [1934] Ch. 1.
[4] [1934] P. 189.
[5] *Infra*, p. 335.
[6] E.g. McGregor, §1023.
[7] *Infra*, pp. 322–323.

plaintiff may recover for loss of profits only where that loss could not reasonably have been avoided. Where there is a market available for the goods in question, it is assumed that on non-delivery the plaintiff might reasonably have gone to the market to purchase a substitute with which he could have fulfilled his sub-contract. His loss then is the price which he would have had to pay for the substitute—the "market value" of the goods.[1] Where there is no available market for the goods in question, or where in all the circumstances of the case the purchase of a substitute is deemed unreasonable, notwithstanding the decision in *The Arpad*, the plaintiff should recover for his lost profits.

The same problems do not exist where general loss of business is pleaded, and consistently with the Admiralty cases,[2] where the plaintiff had intended to sell the chattel, or to put it out to some profitable use, he may recover a sum representing the loss of the general profits he would have earned.[3] It is by this method, as has been noted, that the courts can cater for fluctuations in the "value" of a chattel, by awarding the plaintiff a sum for the loss of an opportunity to sell the chattel at the higher "value".[4]

From any sum claimed by way of lost profits a deduction will have to be made for the saving of expenses which the plaintiff would have incurred to earn his profits.

(c) Detention

The plaintiff may, as an alternative to compensation for loss of profits, claim a sum for the mere detention of his property. This is particularly important in cases of redelivery where it may represent the plaintiff's only substantive loss. It is not surprising, therefore, that the recognition of damages for detention in misappropriation cases[5] preceded that in repair cases[6] by over sixty years. It is true that there is little modern authority for allowing compensation for detention in conversion[7] (as opposed to detinue), but in principle there is no reason to distinguish between the actions in this respect. The deprivation of possession following the defendant's tortious conversion is just as much a "consequential loss" as the loss of profits on sale. The method

---

[1] Of course, if the plaintiff has not yet paid for the goods, the measure will be the difference between the contract price and the price at which the substitute could have been bought.

[2] E.g. *The Risoluto* (1883), 8 P.D. 109.

[3] *Strand Electric and Engineering Co.* v. *Bristol Entertainments*, [1952] 2 Q.B. 246; *Astley Industrial Trust* v. *Miller*, [1968] 2 All E.R. 36.

[4] *Supra*, p. 147.

[5] *Moon* v. *Raphael* (1835), 2 Bing. N.C. 310.

[6] *The Greta Holme*, [1897] A.C. 596. See supra, p. 138.

[7] In *General and Finance Facilities* v. *Cooks Cars*, [1963] 1 W.L.R. 644, at p. 649, DIPLOCK, L.J. recognized that "consequential damages" might be awarded but was not more specific.

generally adopted for assessing an award for detention is the cost of hiring a reasonable substitute.[1] From this figure must be deducted a sum representing any expenses he would have incurred if he had kept the chattel in his possession.[2] Where, however, it would not be reasonable for the plaintiff to hire a substitute—for example, where, as with an ornament, he does not put the chattel to any active use—interest on the capital "value" of the chattel would appear to be the most likely measure.[3]

(d) Other consequential losses

The ordinary depreciation in the "value" of the article during the defendant's wrongful detention should be absorbed into damages for detention. If the chattel had remained in the plaintiff's possession, the same depreciation would have occurred: the plaintiff's substantive loss is the inability to benefit from the possession of the thing during the period of detention. If, however, through the defendant's neglect, depreciation is greater than it would have been under proper care, the plaintiff is entitled to additional compensation for this loss.[4] The plaintiff may, of course recover any expenses necessarily or reasonably incurred as a result of the deprivation of his chattel.[5] Finally, it is possible that the plaintiff may recover a sum for loss of reputation or credit resulting from the misappropriation.[6] This will be appropriate where the property appropriated by the defendant in some way enhanced the credit or reputation of the plaintiff[7] or where a wrongful distress in satisfaction of an alleged unpaid debt lowers the reputation of the plaintiff in the estimation of his customers.[8]

V DAMAGE TO LAND

1 Introduction

The common law has traditionally regarded remedies for injuries to real property as distinct from those applicable for injuries to personal property. Consistently, the authorities on the quantification of com-

---

[1] *Davis* v. *Oswell* (1837), 7 C. & P. 804; *Matthews* v. *Heintzmann & Co.* (1914), 16 D.L.R. 522.

[2] *Davis* v. *Oswell, supra.*

[3] As in the repair cases for the detention of non-profit-earning chattels: *supra*, p. 140.

[4] *Hall & Co.* v. *Pearlberg*, [1956] 1 All E.R. 297.

[5] *Piggott* v. *Birtles* (1836), 1 M. & W. 441.

[6] On damages for loss of reputation see, generally, *infra*, pp. 230–246.

[7] E.g. in conversion of copyright, *Caxton Publishing Co., Ltd.* v. *Sutherland Publishing*, [1939] A.C. 178.

[8] *Smith* v. *Enright* (1893), 63 L.J.Q.B. 220.

pensation for damage to land have, with some exceptions,[1] paid little heed to the case-law on damage to chattels. It may be conceded that there are certain aspects of land which require special considerations. Land, unlike a chattel is "permanent, almost indestructible, and capable of almost infinite division and subdivision."[2] But where, for example, the plaintiff sues for damage to, or destruction of, buildings (which for legal purposes is regarded as damage to land) it is difficult to discover adequate reasons for applying a rule different from that which governs compensation for damage to chattels.

2 Basic loss

(a) General

It has been seen that the basic loss consequent on damage to chattels was assessed by reference to the restitutionary measure of cost of repairs. For the destruction or misappropriation of chattels, "the value of the thing at the time of the tort" was laid down as the general rule. On closer examination, this formula left it to the court to choose which of several methods of quantification were to be adopted. In essence, it might be said that, apart from cases of "special value" or "capitalized potential", the court had to choose between the selling prices of the chattel and the cost of replacing the chattel (whether by purchasing an equivalent article, adapting a similar article or by reconstruction). It was suggested that, broadly speaking, the choice should depend on whether the plaintiff held the chattel for his own beneficial use, or whether he intended to gain some pecuniary advantage from it, generally by sale.[3] In the cases on damage to land, rivalry between the two methods has been very much to the fore. A variety of views has been adopted.[4]

(i) Some consider the diminution in the saleable "value" of the land to be the only proper measure.[5]

(ii) Others have preferred the cost of replacement method.[6]

(iii) A third group considers that "depreciation in value" is the

---

[1] E.g. *Hutchinson* v. *Davidson*, 1945 S.C. 395; *Hollebone* v. *Midhurst and Fernhurst Builders*, [1968] 1 Lloyd's Rep. 38.
[2] Lawson, *Introduction to the Law of Property*, p. 19.
[3] *Supra*, p. 129.
[4] Cf. Legh Jones & Pickering (1970), 85 L.Q.R. 513, at pp. 524–527.
[5] *Hosking* v. *Phillips* (1848), 3 Exch. 168; *Whitham* v. *Kershaw* (1886), 16 Q.B.D. 613; *Moss* v. *Christchurch Rural District Council*, [1925] 2 K.B. 750.
[6] *Duke of Newcastle* v. *Hundred of Broxstowe* (1832), 4 B. & Ad. 273; *Cooper* v. *Railway Executive*, [1953] 1 W.L.R. 223; *Harbutt's Plasticine* v. *Wayne Tank*, [1970] 1 Q.B. 447, *per* LORD DENNING, M.R. at p. 468, *per* CROSS, L.J. at p. 476.

basic measure, but that cost of replacement may be used as evidence of that depreciation.[1]

(iv) Finally, some regard them as alternative measures, the choice between which depends on the facts of the particular case.[2]

It is suggested that the flexible fourth approach (iv) is to be preferred. Unlike (i) and (ii) it recognizes that one method will not be appropriate for all cases. Method (i) will not suffice since the property may have no available "market value". Method (ii) can hardly apply where the plaintiff held the land only for sale. The view expressed in (iii) either misconceives the nature of the problem or is indistinguishable from (iv): "depreciation in value" as contrasted with the "cost of replacement" can only refer to the selling price of the property, for which the cost of replacement is generally not evidence.

(b) Diminution of selling price or cost of replacement

If, as seems likely, the fourth approach (iv) is the correct one, the question arises as to what should determine whether the diminution of selling price or cost of replacement is to be adopted. In some cases, the actual circumstances by themselves are sufficient to determine the choice without reference to any guiding principle. Thus, if there is no market for the property, the cost of replacement should be adopted.[3] Conversely, if for some reason, replacement or restoration is impossible,[4] or unreasonable (in an economic sense),[5] the award should be based on the diminution of the selling price. Apart from such factual necessities, are there any general criteria which may be applied? There has been little attempt in the case-law to lay down any real guidance. It is, however, suggested that a test, similar to that which was proposed for the analogous problem in awards for the destruction[6] or misappropriation[7] of chattels may be reconciled with almost all the decided cases. If the plaintiff holds the land primarily as an *economic* asset,[8] then the doctrine of *restitutio in integrum* requires that he be awarded a sum based on the diminution of the selling price. This would arise where,

---

[1] *Stevens* v. *Abbotsford Lumber*, [1924] 1 D.L.R. 1163; *Hutchison* v. *Davidson*, 1945 S.C. 395, *per* LORD RUSSELL at pp. 407–408.

[2] *Murphy* v. *Wexford County Council* (1921), 2 I.R. 230; *Hutchison* v. *Davidson, supra, per* LORD MONCRIEFF at pp. 410–411; *Hollebone* v. *Midhurst and Fernhurst Builders*, [1968] 1 Lloyd's Rep. 38; *Harbutt's Plasticine* v. *Wayne Tank, supra, per* WIDGERY, L.J. at p. 473; *Taylor* v. *Auto Trade Supply*, [1972] N.Z.L.R. 102.

[3] *Murphy* v. *Wexford County Council, supra.*

[4] This appears to have been the case in *Spicer* v. *Smee*, [1946] 1 All E.R. 489.

[5] *Taylor* v. *Auto Trade Supply, supra*; *Hole & Son* v. *Harrisons of Thurnscoe* (1972), 116 Sol. Jo. 922.

[6] *Supra*, p. 129.

[7] *Supra*, p. 145.

[8] As must be the case where the property was in any event to be demolished: *Hole's* case, *supra.*

for example, he was a reversioner[1] or where he intended eventually to sell or sublet the property. Where, on the other hand, the plaintiff used and intended to continue to use the land for his own purposes, then he should be entitled to a sum based on the cost of replacement.[2]

(c) Cost of replacement must be reasonable

It should be added that, as in all cases where the quantification of damages is based on restitution, the sum payable must be reasonable. If the cost of exact restitution is disproportionately high, the plaintiff must rest content with a sum which will provide him with a sufficiently approximate equivalent of what has been lost.

(d) Replacement increases value of property

It has been held that no deduction should be made from the plaintiff's award for any increase in the value of the property resulting from replacement.[3] The same rule applies in actions for damage to chattels and it has been critically evaluated in that context.[4]

(e) Plaintiff with limited interest

As regards misappropriation of chattels, it was seen that, as a general rule, a plaintiff with a limited interest could recover "full" value, at least where he was in possession of the thing at the time of the tort.[5] Here the plaintiff is claiming not for deprivation of possession but for damage to his property, and the extent of his recovery is limited by the extent of his interest in it. The court is wary of duplicating compensation for the same items of loss merely because there is more than one person interested. It has therefore been suggested[6] that where there is a division of interests in the land damages, the court ought first to ascertain what loss is caused to the estate as a whole and then to apportion the compensation among those persons interested. It remains to consider how the award is to be apportioned.

(i) *Mere occupiers* An occupier with no proprietary interest may recover such a sum as will represent the loss to his use and enjoyment of the land during his term of possession. Thus in the old case of *Bedingfield* v. *Onslow*[7] where a claim was brought for the severance and removal of trees, it was held that while the reversioner could recover the "value" of the timber, the tenant in possession should receive a sum for the

---

[1] *Hosking* v. *Phillips* (1848), 3 Exch. 168; *Moss* v. *Christchurch Rural District Council*, [1925] 2 K.B. 750.
[2] *Hutchinson* v. *Davidson*, *supra*; *Hollebone's* case, *supra*; *Harbutt's Plasticine* v. *Wayne Tank*, *supra*.
[3] *Harbutt's Plasticine* v. *Wayne Tank*, *supra*.
[4] *Supra*, p. 134.
[5] *Supra*, p. 154–157.
[6] *Rust* v. *Victoria Graving Dock Co.* (1887), 36 Ch.D. 113, at pp. 130 and 135.
[7] (1685), 3 Lev. 209.

deprivation of "shade, shelter and fruit." Such losses may be quantified by ascertaining the loss in rent that the *reversioner* would sustain if he were to let the land in its damaged condition.

(ii) *Reversioner*   The reversioner will be able to recover only to the extent that his permanent interest in the property has been injured. Whether or not the property is "permanently injured" is a question of fact.[1]   To give contrasting illustrations: in *Rust* v. *Victoria Graving Dock Co.*,[2] flood damage which would be restored before the reversioner would be entitled to re-enter into possession did not constitute permanent injury; but in *Mayfair Property* v. *Johnston*[3] the embedding of the foundation of a wall in the land was "permanent" and the reversioner could recover.   Damages will be awarded according to the principles considered above.[4]

3   Consequential losses
(a)   General

In general the principles as to consequential loss developed in relation to damage to chattels apply also to damage to land.   Thus the plaintiff is entitled to (i) any reasonable expenses he incurred as a result of the tort;[5] (ii) any loss of profits which was prevented from earning through the damage to his land;[6] (iii) damages for the loss of use of the property to the extent that his use and enjoyment of the property was impaired by the tort.[7]   Three areas of consequential loss, however, call for special comment.

(b)   Losses capable of constituting a separate action

In several early cases the question arose whether losses which were capable of giving rise to an independent cause of action in tort might as an alternative be the object of compensation as consequential damages for an injury to land.   For example,[8] if a man trespassed on your land and seduced your daughter, could you in an action for trespass recover losses arising from the seduction?   In most cases the court was happy to compensate the plaintiff for such losses.[9]   It did, however, stop short of allowing under this head an award for loss of reputation.[10]

---

[1] *Young* v. *Spencer* (1829), 10 B. & C. 145.
[2] (1887), 36 Ch.D. 113.
[3] [1894] 1 Ch. 508.
[4] *Supra*, p. 155.
[5] *Grosvenor Hotel* v. *Hamilton*, [1894] 2 Q.B. 836.
[6] *Rust* v. *Victoria Graving Dock*, *supra*;   *Campbell* v. *Paddington Corporation*, [1911] 1 K.B. 869.
[7] *Spicer* v. *Smee*, [1946] 1 All E.R. 489.
[8] *Bennett* v. *Allcott* (1787), 2 Term Rep. 166.
[9] *Bennett* v. *Allcott, ibid.*;   *Anderson* v. *Buckton* (1719), 1 Stra. 192 (infection of chattel);   *Pritchard* v. *Long* (1842), 9 M. & M. 666 (conversion of chattels).
[10] *Bracegirdle* v. *Orford* (1813), 2 M. & S. 77.   See also *Marquis of Granby* v. *Bakewell Urban District Council* (1923), 87 J.P. 105.

(c) Aggravated damage

It did not follow that this latter type of loss would go uncompensated. It could properly be pleaded as an element of aggravated damage. Where the defendant's conduct adds insult to the basic injury to property, the plaintiff may be awarded a sum for his justifiable grievance.[1]

(d) Anticipated loss

The general rule, as in all actions of tort, is that the plaintiff may recover not only for the losses he has sustained, but also for those which he is expected to sustain, subject to the rules as to certainty. A qualification of particular significance in the present context is that the principle does not apply where damages are awarded for a continuing tort (e.g. nuisance). The principle and its qualification have already been discussed[2] and no further elaboration is necessary.

VI WRONGFUL OCCUPATION OF LAND

1 Introduction

Where the defendant wrongfully occupies the plaintiff's land, this situation is analogous to that in which he misappropriates the plaintiff's chattel; the plaintiff seeks compensation for the deprivation of possession and all losses which flow from that. The rules governing the assessment of damages are, in general, the same.

2 Basic loss—permanent deprivation

The one major difference between the land and chattel cases is that in almost all of the former cases the plaintiff will be claiming damages only for temporary deprivation, while in the latter cases he very frequently seeks compensation for permanent deprivation. This difference arises from the fact that land is permanent, and provided the plaintiff can prove sufficient interest he will almost always recover the property *in specie*. There are two exceptions to this: one apparent and one real. The apparent exception is compensation for the compulsory purchase of land. But this is not an award of damages[3] and thus does not come within the scope of this book.[4] A real exception will

---

[1] *Davis* v. *Bromley Urban District Council* (1903), 67 J.P. 275; and see *Huxley* v. *Berg* (1815), 1 Stark. 98 where the nervous shock to the plaintiff's wife resulting from the defendant's violent entry furnished evidence of aggravation of damage but did not itself constitute a substantive head of consequential loss. See, generally, *infra*, pp. 237–238.

[2] *Supra*, pp. 11–12.

[3] *Supra*, p. 1.

[4] It is, however, interesting to note that the principles on which compensation for the compulsory purchase of land is assessed are very similar to the principles

exist where, although the plaintiff can show a valid interest, he is denied specific recovery. He will thus be entitled to damages for the permanent deprivation of his land. This may occur, for example, where the defendant has guaranteed a good title to a third party purchaser who is at the time of the action in possession of the land.[1] In such circumstances the plaintiff will be entitled to the "market value" (i.e. the selling price) of the property at the time of the wrongful assumption of title.[2]

3 Consequential losses—temporary deprivation

In the great majority of cases, the plaintiff will be able to recover the land. The assessment of his loss will then be governed by the principles which are applied to the temporary misappropriation of chattels (i.e. where the chattels have been redelivered).[3] The plaintiff is limited to compensation for consequential losses. These may be considered under the usual heads.

(a) Loss of profits

The plaintiff is entitled to a sum representing the profits he would have made if the land had not been occupied by the defendant.[4] But deductions must be made for those expenses which the plaintiff would have incurred in order to secure those profits.[5]

(b) Loss of use

If the plaintiff himself would, but for the wrongful occupation, have been in possession, then he is entitled to compensation for the loss of the use and enjoyment of his land. The usual method of assessing this is to award him such a sum as would have been paid to him as rent if the defendant had been a lawful tenant.[6] One problem which has exercised the judicial mind arises where the defendant occupied a part of the land which the plaintiff owner would not himself have used. A frequent example was the unauthorized mining of coal under the plaintiff's land. Independently of compensation for the coal which the defendant had wrongfully severed, might the plaintiff also recover for the mere use of his land, even though he himself might have made no use of that part of it? There is a conflict of authority, but the

---

assessing common law damages. For a detailed account, see Cripps, *Compulsory Acquisition of Land*, Chaps. 18–24.

[1] *Spencer* v. *Registrar of Titles* (1910), 103 L.T. 647.
[2] *Ibid.*
[3] *Supra*, pp. 159–162.
[4] *McArthur & Co.* v. *Cornwall*, [1892] A.C. 75.
[5] *Ibid.*
[6] *Hall* v. *Pearlberg*, [1956] 1 All E.R. 297.

balance seems in favour of such an award.[1] The merits of the prevailing view may be considered by weighing the undesirability of allowing the plaintiff to recover for a loss which he did not in fact suffer against the impracticability of determining exactly what constitutes the "use" of land.

(c) Expenses and other consequential losses

The plaintiff may, of course, recover for expenses and any other losses resulting from the deprivation of possession, provided that they do not infringe the rules as to certainty, mitigation and remoteness.

---

[1] *Martin* v. *Porter* (1839), 5 M. & W. 351; *Hilton* v. *Woods* (1867), L.R. 4 Eq. 432; *Jegon* v. *Vivian* (1871), L.R. 6 Ch. App. 742; *Whitham* v. *Westminster Brymbo Coal and Coke Co.*, [1896] 2 Ch. 538; cf. *obiter* in *Livingstone* v. *Rawyards Coal Co.* (1880), 5 App. Cas. 25, at p. 38.

CHAPTER SIX

Injuries to the Person and to Reputation

A PERSONAL INJURIES

I INTRODUCTION

There is no equivalent area of the law of damages which has provoked so much attention in recent years as that concerned with personal injuries. The chief reason is the vast amount of litigation in personal injury cases, a significant proportion of which is concerned solely with questions of compensation. In each legal system this has the effect of generating a "damages information service": practitioners must be kept up to date with all the latest information on personal injury awards, so that they might advise their clients as to the "going rate" for each category of injury.[1] The subject has attracted the attention of the actuary and the economist, the one seeking to provide a statistically based estimate of the plaintiff's loss, the other to prophesy on the future economic climate of the country.[2] For several years now the Law Commission has been examining certain allegedly unsatisfactory aspects of the law,[3] although at the time of writing it has yet to advance any definite recommendations.

A second reason for the great interest shown in the subject is the growing feeling that the tort system is not the most appropriate method of dealing with formidable social problems created by accidents and by personal injuries in particular.[4] Questions as to the nature and extent

---

[1] England: Kemp and Kemp, *The Quantum of Damages* (3rd Edn.), Vol. 1; *Current Law*. Canada: Goldsmith, *Damages for Personal Injury and Death*. Australia: *Legal Monthly Digest*. South Africa: Corbett, *The Quantum of Damages* (2nd Edn.). France: *Gazette du Palais*.
[2] E.g. *Mitchell* v. *Mulholland* (No. 2), [1972] 1 Q.B. 65.
[3] See Working Papers 19, 27 and 41.
[4] A vast literature of this subject has accumulated. See, especially, Elliott and Street, *Road Accidents*; Atiyah, *Accidents, Compensation and the Law*; Keeton & O'Connell, *Basic Protection for the Traffic Victim*; Tunc 11 I.E.C.L., Chap. 14.

of compensation form an important part of these discussions. Comparisons are made with the standards prevailing in other compensation systems, especially the social security benefits.[1] Beneath everything lurks a fundamental policy issue: who is paying for the compensation? It lies, of course, beyond the scope of this work comprehensively to deal with these questions, but it is to be hoped that the discussion of the principles of quantification which follows[2] will at the very least serve to make the reader aware of the impact which such questions have on the development of the law.

Discussion of the subject will be divided into the usual categories of pecuniary and non-pecuniary loss. This division is standard with writers and indeed is the only convenient way of approaching the subject but it is to be noted that it was only recently that the division was universally accepted into judicial practice.[3] Before then the courts were generally reluctant to subdivide awards of general damages into pecuniary and non-pecuniary elements.[4] Even now, there are problems as to the relationship between the two, and the courts scrutinize claims carefully for the possibility of overlap.[5]

II THEORIES OF COMPENSATION

The *restitutio in integrum* doctrine requires that the plaintiff be put in the position he would have been in if the tort had not been committed. This means that he must be indemnified not only for the loss of those assets which at the time of the accident he already possessed but also for those which he would have acquired at some time in the future. Thus stated, it will be apparent that the tort system differs significantly in its standard of compensation from that available under other compensation schemes.[6] In particular its awards far exceed those available under what is known as the "Beveridge" theory of compensation:[7] that a mean standard of compensation should be

---

[1] See especially Atiyah, *op. cit.*, Chaps. 15–16.

[2] Also compensation for death which is treated along with other pure economic injuries in Chap. 5, *infra*, pp. 264–278.

[3] *Jefford* v. *Gee*, [1970] 2 Q.B. 130, *infra*, p. 214.

[4] E.g. *Watson* v. *Powles*, [1968] 1 Q.B. 596. "The award of damages is ... an award of one figure only, a composite figure, made up of several parts. . . . At the end all the parts must be brought together to give fair compensation for all the injuries." *Per* LORD DENNING, M.R., *ibid.*, at p. 603.

[5] E.g. *Smith* v. *Central Asbestos*, [1972] 1 Q.B. 244, *infra*, pp. 221–222.

[6] See generally Atiyah, *op. cit.*, Chap. 22.

[7] Beveridge Report on Social Insurance and Allied Services. Cmd. 6404 (1942). George, *Social Security, Beveridge and after*, pp. 5–11.

paid to all injured persons;[1] or under those compensation schemes which seek to maintain the injured person at the standard of living he enjoyed at the time of the accident.[2]

Even though it is clear that common law damages must reflect potential as well as existing benefits, there is still much room for divergent attitudes within the doctrine. A brief introduction to three such views[3] will here be offered; their practical consequences will emerge in the course of the discussion.

(i) *Conceptual* On the first view, the human personality is seen as a combination of a number of economic and non-economic assets. The object of damages is to restore all the elements in the combination to the *status quo ante*. The standard is objective and abstract: a "value" is ascribed to each personality asset. No account is taken of the social, psychological or moral attitudes of the victim.

(ii) *Personal* On the subjective personal view, a person's life and body cannot be "valued" in isolation from its context. The court has regard to the individual circumstances of each case. It takes into account the plaintiff's actual intentions before the accident, and his actual condition (moral as well as physical) after the accident.

(iii) *Functional* The third view accepts the premise of the personal view that the court should have regard to the individual features of the plaintiff's case—but takes the process further. The emphasis is on how the damages will be used to improve the victim's lot. It sees the object of the compensation as being what money will buy rather than the money itself.

III PECUNIARY LOSSES I: BASIC LOSSES

1 Classification

In dealing with property injuries it was found convenient to classify the heads of damages into basic and consequential losses. The distinction reflected the dual function of the award of damages: to restore the property to the condition it was in before the tort, and to compensate the plaintiff for the loss of any profits which he would have earned from the use of the property if it had been available. An analogous distinction may be applied to personal injuries. The plaintiff's basic losses

---

[1] To a large extent this was adopted in the National Insurance (Industrial Injuries) Act 1946: George, *supra*, at pp. 33–39.
[2] This, in practice, the effect of introducing an earnings-related supplement. Atiyah, *supra*, Chap. 15.
[3] Cf. Ogus (1972), 35 M.L.R. 1.

are his outgoings, in particular the expenses involved in the process of healing and cure—the nearest equivalent to the "cost of repairs" measure in property cases. His consequential losses are his loss of earnings and loss of other pecuniary advantages which would have been available to him if he had not been injured.

2 Past losses

To restore a person to his exact mental and physical condition immediately prior to the accident is, in general, impossible. But insofar as recovery or cure will ameliorate the plaintiff's condition, the law will order the defendant to pay such a sum of money as is reasonable and necessary for that purpose. In *Phillips* v. *London and South Western Rail Co.*,[1] the first important English authority on personal injury damages, COCKBURN, C.J. prescribed that the jury should take into account "the expenses incidental to attempts to effect a cure, or to lessen the amount of the injury."[2] Thus included under this head are such items as medical treatment,[3] nursing fees,[4] medical appliances,[5] institutional care,[6] extra domestic help,[7] and the increase of living expenses generally.[8] To recover compensation for expenses three conditions must be satisfied.

(a) The expenditure must be reasonably necessary

The item claimed must be reasonably necessary in the sense that it must serve to ameliorate the plaintiff's condition. Thus in one case the question for the court was whether a plaintiff (in 1938) was entitled to claim £2 2s. per week for taxi fares to and from her place of employment.[9] Another oft-disputed claim is for the expenses of relatives travelling to and staying with the injured party for the purpose of comforting him or offering him physical assistance. The tendency is to allow this claim only where medical opinion considers it necessary for the plaintiff's recovery.[10]

---

[1] (1879), 4 Q.B.D. 406, affirmed (1879), 5 Q.B.D. 78 and (1879), 5 C.P.D. 280.
[2] (1879), 4 Q.B.D. 406, at p. 408.
[3] *Roach* v. *Yates*, [1938] 1 K.B. 256.
[4] *Oliver* v. *Ashman*, [1962] 2 Q.B. 210.
[5] *S.* v. *Distillers Co.*, [1969] 3 All E.R. 142.
[6] *Cutts* v. *Chumley*, [1967] 2 All E.R. 89.
[7] *Wattson* v. *Port of London Authority*, [1969] 1 Lloyd's Rep. 95.
[8] *Shearman* v. *Folland*, [1950] 2 K.B. 43.
[9] *Pitt* v. *Jackson*, [1939] 1 All E.R. 129; it was held to be a reasonable item of expenditure since (i) the plaintiff's injuries prevented her using public transport, (ii) it was difficult to find either alternative employment or suitable accommodation nearer her work.
[10] *Schneider* v. *Eisovitch*, [1960] 2 Q.B. 430; *Wilson* v. *McLeay* (1961), 106 C.L.R. 523; *Bresatz* v. *Przibilla* (1962), 108 C.L.R. 541.

(b) The amount paid or payable must be reasonable

It is a corollary of the doctrine of mitigation[1] that the plaintiff in incurring expenses for treatment and recovery should pay no more than was reasonable in the circumstances. This requirement has been impliedly recognized by the legislature.[2] It is, of course, difficult to generalize on the standard of reasonableness applied, but the present practice of the English courts would seem to indicate that the test is by no means strict. A typical instance is *Winkworth* v. *Hubbard*:[3]

> P, a Canadian stockbroker, manager of his firm's European department, was very seriously injured while water-skiing at Monaco. He received emergency treatment in Monaco but, desirous of having "the very best possible medical and surgical attention that could be obtained", he was then taken to a specialist in New York, before returning to Canada. STREATFIELD, J. considered that in the circumstances it was reasonable for the plaintiff to go to New York to receive his treatment, and to incur hospital charges there of £5328. But he held that the cost of two rubber-tipped canes, at £4 10s. each was excessive (it would "cause an Englishman to rebel") since they could be bought at 12s. 6d. a piece.[4]

In a country where free medical treatment is provided by the National Health Service, it might have been thought that to incur expenses as a private patient would in many cases be regarded as unreasonable. Indeed, in 1942, Beveridge had already anticipated the argument:

> "it can be argued . . . that if comprehensive medical treatment is available for every citizen without charge quite irrespective of the cause of his requiring it, he ought not to be allowed, if he incurs special expenses for medical treatment beyond the treatment generally available, to recover such expenses in an action for damages."[5]

But the Monckton Committee,[6] after examining the matter in some depth, came to no such conclusion. While appreciating the force of the argument that:

> "if a defendant could convince the Court that medical or other services were available free of charge to the plaintiff through a public service with which a reasonable man in the plaintiff's position ought to have been content, it would be the duty of the Court to hold that the de-

---

[1] *Supra*, pp. 85–92.
[2] Law Reform (Personal Injuries) Act 1948, s. 2(4); *infra*, p. 175.
[3] [1960] 1 Lloyd's Rep. 150.
[4] Cf. *Roberts* v. *Roberts* (1960), *Times*, March 11th.
[5] Beveridge Report on Social Insurance and Allied Services, Cmd. 6404 (1942), para. 262.
[6] Final Report of the Departmental Committee on Alternative Remedies, Cmd. 6860 (1946).

fendant was not liable for expenditure incurred by obtaining similar services from other sources"[1]

they nevertheless felt[2] that it was outweighed by two other considerations: (1) that the task of a court in deciding between the merits of a State or private treatment was too difficult; and (2) that it would be "inconsistent with the liberty of the individual" to take private treatment and yet not be able to claim for the cost of it from the tortfeasor.

It was clearly these latter sentiments which swayed Parliament, for section 2(4) of the Law Reform (Personal Injuries) Act 1948 provides:

> "In an action for damages for personal injuries ... there shall be disregarded, in determining the reasonableness of any expenses, the possibility of avoiding those expenses or part of them by taking advantage of facilities available under the National Health Service Act 1946. . . ."

It may yet be doubted whether the statutory solution is the best one.[3] It seems to ignore the fact that a large segment of society is, albeit indirectly, carrying the burden of tort liability, and that as a consequence of section 2(4) of the 1948 Act it must subsidize both public and private medical treatment. Moreover where the plaintiff is a member of a scheme which covers the cost of private medical treatment he may still recover the cost of the treatment in damages (as private insurance benefits are not taken into account)[4] so that, in effect, he is receiving *twice* the sum necessary for the *private* treatment.[5]

Of course, cases may be envisaged in which the provision of private treatment is reasonable and necessary for the plaintiff's recovery. But if section 2(4) were to be repealed there would be nothing to prevent the award of the expenses so incurred. The ordinary test of reasonableness would apply. What is objectionable in the statutory rule is that the availability of National Health facilities *must* be ignored.

(c) The plaintiff must be under a legal or moral obligation to pay the expenses

In determining the award for the cost of recovery, the question arises whether the plaintiff is entitled to include the cost of benefits or services *received* but not *paid for*. For example, the plaintiff's aunt may voluntarily nurse and attend the plaintiff during the period of recovery. Is he entitled to a sum representing the cost of this service? The question has a bearing on issues of some theoretical importance which

---

[1] *Ibid.*, para. 55.
[2] *Ibid.*, para. 56.
[3] See also Atiyah, *op. cit.*, pp. 442–443.
[4] *Bradburn* v. *Great Western Rail Co.* (1874), L.R. 10 Ex. 1, *infra*, p. 223.
[5] Atiyah, *op. cit.*, p. 443.

are to be discussed later in this book.¹ Suffice it at this stage to observe that the answer to the question will depend on which of two approaches to pecuniary loss the law adopts. If the *conceptual* approach holds sway, the court will look to the *objective* cost of the plaintiff's recovery—it will attempt to set a "value" on the services and expenses reasonably necessary to effect the plaintiff's recovery. Alternatively the law may prefer the *personal* approach, according to which damages are payable for the expenses which the plaintiff actually incurred in the past, and those which he is likely actually to incur in the future. It is at once apparent that if the former approach is adopted, the plaintiff is entitled to recover the cost of the service, whether or not he is under an obligation to pay for it. Such is the position generally taken by the courts in the United States of America.² In England, on the other hand, the personal approach is favoured: the plaintiff is entitled to compensation only for such liabilities as he is under an obligation to pay. Thus under section 2(4) of the Law Reform (Personal Injuries) Act 1948 (considered above)³ he may recover for the expenses of private treatment which he has actually incurred, but he may not claim for the "value" of the services provided.⁴

It remains to discover what the scope of this "obligation to pay" must be. English law is remarkably uncertain on the point. Three views emerge from the case-law.

(i) According to PAULL, J. in *Schneider* v. *Eisovitch*⁵ the obligation must be to assign to the third party what is awarded as damages under this head. Provided that in addition the services provided by the third party were a reasonably necessary consequence of the defendants' tort, and that their cost was reasonable, the accident victim can recover.

(ii) For the courts in *Roach* v. *Yates*⁶ and *Wattson* v. *Port of London Authority*⁷ on the other hand, the essential requirement was that the plaintiff should have been, at the time of the service, under a moral obligation to pay for them. This will usually arise, as in the two cases cited, where the benefactor has voluntarily given up some remunerative employment.⁸

---

¹ (i) Whether a plaintiff is awarded damages for loss of earnings or lost earning capacity, pp. 184–186; (ii) the extent to which a third party who indemnifies the accident victim against his losses may be reimbursed, pp. 278–282; (iii) the theoretical basis of damages for non-pecuniary loss, pp. 194–196.

² See McCormick, pp. 323–325.

³ P. 175.

⁴ *Harris* v. *Bright's Asphalt Contractors*, [1953] 1 Q.B. 617; see also *Lindstedt* v. *Wimborne S.S. Co.* (1949), 83 Ll.L. Rep. 19.

⁵ [1960] 2 Q.B. 430. See also *Dennis* v. *London Passenger Transport Board*, [1948] 1 All E.R. 779.

⁶ [1938] 1 K.B. 256.

⁷ [1969] 1 Lloyd's Rep. 95.

⁸ See also *George* v. *Pinnock*, [1973] 1 W.L.R. 118.

(iii) The most restrictive view originally expressed by DIPLOCK, J. in *Gage* v. *King*[1] and recently affirmed by MAY, J. in *Haggar* v. *De Placido*[2] is that the plaintiff should only recover where he was under a *legal* obligation to pay the third party.

Even though the third view has the more recent following[3] and is the easiest to apply, it may yet be doubted whether it constitutes the best solution to the problem. The difficulty is that services voluntarily undertaken do not, in English law, give rise to a legal obligation in the person benefited: we have no doctrine of *negotiorum gestio*.[4] Unless, therefore, the volunteer is himself to be given a right of action against the tortfeasor—which sadly is not generally the case,[5] though recommendations to this effect have been urged[6]—there seems to be every justification in extending the remedy of the accident victim beyond cases where he was under a legal obligation to pay for the services.

3 Future losses

Finally the question arises as to the recoverability of future and, therefore, necessarily uncertain expenses. The court must, of course, according to the ordinary principles of certainty and with the aid of medical evidence, attempt to predict what will be the plaintiff's needs[7] and the future cost thereof.[8] Among the factors to be considered is, for example, whether the kind of institution where the plaintiff is receiving treatment may become unavailable in the future, or whether an improvement in national health service facilities will nullify the expenses.[9]

III PECUNIARY LOSSES II: CONSEQUENTIAL LOSSES

1 Introduction

The most important head of damages in a personal injury claim is

---

[1] [1961] 1 Q.B. 188.
[2] [1972] 2 All E.R. 1029.
[3] But see *George* v. *Pinnock*, *supra*.
[4] *Falcke* v. *Scottish Imperial Insurance Co.* (1886), 34 Ch. D. 234.
[5] *Infra*, pp. 278–282.
[6] 11th Report of the Law Reform Committee Cmnd. 2017 (1963); Law Commission Working Papers Nos. 19 and 41.
[7] Although the court is to resist the temptation of blindly accepting the views of medical practitioners, the question is always: what is the plaintiff reasonably likely to spend? *Per* BARWICK, C.J., *Robinson (Grafton), Pty., Ltd.* v. *Carter* (1968), 41 A.L.J.R. 327, at p. 329.
[8] In estimating the future cost of e.g. medical services, the court should not take account of inflation since this should, under normal circumstances, be counter-balanced by a corresponding rise in the value of investments: SIR GORDON WILLMER in *Mitchell* v. *Mulholland* (No. 2), [1972] 1 Q.B. 65, at p. 88, see also *infra*, pp. 192–193.
[9] *George* v. *Pinnock*, *supra*.

for the plaintiff's lost opportunity of earning a profit. In the ordinary case this will comprise his lost wages or salary, but it will also include cases of loss of business profits, where, for example, the injured party ran a one-man company and his disability affected the profitability of the firm.[1]

It is necessary first to distinguish between those losses which, at the time of judgment,[2] have already accrued and those which are likely to accrue in the future. Although there is no difference in the theory of quantification,[3] yet past pecuniary losses are almost always pleaded as special damages[4] and being more certain present fewer problems of assessment.

2   Past losses

(a)   Basic measure

Application of the *restitutio in integrum* doctrine gives rise to a simple proposition: the plaintiff is to be awarded the difference between what he would have been able to earn if he had not been injured and what he has been able to earn since the accident.[5] The figures concerned are *net earnings*; they do not include, for example, contributions to the National Insurance Fund.[6]

(b)   Loss of earnings or loss of earning capacity

It is usually stated, especially in practitioners' manuals,[7] that losses up to the date of trial must be pleaded and proved as special damages. There is, indeed, authority for the proposition that a plaintiff claiming compensation for loss of past earnings should plead it as special damages and as such it should not form part of an award of general damages.[8] But this does not conclude the matter for it is arguable that even as regards losses already accrued[9] the plaintiff may claim for his *loss of earning capacity* which as an element in general damages will not need to be specifically pleaded or proved.[10] There is an *obiter dictum* to the

---

[1] E.g. *Ashcroft* v. *Curtin*, [1971] 3 All E.R. 1208.

[2] For the problems of specific evidence admissible after the date of judgment see *supra*, pp. 16–18.

[3] See DIPLOCK, L.J.'s observations in *Fletcher* v. *Autocar and Transporters*, [1968] 2 Q.B. 322, at p. 344.

[4] *Infra*, pp. 178–181.

[5] *Phillips* v. *London South Western Rail Co.* (1879), 5 Q.B.D. 78 affirming (1879), 4 Q.B.D. 406.

[6] *Cooper* v. *Firth Brown*, [1963] 2 All E.R. 31. The incidence of tax liability has been considered, *supra*, pp. 107–115.

[7] McGregor, §1048; Kemp and Kemp, pp. 20–21.

[8] *Ilkiw* v. *Samuels*, [1963] 2 All E.R. 879.

[9] For future losses see *infra*, pp. 184–187.

[10] Street, pp. 44–55; Parsons (1955), 28 A.L.J. 563, at pp. 571–572; Jolowicz [1960] C.L.J. 214, at pp. 218–222.

effect that this is a perfectly proper approach[1] but in practice loss of earning capacity has only been admitted for past losses where the plaintiff's earnings were speculative or irregular. Where he received a regular wage or salary, his loss of earnings up to the time of the trial is invariably pleaded as special damages and loss of future earnings as general damages.[2] The question whether a plaintiff may be allowed to claim for the impairment to his capacity rather than for loss of earnings is not merely a verbal one. It may have important consequences on the quantification of the award. The most significant of such consequences affect future losses and will be considered under that head.[3] But two aspects of assessment of past losses may likewise be affected.

(i) *Certainty* A claim under general damages allows the court more flexibility in quantifying the plaintiff's loss. On the one hand, it permits an award for the loss of a chance to earn remuneration. In *Mulvaine* v. *Joseph*:[4]

P, an American professional golfer, while on a European tour injured his hand in an accident for which D was responsible. He was awarded £1000 for *inter alia* the loss of the chance of winning prize money.[5]

On the other hand, the court should take into account the contingencies of life, such as unemployment, ill health or an early death which would have prevented the plaintiff earning the anticipated sum.[6] Conversely it is in the nature of special damage that a much higher standard of certainty is required: the losses claimed under it must be pleaded with complete accuracy and must be susceptible of the most exact proof.[7] Yet too rigid an adherence to this rule would exclude almost all cases of lost earnings. There is always an element of uncertainty: the court has still to predict what the plaintiff would have earned if there had been no accident. Not surprisingly, the courts have refused to take the rule too literally. Where, for example, the plaintiff is on piece work,[8] or where his remuneration would have depended on whether or not he would have continued in a special work-category,[9] they have been quite content to fall back on average pre-accident earnings.[10] Faced with a

---

[1] WILLMER, L.J. in *Ilkiw* v. *Samuels, supra,* at p. 887.
[2] E.g. *Mulvaine* v. *Joseph* (1968), 112 Sol. Jo. 927, *infra* and see the authorities cited in n. 10, p. 178, *supra.*
[3] *Infra,* pp. 184–187.
[4] (1968), 112 Sol. Jo. 972.
[5] The principle applied to this head of damages was first adumbrated in *Chaplin* v. *Hicks,* [1911] 2 K.B. 786, *supra,* p. 83.
[6] See the cases cited, *infra,* p. 188.
[7] *Supra,* p. 4. See also *Ashcroft* v. *Curtin,* [1971] 3 All E.R. 1208.
[8] *Rouse* v. *Port of London Authority,* [1953] 2 Lloyd's Rep. 179.
[9] *Barry* v. *British Transport Commission,* [1954] 1 Lloyd's Rep. 372.
[10] *Per* COCKBURN, C.J., *Phillips* v. *London and South Western Rail Co.* (1879), 4 Q.B.D. 406, at p. 408.

claim for lost profits by the owner of a one-man business, however, they have been reluctant to infer general business losses.[1] Even though it be highly probable that the plaintiff's disability had a damaging effect on the company's profitability, the plaintiff must produce clear reliable accounts as evidence of such loss, otherwise it will be impossible to quantify.[2] On the question whether the general contingencies are to be taken into account in determining the amount to be awarded by way of special damage, the position is somewhat unclear. Certainly there are dicta to the effect that such possibilities as unemployment,[3] or the aggravation of a pre-existing physical disability should be reflected in the award.[4] Yet in practice, especially where the parties make a settlement out of court, it would seem that such contingencies are often ignored.[5]

(ii) *Actual losses*   The problems arising from the situation in which the plaintiff's loss is made good by a third party are considerable and later in this chapter a full analysis will be offered.[6] But one aspect calls for discussion here. Special damage is confined in principle to actual losses sustained not those which are speculative or notional. Where, therefore, a third party has indemnified the plaintiff's loss, it can be argued that the plaintiff has sustained no "actual loss" and he should not recover. On a claim for general damages, on the other hand, it may be claimed that whether or not the plaintiff has enjoyed a compensating advantage from a collateral source, his earning capacity has still been impaired. Now, of course, it cannot be maintained that the complex problems of compensating advantages can be solved by the technical legal distinction between loss of earnings and loss of earning capacity. Yet it is sad to relate that an obsession with the nature of special damage has in one case been allowed to determine an issue which involved a wide range of legal and policy issues.[7] In *Metropolitan Police District Receiver* v. *Croydon Corporation*[8]

> Ds were liable in negligence for an injury inflicted on P. P recovered damages from Ds but the award did not include anything for loss of wages, as during his period of incapacity P's employer X had continued to pay P his full wages. X brought an action against Ds for the payments he had made to P, claiming that Ds' liability to P had been reduced by X's payments, and that therefore Ds had been unjustly

---

[1] *Ashcroft* v. *Curtin, supra.*
[2] *Ibid., per* EDMUND DAVIES, L.J., at p. 1214.
[3] *Wilkins* v. *Brocklebank*, [1961] 2 Lloyd's Rep. 110.
[4] *Cutler* v. *Vauxhall Motors*, [1971] 1 Q.B. 418, at pp. 423 and 426.
[5] See Street, pp. 46–47, and the Law Commission Working Paper No. 41, para. 15.
[6] *Infra*, pp. 222–230.
[7] Jolowicz, *supra*, at pp. 220–221.
[8] [1957] 2 Q.B. 154.

enriched at X's expense. The claim was rejected by the Court of Appeal mainly on the ground that since P had not sustained an "actual loss" of his wages, Ds *eo tanto* were not liable.

The reasoning in this case has not (fortunately) been extended to situations in which the injured party was under a legal[1] or moral[2] duty to assign the benefit of the award to the third party who made good his losses. The argument that in these circumstances the plaintiff had not sustained an "actual loss" has not been sympathetically received.[3]

(c) Mitigation

The ordinary principles of mitigation apply: the plaintiff must have acted reasonably in attempting to minimize his losses, but the burden is on the defendant to establish that the plaintiff did not so act,[4] and the strength of the presumption that he did act reasonably makes the burden a difficult one to shift.[5] The standard of reasonableness must make allowances for the plaintiff's *actual* knowledge of the possible courses of conduct open to him. Thus where an injured party did not realize (and was not advised) that she was entitled to a social security benefit, it was held that her failure to claim the benefit was not unreasonable and hence the appropriate deduction was not made.[6] In some cases the difficult question has arisen whether the plaintiff acted reasonably in refusing to undergo a medical operation. The court must, of course, rely heavily on expert evidence but it does not generally reduce damages where there were some doubts as to the prospects of a successful operation,[7] and it usually prepared to make allowances for the plaintiff's physical and mental idiosyncracies.[8]

Another claim frequently advanced by defendants is that the plaintiff did not take reasonable steps to find alternative employment which would accommodate the disability from which he suffered. The guide-lines for determining the type of employment and the scale of remuneration which the plaintiff might reasonably seek have received greater attention in the contractual action for wrongful dismissal, to which reference should be made.[9] Recent tort cases have dealt with the parallel issue whether the plaintiff might reasonably undergo training for a new

---

[1] *Allen v. Waters*, [1935] 1 K.B. 200.
[2] *Dennis v. London Passenger Transport Board*, [1948] 1 All E.R. 779.
[3] See DENNING, J., *ibid.*, at p. 779.
[4] *Stafford v. Antwerp S.S.*, [1965] 2 Lloyd's Rep. 104.
[5] *Per* VISCOUNT SIMON, L.C., *Steele v. Robert George & Co.* (1937), *Ltd.*, [1942] A.C. 497, at p. 501.
[6] *Eley v. Bedford*, [1972] 1 Q.B. 155.
[7] E.g. *Savage v. Wallis*, [1966] 1 Lloyd's Rep. 357.
[8] E.g. *Steele v. Robert George & Co.* (1937), *Ltd.*, *supra*; cf. the surprisingly harsh decision in *Marcroft v. Scruttons*, [1954] 1 Lloyd's Rep. 395.
[9] *Infra*, pp. 329–330.

category of employment. There are many factors to be taken into account: for example, the prospects of employment in the new category of work and the scale of remuneration; the capabilities of the plaintiff; the length of training necessary; the availability of alternative modes of employment, in particular whether the plaintiff has received a specific offer of a job for which he was suitable. In *Luker* v. *Chapman*[1] these last factors proved decisive:

> P, a telephone engineer, was unable as a result of the accident to continue in the same job. His employers offered him a clerical job. He refused because he wanted to train to become a teacher. BROWNE, J. "reluctantly" came to the conclusion that he should reasonably have accepted the offer of a clerical job.

In *Rowden* v. *Clarke Chapman*[2] it was held to be reasonable for the plaintiff to train for a new category of work for which there were good prospects of employment and which was the only feasible alternative to remaining in his previous job where his prospects of continuous and full employment were rather uncertain.

3 Future losses

That an injured person should be entitled to compensation for the loss of future opportunities to earn has never been in doubt but the necessarily speculative nature of the award has given rise to considerable difficulty. Jury awards have in practice wholly disappeared in England and the courts must now award a separate sum for future pecuniary loss[3] but the problem still remains whether judges should aim at a more scientific, statistically based figure or rest content with the more intuitive notion of "fair and reasonable" but not "perfect" compensation.[4]

This section will be concerned mainly with the loss of wages and salary, but it is necessary to observe that the loss of any prospective profit, even the loss of an opportunity to invest in a profitable undertaking,[5] is in principle recoverable. The typical case is that of an owner of a small company claiming that the profits of the firm diminished as a result of his inability to work. In the early days, consonant with the doctrine of certainty then prevailing, it had to be shown that the plaintiff's injury prevented him or his firm gaining a profit under

---

[1] (1970), 114 Sol. Jo. 788.
[2] [1967] 3 All E.R. 608.
[3] *Jefford* v. *Gee*, [1970] 2 Q.B. 130.
[4] *Per* LORD DENNING, M.R., *Fletcher* v. *Autocar and Transporters*, [1968] 2 Q.B. 322, at pp. 335–356, and see *infra*, pp. 207–208.
[5] *R.* v. *Jennings* (1966), 57 D.L.R.(2d) 644.

an *existing* contract.[1] This limitation has now been removed:[2] the remaining (and not inconsiderable) obstacles are causation and certainty. It must be proved to the satisfaction of the court that the future prospects of the firm have been seriously affected and that this resulted from the plaintiff's disability and not from other causes.[3] The possibility that a wage-earner might have set up a business of his own is something which theoretically may qualify for compensation but which in practice is likely to be too uncertain to merit an award.[4] The doctrine of mitigation applies to this as to other heads and if the plaintiff might have avoided the loss or part of it by employing a substitute, then the cost of the replacement and not the loss of profits will be the appropriate measure.[5]

As regards this and the more common loss of wages or salary, the basic principle of quantification follows from the doctrine of *restitutio in integrum*: the plaintiff is to be awarded the difference between what he would have been able to earn if he had not been injured and what he is likely to earn in his post-accident condition.[6] Unlike the action in contract for wrongful dismissal,[7] the award is not limited to such remuneration as the plaintiff would be *contractually* entitled to receive but will include all his reasonable expectations including overtime and bonus payments.[8] The basic principle is a simple one but its practical application may involve consideration of a number of issues which often must exercise the courts' arithmetical and predictive faculties.

(a) Causation and mitigation

Of course, it must be shown that the plaintiff's loss of income will substantially result from the accident for which the defendant is liable and not from some extraneous cause such as a latent physical disability which would in any case have impaired the capacity to earn.[9] Nor is the defendant responsible for such consequences as result from the plaintiff's own failure reasonably to mitigate his loss by, for example, refusing to undergo an operation.[10]

---

[1] *Priestley* v. *MacLean* (1860), 2 F. & F. 288.
[2] E.g. *Webb* v. *Comer*, [1956] C.L.Y. 2364.
[3] *Lee* v. *Sheard*, [1956] 1 Q.B. 192; *Ashcroft* v. *Curtin*, [1971] 3 All E.R. 1208.
[4] *Domsalla* v. *Barr*, [1969] 3 All E.R. 487.
[5] *Owen* v. *Sykes*, [1936] 1 K.B. 192, cf. *supra*, p. 92.
[6] *Phillips* v. *London South Western Rail Co.* (1879), 4 Q.B.D. 406, affirmed (1879), 5 Q.B.D. 78 and (1879), 5 C.P.D. 280.
[7] *Infra*, pp. 311–312.
[8] E.g. *Mitchell* v. *Mulholland (No. 2)*, [1972] 1 Q.B. 65.
[9] E.g. *Cutler* v. *Vauxhall Motors*, [1971] 1 Q.B. 418; and see generally *supra*, p. 63.
[10] *Supra*, p. 181.

(b)   Unexploited earning capacity

To what extent may the plaintiff recover for an earning potential which, up to the time of the accident, he had not fully exploited? This is one aspect of the more general question of whether the award in a personal injury action is for loss of earnings or loss of earning capacity.[1] Resort to the various theoretical foundations of the award[2] is revealing. Advocates of the *conceptual* approach would insist that the capacity to earn is itself a benefit of economic value which if impaired or destroyed must be fully indemnified independently of whether or not the plaintiff would actually have exploited his capacity. On the *personal* view, however, the task would be to determine how much would have been earned if the injury had not been inflicted. On a third view the earnings at the time of the accident are regarded as conclusive of the plaintiff's potential and no account is taken of future prospects. This third view has no adherents in the common law world, although several social security systems subscribe to it.[3] It does not compensate the plaintiff's actual loss and it must be regarded as a concession both to the evidentiary problem of establishing with sufficient certainty the plaintiff's full potential and the economic burden which results from a more generous approach. The choice between the other two approaches is not so obvious.

The American courts have for some time stated a clear preference for the *conceptual* approach:[4]

> "Human nature is so constituted that physical labour in some form is essential to health and happiness, and to be deprived of the power to work is one of the most serious personal injuries, independent of the pecuniary benefits that such labor may confer."[5]

In Australia judges have been at pains to explain that damages are awarded for lost earning capacity rather than for lost earnings,[6] and yet the theory is not taken to its logical conclusion. Thus a man of independent means who would not have fulfilled his earning potential is not entitled to recover for his lost earning capacity.[7] Though sometimes expressed in terms of lost earning capacity, these awards of damages are, in fact, perfectly consistent with the *personal* approach.

---

[1] Cf. *supra*, p. 178.
[2] Cf. *supra*, p. 172.
[3] *Supra*, n. 2, p. 172.
[4] McCormick, pp. 299–300.
[5] *Per* PRACE, C.J., *Perrigo* v. *City of St. Louis*, 84 S.W. 30, at p. 34 (1904).
[6] See especially, *Robinson (Grafton) Pty., Ltd.* v. *Carter* (1968), 41 A.L.J.R. 327, *per* BARWICK, C.J. at pp. 330–331 and *O'Brien* v. *McKean* (1968), 42 A.L.J.R. 223, *per* BARWICK, C.J. at p. 225, *per* WINDEYER, J. at p. 229.
[7] *Per* SMITH, J., *Tzouvelis* v. *Victorian Railways Commissioners*, [1968] V.R. 112, at p. 130.

This is substantially true also for the English courts: though they are tentatively feeling their way to a doctrine of lost earning capacity,[1] this is only to justify the award of substantial damages to plaintiffs who are too young to have earned,[2] or who cannot produce direct evidence of their future loss.[3] It seems clear that English judges, like their Australian brethren, will not award damages for an as yet unused earning capacity unless it is reasonably certain that that capacity would, but for the accident, have been exploited in the future.[4] This is well illustrated by the cases on young unmarried women. In *Heath* v. *Flouty*[5]

> P, a girl aged 16, was very seriously injured in a road accident. For the purpose of ascertaining her future loss the court accepted the evidence that she was likely (1) to have earned a salary of £1000 to £1700 a year as a teacher when qualified, (2) after 5 or 6 years to have given up teaching in order to get married, (3) to have returned to teaching when her family had grown up.

In short, consistently with the personal approach the courts must still ask the question: what would the plaintiff have earned if he had not been injured? As far as this aspect of quantification is concerned, flirtation with the loss of earning capacity doctrine seems to be unnecessary and misleading.

(c) The lost years[6]

Another problem which has been discussed in terms of the loss of earnings/loss of earning capacity dichotomy arises where a plaintiff's life has been shortened by the accident: should he recover for the loss of earnings during the period when it is anticipated that he will no longer be alive? After several conflicting decisions[7] the conclusion was reached in *Oliver* v. *Ashman*[8] that he may not: compensation is to be limited to the earnings lost during the period that the plaintiff is likely to remain alive. The limitation has never been accepted in the

---

[1] E.g. *Gardner* v. *Dyson*, [1967] 3 All E.R. 762; *Patel* v. *Edwards*, [1970] R.T.R. 425.
[2] E.g. *S.* v. *Distillers Co.*, [1969] 3 All E.R. 1412.
[3] *Patel* v. *Edwards, supra.*
[4] See the *obiter dictum* of DIPLOCK, L.J. in *Browning* v. *War Office*, [1963] 1 Q.B. 750, at p. 766. But see now *Field* v. *British European Airways, Ltd.* (1973), *Times*, 1st March.
[5] 1970 C.A. No. 461 *Kemp & Kemp* 10th Cum. Supp. to 3rd Edn., Chap. 13.
[6] Fleming (1963), 50 Calif. L.R. 598; Law Commission Working Paper No. 41, paras. 52–58.
[7] *Roach* v. *Yates*, [1938] 1 K.B. 256 (recovery); *Harris* v. *Bright's Asphalt*, [1953] 1 Q.B. 617 (no recovery); *Pope* v. *Murphy*, [1961] 1 Q.B. 222 (recovery).
[8] [1962] 2 Q.B. 210; followed in *Wise* v. *Kay*, [1962] 1 Q.B. 638.

United States of America[1] and was decisively rejected by the High Court of Australia.[2] To evaluate the merits of the rule in *Oliver* v. *Ashman* (as it has become known) and the possible alternatives involves a consideration of the problem from different vantage points.

(A) Assessing damages on the basis of *lost earning capacity* would involve a rejection of the rule. The economic value of a man's earning potential has been impaired whether or not he will be alive to suffer the consequences.[3] But the rule would then derive support from the opposing theory that the basis of the compensation is the plaintiff's *actual lost earnings*: if he will not be alive, he will not have lost his earnings.[4]

(B) The *conceptual* approach, according to which the loss is to the plaintiff's estate which is independent of his life, would deprecate the rule;[5] whereas the *personal* approach, concentrating on the plaintiff's actual losses and the *functional* approach, making compensation dependent on the benefit derived from the award,[6] would sustain it.

(C) The argument that the tortfeasor should not benefit from the consequences of having inflicted a more serious injury could be employed to attack the rule but it is of course based on punitive considerations which are irrelevant to the law of tort.

(D) The most forceful objection to the rule resides in the fact that the persons who would have benefited from the victim's earnings during his "lost years" are not indemnified for their loss.[7] On the one hand they have no action during his lifetime.[8] On the other hand an action under the Fatal Accidents Acts which might otherwise be brought when the victim dies is barred by his own successful action.[9] The plight of the dependants is amply illustrated by *Murray* v. *Shuter*[10] [January 1969 P, aged 31, sustained brain damage in accident. P remained unconscious but action against D was brought and trial on damages was fixed for 17 May, 1971. In February, 1971, medical prognosis set P's life expectancy at probably a few months but certainly at no more than a year. The trial judge was asked to adjourn the trial on the ground that if heard before P's death, the rule in *Oliver* v. *Ashman* would apply and P's dependants would suffer. The Court of Appeal ordered the postponement of the trial until June, 1972, so that, once P had died, the dependants would get the "full compensation . . . which they ought to have."][11] It is true that in *Wise* v. *Kay*,[12] SELLERS, L.J. envisaged that

---

[1] 22 Am. Jur. 2d § 92 and the cases cited there at n. 14.
[2] *Skelton* v. *Collins* (1966), 115 C.L.R. 94.
[3] *Per* WINDEYER, J., *ibid.*, at p. 129.
[4] *Per* HOLROYD PEARCE, L.J., *Oliver* v. *Ashman*, *supra*, at p. 228.
[5] *Per* STREATFIELD, J., *Pope* v. *Murphy*, *supra*, at p. 231.
[6] *Per* WILLMER, LJ., *Oliver* v. *Ashman*, *supra*, at p. 237.
[7] Fleming, *supra*, n. 6, p. 185; Law Commission Working Paper No. 41.
[8] See, generally, *infra*, pp. 278–280.
[9] An application of the "once-for all" rule: *supra*, pp. 10–11.
[10] (1971), 115 Sol. Jo. 774.
[11] *Per* LORD DENNING, M.R., *ibid.*
[12] [1962] 1 Q.B. 638, at p. 646.

if a man had prior to the accident habitually put aside a sum of money to provide for his dependants then he might be able to recover for the loss of the opportunity to continue to do so; but there is little evidence that the courts have taken up the suggestion.[1]

It is submitted that the shortcomings of the rule brought to light in (D) constitute a sufficient ground for abolishing or at least modifying the rule.　Three proposals have been made[2]

(I) The dependants might bring an action under the Fatal Accidents Acts on the death of the plaintiff notwithstanding that he had himself during his lifetime recovered damages.

(II) The plaintiff could recover for his lost earnings during the lost years less the proportion which he would have spent on himself.[3]　In other words, he would recover compensation for his dependants' loss and would be expected to confer the benefit of the award on them.

(III) The dependants could be joined to the plaintiff's action.　A sum would be awarded to compensate for their loss during the lost years. The money would be paid into court where it would earn interest during the remaining years of the plaintiff's life, and on his death it would go to the dependants in proportions decided by the judge at the original trial.

The problems of causation, limitations and evidence make (I) quite unacceptable.　Of the other two, (III), though more closely identified with losses actually sustained by the plaintiff and his dependants, could be implemented only by major administrative changes.　(II), the best solution within the framework of existing procedure, would carry with it the risk of overcompensation, and the possibility that the plaintiff might spend the award during his lifetime.

(d)　Certainty[4]

An award of damages for future losses involves two predictions: (1) what would the plaintiff have earned if he had not been injured? (2) what is he likely to earn?　Both necessarily involve elements of uncertainty which must be taken into account in quantifying the loss. Thus under (1) such contingencies as sickness, disablement, strikes and unemployment will go to reduce the award.[5]　Of factors tending to

---

[1] The award of £1000 for this loss in *Richards* v. *Highway Ironfounders*, [1955] 1 W.L.R. 1049 was set aside by the Court of Appeal.
[2] Law Commission Working Paper No. 41, para. 57.
[3] This was the solution adopted in *Skelton* v. *Collins* (1966), 115 C.L.R. 94.
[4] Street, pp. 120–125.
[5] Street, *ibid.*, after a thorough investigation of the working days lost through these factors in the 1950s, estimated that for the average male employees in England the total deduction for contingencies should be about 3½ per cent. More recently an actuary (Prevett (1972), 35 M.L.R. 129, at p. 130), has in-

increase the award, the plaintiff's prospects of promotion provide the clearest example.[1] A second possibility, inflation, will be discussed below.[2] Thirdly, the plaintiff may attempt to show that his earnings would have increased through a growth in productivity in his particular trade or industry. Of course the matter is speculative but it was taken into account in *Stafford* v. *Antwerp S.S.*:[3] MACKENNA, J. was convinced that "stevedores are more likely to receive increases in their rates of pay than light workers."[4] Even more speculative is the prediction made by expert economists that there will be a national growth in real wages, that the real income of the population will rise faster than consumer prices. So far the courts have rejected evidence of this kind: "'national tendencies', without more are surely too vague to enable one to calculate with anything approaching precision what in this respect is likely in any particular case."[5] "It is cancelled out by an equal and opposite chance that such development will not occur at all".[6]

Finally mention must be made of those factors which render uncertain predictions under (2) as to what the plaintiff is likely to earn. To *increase* damages the court should take into account the possibility of a deterioration in the plaintiff's physical or mental condition,[7] or the possibility that unemployment may affect prospects in his new category of work.[8] Conversely, to *reduce* damages, the judge may advert to the possibility that, contrary to expectations at the time of the trial, the plaintiff's condition will ameliorate[9] or that the award of a capital sum will enable him to set up a small business which will more than eradicate his loss.[10]

(e) Method of quantification: multiplier or actuarial?

(i) *The multiplier* The traditional method of quantifying the loss is to multiply the lost net average annual income (the multiplicand) by the number of years during which the loss will last (the multiplier). The multiplier and the multiplicand will be ascertained according to

---

dicated that in practice he rarely deducts more than 2 per cent., though in one case, *Mitchell* v. *Mulholland* (*No.* 2), [1972] 1 Q.B. 65, this figure was considered to be too low.

[1] *Mitchell's* case, *supra*.
[2] Pp. 192–193.
[3] [1965] 2 Lloyd's Rep. 104.
[4] *Ibid.*, at p. 108. See also *Mitchell's* case, *supra, per* EDMUND DAVIES, L.J. at pp. 80–81, *per* WIDGERY, L.J. at p. 83, *per* SIR GORDON WILLMER, at p. 87 and *O'Brien* v. *McKean* (1968), 42 A.L.J.R. 223, *per* BARWICK, C.J., at p. 225.
[5] *Per* EDMUND DAVIES, L.J., *Mitchell's* case, *supra*, at p. 80.
[6] *Per* WIDGERY, L.J., *ibid.*, at p. 84.
[7] *Littler* v. *G. L. Moore* (*Contractors*), [1967] 3 All E.R. 801.
[8] *Cheesman* v. *Furness, Withy*, [1969] 1 Lloyd's Rep. 315; *Elliott* v. *Corporation of Preston*, [1971] 2 Lloyd's Rep. 328.
[9] *Winkworth* v. *Hubbard*, [1960] 1 Lloyd's Rep. 150.
[10] *Lindstedt* v. *Wimborne S.S. Co.* (1949), 83 Ll.L. Rep. 19.

the principles already discussed, in particular the doctrine of certainty. Thus the multiplicand will include an allowance for any prospect of increased earnings,[1] while the multiplier must be scaled down to account for first the contigencies of life[2] and secondly the advantage of receiving a capital sum now instead of income over a prolonged period.[3]

> *Illustration*[4] P, a planning engineer aged 32 is totally disabled by injuries sustained in an accident for which D is liable.
>
> Earnings at time of accident (including insurance and
> pension rights) = £1,211 (A)
> taking into account prospects of promotion = £1,325 (B)
> Working-life expectancy from date of trial (when
> aged 36) = 29 (C)
> scaled down to account for (i) contingencies and
> (ii) receipt of lump sum = 14 (D)
> Award for lost future earnings = £1,325 × 14 = £18,550

This technique may be criticized.[5] In the first place, it may be argued that the multiplier method is too imperfect an instrument for calculating the present worth of future lost income:[6] the annuity certain (B) multiplied by the working-life expectation in no way correlates to the present value of the plaintiff's loss. A deduction has to be made—thus (D)— but since the starting figure is imprecise and the rate of discount is largely instinctive, the resultant figure will be somewhat arbitrary. Secondly, the reduction for "contingencies" seems often excessive.[7] Judges tend to forget that unexpected events may serve to aggravate as well as diminish the plaintiff's loss.[8] It is not unknown for judges to make the mistake of deducting for a contingency from a sum which as representing an "average" has already taken into account the contingency. Thus in *Pope* v. *Murphy*[9] the trial judge extracted a life-expectancy figure from the statistical tables and then scaled it down to allow for the possibility that the plaintiff might die before he reached that age.

---

[1] *Supra*, p. 188.
[2] *Supra*, p. 187.
[3] *Phillips* v. *London South Western Rail Co.* (1879), 5 Q.B.D. 78 and many others.
[4] Based on *Mitchell* v. *Mulholland (No. 2)*, [1972] 1 Q.B. 65.
[5] See especially: Street, Chap. 5; Phillips (1965), 109 Sol. Jo. 722; Law Commission Working Paper No. 41, paras. 162–166; Prevett (1972), 35 M.L.R. 140.
[6] Phillips, *supra*; Prevett, *supra*.
[7] Street, *supra*.
[8] Cf. WIDGERY, L.J. in *Mitchell* v. *Mulholland (No. 2)*, *supra*, at p. 84: "the chance that a particular development may occur is not to be taken into account if it is cancelled by an equal and opposite chance that such development will not occur at all."
[9] [1961] 1 Q.B. 222; and see the remarks of SIR GORDON WILLMER in *Mitchell's* case, *supra*, at pp. 85–86.

(ii) *Actuarial techniques*[1]   Actuarial techniques cannot provide a complete answer to the problems created by future losses, but they can assist the court in determining with greater accuracy certain aspects of the quantification process.   They can only be used as a reliable guide where two conditions are satisfied.   These are that the future rate of income loss is reasonably certain and that the plaintiff has sustained no substantial loss of life expectancy.   The latter requirement is to cater for the rule in *Oliver* v. *Ashman*.[2]   Within these limits the court may have access to tables which indicate the present value of the future loss of income continuing up to the normal age of retirement.[3]   The tables are based on the following variables:

(1) *Mortality* according to (A) the age and (B) the sex of the plaintiff, and (C) whether his/her work is high-risk or low-risk.

(2) *Capitalization* according to whether or not the income payable on the capital sum will attract (A) tax at the standard rate or (B) little or no tax.

The court selects the appropriate figure from the permutation of 1A, 1B and 1C with 2A or 2B.   With or without expert assistance it should then modify the sum to take account of other factors.   These include:

(1) *Contingencies of life*   The contingency of an early death has already been accounted for but a deduction should be made for the possibilities of strikes, unemployment and disability.   The discount should be at a rate somewhere between 2% and 6%.[4]

(2) *Promotion and progression in real earnings*   Conversely the sum should be increased to account for prospects of progressive gains.[5]

(iii) *Judicial attitudes*   At first sympathetic to actuarial assistance, especially in Chancery cases,[6] the English courts are now extremely reluctant to advert to actuarial evidence.[7]   In three important recent

---

[1] See the authorities cited on pp. 185–187, *supra*, also Kemp & Kemp, Chap. 4; Walker (1967) 111 Sol. Jo. 223; Traverse (1956), 29 A.L.J. 517; Howroyd & Howroyd (1958), 75 S.A.L.J. 65; Peck & Hopkins (1969), 44 Wash. L.R. 351; Dublin & Lotka, *The Money Value of a Man*; Law Commission Working Paper No. 27.

[2] *Supra*, pp. 185–187; but even in this case actuarial evidence will be of help provided that the court can estimate with reasonable exactitude the reduction in the life expectancy.

[3] Specimens are set out in Kemp & Kemp, pp. 40–51 and as Appendix B to Working Paper No. 27, *supra*.

[4] *Supra*, pp. 187–188, Street, pp. 120–125 and Prevett (1972), 35 M.L.R. 140, at pp. 150–151.

[5] *Supra*, p. 188.   The methods of accounting for inflation are considered *infra*, pp. 192–193.

[6] E.g. *M'Donald* v. *M'Donald* (1880), 5 App. Cas. 519.

[7] *Watson* v. *Powles*, [1968] 1 Q.B. 596; *Fletcher* v. *Autocar and Transporters*, [1968] 2 Q.B. 322.

cases,[1] they have reaffirmed allegiance to the traditional multiplier method—actuarial evidence should be admitted, if at all, only as a crosscheck to the result reached by employing the multiplier.[2] It may be that the reluctance to admit actuarial techniques results from a fear that the independence and autonomy of the judiciary is being threatened. The attitude may more legitimately be related to the efforts of the courts to keep down the length and cost of personal injury trials[3] and to restrain the awarding of very large sums.[4] Whatever be the real cause, the theoretical grounds on which judges purport to reject such evidence are not always satisfactory. The main objection appears to be that the actuarial method presents a false image of scientific accuracy. Typical are the remarks of LORD PEARSON in *Taylor* v. *O'Connor*.[5]

"there are too many variables and there are too many conjectural decisions to be made before selecting the tables to be used. There would be a false appearance of accuracy and precision in a sphere where conjectural estimates have to play a large part. The experience of practitioners and judges in applying the normal method is the best primary basis for making assessments."

The actuary is of course ready to concede that a modification to the *prima facie* figure extracted from the tables will in most cases be necessary to allow for such factors as the contingencies of life.[6] But more than this he will argue that far from conflicting with the traditional multiplier method, the actuarial approach attempts to make that method more realistic and less subject to error.[7] Another favourite criticism is that the actuarial method does not pay sufficient attention to the particular circumstances of the plaintiff's life: they are based on the notion of the "average man".[8] There is a two-fold answer to this. In the first place it must be of some value to know what the solution for the average man should be so that should the court decide to depart from

---

[1] *S.* v. *Distillers Co.*, [1969] 3 All E.R. 1412; *Taylor* v. *O'Connor*, [1971] A.C. 115; *Mitchell* v. *Mulholland* (*No.* 2), [1972] 1 Q.B. 65.

[2] American courts have predictably been more ready to admit actuarial evidence: Annotation 79 A.L.R. 2d. 27 § 2. In Australia the effect of such evidence on juries has caused some problems (e.g. *Robinson* (*Grafton*) *Pty.*, *Ltd.* v. *Carter* (1968), 41 A.L.J.R. 327) but judges seem generally more favourably disposed towards the actuary than their English counterparts: E.g. *Tiliakos* v. *Trikilis* (1969), 14 F.L.R. 406.

[3] See, e.g. *S.* v. *Distillers Co.*, *supra*.

[4] See especially *Fletcher* v. *Autocar and Transporters*, *supra*.

[5] [1971] A.C. 115, at p. 140. For other observations to the same effect see, in the same case, LORD MORRIS at p. 134 and LORD GUEST at p. 135; in *Fletcher's* case, *supra*, DIPLOCK, L.J. at pp. 346–347; in *Mitchell's* case, *supra*, EDMUND DAVIES, L.J. at p. 77 and WIDGERY, L.J. at pp. 82–83.

[6] *Supra*, p. 190.

[7] Prevett (1972), 35 M.L.R. 140, at p. 145.

[8] See, e.g. in *Mitchell's* case, *supra*, EDMUND DAVIES, L.J. at p. 77 and SIR GORDON WILLMER at pp. 85–86.

the norm it may know what the norm is. Secondly, the danger in ignoring the average is that the court may also ignore the fact that the "average" is calculated on bad cases as well as good, and that there exists the possibility that the uncertainties of life may turn out to favour just as much as to prejudice the plaintiff.[1]

(iv) *Conclusions*   The Law Commission has encouraged the increased use of actuarial techniques.[2]   The plaintiff should be "entitled to rely upon the evidence of actuaries and upon approved actuarial tables to an extent which the Court considers appropriate in the particular case."[3] On the basis of the arguments considered above, it does indeed seem desirable to pay greater heed to results achieved by actuarial methods. However there is one aspect of the matter which should not be forgotten. To employ individual actuaries on individual cases will increase both costs and delays.   In a system where civil procedure is based on the adversary theory, the resort by one party to actuarial evidence will frequently induce his opponent to do the same with the inevitable spiralling of costs.   It is submitted that unless an actuary is employed as a court official,[4] use of actuarial methods should be restricted to consultation of approved tables, the figures derived from which being then modifiable at the courts' discretion.

(f) Inflation[5]

It is obvious that damages must keep pace with inflation in the sense that awards in previous cases must be read subject to the declining value of money.[6]   The more difficult question is whether (and if so how) compensation for future loss should take into account predicted rates of inflation.   The common law systems have not yet formulated a definitive approach to the problem.   There would appear to be four possibilities.

(i) Future inflation can be disregarded entirely.[7]   Such a conclusion can be reached by strict adherence to a nominalist theory of damages awards[8] (the plaintiff is awarded the present "value" of his loss at the the time of judgment which must be expressed in the prevailing rate of currency) or by a harsh application of the doctrine of certainty: "we

---

[1] Cf. Sir Gordon Willmer, *ibid.*, at p. 86.
[2] Working Paper No. 41, paras. 174–176.
[3] *Ibid.*, para. 176.
[4] This could be accomplished more economically if, as has been suggested, (p. 10) a damages tribunal manned by a lawyer, a doctor and an actuary were to replace the ordinary court for the purpose of quantifying personal injury awards.
[5] Street, pp. 125–127;   Law Commission Working Paper No. 41, paras. 177–190;   Prevett (1972), 35 M.L.R. 140, at pp. 151–154.
[6] *Infra*, p. 212.
[7] E.g. *Warner* v. *Royal Mail Lines*, [1970] 2 Lloyd's Rep. 353.
[8] See Mann, *The Legal Aspect of Money* (3rd Edn.), pp. 103–114.

cannot know the way the world is going."[1] But neither approach would be sympathetically received by a plaintiff who finds that as a consequence of inflation his award of damages is insufficient to meet his needs.

(ii) At the other extreme, estimates of the plaintiff's loss of future income should be increased for each year by a percentage determined by an economist. This approach has been generally condemned by the courts.[2] There is a small body of opinion that holds that some direct allowance should be made for inflation,[3] but none would seem to welcome highly speculative evidence provided by an economist.[4]

(iii) The most popular view is that protection against future inflation should be sought in investment of the capital sum awarded: "experience of twenty years of inflation has shown that its effects can be offset to some extent at any rate by prudent investment in buying a home, in growth shares, or in the short-term high interest bearing securities."[5] In ordinary economic circumstances the level of inflation should be reflected in the returns on investment.[6] Allowance is made for inflation, on this view, in the process of capitalization of lost income. It will be recalled that a discount is made from the *prima facie* figure to allow for the advantage of receiving a capital sum instead of income.[7] The rate of discount is determinable according to the amount of interest accruing from investment of the capital sum. To guard against inflation, then, the discount should be made at a low rate, on the basis of the interest which would accrue on good growth securities rather than on those which were intended primarily to secure income.[8]

(iv) It should be observed, finally, that the problem of inflation is an acute one only within the context of a system committed to the lump-sum method of awards. Were a periodical payment system to be introduced,[9] the payments could be linked to a cost-of-living index.

---

[1] *Per* DIPLOCK, L.J., *Fletcher* v. *Autocar and Transporters*, [1968] 2 Q.B. 322, at p. 348.
[2] *Mallett* v. *McMonagle*, [1970] A.C. 166; *S.* v. *Distillers Co.*, [1970] 3 All E.R. 1412; *Mitchell* v. *Mulholland (No. 2)*, [1972] 1 Q.B. 65; *Gray* v. *Deakin*, [1964] N.Z.L.R. 852; *O'Brien* v. *McKean* (1968), 42 A.L.J.R. 223; *Tzouvelis* v. *Victorian Railways Commissioners*, [1968] V.R. 112.
[3] E.g. *Taylor* v. *O'Connor*, [1971] A.C. 115, *per* LORD REID, at pp. 129–130.
[4] *S.* v. *Distillers Co.*, *supra*; *Mitchell's* case, *supra*.
[5] *Per* LORD DIPLOCK, *Mallett* v. *McMonagle*, *supra*, at p. 175. See also LORD PEARSON in *Taylor* v. *O'Connor*, *supra*, at pp. 144–145.
[6] *Per* SIR GORDON WILLMER, *Mitchell's* case, *supra*, at p. 87. Cf. in 1970 though prices went up, the capital value of securities fell: Law Commission Working Paper No. 41, para. 189.
[7] *Supra*, p. 189.
[8] See LORD DIPLOCK's analysis in *Mallett* v. *McMonagle*, *supra*, at pp. 175–176. Allowance must be made for tax payable on the income: *Taylor* v. *O'Connor*, *infra*, p. 271.
[9] Cf. *supra*, pp. 12–14.

IV NON-PECUNIARY LOSSES

1 Introduction

(a) Recoverability of non-pecuniary losses

A man who is physically injured in an accident will generally lose
more than mere pecuniary advantages. He may lose the function of a
part of his body. He may be permanently or temporarily disfigured.
He may have experienced pain and suffering. His enjoyment of life
may be impaired by the consequences of his injuries. The task of
compensating these aspects of personal injuries is highly problematical.
But it has never been questioned that in English law the plaintiff should
recover compensation for his non-pecuniary losses. In one of the
first cases to be reported on the measure of damages for personal
injuries,[1] COCKBURN, C.J. propounded the rule that in assessing compensation,

> "the jury should take into account two things: first, the pecuniary loss
> (the plaintiff) sustains by his accident; secondly, the injury he sustains
> in his person, or his physical capacity of enjoying life."[2]

(b) Basis of compensation for non-pecuniary losses

Although compensation for pecuniary losses poses problems of some
technical difficulty, the basis of assessment has always been clear: the
award seeks to put him in the *economic* position he would have been in
but for the accident. *Ex hypothesi*, compensation on this restitutionary
basis is impossible in the case of non-pecuniary losses. The court
cannot order that the defendant redeliver to the plaintiff the leg or eye
which he has lost. Mental pain and anguish which he has suffered
cannot be obliterated. Years cannot be added to a life which has been
irretrievably shortened. *Restitutio in integrum*, in its ordinary sense,
is impossible. This has led one judge to the extreme of saying that the
remedy should not really be called "damages".[3] Whatever be its correct appellation it is clear that the remedy exists and that some basis
for its assessment must be found.

The judges are, in general, hesitant to venture beyond the "principle"
that the task of the court (judge or jury) is to award "fair and reasonable
compensation". For example, it has been said that

> "damages must be real and amount to what the ordinary, reasonable
> man would regard as fair and sensible compensation for the injuries
> suffered."[4]

---

[1] *Fair* v. *London and North Western Rail Co.* (1869), 21 L.T. 326.
[2] *Ibid.*, at p. 327. See also *Phillips* v. *London and South Western Rail Co.*
(1878), 4 Q.B.D. 406 affirmed (1879), 5 Q.B.D. 78 and (1879), 5 C.P.D. 280.
[3] *Per* HARMAN, L.J., *Warren* v. *King*, [1964] 1 W.L.R. 1, at p. 9.
[4] *Per* SALMON, L.J., *Gardner* v. *Dyson*, [1967] 1 W.L.R. 1497, at p. 1501.
Among many other statements to the same effect see e.g., BRETT, J. in *Rowley*

Not only is this vague criterion of little help in actually determining on a figure, but it offers no assistance on the more fundamental problem as to what is to be the general basis of assessment. As DIPLOCK, L.J. has said, "the rational principles upon which damages . . . are to be assessed . . . tend . . . to be obscured by familiar phrases which lawyers use but seldom pause to analyse."[1] What then are the "rational principles?" What object is to be pursued in the award of damages for non-pecuniary losses? Three approaches may be distinguished.

(i) *Conceptual approach* The first approach is conceptual and objective. It has its analogy in property injury cases. The plaintiff's life, his faculties, his capacity for enjoying life, his freedom from pain and suffering are all "value" personal assets, akin to his house, his shares or his china vase. To deprive him of one or more of these assets is to deprive him of something to which he has a "proprietary right". Each asset bears an objective "value" which is fully recoverable in the case of loss, even if the plaintiff is unaware of his loss.[2]

(ii) *Personal approach* The second approach rejects the premise on which the conceptual approach is based, that human life and the human personality can be "valued" independently of an individual's feelings. Measurement can only be made in terms of human happiness. An award for non-pecuniary losses should not therefore attempt to ascertain the objective "value" of what the plaintiff has lost—it should seek to assess in monetary terms his past, present and future loss of pleasure and happiness.[3]

(iii) *Functional approach* The third approach adopts the premise of the personal approach, that the sole concern of the court is with the plaintiff's pleasure or happiness, but it prescribes a different standard of compensation. Damages for non-pecuniary loss may be justified only to the extent that they might effectively be employed to provide the plaintiff with some measure of consolation. The court, therefore, should not attempt to set a "value" on the loss of happiness. It should instead award the plaintiff such a sum as might be used to provide him with reasonable solace for his misfortunes.[4]

In short, the differences between these approaches may be summarized by asserting that the award is measured in (i) by the extent of *the*

---

v. *London and North Western Rail Co.*, (1873), L.R. 8 Ex. 221, at p. 231; ORMEROD, L.J. in *Scott* v. *Musial*, [1959] 2 Q.B. 429, at p. 443.

[1] *Wise* v. *Kay*, [1962] 1 Q.B. 638, at pp. 663–664.

[2] See the description of this approach by LORD DEVLIN in *West & Son* v. *Shephard*, [1964] A.C. 326, at p. 355 and the opinions of LORD MORRIS and LORD PEARCE in that case.

[3] DIPLOCK, L.J. in *Wise* v. *Kay, supra*, at pp. 663–676; LORDS REID and DEVLIN in *West* v. *Shephard, supra*, at pp. 340–343, 353–363.

[4] See, e.g. WINDEYER, J. in *Teubner* v. *Humble* (1963), 108 C.L.R. 491, at p. 507.

injury, in (ii) by the extent of *the loss of happiness* and in (iii) by the extent to which *money can provide the plaintiff reasonable solace*. The application of these approaches to the heads of damages for non-pecuniary loss will be considered in the appropriate context.

(c) Heads of damages for non-pecuniary losses

Compensation for non-pecuniary loss is always awarded by way of general damages. The general practice of the courts is not to sub-divide the award under the various heads of non-pecuniary loss.[1] It is therefore impossible to state with absolute certainty the types of non-pecuniary loss which might be taken into account. Further, the classi-fication of heads of damages must to a certain extent depend on which of the theoretical approaches outlined above is adopted. Thus, for example, to be wholly consistent with the conceptual approach, the loss of a faculty (e.g. the loss of a limb) must be distinguished from loss of amenities (i.e. deprivation of the use of the lost limb). On the personal approach, on the other hand, it might well be argued that all non-pecuniary losses constitute a loss in happiness which, for the pur-poses of assessment, cannot be treated differently from pain and suffering. Nevertheless it has been found convenient to consider the modes of assessment under the three conventional heads: (A) pain and suffering/inconvenience; (B) loss of expectation of life; (C) loss of faculties/loss of amenities. These will be examined in turn.

2   Pain and suffering—inconvenience

(a) Theoretical approaches

The plaintiff has, as a result of his injuries, been subjected to pain and suffering. Those favouring the conceptual and personal approaches will reach a similar conclusion. The plaintiff is to be awarded sub-stantial damages, on the conceptual view because he has been deprived of one of his personal assets, freedom from pain, on the personal view because the injury has directly given rise to a loss of happiness of which the plaintiff is keenly aware. Those adopting the functional approach might, however, draw a distinction between past and future pain. It might be argued that no award should be made for past suffering, since the monetary payment of damage could in no way alleviate the plain-tiff's grievance. In contrast, a substantial award should be made in the case of future suffering, to give the plaintiff as much solace and recompense as money might buy. But such a distinction would provoke

---

[1] E.g. *Watson* v. *Powles*, [1968] 1 Q.B. 596; cf. *Hett* v. *W. and C. French*, [1971] C.L.Y. 3250.

the formidable objection that it would encourage the defendant to delay proceedings as much as possible.

(b) Scope of award

It has always been clear that in English law the plaintiff is to be compensated for pain and suffering, past, present and future.[1] But it is not automatically added to any award for personal injuries. There must be "clear evidence of reasonably prolonged suffering."[2]

Compensation under this head has also been extended to cases of physical discomfort or inconvenience even where no actual physical injury has been sustained. Thus in *Bailey* v. *Bullock*,[3] as a result of the defendant solicitor's negligence in failing to take proper steps to evict tenants from the plaintiff's premises, the plaintiff and his family had for two years been living in uncomfortable circumstances. £300 was awarded for "discomfort and inconvenience".

It seems, however, that recovery does not encompass cases of mental suffering which do not have their origin in some physical or physiological injury. In *Bailey* v. *Bullock*,[3] the trial judge laid great stress on the fact that he was compensating for *physical* inconvenience and not for mental distress. In *Hinz* v. *Berry*[4] the plaintiff suffered nervous shock while witnessing an accident in which her husband was killed and her two children were injured. For some considerable time thereafter she was in a state of mental depression. The award of £4000 for her condition was upheld by the Court of Appeal. Mental depression was a recognizable psychiatric illness and as such was distinguishable from mere "sorrow and grief" for which the plaintiff would not have recovered.

It is submitted that this distinction between "sorrow and grief" on the one hand and "psychiatric illness" on the other is difficult not only to maintain in practice but also to justify in theory.[5] It is, of course, a consequence of the common law's reluctance to award damages for *solatium*.[6] But why, it may be asked, does the law offer relief to a plaintiff who grieves selfishly over his own misfortunes but not to one whose anxiety is caused by the fate of another? Does it rest on a tacit assumption that mental distress unaccompanied by some physical or

---

[1] *Heaps* v. *Perrité*, [1937] 2 All E.R. 60.
[2] *Per* HODSON, J., *Bishop* v. *Cunard White Star*, [1950] P. 240, at p. 247.
[3] [1950] 2 All E.R. 1167.
[4] [1970] 2 Q.B. 40; see also *Lucy* v. *Mariehamns Rederi*, [1971] 2 Lloyd's Rep. 314.
[5] In *Cutts* v. *Chumley*, [1967] 2 All E.R. 89, the distinction clearly did not appeal to WILLIS, J. who was not deterred from awarding substantial damages for pain and suffering by the fact that the plaintiff's mental anguish was unaccompanied by bodily pain.
[6] But see now *Jarvis* v. *Swans Tours, Ltd.*, [1973] 1 All E.R. 71, *infra*, p. 309.

physiological disorder is somehow unreal? Or is it provoked by the fear that admittance of the claim would give rise to vexatious litigation? Neither proposition seems to be borne out by the available evidence. Advances in psychological studies deny the validity of the first assumption,[1] while the second must succumb to the experience in Scotland where damages for *solatium* have for a long time been available without any noticeably embarrassing consequence.[2]

(c) Mode of assessment

The task of assessing damages for pain and suffering is typical of those involved with imponderable and intangible losses. Consistently with either the conceptual or the personal approaches the courts attempt to quantify the intensity and duration of the plaintiff's distress. Although efforts are being directed towards a scientific evaluation of this phenomenon,[3] under existing conditions it is clear that no real criterion for measurement exists, and the court must perforce derive guidance solely from the standard level of awards in comparable cases. A practitioners' manual[4] keeps judges informed of recent awards and the Court of Appeal may interfere if it considers that a figure is totally inconsistent with the general level of awards.[5] A general consideration of the "conventional award" method of assessment will be offered in relation to loss of amenities.[6]

(d) Critique

Damages for pain and suffering can hardly be assessed on any scientific basis. There is no method of objectively assessing pain. Everything must depend on evidence both of the victim himself and his medical attendants. But how does one translate linguistic concepts like "very severe" or "harrowing" pain into monetary units? How can we relate what medical opinion means by "severe pain" to what the victim, or the man on the Clapham omnibus describe as "severe pain"? There are no answers to such awkward questions. In the United States of America where jury trials still greatly persist and where awards are notoriously capricious, attempts have been made to find a more objective basis for assessment.[7] As indicative of the futility of most of these attempts, two suggested approaches may be briefly described.

---

[1] Smith (1943), 30 Virg. L.R. 192.
[2] See generally Walker, *Law of Damages in Scotland*, pp. 579–580.
[3] Olender, [1962] Duke L.J. 344, at pp. 360–366.
[4] Kemp & Kemp, *The Quantum of Damages*, Vol. 1 (3rd Edn.). Details of personal injury awards are also to be found in Current Law.
[5] E.g. *Crawford* v. *Erection and Engineering Services* (1953), C.A. No. 254, Kemp & Kemp, Vol. 1 (2nd Edn.), p. 684, damages for pain and suffering reduced from £1000 to £500.
[6] *Infra*, pp. 214–215.
[7] See, e.g. Plant (1958), 19 Ohio S.L.J. 200; Olender, [1962] Duke L.J., 344.

(i) *Per diem approach* In some jurisdictions, an approach based on awarding a fixed amount for each period of pain and suffering is favoured. Thus in *Imperial Oil* v. *Drlik*[1] the following formula was approved by the U.S. Court of Appeals: $100 a day for the first month following the accident, $50 a day for the second month, $20 a day for the next four months, and $100 a month for the balance of life expectancy. In other jurisdictions the approach has been rejected. The objections are clear. The method proceeds from the assumption that severity of pain and suffering (and thus the element primarily to be compensated for) lies chiefly in its temporal aspect. Secondly, its objective arithmetical process has no rational foundation on which to rest. The figures chosen for the calculation are as arbitrary as those reached by any other method: "to permit a *per diem* evaluation of pain, suffering and disability would plunge the already subjective determination into absurdity by demanding accurate mathematical computation of the present worth of an amount reached by guesswork."[2]

(ii) *Barter approach* Almost universally condemned is the process by which the jury (or the court) is invited to consider what sum would have been sufficient to induce a reasonable person voluntarily to submit to the pain experienced by the plaintiff, or what it would cost to hire someone to undergo such suffering.[3] The defect (among others) of this method lies in its assumption that "market conditions" are in any way relevant to the assessment of non-pecuniary losses. To attempt to ascertain the monetary "value" of what the plaintiff has suffered, and award that sum by way of damages presupposes that the object of this award is to return to the plaintiff what he has lost, but as has already been indicated, in the context of non-pecuniary losses, *restitutio in integrum* cannot be applied. Furthermore, the notion that the willingness to submit to pain and suffering has a "market value" is of course, wholly artificial. The "barter" method, applied to pain and suffering, depends entirely on an instinctive emotive response.

It is arguable that the only non-pecuniary loss for which a plaintiff should recover compensation is pain and suffering: that is to say, that the basis of loss of amenities and loss of expectation of life is mental pain and anguish. If this view is accepted, there should be no special award for pain and suffering, but all non-pecuniary loss should be assessed according to the principles discussed under loss of amenities.[4]

---

[1] 234 F.(2d) 4 (1956).
[2] *Per* CHRISTIANSON, J., *Ahlstron* v. *Minneapolis Ste. M.R. Co.*, 68 N.W. (2d) 873, at p. 891 (1955).
[3] *Baker* v. *Pennsylvania Co.*, 21 A. 979 (1891).
[4] *Infra*, pp. 206–218.

3 Loss of expectation of life[1]

(a) Introduction

A serious physical injury may have the effect of shortening a man's expectation of life on earth. Should the victim be entitled to compensation for this loss as a separate head of damages? The answer to this question will vary according to the theoretical approach to compensation which is adopted.

(i) According to the *conceptual* approach, a man is entitled as of right to his natural span of years on earth.

> "A man has a legal right in his own life . . . a legal right that his life should not be shortened by the tortious act of another. . . . His normal expectancy of life is a thing of temporal value, so that its impairment is something for which damages should be given."[2]

It should follow from this view that damages should be awarded on the basis of the number of years of life of which the plaintiff has been deprived.

(ii) On the *personal* view, the only loss for which compensation is appropriate is loss of happiness. To the situation in which an individual's life is shortened, it would seem that, on the basis of this view, two alternative reactions are possible. First, as in the conceptual approach, it might be maintained that an individual has a right to his normal span of years, but that, in compensating for any impairment of that right, the court should have regard only to the amount of happiness which has been lost. This is the approach at present adopted by English law as expressed in the House of Lords decision in *Benham* v. *Gambling*.[3] Alternatively, the argument based on the pleasure/pain axis could be extended further, so that the plaintiff should be compensated only for unhappiness which he actually experiences. After his life has ended, there is no empirical evidence to show that he may experience either happiness or unhappiness. The court must confine its activity to compensating unhappiness actually experienced during the plaintiff's lifetime. Thus the only compensatable element of loss, on this view, is the grief and anguish suffered in apprehension of the early curtailment of life. In other words, damages for loss of expectation of life should be nothing more than an addition to the award for pain and suffering.[4]

(iii) The *functional* approach would, for the most part, coincide with this last approach, but the argument would be taken a step further.

---

[1] Kahn-Freund (1941), 5 M.L.R. 81.
[2] *Per* LORD WRIGHT, *Rose* v. *Ford*, [1937] A.C. 826, at pp. 847–848.
[3] [1941] A.C. 157, *infra*, pp. 201–205.
[4] ROCHE, L.J. in *Flint* v. *Lovell*, [1935] 1 K.B. 354, at pp. 366–367.

To recover damages under this head, the plaintiff must show not only that he has suffered or will suffer from grief at the prospect of an early ending to his life, but also that a reasonable sum of money spent for his own benefit would provide him with solace.

(b) Case-law developments to 1941

Substantial damages were awarded under this head for the first time in *Flint* v. *Lovell*[1]

P aged 70, with a life expectation of 8 to 9 years was seriously injured as a result of which he was not expected to live for longer than another year. In approving an award of £4000 general damages, the majority of the Court of Appeal held that the trial judge had rightly taken into account the shortening of life as a separate head of damages. ROCHE, L.J. expressing some doubt as to this view, was of the opinion that the only legitimate ground for compensation was the loss of happiness arising from the prospect of an earlier death.

It seems therefore that whereas the majority, in this case, adopted the conceptual approach, ROCHE, L.J. preferred the second personal approach.

In *Rose* v. *Ford*[2] in a case where a woman, aged 20 had died shortly after being injured in a road accident, two questions came to be decided by the House of Lords: (i) whether *Flint* v. *Lovell* had been correctly decided, and (ii) whether it should be extended to an action by a personal representative suing on behalf of the dead victim's estate under the Law Reform (Miscellaneous Provisions) Act 1934.[3] Both questions were unanimously answered in the affirmative. *Flint* v. *Lovell* was approved in terms appropriate only to the conceptual approach.[4] Even LORD ROCHE, since promoted to the higher court, abandoned the view he had expressed in *Flint* v. *Lovell*.[5]

(c) *Benham* v. *Gambling* and its interpretation

In *Rose* v. *Ford* LORD ROCHE had confessed to an "apprehension lest this element of damage may now assume a frequency and a prominence in litigation far greater than is warranted in fact, and becoming common form may result in the inflation of damages in undeserving cases. . . ."[6] By the time the House of Lords came to re-examine the

---

[1] [1935] I K.B. 354.
[2] [1937] A.C. 826.
[3] On this aspect of the case see *supra*, pp. 118–119.
[4] See in particular the opinions of LORD WRIGHT (*ibid.*, at pp. 840–853) an extract from which has been quoted above (p. 200), and LORD RUSSELL (*ibid.*, at pp. 836–840).
[5] *Ibid.*, at pp. 853–854, 858–859.
[6] [1937] A.C. 826, at pp. 861–862.

question some four years later,[1] it was apparent that his fear had been justified. The head of damages had figured dramatically in a number of cases decided in the interim.[2] Four figure sums had been awarded for this item alone.[3] Two important modifications to the existing law were made in *Benham* v. *Gambling*.[4] First, the House of Lords shifted the basis of calculation from the arithmetical objective conception of the number of years lost to the subjective conception of the loss of prospective happiness:

> "the thing to be valued is not the prospect of length of days, but the prospect of a predominantly happy life."[5]

Secondly, it laid down that in quantifying this loss

> "very moderate figures should be chosen . . . a lower standard of measurement than has hitherto prevailed. . . ."[6]

In the actual case an award for an infant of two and a half years was reduced from £1200 to £200.

It is now proposed to examine in greater detail points arising from the decision in *Benham* v. *Gambling* as seen in the light of subsequent case-law.

(i) *Nature of approach*   There has been a marked difference of judicial opinion as to the approach to the problem of quantification laid down in *Benham* v. *Gambling*. Some judges have pointed to the first proposition, that the court must look to the "prospect of happiness" and argued that it thereby envisaged a subjective approach.[7] Others preferred to stress the second proposition and asserted that, as an objective measure (£200) was formulated by the House of Lords, the decision in effect brought to an end any investigation into "happiness".[8] In fact, the correct view would seem to be that the approach is both subjective and objective at the same time.[9] Certainly the basis of the award is the

---

[1] *Benham* v. *Gambling*, [1941] A.C. 157.
[2] *Trubyfield* v. *Great Western Rail Co.*, [1937] 4 All E.R. 614; *Morgan* v. *Scoulding*, [1938] 1 K.B. 786; *Roach* v. *Yates*, [1938] 1 K.B. 256; *The Aizkarai Mendi*, [1938] P. 263; *Mills* v. *Stanway Coaches*, [1940] 2 K.B. 334.
[3] *Turbeyfield's* case, *supra*, £1500; *Morgan* v. *Scoulding*, *supra*, £1000; *Mills* v. *Stanway Coaches*, *supra*, £1000.
[4] [1941] A.C. 157.
[5] *Per* LORD SIMON, *ibid.*, at p. 166.
[6] *Per* LORD SIMON, *ibid.*, at p. 168.
[7] E.g. DIPLOCK, L.J. in *Wise* v. *Kay*, [1962] 1 Q.B. 638, at pp. 666–667; LORD MORRIS in *Yorkshire Electricity Board* v. *Naylor*, [1968] A.C. 529, at pp. 544–545.
[8] E.g. SELLERS, L.J. in *Wise* v. *Kay*, [1962] 1 Q.B. 638, at pp. 648–651; KITTO, J. in *Skelton* v. *Collins* (1966), 115 C.L.R. 94, at pp. 97–98.
[9] See, especially, SALMON, L.J. in *Naylor* v. *Yorkshire Electricity Board*, [1967] 1 Q.B. 244, at pp. 256–261 and on appeal, *sub nom. Yorkshire Electricity Board* v. *Naylor*, [1968] A.C. 529, at pp. 548–550.

subjective concept of the happiness of the individual, and this will vary from case to case, but the courts must have an objective figure to serve as a "prototype" from which they can depart where the circumstances require it.[1] This is none other than the first personal approach, as described above: a theoretical basis in the subjective element of "happiness" but an objective conception of an individual's right to the happiness which the enjoyment of a full and normal life should bring him.

(ii) *Living plaintiff or survival action* It has been widely recognized[2] that an important factor which persuaded the House of Lords to arrive at the low figure of £200 was the fact that, as in *Rose* v. *Ford*,[3] the victim had died and the plaintiffs were his personal representatives. A large windfall to the undeserving successors was, if possible, to be avoided. But was the conventional award to be regarded as appropriate where the plaintiff was still living at the time of the action? It is, perhaps, possible, though strained, to interpret the words of Viscount Simon as recognizing the distinction between the dead and living victim,[4] but subsequent decisions have uniformly suppressed attempts to increase the award on the ground that the plaintiff was still living.[5]

(iii) *Quantification of "prospect of happiness"* As has already been indicated, subject to the age ((iv) *infra*) and currency ((v) *infra*) factors, the figure laid down in *Benham* v. *Gambling* has been the conventional award for the loss of expectation of life, to be departed from only in exceptional circumstances. Indeed, one judge, apparently, would be prepared to make the award even more mechanical: "it would lead to highly desirable certainty . . . if judges listened in silence to argument, and simply awarded £500 without giving any reasons at all."[6] Others have not so readily disposed of the assessment of "happiness". Thus in *Hart* v. *Griffiths-Jones*,[7] the trial judge took into account that the father of the victim—a child aged four—was a hawker and would have had some difficulty in looking after the child, had it survived. In *Burns* v. *Edman*,[8] there was evidence that for some years previous to his death the victim had involved himself in criminal activities and Crighton, J.

---

[1] It appears that the courts will only be prepared to depart from the conventional figure in exceptional circumstances. See (iii), *infra*.
[2] E.g. Sellers, L.J. in *Wise* v. *Kay*, *supra*, at pp. 647–648 and Lord Devlin in *Yorkshire Electricity Board* v. *Naylor*, *supra*, at p. 550.
[3] [1937] A.C. 826.
[4] At [1941] A.C. 157, at p. 168, he observes that "stripped of technicalities the compensation is not being given to the person who was injured."
[5] *Oliver* v. *Ashman*, [1962] 2 Q.B. 210, at p. 231; *Wise* v. *Kay*, [1962] 1 Q.B. 638, at pp. 648–649; *Yorkshire Electricity Board* v. *Naylor*, [1968] A.C. 529.
[6] Per Russell, L.J., *Cain* v. *Wilcock*, [1968] 1 W.L.R. 1961, at p. 1966.
[7] [1948] 2 All E.R. 729.
[8] [1970] 2 Q.B. 541.

felt himself "entitled to take judicial notice of the fact that the life of a criminal is an unhappy one."[1] Any attempt, however, to base the assessment of "happiness" on any rational criteria founders on encountering the rule propounded in *Benham* v. *Gambling* that for the purposes of an award for the loss of expectation of life the future financial and social circumstances of the victim are to be ignored: "lawyers and judges may here join hands with moralists and philosophers and declare that the degree of happiness to be attained by a human being does not depend on wealth or status."[2] Clearly, if the rule were otherwise, there would be a danger of overlap between pecuniary and non-pecuniary loss, but if such factors as financial or social status (which most people would admit to being important inducements to happiness)[3] are to be ignored, then it would seem that the law has at once abandoned the possibility of rational quantification.

(iv) *Age of victim*   In rejecting the arithmetical approach based on the number of years of life lost and in establishing a conventional sum, the House of Lords did not go so far as to suggest that the age of the victim was totally irrelevant. Indeed Viscount Simon made clear that the appropriate figure for a very young child whose future was uncertain should not necessarily apply to an adult of "settled prospects."[4] The House of Lords, in its most recent review of this head of damages, considered that the conventional figure as laid down in *Benham* v. *Gambling* (subject to modification for the decline in the value of money) was to be regarded as the norm and only to be departed from in cases of definite abnormality.[5] Such cases would exist where the victim was an infant not yet past the risk of childhood,[6] or at the other end of the life span, where his prospect of years was most significantly reduced.[7]

(v) *Decline in value of money*   It is clear that if a conventional sum is to be the norm, then it must consistently respond to any changes in the value of the currency in which it is expressed. This has always been

---

[1] *Ibid.*, at p. 546.
[2] Per VISCOUNT SIMON, [1941] A.C. 157, at p. 167.
[3] Kahn-Freund (1941), 5 M.L.R. 81, at pp. 95–96.
[4] [1941] A.C. 157, at p. 167.
[5] *Yorkshire Electricity Board* v. *Naylor*, [1968] A.C. 529, at pp. 544–545, 547, 549.
[6] *Ibid.*, at p. 545 (LORD MORRIS), at p. 547 (LORD GUEST) and at p. 548 (LORD DEVLIN). This factor effectively reduced the award in *Hart* v. *Griffiths-Jones*, [1948] 2 All E.R. 729 (child aged 4 years); *Oliver* v. *Ashman*, [1962] 2 Q.B. 210 (child aged 20 months) and *Cain* v. *Wilcock*, [1968] 3 All E.R. 817 (child aged 2½ years).
[7] [1968] A.C. 529, at p. 549. Damages were reduced on this ground in *Mortiboys* v. *Skinner*, [1952] 2 Lloyd's Rep. 95 ("early 60s") and *Stanton* v. *Youlden*, [1960] 1 All E.R. 429 ("late 60s").

recognized by the courts.[1] Thus in 1967 the normative figure of £200 established in *Benham* v. *Gambling* had risen to £500.[2]

(d) Critique

Any principle of law which attempts to set a price on such imponderables as "life" and "happiness" can hardly fail to provoke serious criticism. Thus, it has been persuasively argued that, "in assuming the task of measuring the value of life, or of 'happiness' in terms of money, the law has transgressed the boundaries of its province."[3] The present position adopted by English law is open to attack on several fronts.

(i) *Legal interests in life expectancy* The primary assault may be directed against the law's partial adherence to the conceptual approach, as a result of which recover for "lost years" is allowed. It may be argued that a person has no "proprietary right" to his full life span of "three score and ten" years,[4] that the law can compensate the victim of an accident only for a loss which he has actually suffered or will actually suffer. The law can hardly take cognizance of losses suffered at a metaphysical or intangible level. It cannot be said that, in a *material* sense, the victim *suffers* a loss where he is deprived of a number of years on earth. He will not be living to appreciate his loss. On this view, compensation should be directed only to the loss of happiness produced by awareness of a shortened life.[5]

(ii) *Recovery by estate* At the very least, it might be argued, this head of damages should not be available where the victim has died before the commencement of the action. To allow the beneficiaries of the victim's estate to recover for what was, at best, a dubious loss, seems repugnant to common sense.[6]

(iii) *Quantification of award* Even if the objections to the availability of the award are overreached, the method of quantifying the award may be criticized. The *Benham* v. *Gambling* rule stipulating a conventional award is a compromise between the objective (conceptual) and the subjective (personal) approaches, and is truly consistent with neither. If

---

[1] E.g. *Hart* v. *Griffiths-Jones, supra*; *Wise* v. *Kay*, [1962] 1 Q.B. 638; *Yorkshire Electricity Board* v. *Naylor, supra*.

[2] *Andrews* v. *Freeborough*, [1967] 1 Q.B. 1; *Yorkshire Electricity Board* v. *Naylor, supra*.

[3] Kahn-Freund, *loc. cit.*, p. 87.

[4] Psalms, xc. 10.

[5] As *per* ROCHE, L.J. in *Flint* v. *Lovell*, [1935] 1 K.B. 354, at pp. 366–367.

[6] The Law Commission has suggested (Working Paper No. 41, para. 66) that damages for loss of expectation of life should not survive for the benefit of the estate. For the effect of non-pecuniary losses in survival actions generally, see *supra*, pp. 118–119.

the objective view were to be adopted, then the calculation would be based on the number of years lost. If the subjective view were to prevail, then the necessary inquiry into loss of happiness would, rationally, require an investigation into the victim's social and financial circumstances. As has been shown, the law, at present, adopts neither position and is, in theory at least, difficult to justify. In practice, on the other hand, since the loss itself is so questionable and obscure, there is much to be said for the adoption of a small conventional sum and on this ground LORD DEVLIN's suggestion[1] that the legislature should fix a sum to be applied in all cases is worthy of support.

4 Loss of faculties—loss of amenities[2]

(a) Introduction

The third type of non-pecuniary loss which may arise from personal injuries has been variously described as "the injury itself", "loss of faculties" or "loss of amenities".[3] The object of the award is to compensate the plaintiff for the physical disability sustained as a result of the accident, and the effect of that disability on his enjoyment of life.

Again it will be useful to begin by contrasting the possible theoretical approaches in this head of damages.

(i) *Conceptual approach* The exponent of the first approach would hold that each part of the body has an objective value the loss or impairment of which entitles the plaintiff to a substantial sum, quite independently of any consequent loss of happiness.[4] A tariff system can then be adopted which would prescribe a certain sum for each part of the body, and the extent of injury to each part. This method of compensation was in force over a thousand years ago in the laws of King Alfred.[5]

(ii) *Personal approach* According to the second view, the calculation

---

[1] *Yorkshire Electricity Board* v. *Naylor*, [1968] A.C. 529, at p. 550 and cf. Law Commission, *loc. cit.*, paras. 59–64.

[2] This section closely follows an article published by the author in (1972), 35 M.L.R. 1.

[3] Street, pp. 62–67, lists as separate heads (i) loss of amenities, (ii) loss or impairment of physiological functions, (iii) loss or impairment of anatomical structures. Such distinctions are elusive both in theory and in practice, and have never been recognized by the courts.

[4] See, especially, SELLERS, L.J. in *Wise* v. *Kay*, [1962] 1 Q.B. 638 at pp. 644–654 and LORD MORRIS in *West & Son* v. *Shephard*, [1964] A.C. 326, at pp. 344–353.

[5] Ed. Thorpe, *Ancient Laws and Institutes of England*, pp. 93–101. Specimen examples of the "bot" payable: broken arm above the elbow, 15s; loss of thumb, 30s.; loss of arm below elbow, 80s.

should be based entirely on the loss of happiness resulting from the physical disability.[1] Three important consequences follow: in marked contrast to the conceptual approach (I) the right to compensation under this head would not pass to the injured party's survivors on death; (II) the plaintiff would recover nothing in circumstances in which he was unaware of his loss (e.g. he remained in a state of unconsciousness until his death); (III) "loss of amenities" so interpreted would be merely an extension of the award for pain and suffering; both at root depend on loss of pleasure.

(iii) *Functional approach*   As with other non-pecuniary losses, the functional approach adopts the premise of the personal approach but directs it to a different conclusion. The plaintiff should receive such a sum of money as will provide him with reasonable solace for the loss of pleasure resulting from the physical disability.[2]

The English law on this subject is not perfectly consistent with any of these approaches, but as will be seen from the ensuing discussion, it has a strong leaning towards the conceptual approach.

(b)   Method of quantification

There is, of course, no logical objective basis for expressing a non-pecuniary loss in pecuniary terms. "No money can compensate for the loss. Yet compensation has to be given in money. The problem is insoluble."[3] How then has the law been able to lay down principles to accommodate this problematic situation?

(i) *Fair and reasonable compensation*   When, towards the end of the nineteenth century it was put beyond doubt that damages for non-pecuniary loss might properly be awarded,[4] the only guidance to quantification offered by the court was that the sum should be "fair and reasonable compensation" for the injury sustained.[5] Used predominantly in directions to juries, this vague and all-embracing formula was but an attempt to conceal the fact that the law lacked any yardstick whereby damages could be assessed. That the formula was an empty

---

[1] See, especially, the dissenting judgment of DIPLOCK, L.J. in *Wise* v. *Kay*, *supra*, at pp. 663–676, and LORDS REID and DEVLIN in *West* v. *Shephard*, *supra*, at pp. 340–343, 353–363.
[2] Traces of this approach are to be found *per* LORD DEVLIN in *West* v. *Shephard*, *supra*, n. 1 and *per* LORD DENNING, M.R. and DIPLOCK, L.J. in *Fletcher* v. *Autocar and Transporters, Ltd.*, [1968] 2 Q.B. 322, at pp. 336, 352. Its most unequivocal advocate, however, has been the Australian High Court judge WINDEYER, J. See, especially, *Skelton* v. *Collins* (1966), 115 C.L.R. 94, at pp. 130–133.
[3] *Per* LORD DENNING, M.R., *Ward* v. *James*, [1966] 1 Q.B. 273, at p. 296.
[4] *Phillips* v. *London and South Western Rail Co.* (1879), 4 Q.B.D. 406 affirmed 5 Q.B.D. 78.
[5] *Per* COCKBURN, C.J. (1879), 4 Q.B.D. 406, at p. 408.

shell, without any substance, is aptly illustrated by PAULL, J.'s direction to the jury in *Scott* v. *Musial*.[1]

> "It is not going to be a grossly extravagant sum in the sense that you would say: 'I would not have that happen to me for a million pounds'. . . . Obviously it is not going to be a small sum, but, of course, not absurdly extravagant. . . . You must take some sum which you think is reasonable for the defendant to pay and for the plaintiff to receive, and I can help you no further than that."

(ii) *Conventional awards—the "pragmatic solution"*   In England jury trials of personal injury actions have almost completely disappeared.[2] The predictable result has been that level of awards have become standardized.   The judiciary have ready access to current sizes of awards in all cases of personal injuries.[3]   The courts soon began to abandon their appeal to the fiction of "fair and reasonable compensation".   It was frankly recognized that in dealing with the incommensurables of non-pecuniary losses, "the courts are compelled to make a pragmatic solution. They have done so by fixing an arbitrary standard of monetary compensation."[4] Uniformity and predictability of compensation can only be achieved by reference to an empirical scale of awards[5] which is derived from "the general consensus of opinion of judges trying these cases."[6] Thus by consulting the standard reference works, a judge, or indeed a legal adviser, can obtain a rough guide as to the kind of sums awarded for all types of personal injury conditions from minor burns to multiple brain injuries, and make his estimate accordingly.[7]

From the theoretical standpoint, the question then arises as to whether the present English practice is nothing more than a return to the Anglo–Saxon concept of "bot" whereby each part of the body had an objective "value" which the defendant should offer as compensation should he deprive the plaintiff of the use or enjoyment of it[8]—whether, indeed, the English approach to loss of amenities is purely "conceptual".
To answer this question, the pragmatic approach must be subjected to

---

[1] [1959] 2 Q.B. 429, at p. 432. The appeal against the jury's award was dismissed.
[2] In 1965 it was estimated that jury trials were ordered in only about 2 per cent. of personal injury cases: *Ward* v. *James*, [1966] 1 Q.B. 273, at p. 290. The figure today must be even smaller.
[3] See, *supra*, n. 1, p. 170.
[4] *Per* DIPLOCK, L.J., *Every* v. *Miles* (1964), C.A. No. 261 quoted by Kemp & Kemp, Vol. 1 (3rd Edn.), p. 6.
[5] *Per* LORD DENNING, M.R., *Ward* v. *James*, *supra*, at p. 300.
[6] *Per* DIPLOCK, L.J., *Hennell* v. *Ranaboldo*, [1963] 1 W.L.R. 1391, at p. 1393.
[7] Of course there are a large number of cases which do not fall within traditional categories and are not reported. But experienced practitioners in the field acquire an "instinct" for the appropriate figure.
[8] See n. 5, p. 206, *supra*.

closer scrutiny in order to ascertain those aspects of the technique which are objective and those which are subjective.

(iii) *Objective aspects of the "pragmatic solution"* There are certain aspects to the English method of assessment which clearly point to the conceptual approach.

The "tariff system" The availability of, and constant judicial resource to, exhaustive compilations of current awards in personal injury cases suggests the possibility that in practice a "tariff system" operates to "objectify" awards of damages for non-pecuniary losses. Further evidence for this may be sought in the decisions of the Court of Appeal whose function it is to maintain a general conformity of awards.[1]

Extent or gravity of injury Although no rational basis for quantification can be discovered, and although it has been stated that the standard of conventional awards are "arbitrary", nevertheless the graduation of awards must be based on certain assumptions. What, for example, is the relationship between an award of £1250 for the loss of an index finger[2] and an award of £6250 for a condition in which serious facial and jaw injuries had left the plaintiff moderately disfigured and unable to bite hard?[3] The conventional and most obvious explanation is that the greater sum is to be paid as compensation for the "more serious" injury, that is to say, that the award must be commensurable with the degree of deprivation caused to the plaintiff by his injury.[4] At first glance this might seem a sufficient test. It is most clearly adopted in the field of social security benefits.[5] A moment's reflection, however, reveals that the attempted explanation is not, in any rational sense, adequate. In *Jones v. Griffith*,[6] as a result of an accident, the plaintiff was subject, *inter alia*, to epilepsy attacks. The Court of Appeal attempted to correlate the "ceiling figure" for epilepsy (£10,000 to £11,000) with the conventional sums awarded for loss of a limb and were evidently happy with the conclusion that the former sum was "twice the conventional figure for the loss of a limb and nearly four times as much as the conventional figure for the loss of an eye."[7] But on what basis can epilepsy be compared with the loss of a limb? The only possible criterion is the extent to which the plaintiff's activities have been

---

[1] *Per* Diplock, L.J., *Hennell v. Ranaboldo*, [1963] 1 W.L.R. 1391, at p. 1393. Thus in 1972 an eye is worth £3000–£4000: *Watson v. Heslop*, [1971] R.T.R. 308.
[2] *Eaves v. Morris Motors*, [1960] 3 All E.R. 656.
[3] *Taylor v. R. V. Chuck (Transport), Ltd.* (1963), 107 Sol. Jo. 910.
[4] *Per* Diplock, L.J., *Fletcher v. Autocar and Transporters*, [1968] 2 Q.B. 322, at p. 340.
[5] S.I. 1964, No. 504, Sch. 2. See, generally, Vester and Cartwright, *Industrial Injuries* (1961).
[6] [1969] 1 W.L.R. 795.
[7] *Per* Sachs, L.J., *ibid.*, at p. 801.

materially affected by his injury.[1] This can only be applied if account
is taken of the special circumstances of the plaintiff's life. The loss of
a leg would mean more to an athlete than to a chess player. The inquiry has become a subjective one. The result must be that the objective
conceptual attempt to put a price on each type of injury cannot, on
rational grounds, be defended.

Victim insensitive to loss The most controversial instance of the
objective/conceptual approach arises where the victim of the accident
is unable to appreciate his loss. This may occur where (i) the victim
has died, or (ii) where he remains unconscious or (iii) where, though
conscious, severe brain injuries have brought about a total insensibility
to the changed condition of life.

It has never been doubted that claims for loss of amenities subsisting
in the victim at the time of his death could be enforced for the benefit
of his estate under the Law Reform (Miscellaneous Provisions) Act
1934.[2] The statutory provisions make no exception for this head of
damages.[3] The cases where the plaintiff is still alive at the time of the
action, on the other hand, provoked some doubts. Was it essential that
the plaintiff should be conscious of his plight? This question, of
course, constituted a direct challenge to the objective/conceptual
approach. If the award were substantially to be reduced on the ground
that the plaintiff was not aware of his condition, the basis of the award
must really be loss of happiness or loss of pleasure. In two crucial
cases in the early 1960s the question was mooted and decided in favour
of the objective approach.

In *Wise* v. *Kay*,[4] the plaintiff, who had been very seriously injured in
a road accident, sustained permanent brain damage and for three and
a half years remained helpless and unconscious. She had never been
aware of her condition, and there was no prospect of recovery. As
SELLERS, L.J. remarked, "no one could be nearer to death and survive."[5]
An appeal against, *inter alia*, an award of £15,000 for loss of amenities
was, DIPLOCK, L.J. dissenting, dismissed. The fact that the plaintiff
could not appreciate her loss was regarded by the majority as irrelevant.

This decision was approved by the House of Lords some seventeen
months later in the somewhat similar case of *West & Son* v. *Shephard*.[6]
Here the plaintiff, though conscious, only to a limited extent appreciated
her condition. The award of £17,500 general damages based on the
ruling in *Wise* v. *Kay* was by a narrow majority (LORDS REID and
DEVLIN dissenting) approved.

---

[1] *Per* DIPLOCK, L.J., *Fletcher* v. *Autocar and Transporters, supra*, at p. 340.
[2] *Rose* v. *Ford*, [1937] A.C. 826, *supra*, p. 116.
[3] See further, *infra*, p. 214.
[4] [1962] 1 Q.B. 638.
[5] *Ibid.*, at p. 644.
[6] [1964] A.C. 326.

At heart these two decisions reaffirmed the traditional conceptual approach to loss of amenities. The plaintiff was, in effect, claiming for the loss of a personal asset, a thing of intrinsic "value", the calculation of which was dependent on the extent and gravity of the injury.

> "The practice of the courts . . . has been to treat bodily injury as a deprivation which in itself entitles a plaintiff to substantial damages according to its gravity."[1]

The assessment of the loss will not be affected by the fact that the plaintiff does not appreciate that he has suffered any loss.

> "The fact of unconsciousness does not . . . eliminate the actuality of the deprivations of the ordinary experiences and amenities of life which may be the inevitable result of some physical injury."[2]

One may express this viewpoint in another way by recognizing that it regards the human personality as a combination of a large number of patrimonial rights which are independent of "feelings" or "sentiments". The deprivation of any of these rights entitles the human personality, which on this view includes a person's estate as being merely an extension of his patrimonial rights, to full and substantial compensation.

The adoption of this approach necessarily entailed a rejection of the two other theoretical approaches outlined above.[3] A critical evaluation of these decisions and their reasoning will be offered at the end of this section. Suffice it, at this stage, to observe that they have been followed,[4] though sometimes with reluctance,[5] in the English courts, but the High Court of Australia has most explicitly rejected them.[6]

(iv) *Subjective aspects of the "pragmatic solution"* It might appear from the analysis above that the quantification of awards for loss of amenities has become the almost automatic application of an objectively assessed tariff. But there are two aspects involved in the standard approach of the courts which indicate that in response to both theoretical and practical requirements, a certain amount of subjectivity must enter into the court's process of assessment.

Social and economic conditions It is, of course, obvious that the conventional sums generally adopted by the courts cannot be good for all

---

[1] *Per* LORD PEARCE, *ibid.*, at p. 365.
[2] *Per* LORD MORRIS, *ibid.*, at p. 349.
[3] *Supra*, pp. 206–207.
[4] *Hindmarsh* v. *Henry Slater* (1966), 110 Sol. Jo. 429; *Andrews* v. *Freeborough*, [1967] 1 Q.B. 1; *Povey* v. *Governors of Rydal School*, [1970] 1 All E.R. 841; cf. *Swift* v. *Prout* (1964), 108 Sol. Jo. 317 (an inadequately reported decision but difficult on any account to reconcile with *Wise* and *West*).
[5] *Andrews* v. *Freeborough, supra, per* WILLMER, L.J., at p. 12; *per* DAVIES, L.J., at p. 18; *per* WINN, L.J., at pp. 20–26.
[6] *Skelton* v. *Collins* (1966), 115 C.L.R. 94.

times and all places.   They are relative to the prevailing social and
economic conditions.   Thus the level of awards must keep pace with
inflation,[1] and may vary from country to country.[2]

Enjoyment of life   The very fact that the term "amenities" is generally
used to describe this head of damages implies that the extent or
gravity of the injury is not the sole factor to be taken into account.   The
award should also reflect the uses to which the plaintiff put the part of
his body injured in the accident and of which he is now deprived.

> "The standard of comparison which the law applies . . . is based . . .
> upon the degree of deprivation—that is, the extent to which the victim
> is unable to do those things which, but for the injury, he would have
> been able to do."[3]

Consequently, the court must look at the circumstances of the plaintiff's
life prior to the accident to see whether he indulged in any special
activities which he is now prevented from pursuing:

> "if, for instance, the plaintiff's main interest in life was some sport or
> hobby from which he will in future be debarred, that too increases the
> assessment."[4]

There are very many instances of such special activities being pleaded[5]
and as a result the court is generally persuaded to select a figure above
the "tariff' figure for the injury in question.   These intangible, subjective, factors extend also to social and sexual relationships: if the
plaintiff's injuries make intercourse (social or sexual) more difficult,
then this too must be taken into account.[6]   Finally, the fact that the
plaintiff has been forced to give up work which he was enjoying for a
less interesting job is a sufficient ground for awarding him substantial
damages, quite independently of any loss of earnings.[7]

5 Critique

It is now proposed critically to evaluate the principles outlined
above.

---

[1] *Aiken* v. *Port of London Authority*, [1963] 1 Lloyd's Rep. 44; *Yorkshire
Electricity Board* v. *Naylor*, [1968] A.C. 529.

[2] *Jag Singh* v. *Toong Fong Omnibus Co.*, [1964] 1 W.L.R. 1382.

[3] *Per* DIPLOCK, L.J., *Fletcher* v. *Autocar and Transporters*, [1968] 2 Q.B. 322,
at p. 340.

[4] *Per* LORD PEARCE, *West & Son* v. *Shephard*, [1964] A.C. 326, at p. 365.

[5] Some specimen examples: walking (*Cole* v. *Bullivant*, [1967] C.L.Y. 1169);
playing the organ (*Page* v. *London Transport Board*, [1965] C.L.Y. 1076); golf
and gardening (*Osborn* v. *Squire*, [1966] C.L.Y. 3334); swimming, playing
cards, sorting out coins (*O'Callaghan* v. *Tersons*, [1966] C.L.Y. 3351); dancing
(*Goodall* v. *Richard Shops*, [1965] C.L.Y. 1145).

[6] See especially *V.* v. *C.* (1972), 26 D.L.R.(3d) 527.   The courts are particularly sensitive to the plight of young unmarried women: e.g. *Duggan* v.
Parmenter, [1965] C.L.Y. 1059.

[7] *Hearnshaw* v. *English Steel Corporation* (1971), 11 K.I.R. 306.

(a) The conceptual approach

It has been seen that, subject to certain qualifications, English law adopts the conceptual approach. This may be criticized on several grounds.

(i) *Philosophical premise* The approach rests on the assumption that each part of the body has an objective "value" which is independent of the use or enjoyment to be derived from it. The integrity of the body becomes something sacrosanct. The functions and pleasures of the body are relegated to a status of minor importance. It is difficult to characterize the exact nature of this metaphysical doctrine[1] but it would seem hardly to accord with the usual role that the law seeks to play in its daily concern with human life. It is submitted that the courts should rest content with the realities of human existence, should have regard to the affect of the injury on the plaintiff's enjoyment of life, should pursue the utilitarian ideals of happiness and pleasure.[2]

(ii) *Distinction between "injury" and "loss"* The second criticism is not unconnected with the first. It will be recalled that in classifying the various elements in an action for damages, it was suggested,[3] that the law should carefully distinguish three aspects: (i) the breach of an obligation; (ii) the injury; and (iii) the loss. In *quantifying*[4] the award of damages, the court should be concerned simply with the third head. In the present context, however, it is evident that the court with its dogma of "the greater the injury, the greater the damages" is basing its assessment on the second item. The incorrectness[5] of this approach might be illustrated by applying it by analogy to a case of injury to property. Compensation for damage to a vehicle would, for example, be based not on the cost of repairs plus loss of use,[6] but on the extent of the injury: $£x$ for a broken axle, $£y$ for a shattered windscreen.

(iii) *A punitive element?* An argument which is sometimes expressed to support the view that compensation should be assessed according to the extent of the injury is that it is unjust that the defendant should pay less where the injury is more severe. In *Wise* v. *Kay*,[7] UPJOHN, L.J. said,

---

[1] In *Skelton* v. *Collins* (1966), 115 C.L.R. 94, at p. 130, WINDEYER, J. referred to the Cartesian doctrine of distinguishing between "injuries to body and mind". Cf. WINN, L.J. in *Andrews* v. *Freeborough*, [1967] 1 Q.B. 1, at p. 22.

[2] *Per* DIPLOCK, L.J., *Wise* v. *Kay*, [1962] 1 Q.B. 638, at p. 666; *per* TAYLOR, J., *Skelton* v. *Collins*, *supra*, at p. 112.

[3] *Supra*, pp. 1–2.

[4] In contrast to establishing liability.

[5] "Compensable loss depends not only on the severity of the injury but on the consequences for the individual." WINDEYER, J. in *Thatcher* v. *Charles* (1961), 104 C.L.R. 57, at p. 71. See also McGregor, n. 2, p. 214, *infra*.

[6] See *supra*, pp. 132–140.

[7] [1962] 1 Q.B. 638, at p. 659.

"it would, I think, be a great slur upon the law, if the complete doctrine is that it is cheapest to kill but if you cannot kill then reduce damages by injuring him so severely that it is most improbable that he can personally use the damages."

But, as has been pointed out by several judges[1] and writers[2] this is improperly to introduce a punitive element into the task of compensation. The duty of the court is to award the plaintiff such money as will compensate him for the losses he has actually sustained, not to nominate a sum which it thinks that the defendant ought to pay.

(iv) *Windfall to dependants* From a social standpoint, the approach as manifested in the *Wise* or *West* situation, that is, where the victim has either died or is as near to death in terms of consciousness or awareness of plight as makes no difference, produces unfortunate consequences. Very large sums of money which are ostensibly intended to compensate the victim for his misfortunes cannot be used for his benefit. The persons who benefit are his dependants or near relatives. The anomaly is obvious.[3]

(v) *The "tariff system"* Even if the theory of the conceptual approach is accepted, it is arguable that its method of application is neither wholly efficacious nor internally consistent. There is, on the one hand, the difficulty referred to above[4] of finding a suitable criterion for judging the gravity of the injury (e.g. which is the greater injury, the loss of an arm or the loss of an eye?) On the other hand the judicial tariff cannot operate efficiently unless the sum awarded for each category of injury is readily available. Until recently, the courts were unwilling to itemize awards. In particular they were reluctant to apportion general damages between lost future earnings and non-pecuniary losses.[5] Following the decision in *Jefford* v. *Gee*,[6] for the purpose of determining the interest payable on damages awards the courts must now apportion between pecuniary and non-pecuniary losses.[7] Judges do now itemize awards,[8] but the itemization does not always appear in the reports of cases,[9] and though they may be current

---

[1] E.g. *West* v. *Shephard*, [1964] A.C. 326, *per* Lord Reid, at p. 342, *per* Lord Devlin, at p. 362.

[2] E.g. McGregor (1965), 28 M.L.R. 629, at pp. 641–653.

[3] See also *supra*, pp. 118–119.

[4] *Supra*, p. 209.

[5] See e.g. *Watson* v. *Powles*, [1968] 1 Q.B. 596.

[6] [1970] 2 Q.B. 130.

[7] See, also, *George* v. *Pinnock*, [1973] 1 W.L.R. 118.

[8] Some judges have taken recognition of the "tariff" even further. In *Hett* v. *French*, [1971] C.L.Y. 3250, Cairns, L.J. subdivided an award of £8500 into £3000 for loss of sight, £2000 for loss of taste and smell, £1750 for deafness, £500 for wrist injury, £250 for risk of epilepsy and £1000 for pain and suffering.

[9] This will be confirmed by a survey of the numerous decisions listed in *Current Law*.

among expert practitioners in the field, a wider circulation would seem to be desirable.

6 Suggestions for reform

It should be apparent that the methods of assessing damages for loss of amenities at present adopted by English law can be heavily criticized both on theoretical and on practical grounds. It remains, in the light of the criticisms made above, to consider ways in which the system might be improved.

(i) *Retention of conceptual approach* It follows from what was said in the preceding section that even if no change were felt desirable in the theoretical basis, nevertheless there is room for improvement within the conceptual doctrine. Once it has been accepted that the artificial process of "valuing" different kinds of injury is the appropriate method, there seems little point in resisting a complete adherence to the fiction by establishing a detailed and reliable tariff system. The practical advantages would be in the time and expense involved in the prediction and assessment of awards. The tariff would consist of an exhaustive list of injuries, set out under medical advice with each item expressed as a percentage of total disability.[1] A variable would distinguish temporary from permanent injuries. The amount of compensation payable for each form of disability would then be geared to a cost of living index. The question would then arise whether the award of the appropriate figure should be automatic or whether the trial judge should be given a limited power to vary the amount.[2] If the conceptual approach is to be preferred and if the main object of the tariff is to avoid uncertainty, it is surely self-defeating to suggest that the courts should be permitted to diverge from the statutory norm. On the other hand, greater flexibility would allow the judge to be guided by the personal or functional approaches the merits of which are not to be considered.

(ii) *Adoption of personal approach*[3] A more radical proposal would be to shift the theoretical basis of the award from the conceptual to the personal doctrine. Compensation would be assessed according to the diminution of happiness experienced by the plaintiff as a result of his injuries. The court would start with the "average" figure in the

---

[1] Useful models are: (a) the statutory tariff for disablement benefits under the National Insurance Industrial Injuries Scheme, n. 5, p. 209, *supra*. But it is not sufficiently detailed; and (b) the *barème indicatif d'invalidité* of the French Workmen's Compensation Legislation (see *Juris-Classeur des Accidents du Travail*) but it is to be noted that each type of disability carries with it a range of percentages any one from which the trial judge may in his unfettered discretion select.

[2] Working Paper No. 41, para. 102.

[3] See New Zealand's Accident Compensation Act 1972, s. 120 (7).

statutory tariff as representing the amount of unhappiness that is likely to be inflicted for that category of injury on the reasonable man. This would then be variable according to the court's view of how the plaintiff's enjoyment of life had been, and would in the future be, affected by the accident. The anomalies arising from the conceptual approach would disappear: compensation would be based on the "loss" rather than on the "injury"; there would be no question of any punitive considerations applying; the dependants would receive no windfall;[1] and the victim would recover compensation only to the extent that he appreciated his condition.

The chief objection raised to the personal approach in the *Wise* and *West* decisions was impracticability.

> "The inquiry into damages would become . . . an investigation of the inner feelings and outward manifestations of conduct . . . which inquiries were found invidious, and undesirable and as a matter of proof well-nigh unattainable."[2]

But the fear is almost certainly exaggerated. The assumption that the new approach would be purely subjective and thus highly elusive would be unfounded if the statutory tariff were the basis for the award. The ordinary case would be unaffected by the theoretical shift, since *ex hypothesi* the plaintiff in the ordinary case would sustain the "ordinary" amount of unhappiness. The change would be clearly felt only in the extreme cases where the plaintiff suffers little or no unhappiness, as where he remains unconscious, or a peculiarly abnormal degree of unhappiness; and it is in these areas that the need for reform is greatest.

(iii) *Adoption of functional approach*   The adoption of the functional approach would involve the greatest departure from the present position. The statutory figure would be variable according to the amount necessary to afford the plaintiff reasonable solace for his unhappy condition. In *West & Son* v. *Shephard*,[3] LORD DEVLIN thought that it would be proper for the court to

> "provide such a sum as would ensure that for the rest of her life the plaintiff would not within reason want for anything that money could buy. That would not be perfect; it would not be full; but it would be as much as money could fairly do."[4]

---

[1] The Law Reform (Miscellaneous Provisions) Act 1934, which allows personal representatives to recover for non-pecuniary losses sustained by the deceased, would have to be amended; cf. Law Commission Working Paper No. 41, para. 67.

[2] *Per* SELLERS, L.J., *Wise* v. *Kay*, [1962] 1 Q.B. 638, at p. 649. The objection has been adopted by the Law Commission, Working Paper No. 41, para. 89.

[3] [1964] A.C. 326.

[4] *Ibid.*, at p. 357.

As with the personal approach, this would remove the anomalies from the present law. But in addition, adherence to the functional approach would seem to carry with it one further advantge. By insisting that the money awarded serve some useful purpose, the theory draws nearer to the fundamental notion of *restitutio in integrum*. The award, though it may fail to restore to the plaintiff the happiness which he has actually lost, attempts the next best thing by supplying him with the means to obtain some alternative pleasure. Compensation lies not in the damages award itself but what the plaintiff can do with that money.

It remains to consider the objections which have been or may be brought against this view. The main objection to the personal approach, impracticability, might be raised again. It is said that it is too difficult to define what is meant by the plaintiff being able to "use" the money.[1] There are a variety of "uses" which would satisfy this requirement and it would be for the court to determine whether a particular "use" was a reasonable method of alleviating the plaintiff's grief. It must not be forgotten that the doctrine of mitigation requires the plaintiff to take such steps as are reasonable to mitigate his loss.[2] The second objection might be the traditional view long held by the courts and confirmed in *West* v. *Shephard*[3] that in quantifying damages the court must not be influenced by the use to which the money might be put. The court, it was emphasized, has never exercised control over what the plaintiff did with the money, unless he was insane[4] or an infant.[5] But the argument surely contains a non-sequitur. It does not follow from the admitted rule that the court cannot control the disbursement of an award in the hands of the plaintiff, that in assessing the quantum of damages it should not be influenced by the use to which the compensation is likely to be put. There is no suggestion that once the award has been assessed, the court will in any way interfere with what the plaintiff actually does with the money. Further, despite the dicta in *West* v. *Shephard*[6] it is clear that on other quantification questions the court has estimated what benefits the plaintiff will derive from his award.[7] Finally, it is probable that in most cases the functional approach would operate to limit rather than to increase awards for loss of amenities. But this might be regarded as a desirable consequence. In an era when the call to spread the ambit of compensation over a wider area is at its loudest, it is not

---

[1] Working Paper No. 41, para. 91.
[2] *Supra*, pp. 85–93.
[3] *Supra, per* LORD REID, at pp. 341–342; *per* LORD MORRIS, at p. 349; *per* LORD PEARCE, at p. 364; *contra* LORD DEVLIN, at p. 363.
[4] Mental Health Act 1959, s. 102(2).
[5] E.g. *M.* v. *Lester*, [1966] 1 All E.R. 207.
[6] *Supra*, n. 3.
[7] The capitalization of lost future income, *supra*, pp. 189–192, and the prevention of overlap between pecuniary and non-pecuniary losses, *infra*, p. 221.

without significance that at the same time there is a feeling that non-pecuniary awards may be too high.[1]

V DEDUCTION FOR COMPENSATING ADVANTAGES

1 Introduction

As a general principle compensating advantages resulting from the accident for which the tortfeasor is liable should be set off against the losses for which compensation is payable.[2] The principle is, in its essence, a simple one, yet its application in the field of personal injuries has given rise to difficulty of some magnitude and prolonged controversy.[3] The reason for this is that a decision in any given situation as to whether or not a deduction should be made for a compensating advantage necessarily provokes some fundamental questions as to the role of the tort system in a welfare state: what is meant by "compensation"? what section of the community should primarily bear the cost of personal injury awards? The matter is further complicated by the fact that in a situation in which a third party reduces in whole or in part the losses sustained by the accident victim he may himself have an action against the tortfeasor for the losses he has sustained. For the purposes of exposition a distinction will be drawn between (i) savings on expenses for which the plaintiff would otherwise have been liable and (ii) indemnity of losses by collateral sources.

2 Savings on expenses

The plaintiff, had he not been injured, would have been liable for certain expenses. As a result of his injuries he will no longer incur these liabilities. In principle the saving on the expenses should be deducted from his award. Three different factual situations must be considered.

(a) Taxation

The plaintiff would have paid tax on income earned. Tax is not payable on damages for personal injuries. There must be deducted from his award for lost earnings, a sum representing the tax which he would

---

[1] See, e.g. Palmer, [1971] Alberta L.R. 169, at p. 181; Keeton & O'Connell, *Basic Protection for the Traffic Victim*, pp. 268–269.
[2] *Supra*, p. 93.
[3] There is a wealth of literature on this subject. See, especially, Fleming, 11 I.E.C.L., Chap. 4; Street, Chap. 4; McGregor (1965), 28 M.L.R. 629; Cooper (1971), 49 C.B.R. 501.

have paid on the income which forms the basis of the award.[1] This rule
has already been examined in some detail.[2]

(b) Living expenses

An injured person bound to spend the rest of his life in a nursing home
may of course recover the costs thereby incurred. He will at the same
time save on the cost of maintaining himself at home. That a deduction
should be made on this account was clearly established by the Court of
Appeal in *Oliver* v. *Ashman*:[3]

> "it would seem *prima facie* quite wrong to have regard to any probable
> future loss of earnings without also having regard, on the other side
> of the account, to the probable saving of what would ordinarily be the
> expenses of life."[4]

Of course, if the plaintiff will still have the expense of maintaining his
family at home, no deductions should be made on that account.[5]
Nevertheless there are two Court of Appeal decisions which appear to
conflict with the clear principle of deduction.

(i) In *Shearman* v. *Folland*[6]

> P, an elderly woman of some means, resided permanently in a hotel
> paying £7 a week for board and lodging. Following the accident, she
> was, for 55 weeks, accommodated in a nursing home the fees for
> which averaged 12 gns. a week. SLADE, J. applying the general
> principle stated above deducted from the award for nursing home fees
> a sum representing the saving on the hotel bills. P's appeal was
> allowed: the Court of Appeal deducted a sum representing only the
> cost of board in the nursing home.

The exact ratio of the decision is difficult to ascertain but there would
appear to be three possibilities. First, "the precise style in which she
would probably or might well have lived is ... a collateral matter"
which does not affect the liability of the defendant.[7] But this is based
on the old view which did not survive *British Transport Commission* v.
Gourley[8] that a financial arrangement between the plaintiff and a third
party being *res inter alios acta* could not be pleaded by a "wrongdoer"

---

[1] *British Transport Commission* v. *Gourley*, [1956] A.C. 185.
[2] *Supra*, pp. 107–115.
[3] [1962] 2 Q.B. 210, *per* WILLMER, L.J., at p. 234; *per* PEARSON, L.J., at
p. 242. See also *Fletcher* v. *Autocar and Transporters*, [1968] 2 Q.B. 322.
[4] *Per* WILLMER, L.J., [1962] 2 Q.B. 210, at p. 235.
[5] *Per* STEVENSON, L.J., *Daish* v. *Wauton*, [1972] 2 Q.B. 262, at p. 270.
[6] [1950] 2 K.B. 43.
[7] *Per* ASQUITH, L.J., *ibid.*, at p. 50.
[8] [1956] A.C. 185, overruling *Billingham* v. *Hughes*, [1949] 1 K.B. 643,
relied on by the Court of Appeal in *Shearman* v. *Folland, supra.*

to mitigate the burden of his own liability. If additional living expenses are regarded as relevant for the purpose of increasing an award,[1] it is difficult to see why a saving on such expenses is irrelevant for reducing the award. Secondly, deduction might lead to absurd results: a millionaire whose ordinary living expenses exceeded the cost of caring for him would make a net financial benefit and a "wrongdoer" should not thereby be freed from paying for the consequences of his tort.[2] This argument is, of course, punitive and for that reason has little to commend it. Moreover, it does not follow that the disabled millionaire would receive nothing. His sole actual but still remediable losses would be pain and suffering (which would include inconvenience) and loss of amenities.[3] Thirdly, there was not sufficient evidence to ascertain the total cost of board and lodging to be deducted,[4] so that the only sum to be deducted was the certain £1 per week representing the cost of food in the nursing home. Even assuming—which is doubtful—that this is a correct application of the doctrine of certainty,[5] the principle behind the award is difficult to justify. Before the accident the plaintiff was paying £x for board and lodging. After the accident she was paid £y medical and nursing expenses and £z for board and lodging. She was awarded £$y-z$ but her true loss was £$y+z-x$.

(ii) In *Daish* v. *Wauton*[6]

> P, a boy aged 5, was very seriously injured. It was envisaged that he would spend the rest of his life in a national health service institution. The argument advanced by the tortfeasor D that a deduction should be made for expenses saved from the award for loss of earnings was rejected.

The Court of Appeal expressed doubts on the dictum in *Oliver* v. *Ashman*.[7] Expenses saved may be set off against expenses incurred, but from loss of earnings should be deducted not the saving of living expenses generally (the court is not concerned with how a man spends his income) but only those expenses which would have been incurred in earning the wages.[8] The distinction between awards for expenses incurred and for lost earnings seems to be an artificial one. A person who lives in a hospital saves on his living expenses whether the hospitalization is free or not. The fortuitous circumstance that he cannot claim damages for expenses does not alter the fact that he has saved on living expenses. To ignore this fact is to ignore the plaintiff's real loss.

---

[1] *Supra*, p. 173.
[2] [1950] 2 K.B. 43, at p. 47.
[3] ASQUITH, L.J. himself makes the point later in the judgment, *ibid.*, at p. 50.
[4] *Ibid.*, at p. 50.
[5] Cf. *supra*, pp. 79–85.
[6] [1972] 2 Q.B. 262.
[7] *Ibid.*, at pp. 267–269.
[8] *Ibid.*, at p. 270.

(c) Overlap of pecuniary and non-pecuniary awards[1]

Since 1970 it has become standard practice for the court to subdivide general damages into pecuniary and non-pecuniary items.[2] In such circumstances there is, it has been claimed, a risk of duplicating compensation for certain items. Recently, the Court of Appeal has drawn attention to two instances.

(i) In *Fletcher* v. *Autocar and Transporters*,[3] LORD DENNING, M.R.[4] and DIPLOCK, L.J.[5] exposed the fallacy of awarding "full" compensation for loss of earnings and for loss of amenities where prior to the accident the plaintiff had spent some of his earnings on a pleasurable activity for the loss of which he has been awarded substantial compensation. If he is no longer able to enjoy the activity, he has saved on the money which otherwise would have been spent on it, and to that extent the award for loss of amenities ought to be reduced. This approach, though theoretically difficult to reconcile with *Shearman* v. *Folland*[6] and *Daish* v. *Wauton*[7] and more remotely with *Wise* v. *Kay*[8] and *West & Son* v. *Shephard*,[9] accords well with the *functional* approach to compensation.[10] For the *Fletcher* rule of deducton to apply, however, it must be clear that the court has awarded some special sum (larger than the conventional tariff figure for the particular disability) to represent the loss of the pleasurable activity on which money was spent.[11] Otherwise in comparison with someone who did not indulge in expensive pastimes the plaintiff would be undercompensated.

(ii) In *Smith* v. *Central Asbestos Co., Ltd.*[12] LORD DENNING, M.R. said:

"When a man is stricken with a disease like asbestosis, it must be a comfort to him to know that he is getting full compensation for loss of his future earnings. It will do something to relieve his distress on being put on light work or put out of action altogether. To that extent the award for loss of amenities may be reduced. The judge also pointed out that high wages often represent "danger money", so that compensation at those rates includes compensation for risks which he no longer incurs when he is on light work."[13]

---

[1] Law Commission Working Paper No. 41, paras. 105–116.
[2] *Supra*, p. 214.
[3] [1968] 2 Q.B. 322. See also *Harris* v. *Harris* (1972), 116 Sol. Jo. 904.
[4] *Ibid.*, at pp. 336–338.
[5] *Ibid.*, at pp. 341–345.
[6] [1950] 2 K.B. 43, *supra*, p. 219.
[7] [1972] 2 Q.B. 262, *supra*, p. 220.
[8] [1962] 1 Q.B. 638, *supra*, p. 210.
[9] [1964] A.C. 326, *supra*, p. 210.
[10] *Supra*, pp. 216–218.
[11] Cf. SALMON, L.J. in *Fletcher's* case, *supra*, at pp. 360–361, 364–365.
[12] [1972] 1 Q.B. 244.
[13] *Ibid.*, at p. 262.

Unlike the *Fletcher* rule, this attitude seems hard to justify. Pain and suffering and loss of amenities are in their nature independent of pecuniary losses. It surely does not follow that the mere knowledge that a loss of earnings has been indemnified of its own accord mitigates any pain and suffering experienced or loss of amenities incurred. The argument based on "danger money" is no easier to defend. It can be argued that the relatively high rates of pay are, in our economic system, necessary to attract men to the job. Alternatively, "danger money" may be regarded as a suitable reward for the more unpleasant aspects of the work while the man is so employed rather than for alleviating him from the consequences of an injury sustained. Indeed it is unrealistic to envisage that a man employed on dangerous work will set aside that part of his remuneration which is regarded as "danger money" as compensation for when he is injured. A man injured while on dangerous work no less than any other injured wage earner has sustained both pecuniary and non-pecuniary losses and should be fully compensated for both.

3   Indemnity of losses by collateral sources

Where the plaintiff (P) is injured in an accident for which the defendant (D) is liable, and P's losses have been reduced in whole or in part by a payment made or a service rendered by a third party (X), two questions may arise for consideration: (1) should the benefit from X be taken into account when assessing D's liability to P? (2) has X a right to recover the value of the benefit conferred? In this section we are concerned strictly only with the answer to (1). The principles governing (2) are considered elsewhere.[1] Although analytically the two questions may be regarded as quite distinct—they have been treated as such by the courts[2]—yet the policy implications of the principles relating to deduction relate so closely to the availability of third party remedies, that no satisfactory solution to the problems posed in (1) can realistically be found without resort to the rules prevailing in (2).[3] It is therefore proposed first to state the rules relating to compensating advantages and then attempt a rationalization of those rules by reference to the theories formulated by the courts, to general policy considerations, and to the availability or otherwise of third party rights.

(a)   The rules

Whether the benefit derived from the collateral source is to be taken into account in assessing damages against the tortfeasor depends on the nature of the benefit.

---

[1] *Supra*, pp. 175–177 and *infra*, pp. 278–282.
[2] A major rationalization of the law on deduction was attempted by the House of Lords in *Parry* v. *Cleaver*, [1970] A.C. 1, but no reference was made to the problem of third party rights.
[3] See, especially, Fleming (1966) 54 Calif. L.R. 1478.

(i) *Gratuitous Benefits*　It is clear that where, as a result of the accident, P receives a gratuitous benefit from X, the value of that benefit is not to be taken into account in assessing P's claim against D. This is so whether the donor is a friend or relative,[1] a charitable organization,[2] or even an employer making good a loss of wages where he was under no legal obligation to do so.[3] The benefit may be in the form of money,[4] or free board and lodging.[5] In neither case will the value of the benefit be deducted from the award. Where X bears the cost of P's medical treatment, P may still recover the sum as part of his award, though he will be under an obligation to repay the donor.[6]

(ii) *Accident insurance*　It has long been settled that a sum received on an accident insurance policy will not be deducted from a personal injuries award.[7]

(iii) *Pensions*　The decision in the House of Lords in *Parry* v. *Cleaver*[8] resolved a conflict of authority[9] as to whether a disablement pension payable to P by his employer was to be deducted. Their Lordships by a bare majority (LORDS MORRIS and PEARSON dissenting) held that disablement pension benefits were not deductible from an award for lost earnings but were to be taken into account in assessing damages for the loss of a retirement pension. For the purposes of this rule no distinction is drawn according to whether (1) grant of the pension was discretionary or obligatory[10] or (2) the employee did or did not contribute to the pension fund.[11] In *Hewson* v. *Downs*[12] the same rules were applied to state retirement pensions.

(iv) *Wages, sick pay and redundancy payments*　Although there is a curious lack of direct English authority on the point[13] it seems that where under his contract of employment P is entitled during his incapacity to the continuance of wages or sick pay, these sums must be deducted from

---

[1] *Liffen* v. *Watson*, [1940] 1 K.B. 556.
[2] *Redpath* v. *Belfast and County Down Railway*, [1947] N.I. 167.
[3] *Hobbelen* v. *Nunn*, [1965] Qd.R. 105.
[4] *Redpath's* case, *supra*.
[5] *Liffen* v. *Watson*, *supra*.
[6] *Schneider* v. *Eisovitch*, [1960] 2 Q.B. 430; *Gage* v. *King*, [1961] 1 Q.B. 188; and see *supra*, pp. 175–177.
[7] *Bradburn* v. *Great Western Rail Co.* (1874), L.R. 10 Exch. 1.
[8] [1970] A.C. 1.
[9] *Payne* v. *Railway Executive*, [1952] 1 K.B. 26 and *Judd* v. *Hammersmith Hospital Board*, [1960] 1 All E.R. 607: pension not deducted; *contra*, *Browning* v. *War Office*, [1963] 1 Q.B. 750.
[10] [1970] A.C. 1, *per* LORD REID, at p. 20, *per* LORD PEARCE, at p. 36.
[11] *Per* LORD PEARCE, *ibid.*, at p. 36.
[12] [1970] 1 Q.B. 73.
[13] Cf. The Australian case *Graham* v. *Baker* (1961), 106 C.L.R. 340.

his award for loss of earnings.[1] It should follow from a recent decision that redundancy payments are also deductible.[2]

(v) *Social security and other state benefits* The position of most social security benefits is governed by section 2(1) of the Law Reform (Personal Injuries) Act 1948 which provides for the deduction from an award for loss of earnings of

> "one half of the value of any rights which have accrued or probably will accrue to him therefrom in respect of industrial injury benefit, industrial disablement benefit or sickness benefit for the five years beginning with the time when the cause of action accrued."

The statutory provision covers injury, disablement,[3] sickness and invalidity[4] benefits, but not unemployment benefits, which must be deducted in full,[5] and not National Health Service facilities which are not to be taken into account at all.[6] Supplementary benefits do not fall within the scope of the subsection and it seems that the present practice is to ignore them altogether.[7] As regards those benefits governed by the statutory provisions, receipt of only five years is to be taken into account,[8] and if the benefit is in the form of a lump sum, the court must ascertain the period it is intended to cover and apportion accordingly.[9] If, on the other hand, the rate for the period of five years is un-

---

[1] In *Metropolitan Police District Receiver* v. *Croydon Corporation*, [1957] 2 Q.B. 154 (*supra*, pp. 80–81) it was assumed throughout that wages paid to P during his incapacity would be deducted from his award against D. The same assumption was made in *Parry* v. *Cleaver*, *supra*, *per* LORD REID, at p. 16; *per* LORD MORRIS, at p. 32; *per* LORD PEARCE, at p. 34. If, however, by the terms of the contract of employment the sum is payable as a form of insurance benefit, it is probably not to be deducted.

[2] *Cheeseman* v. *Bowaters*, [1971] 3 All E.R. 513.

[3] But a constant attendance allowance which may supplement a disablement benefit is not to be taken into account: s. 2(2) of the 1948 Act.

[4] This new category of benefit was added to s. 2(1) of the 1948 Act by Sch. 5 of the National Insurance Act 1971.

[5] *Cheeseman* v. *Bowaters*, [1971] 3 All E.R. 513.

[6] *Daish* v. *Wauton*, [1972] 2 Q.B. 262, *supra*, p. 220.

[7] Following a dictum of LORD REID in *Parry* v. *Cleaver*, [1970] A.C. 1, at p. 14. National Assistance benefits, the precursors of supplementary benefits, were not deductible (*Eldridge* v. *Videtta* (1964), 108 Sol. Jo. 137 and *Foxley* v. *Olton*, [1965] 2 Q.B. 306) but it is sumbitted that they do not support the present practice since the basis of these decisions was the discretionary nature of national assistance and (1) the discretionary element in the supplementary benefit scheme has been much reduced; (2) the distinction between discretionary and non-discretionary pensions was discredited in *Parry* v. *Cleaver*, *supra*. See Casey, [1972] Jurid. Rev. 22. The Law Commission (Working Paper No. 41, para. 129) has recommended that the 50 per cent. deduction rule of the 1948 Act should apply to supplementary benefits.

[8] This includes cases where the benefit is payable although there is no loss of earnings: *Flowers* v. *George Wimpey*, [1956] 1 Q.B. 73.

[9] If the lump sum is payable for life, the court, in order to apportion for the five year period, must estimate the plaintiff's life expectancy: *Hultquist* v. *Universal Pattern*, [1960] 2 Q.B. 467.

certain, it must estimate the value of "any rights which probably will accrue."[1] The statutory provision is mandatory: the trial judge has no discretion whether to deduct or not, nor may he review the insurance officer's decision.[2]

(b) Principle on which rules are based

Has this medley of different rules any underlying theme? The Law Commission has conceded defeat: "there is no acceptable solution to these specific problems which is entirely logical."[3] This may be unduly pessimistic. The process of rationalization must begin with the general principle of deduction: the *restitutio in integrum* doctrine requires that *prima facie* any mitigation of the plaintiff's loss should be set off against his award. If this is the primary principle which explains, for example, why sick pay and unemployment benefits are to be deducted in full, reasons must be adduced for those benefits which are not deducted or are only partially so. Judges and writers have pressed into service a variety of justifications.

(i) *Punitive considerations* The oldest takes its stand on what D should pay rather than on what P should receive. The burden of the "wrong-doer" should not be alleviated by any arrangements which P may have with X.[4] The reasoning cannot survive closer examination and has been abandoned in the most recent decisions.[5] The object of an award of damages is to compensate P for the loss he has suffered, not to punish D for the "wrong" he has committed.

(ii) *Causation* A more popular explanation is founded on principles of causation. It is argued that there is not a sufficient causal connection between D's tort and the benefit conferred by X and that therefore the latter should be disregarded in the assessment of damages. The argument is usually justified to support the rule that gratuitous benefits should not be deducted: the "cause" of the gift was not D's tort but X's benevolence.[6] A wider range of terminology has been employed. Thus it is said that the accident for which D is liable was "the occasion rather than the cause"[7] or the "*causa sine qua non*" rather than the "*causa*

---

[1] *Per* SELLERS, L.J., *ibid.*, at p. 480.
[2] *Flowers* v. *George Wimpey, supra.*
[3] Working Paper No. 41, para. 128.
[4] E.g. *per* TINDAL, C.J., *Yates* v. *Whyte* (1838), 4 Bing N.C. 272, at p. 283; *per* ANDREWS, L.C.J., *Redpath* v. *Belfast & County Down Railway*, [1947] N.I. 167, at p. 175; *per* McTIERNAN, J., *Paff* v. *Speed* (1961), 105 C.L.R. 549, at p. 550.
[5] See especially *British Transport Commission* v. *Gourley*, [1956] A.C. 185; *National Insurance Co.* v. *Espagne* (1961), 105 C.L.R. 569; *Parry* v. *Cleaver*, [1970] A.C. 1.
[6] *Per* ANDREWS, L.C.J., *Redpath's* case, *supra*, at pp. 172–173; *per* SOMERVELL, L.J., *Peacock* v. *Amusement Equipment Co.*, [1954] 2 Q.B. 347, at p. 354.
[7] E.g. MENZIES, J., *Espagne's* case, *supra*, at p. 580.

causans"[1] of the receipt of the benefit.   Others have said that the benefit was *"res inter alios acta"* or *"completely collateral"*.[2]   Finally, some judges, following the reasoning in *Gourley*[3] have inquired whether the benefit was "too remote".[4]   At the outset it is convenient to dispose of one patently unsound notion, that it depends on whether it was foreseeable at the time of D's tort that such a benefit would be received by P.   Clearly, whatever be the force of the arguments based on causation, remoteness in the sense of foreseeability is not at issue.[5]   The existence of a causal link between the accident and the receipt of the benefit would appear to be a necessary but not a sufficient condition for deduction to be made.   It is necessary in the sense that *some* causal link must exist for the benefit to be relevant.   Clearly if P, shortly after his accident, wins a large dividend on the football pools this is not to be taken into account.[6]   But once the existence of a causal link has been proved, the notions of causation do not assist in determining whether or not a benefit is to be deducted.   The distinction between, for example, *causa sine qua non* and *causa causans*, rests on no logical basis[7] and is in any case so vague that it can hardly justify the court treating pensions differently from sick pay.   As LORD PEARCE remarked in *Parry* v. *Cleaver*,[8] "each is certainly a *causa sine qua non* and probably each is entitled to be called a *causa causans*.   Strict causation seems to provide no satisfactory line of demarcation."   In truth, the resort to notions of causation often conceals what are basically policy decisions.[9]

(iii) *Source of benefit*   Perhaps the most popular reason for disregarding a benefit is that it was provided for or earned by P himself.   Most obviously this applies to personal accident insurance.

> "It would be injust and unreasonable to hold that the money which he (P) prudently spent on premiums and the benefit from it should enure to the benefit of the tortfeasor."[10]

The same argument was responsible for the fifty per cent deduction rule in section 2(1) of the Law Reform Act 1948.[11]   Under the National Insurance scheme, as it then was, one half of the contribution was paid

---

[1] E.g. *per* COHEN, L.J., *Payne* v. *Railway Executive*, [1952] 1 K.B. 26, at p. 36.
[2] E.g. *per* PEARSON, L.J., *Parsons* v. *B.N.M. Laboratories*, [1964] 1 Q.B. 95, at p. 141.
[3] [1956] A.C. 185, *per* EARL JOWITT, at p. 199.
[4] *Per* LORD PEARSON, *Parry* v. *Cleaver*, *supra*, at p. 48.
[5] *Per* LORD REID, *ibid.*, at p. 15.
[6] Cf. the contract case *Jebsen* v. *East and West India Dock Co.* (1875), L.R. 10 C.P. 300, *infra*, p. 374.
[7] *Supra*, p. 67.
[8] [1970] A.C. 1, at p. 34.
[9] See McGregor (1965), 28 M.L.R. 629, at p. 632.
[10] *Per* LORD REID, *Parry* v. *Cleaver*, *supra*, at p. 14.
[11] Report of the Committee on Alternative Remedies, Cmnd. 6860 (1946).

by the employee and one half by the employer.[1] In *Parry* v. *Cleaver*[2] the reasoning was applied by analogy to pension schemes. The employee had through his continued service earned the right to the benefit in case of accident. The fact that he had made no financial contribution to the scheme should make no difference. The sum notionally paid by the employer into the scheme is, combined with wages, the price which he is prepared to pay for the employee's services. Nor should a distinction be drawn between voluntary and compulsory pension schemes.[3] If an employee were entitled to retain the benefits only of voluntary schemes, then an employee who had no option but to join the scheme would be unfairly prejudiced. The justification is, however, open to several objections. First, it cannot, of course, account for the rule of non-deduction for gratuitous benefits. This is not by itself fatal. The view of Lord Wilberforce that one should not attempt to reason from one type of benefit to another[4] carries some persuasive force. But the struggle for an all-embracing rationalization should not be given up so easily; and the fact remains that the most significant feature of gratuitous benefits is that they are *not* earned by P. Secondly, if, as seems inevitable,[5] no distinction is drawn between voluntary and compulsory schemes, the argument based on P's foresight, or on the purchase of the benefit "with his own assets" loses much of its force. Moreover, it makes the existing distinction between private pensions schemes and social security schemes even harder to justify. Thirdly, by extending the argument to pensions schemes, the protagonists are setting foot on a slippery slope. If pensions schemes are not to be deducted because the plaintiff has earned the benefit through his past services, why should wages and sick pay be deducted? The distinction propounded by Lord Reid that "wages are a reward for contemporaneous work but that a pension is the fruit . . . of all the money which was set aside in the past in respect of his past work"[6] is, with respect, unconvincing.[7] Some employees negotiate for higher wages and small pension rights, while others prefer lower wages and larger pension rights.

---

[1] *Ibid.*
[2] [1970] A.C. 1.
[3] The point is not directly referred to in the opinions of the majority in *Parry* v. *Cleaver*, though it would seem to follow from their conclusion. It was made explicit in the *Espagne* case (1961), 105 C.L.R. 569 the reasoning in which was adopted in *Parry* v. *Cleaver*.
[4] *Parry* v. *Cleaver*, [1970] A.C. 1, at p. 42.
[5] *Supra*, n. 3.
[6] *Parry* v. *Cleaver*, *supra*, at p. 16.
[7] The distinction was rejected by Lord Denning, M.R. in *Browning* v. *War Office*, [1963] 1 Q.B. 750, at p. 760 and in *Parry* v. *Cleaver*, [1968] 1 Q.B. 195, at p. 207. See also on appeal [1970] A.C. 1 the dissents of Lord Morris at p. 32 and Lord Pearson, at pp. 51–52.

(iv) *Purpose of benefit*[1]   The most convincing explanation of the rules
exempting certain benefits from deduction is that which has regard to
the purpose of the benefit.   The view had its most ample expression
in the Australian case of *National Insurance Co.* v. *Espagne*.[2]   A benefit
conferred by X is to be taken into account unless its purpose, express
or implied, was to provide P with support *in addition* to any claim which
P might have against D.   Now if a gift from X to P is deducted from
P's award against D, it is clear that X's intention to benefit P and not
D has been thwarted.   For private accident insurance to be exempted
from deduction, it must, then, be argued that the contract of insurance
is in the nature of a wager:[3]   P will be rewarded by the payment of an
additional sum if the accident induces both the receipt of the benefit and
tortious liability.   He is investing in the possibility of double recovery.
Similar considerations apply to other benefits.   However, it can hardly
be that the purpose of the benefit as criterion can always provide the
satisfactory answer.   The court may have little evidence from which it
can infer the purpose of the gift.   In such circumstances, it seems inevitable that it will have regard to policy considerations.   Further, the
court may construe the purpose of the benefit to the effect that neither
P nor D should profit from the accumulation of remedies but that the
benefit should revert to its source X.   Even if such an intention is
not clear, the court or indeed the legislature may decide on policy
grounds that this solution would be the most expedient.   Unhappily
not only have the courts in general failed to avail themselves of this
possible solution,[4] but, as is demonstrated elsewhere in this book,[5] the
machinery for effecting the purpose is deficient.

(v) *Policy considerations*   It thus becomes necessary to analyse in broad
outline the policy considerations which should affect the issue.

Wagering   The general policy against the enforcement of wagering
contracts[6] may be relevant.   In the cases of property, marine and fire
insurance there is no possibility of the insured gambling on double
recovery.   He is limited to his actual loss and his insurers may be
subrogated to any claim he may have against a tortfeasor.[7]   A contract
of accident insurance, on the other hand, has invariably been construed

---

[1] Cooper (1971), 49 C.B.R. 63.
[2] (1961), 105 C.L.R. 569, *per* SIR OWEN DIXON, C.J., at p. 573; *per* WINDEYER,
J., at pp. 599–600.
[3] *Per* DIPLOCK, L.J., *Browning* v. *War Office*, [1963] 1 Q.B. 750, at p. 769 and
see *infra*, n. 6.
[4] *Supra*, p. 222.
[5] *Supra*, pp. 175–177 and *infra*, pp. 278–282.
[6] See Treitel, pp. 446–467.
[7] See generally, Ivamy, *General Principles of Insurance Law* (2nd Edn.),
Chaps. 46–47.

as a form of indemnity insurance,[1] but it may be that there is a case for reversing this tradition.

Loss allocation[2]   As has already been suggested, the chief defect of the traditional approach has been the failure to appreciate the wider implications of the three-party situation. It has generally been assumed that the court has only two possible courses of action: either P is allowed to accumulate both his benefit from X and his remedy against D; or the benefit from X will be deducted from his award against D. In fact there is another possibility: X might be allowed to recover the value of his benefit from P[3] in which case no deduction will be made from P's action against D, or directly against D,[4] in which case the sum will be deducted from P's award.

Now the problem as to which of these three solutions should be adopted with regard to any one instance of a collateral source must to a large extent depend on the answer given to the question, who should bear the financial burden of the accident. It is impossible within the scope of this work to do full justice to the complexity of the matter, but a few general observations may be offered.

Solution one.   Both X and D should bear the loss. P is entitled to retain the benefit from both. As has been seen, this solution is widely favoured but it is arguable that it should prevail only where P truly *invests* some of his resources to provide himself with more favourable circumstances in the event of an accident. Where it is adopted on a large scale, then P is over-compensated, and society's economic resources, which are being deployed, through the process of loss distribution, to finance common law awards, are being strained unnecessarily.

Solution two.   X alone should bear the loss. The value of the benefit is deducted from P's award against D. This solution should only be adopted where it is thought desirable, in terms of social justice, that the sources which finance the benefit from X should relieve the burden from those sources which finance common law damages. The strongest case can be made out where X is financed by general taxation e.g. supplementary benefits and to a certain extent national insurance benefits, and where the effects of D's liability are borne by the consumer e.g. to a certain extent, road accidents.

Solution three.   D alone should bear the loss. X has a right to recover the value of his benefit either from P (in which case P's claim against D is unaffected) or from D (in which case the value of the benefit is deducted from P's claim against D). There is a very strong case for

---

[1] Colinvaux, *Law of Insurance* (3rd Edn.), para. 526, but this is only a *prima facie* construction: see *Theobald* v. *Ry. Passengers' Assurance* (1854), 10 Exch. 45.
[2] Atiyah, *Accidents, Compensation and the Law*, Chap. 18.
[3] *Supra*, p. 175.
[4] *Infra*, pp. 278–282.

this solution where X has relatively limited resources, and where those standing behind D are in a better position to carry the burden (e.g. where X is a family unit or a charity). It is arguable that it should also apply where the accident for which D is liable is one resulting from a particular activity, the benefits from which are enjoyed by a certain segment of society, who therefore, on one view of social justice, should alone bear the burden of the accident. Accidents arising from ultra-hazardous activities might fall within this category. The disadvantage of this solution is that the addition of X's cause of action makes the machinery of recovery more cumbersome and more expensive.

B INJURY TO REPUTATION AND TO FEELINGS

I INTRODUCTION

1 Causes of action

If personal injuries create many difficulties for those assessing compensation, the nature of the harm caused is at least tangible and obvious. This certainly cannot be said of the subject-matter of this last section of the present chapter: injury to a man's reputation, his dignity or his feelings. The most important of the torts giving rise to such injuries is defamation which itself distinguishes between two causes of action according to whether the defamatory statement or representation is permanent (libel) or transitory (slander). The chief significance of the distinction for the purposes of the law of damages is that to succeed in the latter action a plaintiff must generally prove special damage.[1] At the end of the chapter consideration will also be given to the torts of false imprisonment and malicious prosecution which, though distinct in character from defamation, nevertheless in practice inflict similar types of harm.[2] The extent to which a plaintiff may recover for loss of reputation as a consequence of torts which primarily protect other interests, notably those in property, is discussed elsewhere in the book.[3]

2 The problem of damages[4]

Defamation actions are notorious for the lack of certainty as to damages awards. The principles that do exist offer no more than the broadest of guidelines. As LORD REID has recently remarked:

---

[1] *Infra*, pp. 242–244.
[2] See LORD DIPLOCK in *Cassell & Co., Ltd.* v. *Broome*, [1972] A.C. 1027, at p. 1124.
[3] *Supra*, pp. 166–167, and *infra*, pp. 260–261.
[4] Samuels (1963), 79 L.Q.R. 63; Ernst and Lindey (1933), 19 Am. Bar. Ass. J. 103.

"any one person trying to fix a sum as compensation will probably find in his mind a wide bracket within which any sum could be regarded by him as not unreasonable—and different people will come to different conclusions."[1]

This unsatisfactory and yet probably irremediable state of affairs results from the combination of several factors.

(a) "Value" of reputation

The impossibility of setting a monetary value on a person's reputation is as crucial as it is obvious.[2] Unlike personal injury actions, the difficulty cannot be alleviated by resort to a tariff. What can "compensation" mean in this context? An application of the ordinary doctrine of *restitutio in integrum* can achieve little. Money cannot restore a man's reputation to its former and rightful condition. Financial advantages cannot eradicate the affront to his dignity. As WINDEYER, J. has pertinently remarked, "a man defamed does not get compensation *for* his damaged reputation. He gets damages *because* he was injured in his reputation. . . ."[3]

(b) Jury trials

Almost all defamation actions in England are tried by juries, and it is a postulate of constitutional law that judges should be slow to interfere with jury awards.[4] The courts have therefore only a limited ability to control and stabilize awards.

(c) Confusion between compensatory, aggravated and exemplary awards

Before the role of exemplary damages was restricted by LORD DEVLIN in *Rookes* v. *Barnard*[5] to his three categories, awards of compensation for injury to reputation frequently included an element whose sole object was to punish the defendant. There was up to 1964 an "extraordinary confusion of terminology reflecting differences in thinking and principle. . . ."[6] Even after the affirmation of Lord Devlin's judgment in *Cassell & Co., Ltd.* v. *Broome*[7] the relationship

---

[1] *Cassell & Co., Ltd.* v. *Broome, supra*, at p. 1085.
[2] "To translate reputations into gold is beyond the capacity of man. We must first find a new Philosophers Stone." Ernst & Lindey, *supra*, at p. 107.
[3] *Uren* v. *John Fairfax* (1967), 117 C.L.R. 118, at p. 150.
[4] The principle was manifest as early as 1677: see *Townsend* v. *Hughes*, 2 Mod. 150. For a recent restatement see *Cassell & Co., Ltd.* v. *Broome*, [1972] A.C. 1027, *per* LORD HAILSHAM, L.C., at p. 1065, *per* LORD REID, at p. 1091; *per* LORD KILBRANDON, at p. 1135; cf. LORD DIPLOCK, at pp. 1122–1123.
[5] [1964] A.C. 1129, at pp. 1220–1233, *supra*, p. 30.
[6] *Per* LORD HAILSHAM, L.C., *Cassell & Co., Ltd.* v. *Broome, supra*, at p. 1069.
[7] *Supra*, pp. 31–32.

between "aggravated" and "compensatory" damages remains somewhat obscure. Indeed this seems to be inevitable so long as it remains impossible to define what "compensation" means when applied to injuries to reputation. The extent to which non-compensatory elements should be admitted into a damages award was fully considered in an earlier chapter.[1] Although the practice was in general condemned, it was conceded that the special features of defamation rendered it difficult, if not actually undesirable, to resist their intrusion.[2] This chapter, however, has been written on the assumption that in this area as in others, the governing the award of damages should pursue the fundamental principle of compensation.

3 Plan of exposition

It follows from these difficulties that no specific methods of assessment can be ventured. The only principles that do exist refer only to those facts in the case to which the jury are entitled to advert and which should influence their minds when selecting a sum of money. It is proposed first to examine the kinds of loss which may result from a defamatory statement and for which damages may be awarded, secondly to consider what factors may be relevant in assessing those damages, thirdly in the light of theoretical conceptions as to the function of compensation to offer some suggestions as to the future development of the law. The chapter will conclude with an account of the special rules applied in slander, false imprisonment and malicious prosecution.

II   TYPES OF LOSS RESULTING FROM INJURY TO REPUTATION

1   Pecuniary losses

The one certain and readily quantifiable element is the pecuniary loss sustained by the plaintiff as a result of the defendant's tort. Specific losses such as out-of-pocket expenses,[3] the loss of particular earnings[4] or the loss of particular contracts[5] are of course recoverable but they should be pleaded and proved as special damage.[6] The plaintiff may in the alternative plead general loss of business as general damages. The standard of certainty required appears to be quite liberal for it will be

---

[1] *Supra*, Chap. 2.
[2] *Supra*, p. 34.
[3] *Skinner* v. *Shapiro*, [1924] W.L.D. 157.
[4] *Longdon-Griffiths* v. *Smith*, [1951] 1 K.B. 295.
[5] *Bateman* v. *Lyall* (1860), 7 C.B.N.S. 638.
[6] *Supra*, pp. 3–4.

inferred where the words were "in their very nature intended or reasonably likely to produce a general loss of business."[1] Where, however, large sums are claimed as business losses, "it is plainly desirable that they should be pleaded, particularized and so far as possible supported by evidence."[2] The point is well illustrated by *Lewis v. Daily Telegraph*[3]

> Two national newspapers (D1 and D2) published a report that the police fraud squad were investigating the affairs of a company (P1) of which (P2) was chairman. No specific evidence of pecuniary loss was submitted to the jury but P2 claimed that he and his company had sustained severe financial damage, and he referred to a sharp decline in the value of the company's shares. In the action against D1, the jury awarded £75,000 to P1 and £25,000 to P2. In the action against D2 (in which there were aggravating factors)[4] P1 was awarded £100,000 and P2 £17,000. The awards were quashed on the grounds that they were out of all proportion to the facts, and were such as would not have been made by twelve reasonable men. The evidence as to loss was "mere hearsay and assertions; and it was entirely undocumented"[5]— the damages were "ridiculously out of proportion to the injury suffered."[6]

This case is also authority for the proposition that the principle of *Gourley*[7] should apply to compensation for pecuniary loss in defamation actions. Insofar as the award of damages reflects the loss of financial benefits, which, if they had been secured, would have attracted tax, the extent of probable tax liability should be taken into account.[8]

2 Non-pecuniary loss

The purpose of this section is to attempt to categorize the various types of non-pecuniary loss which may be consequent on an injury to the reputation. Now it is arguable that such a categorization is artificial since from a practical view the jury will award one sum for the totality of the plaintiff's non-pecuniary loss,[9] and from at least one theoretical standpoint the only remediable loss is a loss of happiness.[10]

---

[1] *Per* BOWEN, L.J., *Ratcliffe v. Evans*, [1892] 2 Q.B. 524, at p. 533, a case of injurious falsehood but considered on this point to apply equally to defamation: see, e.g. *South Hetton Coal v. North Eastern News Association*, [1894] 1 Q.B. 133.
[2] *Per* HOLROYD PEARCE, L.J., *Lewis v. Daily Telegraph*, [1963] 1 Q.B. 340, at p. 376.
[3] *Ibid.*, affirmed on appeal, [1964] A.C. 234.
[4] See *infra*, pp. 237–238.
[5] *Per* DAVIES, L.J., [1963] 1 Q.B. 340, at p. 399.
[6] *Per* LORD DEVLIN, [1964] A.C. 234, at p. 287.
[7] [1956] A.C. 185, *supra*, pp. 107–115.
[8] *Per* LORD REID, [1964] A.C. 234, at pp. 261–262.
[9] *Infra*, p. 239.
[10] *Infra*, p. 240.

But even if the award be predicated on this basis, the jury in selecting an appropriate sum is entitled to take into account the various disadvantages to which the plaintiff was subjected.

(a) Loss of social esteem

The dogma of defamation has it that the defendant's statement should expose the plaintiff to hatred, contempt or ridicule and the law holds it to be a valuable asset that a man should be held in esteem by others. The first type of loss, therefore, depends on nothing which happens to the plaintiff himself but on how others react to the tort. A paradigm case is *Cook* v. *Ward*[1]

> P was represented by D in a local newspaper as a hangman. At a parish meeting which he attended in his capacity as the assistant overseer of the parish, P was made the object of a joke which played on his being represented as a hangman. Evidence of P being subjected to the humiliation of "a general roar of laughter" was admitted as being relevant to the issue of damages.

Clearly the wider the publication of the statement the greater the likelihood of substantial loss in this sense, and therefore the greater the tendency to award a larger sum.[2] Another relevant factor will be the reputation of the plaintiff as it stood at the time of the tort—this is dealt with below[3] under "mitigating factors". Rationally the jury should also take into account the plaintiff's social milieu: some segments of society are manifestly more tolerant of deviant conduct or reputation than others. In an Australian case[4] the court in upholding a high award thought that the jury had rightly taken into account the fact that in a country district an imputation of dishonest dealing against a farmer was likely to have the most serious consequences for him. Less commendable is *Youssoupoff* v. *Metro-Goldwyn-Mayer Pictures, Ltd.*[5]

> P, a former Russian princess, had been portrayed in Ds' film as being seduced by Rasputin. The award of £25,000 was upheld by the Court of Appeal even though P was unable to show that her reputation had in any way suffered, or that she had lost any friends. GREER, L J.

---

[1] (1830), 6 Bing. 409.
[2] See, e.g. the remarks of DEVLIN, L.J. in *Dingle* v. *Associated Newspapers*, [1961] 2 Q.B. 162, at p. 192 (affirmed *sub. nom. Associated Newspapers* v. *Dingle*, [1964] A.C. 371): "the law requires and permits that damages should be measured by the extent of the publication." Dicta to the contrary in *Whittaker* v. *Scarborough Post Newspaper Co.*, [1896] 2 Q.B. 148, at pp. 151–152 seem to have been inspired by punitive considerations.
[3] P. 236.
[4] *Triggell* v. *Pheeney* (1951), 82 C.L.R. 497.
[5] (1935), 50 T.L.R. 581.

thought that the jury were entitled to take into account the high social position that P occupied.[1]

But social position is relevant only to the extent that it exacerbates injury to the reputation. If used for other purposes it can derive support only from the dangerous proposition that the pride of an aristocrat is worth more than the pride of a pauper.

(b) Loss of good health

The plaintiff suffers ill health as a result of the defendant's tort. Might he recover for the consequences? The earlier authorities against recovery were effectually decided on grounds of remoteness.[2] Of course this and the requirement of a causal link between the tort and the loss may prove to be formidable obstacles, but once overcome there seems to be no reason why the plaintiff should not succeed and this has been envisaged *obiter* in a recent decision where the claim was rejected for failing to satisfy the causation test.[3]

(c) Injured feelings

The final category of loss is concerned with psychological reactions of the plaintiff himself. More often as a head of damages it is referred to as aggravated damages.[4] The general principle has been well expressed by PEARSON, L.J.:

> "the natural grief and distress which he may have felt at having been spoken of in defamatory terms, and ... any kind of high-handed, oppressive, insulting or contumelious behaviour ... which increases the mental pain and suffering ... and may constitute injury to the plaintiff's pride and self-confidence: those are proper elements to be taken into account."[5]

The losses for which compensation is payable thus range from actual pain and suffering[6] to loss of dignity and humiliation[7] to annoyance and irritation.[8] The jury is entitled to take into consideration aspects of the defendant's conduct from the time of the tort to the date of the verdict as provoking and aggravating the plaintiff's reactions.[9] There can, of course, be no acid test for proving that the plaintiff's feelings

---

[1] *Ibid.*, at p. 586.
[2] E.g. *Allsop* v. *Allsop* (1860), 5 H. & N. 534.
[3] *Wheeler* v. *Somerfield*, [1966] 2 Q.B. 94, *per* LORD DENNING, M.R., at p. 104. See also the Australian decision of *Rigby* v. *Mirror Newspapers, Ltd.* (1963), 64 S.R.(N.S.W.) 34.
[4] See also *supra*, pp. 29–30.
[5] *McCarey* v. *Associated Newspapers*, [1965] 2 Q.B. 86, at pp. 104–105.
[6] *Barnes* v. *Prudlin* (1667), 1 Sid. 396.
[7] *Cook* v. *Ward* (1830), 6 Bing. 409, *supra*, p. 234.
[8] *Fielding* v. *Variety Incorporated*, [1967] 2 Q.B. 841.
[9] *Infra.*

have been injured.   In most cases it is something to be inferred as the natural and foreseeable consequence of the content of the statement, its publication and other aspects of the defendant's conduct.[1]

III FACTORS MITIGATING OR AGGRAVATING THE AWARD

1 Reputation and conduct of plaintiff

The extent of the plaintiff's loss consequent on injury to his reputation will of course depend on the quality of his reputation before the tort. If the function of the damages award is to restore the plaintiff to his position before the tort, the jury must know what that position was. But the simple proposition that the reputation at the time of the defamation should be taken into account must be modified in the light of the rule in *Scott* v. *Sampson*[2] which has twice been affirmed by the House of Lords.[3] This is to the effect that though *general* evidence of a plaintiff's bad reputation is admissible,[4] neither evidence of *rumours* that the plaintiff had done what the defendant alleged nor evidence of *particular* facts tending to show the plaintiff's bad character is admissible. The laudable objects of so limiting the material available to the jury are "to contain the length of trials within manageable limits, to prevent the jury being avoidably confused as to the bearing of evidence on different issues, and to limit the grosser abuses of too great a liberty of reference given to either plaintiff or defendant."[5] But the rule has the demerit of adding to the overtechnical law of defamation[6] a distinction which is in theory questionable and in practice barely workable. The difficulties are well illustrated by *Waters* v. *Sunday Pictorial*.[7]

In an action by P, an estate agent, against the D newspaper, D sought to plead in mitigation that seven years previously in criminal proceedings LORD GODDARD, C.J. had described P's business as "fraudulent . . .

---

[1] *Per* PEARSON, L.J., *McCarey* v. *Associated Newspapers, supra,* at p. 105.

[2] (1882), 8 Q.B.D. 491.

[3] *Plato Films* v. *Speidel,* [1961] A.C. 1090; *Associated Newspapers* v. *Dingle,* [1964] A.C. 371.

[4] Under Ord. 82, r. 7 (R.S.C.) the defendant requires the leave of the trial judge to give such evidence unless "7 days at least before the trial he furnishes particulars to the plaintiff of the matters as to which he intends to give evidence." The rule complements rather than abrogates the *Scott* v. *Sampson* rule.

[5] *Per* LORD RADCLIFFE, *Plato Films* v. *Speidel, supra,* at p. 1128.

[6] "The law of libel seems to have characteristics of such complication and subtlety that I wonder whether a jury on retiring can readily distinguish their heads from their heels." *Per* RUSSELL, L.J. in *Broadway Approvals* v. *Odhams Press (No. 2),* [1965] 1 W.L.R. 805, at p. 825. See also the remarks of DIPLOCK, L.J. in *Boston* v. *W. S. Bagshaw & Sons,* [1966] 1 W.L.R. 1126, at p. 1135.

[7] [1961] 2 All E.R. 758.

from beginning to end." P sought to have the plea struck out on the ground that under the *Scott* rule it constituted evidence of particular facts. The plea was allowed to stand. The Court of Appeal did not attempt to generalize on the distinction between "general evidence" and "evidence of particular facts" but rested content with the conclusion that the plea did not go beyond what was permissible under the rule.

What, then, is the effect of a concurrent or almost concurrent publication of substantially the same allegation by a third party?[1] The House of Lords in *Associated Newspapers* v. *Dingle*[2] held that though evidence of the third party's publication was admissible for the purpose of negativing malice it was inadmissible for the purpose of mitigating damages. Again there are sound policy reasons for the rule: were it otherwise it would prejudice the plaintiff who was unable to sue the first defamer. But again it leads to practical difficulties: a jury must be told that they may have regard to evidence for one purpose but not for another.[3]

The question finally arises whether the award may be reduced on the ground that the conduct of the plaintiff was such as to provoke the publication. There is an old authority to the effect that evidence of provocation might go to mitigate the plaintiff's loss,[4] but the better view would seem to be that unless it were sufficient to negative liability altogether on grounds of causation or consent, it should operate only to counterbalance any features in the defendant's conduct which would otherwise aggravate the plaintiff's loss.[5]

2 Conduct of defendant

The conduct of the defendant may, indeed, operate to increase the award, for unlike the conduct of the plaintiff, it may directly affect the plaintiff's loss. Since the plaintiff may recover for injury to his feelings, evidence of the defendant's behaviour will be relevant in determining the extent to which the plaintiff suffered legitimate humiliation, irritation and grievance.[6] Thus evidence may be admitted for such factors as: repetition of the allegation,[7] the language of the allegation,[8] the

---

[1] Where the two publications are by *joint tortfeasors* the ordinary rule applies that the damages are to be assessed on the basis of that sum which may be recovered from either tortfeasor, *supra*, p. 37.
[2] [1964] A.C. 371.
[3] See Samuels (1963), 79 L.Q.R. 63, at pp. 84–85.
[4] *Moore* v. *Oastler* (1836), 1 M. & Rob. 451n; *Starkie on Slander and Libel* (3rd Edn.), p. 538.
[5] See *Lane* v. *Holloway*, [1968] 1 Q.B. 379.
[6] There are numerous authorities for this proposition from *Defries* v. *Davies* (1835), 7 C. & P. 112 to *Cassell & Co., Ltd.* v. *Broome*, [1972] A.C. 1027.
[7] *Whitney* v. *Moignard* (1890), 24 Q.B.D. 630.
[8] *Theaker* v. *Richardson*, [1962] 1 All E.R. 229.

manner and mode of the defence, especially any insulting and offensive cross-examination of the plaintiff,[1] the absence of an apology.[2] Not surprisingly this area of the law is bedevilled by the erstwhile confusion between aggravated and exemplary damages.[3] It cannot be sufficiently emphasized that the concern of the jury should not be with the conduct of the defendant *per se* but with the effect which that conduct had on the plaintiff's feelings and pride.[4] The danger is that, by concentrating on the defendant's conduct, the jury will be encouraged to award a large sum which in effect conceals a punitive motivation rather than a smaller sum which may adequately compensate for what is at its most severe an ephemeral loss. Even in *Cassell & Co., Ltd.* v. *Broome*[5] where the House of Lords firmly restricted the award of exemplary damages in defamation cases to the acts of government servants and libels for profits,[6] insufficient attention was paid to the point by some of the majority who upheld LORD DEVLIN's speech in *Rookes* v. *Barnard*.[7] Thus, for example, LORD HAILSHAM, L.C. considered that "the natural indignation of the court at the injury inflicted on the plaintiff is a perfectly legitimate motive in making a generous rather than a more moderate award to provide an adequate solatium",[8] and LORD REID confirmed that the malicious or insulting conduct of the defendant was a sufficient justification for "going to the top of the bracket and awarding as damages the largest sum that could fairly be regarded as compensation."[9] In contrast, the view expressed by LORD DIPLOCK seems more perfectly to accord with the compensatory principle:

> "If malice with which a wrongful act is done or insolence or arrogance with which it is accompanied renders it more distressing to the plaintiff his injured feelings can still be soothed by aggravated damages which are compensatory;"[10]

and he concluded by remarking that

> "an evanescent sense of grievance at the defendant's conduct is often over-valued in comparison with a lifelong deprivation due to physical injuries. . . ."[11]

---

[1] *Watt* v. *Watt*, [1905] A.C. 115.
[2] *Fielding* v. *Variety Incorporated*, [1967] 2 Q.B. 841.
[3] *Supra*, pp. 29–30.
[4] The point was stressed as early as 1866 by BLACKBURN, J. in *Kelly* v. *Sherlock* (1866), L.R. 1 Q.B. 686, at p. 698, but seems to have been largely ignored.
[5] [1972] A.C. 1027.
[6] *Supra*, pp. 34–36.
[7] [1964] A.C. 1129, at pp. 1220–1233.
[8] [1972] A.C. 1027, at p. 1073.
[9] *Ibid.*, at p. 1085.
[10] *Ibid.*, at p. 1130.
[11] *Ibid.*

IV QUANTIFICATION OF NON-PECUNIARY COMPENSATION

1 The problem

The insoluble problem of assessing compensation hardly requires comment. The vain attempts made to apply some form of arithmetical process are almost comically inadequate. In *Greenlands* v. *Wilmshurst*[1]

> Ps, a firm of drapers and furnishers were defamed in a report on their commercial credit published by Ds. The jury awarded £1000. A new trial was awarded on the ground that the award was excessive. HAMILTON, L.J. said: "by no formula or manipulation can £1000 be got at. For any damage really done, £100 was quite enough: double it for the sympathy: double it again for the jury's sense of the defendants' conduct, and again for the sense of Mr. F. E. Smith's (Ds' counsel). The product is only £800."[2]

But even though specific guidance on quantification cannot be provided it is obviously necessary and desirable to examine the theoretical basis of compensation to ascertain, if possible, the object which an award of damages should seek to attain.

2 Theoretical basis

In discussing compensation for non-pecuniary losses consequent on personal injuries it was suggested that there were three possible theoretical approaches.[3] The same analysis can be applied here.

(a) Conceptual approach

Any attempt to set an objective value to each injury to a person's reputation (e.g. £100 for calling a man a rogue, £1000 for calling a woman a whore) is as impracticable and futile as it is theoretically unsound.[4] It follows also that failing an objective basis or a tariff for the various types of loss there is something artificial in separating the categories of loss set out above and adding up the sum appropriate for each. As LORD HAILSHAM, L.C. said in *Cassell & Co., Ltd.* v. *Broome*[5]

> "I do not believe it is desirable or even possible simply to add separate sums together for different parts of the subjective element . . . the whole process of assessing damages where they are 'at large' is essentially a matter of impression and not addition."

---

[1] [1913] 3 K.B. 507.
[2] *Ibid.*, at p. 532.
[3] *Supra*, pp. 194–196.
[4] See the semi-serious attempt by Ernst and Lindey at (1933), 19 Am. Bar Assoc. J. 103.
[5] [1972] A.C. 1027, at p. 1072.

(b) Personal approach

Adoption of the personal approach would involve awarding the plaintiff a round sum for his loss of happiness resulting from the various categories of injury to his reputation. The whole matter would become in effect an assessment of injury to his pride and his feelings. It is apparent from dicta in recent cases that English law[1] is moving close to this position. Distaste for a punitive element in compensation has been balanced by a greater concern for the plaintiff's injured feelings.[2]

(c) Functional approach

Though judges are wont to speak of defamation damages as providing a solatium for a plaintiff's injured feelings,[3] and though disquiet is often expressed at the high level of jury awards[4] there is little evidence of these two issues being connected such as to indicate acceptance of the functional view, that is that the court in estimating the award should have regard to the use to which the money might be put. A solitary trace of this aspect may be found in a dictum of SELLERS, L.J. in *Broadway Approvals* v. *Odhams Press (No. 2)*[5]

> P was the managing director of a mail-order firm which traded in postage stamps. Ds published in their weekly newspaper an article criticizing P's business methods and it was held to be defamatory. The jury awarded P £10,000 but the Court of Appeal considered this to be so excessive that a new trial was ordered.

SELLERS, L.J. having taken into account that (i) the article would have been read by only a proportion of the large number of people who read Ds newspaper and (ii) the article alleged no outrageous conduct by the plaintiff, concluded that the award was "extravagantly out of proportion" to any possible injury to the plaintiff:

> "How can an income of £400 to £500 a year for life be justified by any harm done to Santo (the plaintiff) for such he could obtain with £10,000 and retain the lump sum intact."[6]

---

[1] See especially LORD DIPLOCK in *Cassell & Co., Ltd.* v. *Broome, ibid.*, at pp. 1125–1126.

[2] *McCarey* v. *Associated Newspapers*, [1965] 2 Q.B. 86; *Fielding* v. *Variety Incorporated*, [1967] 2 Q.B. 841; *Cassell & Co., Ltd.* v. *Broome, supra*.

[3] E.g. WINDEYER, J. in *Uren* v. *John Fairfax* (1966), 117 C.L.R. 118, at p. 150; LORD HAILSHAM, L.C. in *Cassell & Co., Ltd.* v. *Broome, supra*, at pp. 1073 and 1076.

[4] A remark by a South African judge GREENBERG, J. (in *Innes* v. *Visser*, [1936] W.L.D. 44, at p. 45) that "the figure of justice carries a pair of scales not a cornucopia" has received sympathetic repetition: e.g. *per* DAVIES, L.J., *Lewis* v. *Daily Telegraph*, [1963] 1 Q.B. 340, at p. 396. See also *Cassell & Co., Ltd.* v. *Broome, supra, per* LORD REID, at p. 1090, *per* LORD WILBERFORCE, at p. 1118; *per* LORD DIPLOCK, at p. 1130.

[5] [1965] 1 W.L.R. 805.

[6] *Ibid.*, at p. 818.

3 Controlling jury awards

Any criticism of the high level of awards at present pertaining in defamation actions involves of course a value judgment which can have no rational basis. Nevertheless the generosity of juries can be evidenced not merely by applying the functional criterion of the use to which the money might be put, but also by comparing awards with those current in personal injury cases. The point has been made (more than once) by LORD DIPLOCK. In *McCarey* v. *Associated Newspapers*[1] he said: "I do not believe that the law today is more jealous of a man's reputation than of his life or limb. That is the scale of values of the duel." An ex-Russian princess was awarded £25,000 in 1935 for the representation in a film that she had been raped some twenty years previously.[2] Taking into account the decline in the value of money it takes a multiple case of physical injuries of the utmost severity combined with intense pain and suffering and pecuniary loss[3] today to approximate to that figure. To say the least it was a curious set of values that was being applied.[4] One may tend to exaggerate the problem by highlighting a few really severe awards, and there is no irrebuttable evidence that juries are more generous than judges, but the feeling remains that awards of damages for loss of reputation are on too high a scale and that some action is necessary to curb them. Three possibilities present themselves.

(a) Functional approach

It might be made mandatory for the jury to take into account the use to which the compensation might be put. This would be theoretically the most satisfactory solution—it would apply the same standards as in personal injury actions (should the author's recommendations be accepted in that area of the law)—but its efficacy might remain suspect while the power of assessing damages still remained with the jury.

(b) Ceiling on awards

Legislation might impose a limit which non-pecuniary damages for injuries to the reputation might not exceed. The difficulty here is that it might encourage juries to award sums on or near this limit.

(c) Abolition of jury's power to award damages

Perhaps the most meritorious suggestion is that the jury's power to

---

[1] [1965] 2 Q.B. 86, at p. 109. See also his remarks in *Cassell & Co., Ltd.* v. *Broome*, [1972] A.C. 1027, at p. 1130 and WILLIAMS, J. in *Advocate Co., Ltd.* v. *Husbands* (1969), 15 W.I.R. 180, at pp. 186–187.
[2] *Youssoupoff* v. *Metro-Goldwyn Mayer* (1935), 50 T.L.R. 581, *supra*, pp. 234–235.
[3] E.g. *Povey* v. *Governors of Rydal School*, [1970] 1 All E.R. 841.
[4] Or was it a case of restitution for unjust enrichment? See *supra*, p. 36.

assess damages should be transferred to the judiciary.[1] This could of course be combined with either (i) or (ii) above. The suggestion does raise the more fundamental question of the role of the jury in civil actions as a whole. There could be practical difficulties in permitting the jury to determine liability without being able to qualify their decision on this point of awarding for example contemptuous damages.[2] But this could presumably be overcome by allowing the jury to recommend to the judge that the plaintiff be awarded only a nominal sum.

V   TORTS OTHER THAN LIBEL

1   Slanders not actionable *per se*

Most slanders are actionable only on proof of special damage.[3] There are two views as to the measure of damages in such cases. The first is that the requirement of special damage limits compensation as well as liability: the plaintiff may recover no more than the special damage which he pleads and proves. The second restricts the requirement of special damages to the question of liability: once the plaintiff has established a cause of action he may recover what compensation he would have recovered if the slander had been actionable *per se* or if it had been a libel.

(a)   Policy

The argument really turns on the nature of the slander action. According to the first view the object of the limitation in slander is to define the scope of protection which the law provides in those slandered. On the second view, it is more to deter vexatious litigation—once the plaintiff is able to show he has a serious grievance he should be fully indemnified. The many attempts made to justify the distinction between libel and slander[4] would appear to support the latter proposition. The common denominator emerging is that a slander assuming a transitory form is more likely to be trivial and harmless.[5] If the policy

---

[1] The Law Society have advocated this reform in their recommendations to the Faulks Committee. See on this question Cornish, *The Jury*, pp. 212–224 and ed. Rubinstein, *Wicked, Wicked Libels*, pp. 140–141.

[2] Cornish, *op. cit.* pp. 220–221.

[3] The exceptional cases in which slanders are actionable *per se* are where the words (i) impute a criminal offence, (ii) impute a contagious disease, (iii) impute unchastity to a woman, (iv) are calculated to disparage in trade or profession: see the standard textbooks on tort and defamation, e.g. Gatley on *Libel and Slander*, (6th Edn.), §§141–186.

[4] See, e.g. those cited in Gatley, *op. cit.*, § 145.

[5] See especially the observations of the Committee on the Law of Defamation Cmnd. 7536 (1948), para. 38. The Committee (with two dissenters) favoured retention of the special rule in slander mainly on the ground that it discouraged trivial complaints.

be then to discourage actions for slander on this basis it does not seem necessary that the rule should operate to limit compensation where it has been proved that the complaint is not a trivial one and that actual harm has been sustained.[1]

(b) Authority

Authority on the point is remarkably indecisive. The majority of English writers[2] prefer the restrictive view but judicial dicta can be invoked to support either.[3] American case-law on the other hand clearly supports the more liberal measure.[4]

(c) Assessment of damages

The present author's view is that the more liberal measure should be applied. Provided that the plaintiff can plead special damage he should be entitled to compensation assessed according to the principle outlined above.[5] Should the restrictive view prevail the plaintiff would be entitled only to such special damage as he could plead and prove. In this context[6] special damage means a loss which is "capable of being estimated in money".[7] This notion has, however, been widely construed to cover, for example, not only general loss of business[8] (i.e. without specific proof of loss of individual customers) but also the loss or postponement of marriage[9] and the loss of the hospitality of friends.[10] It was at one time thought, and some authors still maintain,[11] that special rules of remoteness apply to slander actions but the most widely accepted formulation of the doctrine that the special damage must be the "natural and reasonable result of the defendant's words"[12]

---

[1] Cf. Fleming, *Law of Torts* (4th Edn.), p. 465.
[2] E.g. Gatley, *op. cit.*, § 1388, Clerk & Lindsell on *Torts* (13th Edn.), § 1691, Odgers, *Libel and Slander* (6th Edn.), pp. 315–316; *contra*, Salmond on *Torts* (11th Edn.), p. 247.
[3] For the restrictive view see e.g. Viscount Haldane in *Jones* v. *Jones*, [1916] 2 A.C. 481, at p. 490 and Williams, J. in *Brown* v. *Smith* (1853), 13 C.B. 596, at p. 600; for the liberal view see e.g. Martin, B. in *Dixon* v. *Smith* (1860), 5 H. & N. 450, at p. 453 and Lord Wensleydale in *Lynch* v. *Knight* (1861), 9 H.L.Cas. 577, at p. 598.
[4] See the cases cited in Prosser, *Torts* (4th Edn.), p. 761, n. 10.
[5] Pp. 232–238.
[6] Cf., *supra*, pp. 3–4.
[7] Per Lord Coleridge, C.J., *Chamberlain* v. *Boyd* (1883), 11 Q.B.D. 407, at p. 411.
[8] *Ratcliffe* v. *Evans*, [1892] 2 Q.B. 524.
[9] *Speight* v. *Gosney* (1891), 60 L.J.Q.B. 231.
[10] *Davies* v. *Solomon* (1871), L.R. 7 Q.B. 112 but not the loss of the *society* of friends since this has no pecuniary equivalent: *Argent* v. *Donigan* (1892), 8 T.L.R. 432. The distinction is of course an elusive one.
[11] E.g. McGregor, §§ 1290–1296.
[12] *Chamberlain* v. *Boyd*, *supra*, per Lord Coleridge, C.J., at p. 413, per Bowen, L.J., at p. 417.

may be translated without distorting the meaning into the modern test of "reasonable foreseeability."[1]

2 False imprisonment

The injury which is the essence of an action for false imprisonment is the deprivation of liberty.   But the losses that result are clearly analogous to those for which compensation is sought in a defamation action.

(a) Pecuniary losses

A plaintiff may recover for expenses reasonably incurred.   A typical claim is for the costs of procuring release where these were not awarded in their own right.[2]   He may also recover for being deprived of the opportunity of earning a profit e.g. loss of wages.[3]

(b) Non-pecuniary losses

The three heads of injured feelings[4] loss of good health[5] and loss of social esteem[6] may all be the subject of an award.   The principles discussed above[7] apply equally here: in particular the conduct of the defendant may be taken into consideration as aggravating the injury to the plaintiff's feelings.[8]

3 Malicious prosecution

Here the injury of which the plaintiff complains is being subjected to legal proceedings improperly instituted against him.   Unlike false imprisonment, the tort is derived from the action on the case and is therefore actionable only on proof of special damage.[9]   There is a great deal of judicial discussion of this question and almost nothing on the measure of damages once the cause of action has been established.   As with cases of slander not actionable *per se* it is uncertain whether the plaintiff is entitled to recover more than he is able to plead under special damage.   In slander it was argued that the measure of compensation should not be so restricted.   The position appears to be different here because the ambit of "special damage" is far wider.   In *Roberts* v.

---

[1] *Supra*, pp. 68–71.

[2] *Pritchet* v. *Boevey* (1833), 1 Cr. M. 775.   See also *infra*, pp. 245–246.

[3] *Childs* v. *Lewis* (1924), 40 T.L.R. 870.

[4] *Walter* v. *Alltools* (1944), 171 L.T. 371.

[5] *Lowden* v. *Goodrick* (1791), Peake 64, although the claim was rejected on the ground that it had not been properly pleaded.

[6] *Per* LORD DIPLOCK, *Cassell & Co., Ltd.* v. *Broome*, [1972] A.C. 1027, at p. 1124.

[7] Pp. 233–236.

[8] *Walter* v. *Alltools*, *supra*.

[9] Dworkin (1962), 25 M.L.R. 89.

Savill[1], HOLT, C.J. referred to three types of damage which would render the plaintiff's claim actionable.

> "First, where a man is injured in his fame and reputation . . . the second relates to a man's person, where he is assaulted or beaten, or put under any confinement . . . there is a third sort of damages which a man may sustain in respect of his property. . . ."

(a) Injury to reputation

Although the scope of his head of damage was intended to be confined to cases of slander which were actionable *per se*,[2] it was extended by later decisions to include all cases of injury to the plaintiff's "fair fame".[3] The test is: "was the charge one which necessarily and naturally is defamatory of the plaintiff."[4] Once this equation with defamation is made, damages must be quantifiable on the same basis as libel.[5]

(b) Personal injury

It is clear from Chief Justice Holt's words that this head of damages is concerned as much with what is today regarded as aggravated damages as with personal injuries in the ordinary sense. Both may therefore be the subject of compensation, and the principles of assessment described above[6] will apply.

(c) Property injury

By "injury to property" is meant pecuniary losses.[7] Loss of the opportunity to earn a profit (e.g. earnings) is in principle recoverable.[8] Compensation for expenses reasonably incurred may also be claimed. Yet difficulty has arisen as to whether the plaintiff should recover legal costs beyond those awarded to him in previous proceedings with the defendant. The objection is that the order as to costs must be conclusively determined by the court which tries the action and that the award of a greater sum would infringe the doctrine of *res judicata*. In *Quartz Hill Gold Mining Co.* v. *Eyre*[9] where costs had been incurred in *civil* proceedings, the Court of Appeal were convinced by the argu-

---

[1] (1698), 5 Mod. Rep. 405, at pp. 406–407. There are no less than ten reports of this case but on the strength of DIPLOCK, J.'s remarks in *Berry* v. *British Transport Commission*, [1961] 1 Q.B. 149, at pp. 160–161 the most often cited report (1 Lord Raym. 374) should not be used.
[2] *Per* DIPLOCK, J., *Berry* v. *British Transport Commission, supra*, at pp. 161–162.
[3] E.g. *Rayson* v. *South London Tramways Co.*, [1893] 2 Q.B. 304.
[4] *Per* DIPLOCK, J., *Berry* v. *British Transport Commission, supra*, at p. 166.
[5] *Supra*, pp. 232–238.
[6] Pp. 237–238 and pp. 170–230, respectively.
[7] HOLT, C.J. speaks of "unnecessary expenses" (1698), 5 Mod. 405, at p. 407.
[8] *Per* LUSH, J. *obiter* in *Childs* v. *Lewis* (1924), 40 T.L.R. 870, at p. 871.
[9] (1883), 11 Q.B.D. 674.

ment and rejected the plaintiff's claim for an indemnity. Although the decision is still good law it was criticized in *Berry* v. *British Transport Commission.*[1] The premise of the objection, it was said, is that the order as to costs is intended as a complete indemnity for costs incurred whereas this is manifestly not always so. The usual award of costs is on the "party and party" basis according to which only "such costs as were necessary or proper for the attainment of justice or for enforcing or defending the rights of the party whose costs are being taxed,"[2] are allowed and these will usually fall short of the ordinary damages measure, which is of expenses *reasonably* incurred. But the Court of Appeal in the later case refused to extend the immunity to costs incurred in *criminal* proceedings. The decision in *Eyre* was not of course binding.[3] But more important still the same justification could not support a refusal to grant the remedy: the successful defendant in criminal proceedings is generally not awarded costs. The premise that an order of costs is intended to indemnify the plaintiff cannot apply in this area.[4] Where the cause of action arises out of criminal proceedings, therefore, the plaintiff is entitled to the difference between the costs (if any) which he recovered in those proceedings and the costs reasonably incurred in defence of the prosecution.

---

[1] [1962] 1 Q.B. 306, *per* DEVLIN, L.J. at p. 322–323; *per* DANCKWERTS, L.J., at p. 336.

[2] R.S.C. Ord. 62, r. 28(2).

[3] Although it seems that for DEVLIN, L.J. the decision in *Barnett* v. *Eccles Corporation*, [1900] 2 Q.B. 423 was still an obstacle.

[4] [1962] 1 Q.B. 306, *per* ORMEROD, L.J., at pp. 317–318; *per* DEVLIN, L.J., at pp. 327–328, 330; *per* DANCKWERTS, L.J., at pp. 336–338.

CHAPTER SEVEN

Injuries to Economic Interests

I INTRODUCTION

Any type of injury may result in economic loss. The previous two chapters dealt with the measure of compensation for such losses where they are consequent on injury to the plaintiff's person, reputation or property. This final chapter on tortious damages is devoted to the principles of compensation where the plaintiff suffers only economic harm—where there is no intervening injury to his person, his property or his reputation.[1] The fact that in these cases the distinction between "injury" and "loss", on which great reliance has been placed in other contexts,[2] is no longer a real one has some interesting consequences. In the first place, questions of liability and compensation inevitably run into one another: it is impossible to distinguish between the type of harm and the extent of the harm.[3] Secondly, the principles of quantifying damages have been less well developed:[4] the court, in so many cases, seems concerned simply to ascertain that the plaintiff has sustained *some* economic harm, and awards either that very amount, or a different amount which it instinctively feels is preferable.

The varieties of tortious conduct which may give rise to pure economic injury have been divided into four categories:

(i) In the first, the plaintiff in reliance on a statement by the defendant acts in some way to his own financial detriment.

(ii) The second comprises injuries to the plaintiff's business interests which are consequent on what may be loosely termed "unfair or unlawful competition".

---

[1] For the purposes of liability, there is a lively dispute as to what constitutes "pure economic harm": see, e.g. *S.C.M. (United Kingdom), Ltd.* v. *Whittall & Son, Ltd.,* [1971] 1 Q.B. 337; and *Dutton* v. *Bognor Regis Urban District Council,* [1972] 1 Q.B. 273.
[2] *Supra,* pp. 1–2, 61–62.
[3] *Supra,* p. 61.
[4] This is not true of actions under the Fatal Accidents Acts (*infra,* pp. 264–278) but these are so closely analogous to personal injury claims that most of the principles are the same.

(iii) The third is concerned with injury to the plaintiff's gainful employment which results from the statements or deeds of another.

(iv) The final group deals with cases where the plaintiff's economic injury is parasitic on the injury to or death of a third person.

II ACTIONABLE MISREPRESENTATIONS

1 Forms of liability and losses

This section is concerned with the measure of compensation payable to a plaintiff who by relying on a statement by the defendant acts to his own detriment. To establish a cause of action, the plaintiff must show that the statement came under one of the following heads:

(i) *Fraud* It was a false representation made intentionally or recklessly:[1] or

(ii) *Negligent misrepresentation at common law* It was made negligently in circumstances in which the defendant, being in a special relationship with the plaintiff, owed him a duty of care;[2] or

(iii) *Negligent misrepresentation: statutory remedies* It was an untrue statement contained in a prospectus which induced the plaintiff to take shares or debentures[3] or a misrepresentation which induced the plaintiff to enter into a contract,[4] unless, in either case, the defendant proves that he had reasonable ground to believe and did believe up to the time of the transaction that the facts represented were true;[5] or

(iv) *Innocent misrepresentation* It induced the plaintiff to enter into a contract in circumstances which would have entitled him to rescind the contract but which prompted the court to exercise its statutory power to award damages in lieu of rescission.[6]

Reliance on misstatements may of course give rise to personal or property injury. Should they do so, compensation is assessed according to the principles discussed in the last two chapters.[7] Where no physical injury intervenes, the economic losses resulting from the misstatement

---

[1] *Derry* v. *Peek* (1889), 14 App. Cas. 337.
[2] *Hedley Byrne & Co.* v. *Heller & Partners*, [1964] A.C. 465.
[3] Companies Act 1948, s. 43.
[4] Misrepresentation Act 1967, s. 2(1).
[5] The crucial difference between liability under (ii) and (iii) is that in (ii) the onus of proving negligence is on the plaintiff whereas in (iii) it is for the defendant to show that he has taken reasonable care.
[6] Misrepresentation Act 1967, s. 2(2).
[7] E.g. *Mullett* v. *Mason* (1866), L.R. 1 C.P. 559 (destruction of chattel); *Clay* v. *Crump & Sons*, [1964] 1 Q.B. 533 (personal injuries).

may be divided into the two usual categories of (i) *basic positive losses* = expenses, and (ii) *consequential losses* = loss of profit or the use of property. Before the rules of quantification appliable to these categories are considered, a few observations on the general principles of compensation must be made.

2 *Restitutio in integrum* or loss of bargain ?[1]

Most frequently the plaintiff representee is induced by the representation to enter into a contract. Now the object of an award of tortious damages is to put the plaintiff in the position he would have been in if no tort had been committed, that is, as if he had not entered into a contract with the defendant. This will be achieved by restoring to him what he gave under the contract but compelling him to account for any benefit received under it. For breach of contract,[2] on the other hand, a different mode of compensation is adopted: the plaintiff is awarded such a sum of money as will put him in the position he would have been in if the contract had been performed, in other words, he recovers compensation for his loss of bargain. If, then, the representation can be construed as a contractual term, the plaintiff may sue for breach of contract and he will be entitled to the difference between the value of what he received under the contract and the value of what he should have received if the representation had been true; whereas, if the tortious measure is applied, he will recover only the difference between the value of what he received under the contract and the consideration which he paid for it.

The question thus arises as to which of these two standards of compensation is to be applied to the various causes of action described above.

(a) Fraud

English law is now firmly committed, after some early flirtation with the contractual measure,[3] to the principle that the tortious measure is to be applied in actions of deceit.[4]

(b) Negligent misrepresentation

It seems clear from the case-law that the tortious measure will prevail also in the common law action for negligent misrepresentation.[5]

---

[1] The difference between the two methods of compensation is further discussed, *infra*, pp. 283–288.

[2] See, generally, *infra*, pp. 284–286.

[3] E.g. LORD CAMPBELL, L.C. in *Davidson* v. *Tulloch* (1860), 3 Macq. 783, at p. 790.

[4] *Peek* v. *Derry* (1887), 37 Ch.D. 541, at p. 578 (reversed on another ground (1889) 14 App. Cas. 337); *McConnel* v. *Wright*, [1903] 1 Ch. 546, at p. 554; *Doyle* v. *Olby (Ironmongers)*, [1969] 2 Q.B. 158 (discussed by Treitel in (1969), 32 M.L.R. 552).

[5] *Dodds and Dodds* v. *Millman* (1964), 45 D.L.R.(2d) 472.

There is a long tradition that compensation payable for a misstatement in a prospectus under section 43 of the Companies Act 1943 is assessed as if the statement had been made fraudulently,[1] and for the purposes of liability under section 2(1) of the Misrepresentation Act 1967 the same fiction is made explicit. It follows that the tortious measure applies to both.

(c) Innocent misrepresentation

As regards section 2(2) of the Misrepresentation Act 1967 the position is as yet unclear. There is no authoritative guidance on the measure of damages.[2] Three arguments can be invoked in support of the tortious measure.

(i) An inference that an award under s. 2(2) should be not greater that that prescribed under s. 2(1) may be drawn[3] from s. 2(3) which provides that where a defendant is liable under both s. 2(1) and s. 2(2) "any award under the said subsection (2) shall be taken into account in assessing his liability under the said subsection (1)". The suggestion is that since s. 2(1) lays down a tortious, not a contractual measure, Parliament could not have intended to impose the latter as the basis of compensation. But the hint, even if intended, is at best an equivocal one: it can be interpreted as laying down a different test of remoteness;[4] it may have been designed simply to avoid the possibility of double recovery.

(ii) S. 2(2) gives the court power to award damages in lieu of rescission. Rescission, without a complementary award of damages, does not provide the plaintiff with compensation for the loss of his bargain. It is unlikely that Parliament intended that the alternative remedy should extend the scope of compensation to include this element.

(iii) For the most blatantly improper form of misrepresentation (fraud) the plaintiff may recover compensation only on the tortious basis. It would be somewhat odd if he were to benefit from the generally more generous contractual remedy.[5]

It has been assumed throughout this discussion that the tortious measure is the most appropriate standard of compensation in cases of fraud. But it is interesting to observe that in the United States of America, though the Restatement and a small number of jurisdictions have followed the English rule,[6] the majority of jurisdictions apply the contractual measure,[7] while a third group favours the so-called "flexi-

---

[1] *McConnel* v. *Wright, supra*; *Clark* v. *Urquhart*, [1930] A.C. 28.
[2] See, in general, Atiyah & Treitel, (1967), 30 M.L.R. 369, at pp. 376–377.
[3] Atiyah & Treitel, *ibid.*, at p. 377.
[4] Treitel, *Law of Contract* (3rd Edn.), pp. 305–306.
[5] Atiyah & Treitel, *supra*, at p. 377.
[6] Restatement of Torts, § 549.
[7] See the cases cited and annotation at 13 A.L.R. 3d 885, § 3(a).

bility theory" according to which the trial judge may assess compensation on the basis of either doctrine as the circumstances and the justice of the case requires.[1] It is submitted that the English courts are right in preferring the tortious measure: most of the arguments adduced to support the contractual basis involve punitive or deterrent considerations. The policy of compensation must look askance at the frank admission by one American writer that "many courts have adopted (the contractual measure) because its generally higher awards punish defendants and discourage the practice of fraud".[2] A second argument is based on the expectations of the plaintiff representee: it is said that he is entitled to rely on the truth of the representations so that he might secure the profits expected from the transaction.[3] But this too is unsatisfactory: insofar as the representor may be held to a promise to do or convey what he represented to exist, the promise must be supported by valuable consideration and it will be enforced by a contractual action. To argue that this is a sufficient ground for assessing damages on a contractual basis in a *tortious* action involves a *non-sequitur*.

3 Remoteness

There is some authority for the proposition that the ordinary doctrine of remoteness does not apply to the action of deceit.[4] The question was fully considered in Chapter Three.[5]

4 Quantification

The doctrine of *restitutio in integrum* having been accepted as the basis of compensation, the task of the court is to award the plaintiff such a sum of money as represents the difference between his position resulting from his reliance on the misrepresentation, and his position if no misrepresentation had been made. Pecuniary losses may, as in other torts, be divided into basic losses covering expenditure incurred, and consequential losses for the extent to which the plaintiff has been deprived of opportunities for gain.

(a) Basic losses

Subject to the doctrines of remoteness, mitigation and certainty, the plaintiff may recover any expenses which were incurred as a result of

---

[1] See especially *Selamn* v. *Shirley*, 85 P. 2d 384 (1938).
[2] S.S.P.(olk) (1967), 47 Virg. L.R. 1209, at p. 1211.
[3] *Per* Robb, J., *Walker* v. *Fleming Motor*, 404 P. 2d 929, at p. 934 (1965).
[4] *Doyle* v. *Olby* (*Ironmongers*), [1969] 2 Q.B. 158.
[5] *Supra*, pp. 70–71.

the defendant's misrepresentation. A useful illustration is *Richardson*
v. *Silvester*[1]

> D inserted an advertisement in the Cambrian News to the effect that
> he was willing to let a country estate, when, as he knew, he had no power
> to let the property. P, on the strength of the advertisement, himself
> inspected the property and employed other persons to inspect and value
> it. P recovered his travelling, inspecting and valuing expenses.

More frequently the plaintiff is induced by the representation to
enter into a transaction, usually with the defendant, which proves to be
unprofitable. He should of course recover to the extent that his
patrimony or financial circumstances have been reduced as a result of
the transaction, that is with a deduction for any benefit which the transaction has conferred on him. This measure may, in the alternative, be
formulated as the difference between what he paid and the value of what
he received. Thus in *Dodds and Dodds* v. *Millman*[2]

> P, in reliance on the negligent estimate by D, an estate agent, of the
> profitability of an apartment building, purchased the property from X.
> He was awarded the difference between the price he paid for the
> property $43,000 and its value in his hands $35,000.

Of course, in some cases, the calculation may be more complicated
for the court will have to account for the whole of the plaintiff's outgoings on the transaction and deduct from that all the benefits he
acquired. This is well illustrated by WINN, L.J.'s quantification in
Doyle v. *Olby*[3]

> *Deficits*
>
> | | | |
> |---|---|---|
> | Purchase of business + stock | | = £9,500 |
> | Interest on loan and overdraft + rates | | = £3,000 |
> | TOTAL DEFICITS | | = £12,500 |
> | *Benefits* | | |
> | Sale of business and stock | £4,300 | |
> | Salary and living accommodation | £2,700 | |
> | TOTAL BENEFITS | | = £7,000 |
> | Award = deficits less benefits | | = £5,500 |

A special problem arises where the defendant's misrepresentation
(e.g. under section 43 of the Companies Act 1948) induces the plaintiff
to purchase shares. Without doubt, according to the rule outlined
above, the plaintiff is entitled to the difference between what he paid
for the shares and their value.[4] But what does "value" mean in this

---

[1] (1873), L.R. 9 Q.B. 34.
[2] (1964), 45 D.L.R. (2d) 472.
[3] [1969] 2 Q.B. 158, at pp. 169–170 concurred in by LORD DENNING, M.R.
and SACHS, L.J.
[4] *Twycross* v. *Grant* (1877), 2 C.P.D. 469.

context? and at what time is it to be ascertained? The thorny problem of "value" is with us again,[1] and in truth the answers given by the case-law to these questions are both vague and unsatisfactory. The "well-settled" rule is that the court must take the "real value" of the shares at the time of acquisition.[2] In fact this is but a euphemism for damages at large for the judges have been quick to point out that the "real value" is not ordinarily the "market value" since the market price may itself have been influenced by the defendant's misrepresentation.[3] Little guidance is offered as to how the "real value" is to be assessed except that events subsequent to the transfer may show (i) that the shares were sold at a price which did not represent their "true value"[4] or (ii) that the assets of the company did not correspond in value to the money paid.[5]

A more satisfactory and helpful rule may be formulated if cognizance is taken of the doctrine of mitigation. The plaintiff's true loss may be said to be the difference between the price he paid for the shares and the price which he secured or would have secured if he had sold (or attempted to sell) the shares at such time as the court considers that it was or would have been reasonable to sell the shares. This will probably, though not necessarily, be within a reasonable time of the discovery of the fraud. Such reasoning formed the basis of the award in the recent Canadian case of *Central B.C. Planers* v. *Hocker*.[6]

> D, a securities salesman, believed erroneously that a strike had been made at an oil well. He informed P, a client, of the fact and in reliance on the statement P bought shares in a company with interests in the oil well. P later sold the shares at a loss.

The British Columbia Court of Appeal held that the trial judge had been right to award as damages the difference between the amount paid for the shares and the sum realized when the shares were sold: he had found as a fact that the plaintiff had acted reasonably in selling as he did.

(b) Consequential losses: loss of profit; loss of use

As a result of the misrepresentation the plaintiff may have been deprived of an opportunity to earn a profit. In *Burrows* v. *Rhodes*[7]

> P went to join an invasion force in South Africa in reliance on D's representation that the invasion had the support of H.M. Government,

---

[1] Cf., *supra*, pp. 121–123.
[2] *Peek* v. *Derry* (1887), 36 Ch.D. 541.
[3] *Per* COTTON, L.J., *Peek* v. *Derry*, *supra*, at pp. 591–592; *per* BUCKLEY, J., *Broome* v. *Speake*, [1903] 1 Ch. 586, at pp. 605–606.
[4] *Ibid.*, *per* COTTON, L.J., *Peek* v. *Derry*, *supra*, at p. 592.
[5] *Per* COLLINS, M.R., *Broome* v. *Speake*, *supra*, at p. 623.
[6] (1970), 10 D.L.R. (3d) 541.
[7] [1899] 1 Q.B. 816.

that it would be reinforced by other lawfully appointed forces, and that his services were required for the protection of women and children. P recovered from D, *inter alia*, his loss of earnings.

Equally remediable is the loss of the enjoyment or use of property. For example in *Mafo* v. *Adams*;[1]

P, an occupier under a regulated tenancy of rooms owned by D, was tricked by D into leaving the premises in the belief that alternative accommodation was available to him elsewhere. He was awarded £100 for loss of the regulated tenancy and for the consequent inconvenience.

(c) Non-pecuniary loss: aggravated damages and inconvenience

Non-pecuniary loss is generally consequent on personal injury, but two forms of such loss may result from a pure economic injury. These are: (1) aggravated damages[2] and (2) damages for discomfort and inconvenience.[3] The principles governing the award of both have been considered elsewhere[4] and separate discussion here is not required.

III   INJURY TO BUSINESS INTERESTS

1   Introduction

Under this heading it is proposed to deal with those injuries which result from "unfair or unlawful competition". The courts have not been eager to elaborate principles governing the assessment of damages in this area. It seems to be felt that because the act complained of caused an injury to business profits there is no real problem of quantification save that of proof.[5] A judge faced with an over-elaborate formula and a mass of figures may feel tempted to abandon the arithmetical approach and resort to guessing at a "round sum": "the real problem is, when all the facts are considered and all the considerations on either side are given fair weight, the proper sum at which to estimate the plaintiff's damage."[6] When principles are formulated they tend to be confined to the particular tort which is the subject of the action:

---

[1] [1970] 1 Q.B. 548.
[2] No direct authority for recovery under this head has been found but it may legitimately be inferred from *Mafo* v. *Adams, supra, per* WIDGERY, L.J., at p. 558, that such an award may be made.
[3] *Mafo* v. *Adams, supra.*
[4] *Supra,* pp. 197–198, 237–238.
[5] See, e.g. the remarks of LORD SHAW in *Watson, Laidlow & Co., Ltd.* v. *Pott, Cassels and Williamson* (1914), 31 R.P.C. 104, at pp. 117–118.
[6] *Per* SIR WILFRED GREENE, M.R., *Draper* v. *Trist,* [1939] 3 All E.R. 513, at p. 519.

in this, as in other areas,[1] the courts seem to be obsessed with the cause
of action rather than with applying a general principle. What follows
is an attempt to state some general principles which will be illustrated
by reference to the specific causes of action. First, however, the causes
of action must be summarized, and classified according to the nature of
the tortious conduct.

2 Causes of action

(a) "Unlawful interference" torts

The first group of actions comprise what may be referred to as the
"interference" torts. These are: interference with contract, intimidation, interference by unlawful means and conspiracy. They generally
have as common denominators (1) an intention by the defendant to
injure the plaintiff, (2) the employment of "unlawful means" to achieve
that end, and (3) resulting loss of profitable business to the plaintiff.

(b) Remedies under the Industrial Relations Act 1971

Apart from elaborating special rules for the actionability of the above
torts in industrial disputes, the Industrial Relations Act 1971 intro-
duces the new remedy of "unfair industrial practice".[2] The statute
itself formulates principles of which compensation awarded by the
industrial court or tribunal is to be assessed,[3] but, as will be seen, subject
to certain important limitations, these follow the common law rules.

(c) Injurious falsehoods

The tort most usually known by the name of injurious falsehood is
committed where the defendant makes a false statement to a third
person about the plaintiff causing to the latter some economic injury.
The action for passing off, in which the plaintiff claims that the defendant represented that the goods he was selling were those of the
plaintiff, had its origin in injurious falsehood but, at least as far as the
measure of damages is concerned, is more closely analogous to remedies
for the infringement of rights in immaterial property.

(d) Infringement of rights in immaterial property

There are special torts for the protection of rights in immaterial
property. Three of them, the infringements of trade marks, patents
and copyright, are largely governed by statute.[4] A fourth, which is a

---

[1] See especially misappropriation of chattels, *supra*, pp. 141–142.
[2] Ss. 97–98.
[3] Ss. 116–119.
[4] Especially the Trade Marks Act 1938, the Patents and Designs Act 1949 and
the Copyright Act 1956.

recent judicial creation,[1] makes actionable the passing on of confidential information.

3 Positive losses—expenses

As usual the defendant must account for any expenditure reasonably incurred by the plaintiff and resulting from the tort.[2] Thus in a passing off action when it was established that, as a necessary and reasonable consequence of the defendant's action in selling some of the plaintiff's old and discarded goods as his new goods, the plaintiff incurred expenditure on counter-advertisement, the sum so spent was recoverable.[3] But the court must take care to ascertain that the expense was caused by the tort. In *British Motor Trade Association* v. *Salvadori*[4]

> Ps, in an effort to restrain the inflation of the price of certain cars required all purchasers of such cars to covenant not to resell within 12 months of the purchase. Ds, with the intention of breaking the system, induced certain purchasers to resell their cars to Ds in breach of the covenant. In order to combat this and other attacks on the system, Ps maintained a large investigation department. They successfully claimed from Ds the money spent in "unravelling and detecting the unlawful machinations of the defendants. . . ."[5]

ROXBURGH, J. was ambiguous on the point but it is evident that the plaintiffs would not have recovered the ordinary overheads of running the investigation department. They were entitled to compensation only for those expenses which were directly attributable to the defendant's unlawful activity.

4 Consequential loss—profits

Most frequently, of course, an injury to a business interest will result in a loss of profits. There are three methods of quantifying this item of damages, and selection of the most appropriate method depends on the nature of the plaintiff's injury, the remedy he seeks and the attitude of the court.

(a) Loss of profits on sale

The most obvious and popular method is for the court to attempt to estimate what profit the plaintiff would have made through the sale of

---

[1] See North (1972), 12 J.S.P.T.L. 149.
[2] Under the Industrial Relations Act 1971, s. 116(2) "the loss sustained by the aggrieved party . . . shall be taken to include—(a) any expenses reasonably incurred by him in consequence of the matters to which the complaint relates. . . ."
[3] *A.-G. Spalding & Brothers* v. *A. W. Gamage* (1918), 35 R.P.C. 101.
[4] [1949] Ch. 556.
[5] *Ibid., per* ROXBURGH, J., at p. 569.

his goods or services if the defendant had not committed his tort. In the "interference" torts, this will be a question simply of the production of evidence of lost profits sufficient to satisfy the court.[1] Where, on the other hand, the defendant's tortious activity involves a form of passing off or infringing an immaterial property right, the defendant will himself have exploited the situation to his financial advantage, and the question arises as to the relationship between his profit and the loss of profits claimed by the plaintiff as damages.

Illustration (I) D by the manufacture and sale of certain articles infringes a patent owned by P. P claims that the sales made by D would, but for D's infringement, have been made by P.

Illustration (II) D infringes P's copyright when he incorporates into the production of Christmas cards a sketch designed by P. P claims as damages a proportionate part of the profit made on the sale of the Christmas cards.

The amount of profits made by the defendant may usefully be taken as the starting point in the quantification process.[2] But the court must then reduce the sum by an appropriate part to represent the fact that the plaintiff would not have procured all of the defendant's custom either because a certain proportion of the successful dealing resulted from the defendant's own special exertions,[3] or because he could have made part of the sales without committing a tort,[4] or because other competitors would have captured a share of the market.[5] The scales may be tipped in the reverse direction by other factors: for example, that as a result of the defendant's unlawful competition the plaintiff had to lower his prices in order to minimize his loss of profits[6] (although he must show that he acted reasonably in lowering his prices[7] and that he would in any case have sold at the higher price).[8]

(b) Loss of profits on licence

Instead of himself selling the article in which the special proprietary right exists, the plaintiff may let out at a fixed fee the patented article,

---

[1] E.g. *Goldsoll* v. *Goldman*, [1914] 2 Ch. 603.
[2] This must carefully be distinguished from the equitable remedy of account of profits. The latter is an alternative to damages in cases of infringement of trade marks, patents, or copyright. It will, of course, be to the plaintiff's advantage to select the equitable remedy where the amount of the defendant's profits exceeds his total loss. See, in general, Street, pp. 259–266.
[3] *American Braided Wire* v. *Thomson* (1890), 44 Ch.D. 274.
[4] *United Horse Shoe and Nail Co., Ltd.* v. *Stewart* (1888), 13 App. Cas. 401.
[5] *Alexander* v. *Henry* (1895), 12 R.P.C. 360.
[6] *Birn Brothers* v. *Keene & Co.*, [1918] 2 Ch. 281.
[7] *American Braided Wire* v. *Thomson, supra.*
[8] *Leeds Forge Co., Ltd.* v. *Deighton's Patent Flue Co., Ltd.* (1907), 25 R.P.C. 209.

the trade mark or the copyright material. In such a case his loss, should the right be infringed, is clearly the amount that would have been payable on its lawful use.[1] The great advantage of this method of computing profits is its facility of calculation. There are no complex imponderables or mathematical difficulties. It is undoubtedly for this reason that there has been a tendency to adopt this measure even where the plaintiff was not in the habit of letting out the property on licence but himself sold the goods in question.[2] The same method is apparently to be applied to breach of confidence cases. In *Seager* v. *Copydex* (*No. 2*)[3] LORD DENNING, M.R. suggested that the measure of damages should depend on the nature of the confidential information which the defendant has appropriated: if there was nothing very special about it, then the plaintiff could recover what the defendant would have had to pay for it, a consultant's fee; if the information was so special that it could not be obtained by a consultant, then the defendant would be charged with a capitalization of the royalty which the plaintiff could have obtained on letting it out.[4]

But in this and in other cases where the plaintiff is not in the habit of letting out the property it may be doubted whether, though convenient, this measure accords with principle It does not put the plaintiff in the position he would have been in if no tort had been committed because *ex hypothesi* he would not have earned his profit by letting the thing out. He would have exploited his valuable property right by other means, usually by selling goods and his true loss is then the extent to which that profitable enterprise has been injured.

(c) Loss of business generally

In some cases an award of damages calculated on the basis of either of the two methods described above may be considered inappropriate in the light of the complexity of the plaintiff's business enterprise or the paucity of specific evidence as to lost profits, or the variety of external factors affecting the situation. The courts may then wish to award the plaintiff general damages for "loss of business". An excellent illustration is provided by *Aktiebolaget Manus* v. *Fullwood*.[5]

Ps, a Swedish firm, marketed and sold milking machines under the name of "Manus" (registered as a trade mark). Ds were importers of

---

[1] *Performing Right Society* v. *Bradford Corporation* (1917–23) MacG. Cop. Cas. 309 (copyright); *British Motor Syndicate* v. *Taylor & Son, Ltd.*, [1900] 1 Ch. 577 (patent).
[2] *Per* LORD SHAW in *Watson, Laidlow & Co.* v. *Pott, Cassels and Williamson* (1914), 31 R.P.C. 104, at pp. 119–120 applied in *British Thomson-Houston* v. *Naamlooze Vennootschap* (1923), 40 R.P.C. 119.
[3] [1969] 2 All E.R. 718.
[4] *Ibid.*, at pp. 719–720.
[5] (1954), 71 R.P.C. 243.

the machines and had a licence under a patent to use the trade mark. When the licence expired, Ds continued to manufacture and sell machines under the name of "Manus". It was held that this was an infringement of Ps' trade mark.

DANCKWERTS, J. felt unable to award damages on the basis of a proportionate part of the defendants' profits realized through the sale of the machines.

> "There are so many factors which might affect the results achieved by the defendants which would have nothing to do with the use by the defendants of the name 'Manus' ... I must ... deal with the matter by forming a rough estimate in a way that a jury could properly 'form it', and by assessing, by the best means I can, 'what is a fair and temperate sum'."[1]

There are two possible objections to awards in this form: (1) the need in some torts to prove special damage; (2) the doctrine of certainty.

(i) *Special damage*[2] This obstacle has been overcome partly by legislation, partly by the court's own initiative. For the purposes of establishing liability in the "interference" torts it was essential to show that the plaintiff had suffered *some* damage but the courts did not insist he prove *special* damage.[3] As regards remedies for the infringement of rights in immaterial property, every infringement *per se* is actionable and it follows that special damage need not be pleaded or proved,[4] but in order to recover substantial damages the burden is on the plaintiff to show that he sustained some pecuniary loss.[5] In the injurious falsehood torts, proof of special damage was at first required[6] but a judicial tendency to mitigate the harshness of the rule[7] culminated in the important decision of *Ratcliffe v. Evans*[8] in which a jury award of £120 for general loss of business was upheld by the Court of Appeal. Damages were not at large but the plaintiff need not prove the loss of any particular customer or contract—general loss of business was sufficient.

---

[1] *Ibid.*, at p. 250.
[2] See generally, *supra*, pp. 3–4.
[3] *Exchange Telegraph Co. v. Gregory*, [1896] 1 Q.B. 147 (inducement to breach of contract); *Pratt v. British Medical Association*, [1919] 1 K.B. 244 (conspiracy).
[4] *Exchange Telegraph Co. v. Gregory*, *supra* (copyright); *Meters v. Metropolitan Gas Meters* (1911), 28 R.P.C. 157 (patents); *Rodgers v. Nowill* (1847), 5 C.B. 109 (trade mark).
[5] *Exchange Telegraph Co. v. Gregory*, *supra* (copyright); *Khawan v. Chellaram*, [1964] 1 W.L.R. 711 (patents); *Spalding & Brothers v. A. W. Gamage, Ltd.* (1918), 35 R.P.C. 101 (trade marks).
[6] E.g. *Malachy v. Soper* (1836), 3 Bing N.C. 371.
[7] E.g. *Riding v. Smith* (1876), 1 Ex. D. 91.
[8] [1892] 2 Q.B. 524.

The legislature by section 3 of the Defamation Act 1952 subsequently abolished the requirement of special damage for certain categories of injurious falsehood:

> "(a) if the words upon which the action is founded are calculated to cause pecuniary damage to the plaintiff and are published in writing or other permanent form; or (b) if the said words are calculated to cause pecuniary damage to the plaintiff in respect of any office, profession, calling, trade or business held or carried on by him at the time of the publication."

The principle of *Ratcliffe* v. *Evans* still applies to cases falling outside this provision.

(ii) *Certainty*   In general the ordinary principles of certainty[1] should prevail but it is apparent that at least in cases of intentional injuries to business the courts have been quite lenient in the standard they have applied.   In *Goldsoll* v. *Goldman*[2]

> D induced X to break his contract with P by setting up a rival imitation jewellery business.   P was unable to offer proof of specific loss of profit but NEVILLE, J. held that such loss could be inferred.   The setting up of a rival business must lead to some damage.

At the same time—and this is particularly true since *Rookes* v. *Barnard*[3] —they will strive to restrain the awarding of very high damages where the prospective pecuniary loss is so entirely speculative that the sum must reflect some punitive elements.   In *Fielding* v. *Variety Incorporated*[4]

> Ds described as "flops" two shows which P, a theatre impresario, had promoted.   This was true as regards one of the shows, "Twang", but manifestly untrue of the other, "Charlie Girl".[5]   The master awarded P £10,000 for injurious falsehood on the ground that Ds' statement had adversely affected P's chances of having "Charlie Girl" produced in the U.S.A. The Court of Appeal considered this loss to be "quite fanciful"[6] and damages under this head were reduced to £100.

5   Non-pecuniary losses

Aggravated damages, that is for the plaintiff's justifiable irritation, annoyance and humiliation caused by the defendant's acts may be

---

[1] *Supra*, pp. 79–85.
[2] [1914] 2 Ch. 603.
[3] [1964] A.C. 1129, *supra*, pp. 30–37.
[4] [1967] 2 Q.B. 841.
[5] The show ran for over four years at the Adelphi Theatre, London.
[6] *Per* SALMON, L.J., [1967] 2 Q.B. 841, at p. 856.

awarded.[1] Little material guidance can of course be given on quantum.[2] Perhaps CANTLEY, J.'s direction to the jury in *Moore* v. *News of the World*[3] (a case of false attribution of authorship contrary to section 43 of the Copyright Act 1956) exhausts the subject:

"it will be a small sum . . . not a derisory sum but a small sum . . . something, some gentle, gentle amount for a rather technical cause of action."

£100 was awarded by the jury and the Court of Appeal upheld the award.

6 Limitations on awards under the Industrial Relations Act 1971

If an action is brought in an industrial court or tribunal for injury to business arising from an "interference" tort or other unfair industrial practice, the Court or tribunal is enjoined to award "such amount" as it "considers just and equitable in all the circumstances".[4] That the common law principles of assessment are intended to apply is made clear by the subsequent provision[5] that

"The loss sustained by the aggrieved party . . . shall be taken to include:
(a) any expenses reasonably incurred by him in consequence of the matters to which the complaint relates, and
(b) loss of any benefit which he might reasonably be expected to have had but for those matters,

subject, however, to the application of the same rule concerning the duty of a person to mitigate his loss as applies in relation to damages recoverable under the common law. . . ."

Nevertheless section 117 provides for a special limitation on awards made against trade unions. The ceiling award is regulated according to the membership of the union as follows:

		£
up to 5,000	—	5,000
5,000 to 25,000	—	25,000
25,000 to 50,000	—	50,000
over 100,000	—	100,000

It would be unrealistic to see these limitations in terms of any legal

---

[1] E.g. *Pratt* v. *British Medical Association*, [1919] 1 K.B. 244 (conspiracy); *Moore* v. *News of the World*, [1972] 1 Q.B. 441 (copyright).
[2] For the principles governing the award of aggravated damages generally see *supra*, pp. 237–238. See also *Beloff* v. *Pressdram*, [1973] 1 All E.R. 241.
[3] *Supra*, at p. 450.
[4] Industrial Relations Act 1971, s. 116(1).
[5] *Ibid.*, s. 116(2); but see now on unfair dismissal *Norton Tool Co., Ltd.* v. *Tewson*, [1973] 1 All E.R. 183, *infra*, p. 263.

principle. There are no equivalent ceilings to awards against those organizations which are not registered under the Act. It should be seen more as an inducement to trade unions to register.

IV INJURY TO GAINFUL EMPLOYMENT

1 Introduction

The effect of the defendant's activity may be directly or indirectly to deprive the plaintiff of his employment. For this injury, the common law provides in effect two standards of compensation: (i) the *tortious* standard which, as operative in cases of personal injuries, entitles the plaintiff to an indemnity for his lost earnings, including the benefit of any discretionary elements from which he would most likely have benefited;[1] (ii) the *contractual* standard which limits compensation payable to the plaintiff employee to such benefits as he would have acquired if the defendant employer had exercised his rights under the contract (including the right to terminate the contract on notice) in a way most favourable to himself and least favourable to the plaintiff, with the consequence in practice that the plaintiff can recover only that non-discretionary remuneration which the employer was bound to pay him during the period for which notice of termination of contract should have been given.[2] Within the scope of this chapter there are two types of action which a plaintiff may bring for injury to his employment but in neither case has it been conclusively determined which of the two standards is to apply.

2 "Interference" torts

The less problematical of the two actions are the "interference" torts. A man may lose his job as a result of the defendant's conspiracy, intimidation or inducement to break a contract. Although there is no clear English authority to this effect, it seems most probable that the tortious standard is to be applied and that quantification proceeds on that same basis as for personal injuries.[3] It follows that compensation for earnings beyond the period of notice and for discretionary benefits is recoverable.[4] As with personal injuries, the obstacles to be over-

---

[1] *Supra*, pp. 182–185.

[2] *Infra*, pp. 311–312.

[3] This appears to be the position in the majority of U.S. jurisdictions: see note 30 Col. L.R. 272.

[4] The out-of-court settlement of £4,000 in *Rookes* v. *Barnard* (No. 2) (reported at [1966] 1 Q.B. 176) is some evidence of the suggested position in English law that the tortious and not the contractual measure is applied.

come are certainty and mitigation.[1] The rule in *Addis* v. *Gramophone Co.*[2] prohibiting the award of aggravated damages in the contractual action for wrongful dismissal need not be followed. Indeed, there is express authority for the award of damages for humiliation caused by the defendant's intentional tort.[3]

3 Unfair dismissal

On the basis of a recent decision of the National Industrial Relations Court,[4] it is now clear that the right to compensation for "unfair dismissal" under the Industrial Relations Act 1971 is a right *sui generis*, and the principles of compensation to be applied are referable neither to the tortious nor to the contractual standard. Unlike tort, non-pecuniary losses may not be recovered. Unlike contract, compensation for pecuniary losses appears not to be limited to benefits which the defendant was *bound* to confer on the plaintiff. Finally, section 118 of the Act sets an arbitrary ceiling on awards of 104 weeks pay or £4160, whichever is the less.

V LOSSES CONSEQUENT ON THE DEATH OF OR INJURY TO ANOTHER

1 Introduction

The major problem in this area is liability and not quantification. The only general remedy which applies with certainty is that accruing where the plaintiff seeks compensation for the death of a near relative. Here legislation provided a remedy.[5] The remaining area has been left to judicial inspiration, which here at least has operated in a piecemeal and disjointed fashion. Fortunately the whole matter has been taken up by the Law Commission[6] whose recommendations if implemented, would introduce not only order but also a new and necessary concern for those whose losses are consequent on injury to others.[7]

---

[1] *Supra*, pp. 79–93.
[2] [1909] A.C. 488, *infra*, p. 308.
[3] *Pratt* v. *British Medical Association*, [1919] 1 K.B. 244 (a case of conspiracy). In *Rookes* v. *Barnard*, [1964] A.C. 1129, at pp. 1220–1233 LORD DEVLIN insisted on the distinction between aggravated and exemplary damages (*supra*, pp. 31–34) and the inference can be drawn that it would have been quite proper for the jury to have awarded aggravated damages in that case.
[4] *Norton Tool Co., Ltd.* v. *Tewson*, [1973] 1 All E.R. 183.
[5] Fatal Accidents Act 1846.
[6] Working Papers Nos. 19 and 41.
[7] For their recommendations, see *infra*, p. 282.

2 Fatal Accidents Acts

(a) General

Undoubtedly the most important category of loss incurred by third persons on their own account is that sustained by the dependants of a person killed as a result of the defendant's tort. Unlike almost all other causes of action discussed in this book the defendant's liability here is wholly statutory—the common law knew no action for wrongful death.[1] Even more unusual is the fact that the legislature has also prescribed the measure of damages. Section 2 of the Fatal Accidents Act 1846 provided that:

> "the jury may give such damages as they may think proportioned to the injury resulting from such death to the parties respectively for whom and for whose benefit such action shall be brought".

Now the particular wording of this section does not appear to be significant in itself: that is, it offers little or no guidance to the jury on how to quantify. But the very fact that the measure is in statutory form has provided those judges who on policy grounds have wished to limit the scope of the remedy with an opportunity to justify their conclusion by reference to the fictional "intention of Parliament".[2] However, it will also be seen that in construing the language of section 2, the courts have on the whole developed principles consistent with the ordinary common law rules. In particular compensation under the Fatal Accidents Acts and for personal injuries have been assessed along parallel lines. The only notable exception has been the refusal of the courts to award dependants damages for their own non-pecuniary loss.[3]

(b) Positive losses: expenses

One would have thought there would have been no obstacle to the plaintiff recovering expenses reasonably incurred as a result of the victim's death, but a curiously restrictive construction was imposed on the statutory measure: funeral and other expenses incurred were not allowed as items of damages.[4] As regards funeral expenses, legislation rectified the anomaly, section 2(3) of the Law Reform (Miscellaneous Provisions) Act 1934 providing that "damages may be awarded

---

[1] *Baker* v. *Bolton* (1808), 1 Camp. 493.

[2] This was especially true in the nineteenth century—see *Blake* v. *Midland Rail Co.* (1852), 18 Q.B. 93 and *Dalton* v. *South-Eastern Rail Co.* (1858), 4 C.B.N.S. 296. More surprisingly the device reappeared in the recent case of *Davies* v. *Taylor*, [1972] 1 Q.B. 286, *per* MEGAW, L.J., at p. 297.

[3] *Infra*, p. 272.

[4] *Dalton* v. *South-Eastern Rail Co.*, *supra*; *Clark* v. *London General Omnibus Co.*, [1906] 2 K.B. 648.

in respect of the funeral expenses of the deceased person if such expenses have been incurred by the parties for whose benefit the action is brought". But the doctrine of mitigation is, of course, to be applied, and the expenses so incurred must be reasonable. An over-elaborate and expensive memorial erected over the deceased's grave is not to be charged to the defendant's account[1] although the cost of a simple gravestone may be allowed.[2] The fact that the legislature has intervened to cover funeral expenses goes some way to explain the reluctance of the courts to award damages for other types of expenditure.[3] But as a justification for the immunity it is hardly adequate. There seems to be no argument in principle or in policy for so restricting damages for positive losses. Apart from funeral expenses only one item of expenditure has consistently been allowed and this effectually represents a consequential loss.[4] On the death of a housewife, her immediate family may recover the cost of employing a housekeeper[5] or homehelp[6] to perform some of her functions. In estimating a sum appropriate for this head the court should take into account that the need for such help will gradually diminish as the children grow older and eventually leave home.[7] The possibility that the widower may remarry is also something which should be considered.[8]

(c) Consequential losses: pecuniary benefits

The most important head of loss is the expectation of pecuniary benefits which the deceased would, if he had survived, have conferred on the plaintiffs.

(i) *Proof of dependency* The plaintiff must prove that his relationship with the deceased was such that there was "a reasonable expectation of pecuniary benefit, as of right or otherwise, from the continuance of life".[9] In the ordinary case of the death of a husband (and father) there

---

[1] *Hart* v. *Griffith-Jones*, [1948] 2 All E.R. 729.
[2] *Stanton* v. *Youlden*, [1960] 1 All E.R. 429.
[3] Claims have been rejected for medical expenses (*Boulter* v. *Webster* (1865), 11 L.T. 598), travelling expenses (*Bedwell* v. *Golding* (1902), 18 T.L.R. 436) and for the costs of attending an inquest (*Grice* v. *Tuke* (1940) unreported, see Bingham, *Motor Claim Cases* (6th Edn.), p. 429). There is no direct evidence that the attitude of the courts has changed but it may be of significance that in some cases an agreed amount has been paid by way of special damages which would seem to exceed the probable funeral expenses: see, e.g. *White* v. *B.R.S.* (1970), *Times*, 9th July.
[4] Cf. *infra*, p. 266.
[5] *Berry* v. *Humm*, [1915] 1 K.B. 627; *Jeffery* v. *Smith*, [1970] R.T.R. 279.
[6] *Hurt* v. *Murphy*, [1971] R.T.R. 186.
[7] *Jeffery* v. *Smith*, *supra*; *Hurt* v. *Murphy*, *supra*.
[8] *Hurt* v. *Murphy*, *supra*.
[9] Per POLLOCK, C.B., *Franklin* v. *South Eastern Rail Co.* (1858), 3 H. & N. 211, at p. 214.

is nothing to show beyond the fact of support at the time of death. Problems only arise where there is evidence that the relationship was not permanent or stable. If a wife has been deserted the existence of a legal obligation in the husband to provide for her will not by itself be sufficient: the likelihood of support in the future is a question of fact.[1] In *Davies* v. *Taylor*[2]

> Shortly before his death, H had instituted divorce proceedings against W. W's claim under the F.A. Acts was rejected by the House of Lords on the ground that, though the possibility of a reconciliation could not be ruled out, it was nothing more than a mere speculative chance and, as such, could not form the basis of an award.[3]

Similarly, where the parties felt themselves "obliged" by circumstances to enter rapidly into matrimony and had not at the time of death regularly cohabited together, there existed grounds for a slightly lower award: the court had regard to "the element of instability associated with a shotgun marriage".[4]

Analogous considerations have been applied to the support of illegitimate children. Doubtless it is in principle wrong to visit the sins of the father upon the children, nevertheless the character of the relationship may carry an element of uncertainty which is not present in the ordinary case of legitimate children.[5]

Where the victim of the accident was not the breadwinner of the family those claiming dependency have a harder task in persuading the court that they might reasonably have expected a continuing pecuniary benefit from the deceased. Obviously where a wife has been contributing to the household income there is no problem.[6] Should she have remained at home caring for the home and family a sum representing the "value" of her services may be awarded. As has already been explained,[7] this is likely to be the cost of procuring a substitute to perform the same functions. The most difficult cases arise where parents sue on the death of a child. Where the child is already a wage-earner and contributing to the family income, then, provided that the sum contributed exceeds that spent on the child, the parents have an obviously valid claim,[8] though the court must take into account the possibility that any dependency will be short-lived as the child may

---

[1] *Peters* v. *Overhead, Ltd.* (1934), 27 B.W.C. 190. See also *Barry* v. *McDonald*, [1966] C.L.Y. 3433.
[2] [1972] 3 All E.R. 836.
[3] On the certainty aspect of the case, see *supra*, p. 80.
[4] *Per* Sellers, L.J., *Gadsby* v. *Hodkinson* (1966), 110 Sol. Jo. 834.
[5] *Phipps* v. *Cunard White Star*, [1951] 1 T.L.R. 359.
[6] E.g. *Lucking* v. *Havard*, [1957] C.L.Y. 963.
[7] *Supra*, p. 265.
[8] *Franklin* v. *South Eastern Rail Co.* (1858), 3 H. & N. 211.

leave home and/or get married.[1] What of the case where a child's contribution to the family budget has not yet exceeded the sum spent on him, or more pertinently still, where he has not yet left school? In such cases the courts have been reluctant to award the parents anything: the possibility of the child some time in the future providing for his parents is generally too speculative.[2] But the situation may be different where either the child had expressly undertaken to care for his parents[3] or the parents had been able through financial sacrifice to educate the child to a position where his earning potential greatly exceeded their own.[4] In all other cases of alleged dependency it is a question of fact first whether such dependency existed at the time of death and secondly, having regard to the doctrine of certainty, what prospects, if any, there were of such support continuing.

(ii) *Dependency must be legitimate* Not only must the relationship between the plaintiff and the deceased fall within the bounds set by the Fatal Accidents Acts 1846 to 1959,[5] but it seems also that the source of the benefit emanating from the deceased must have satisfied the dictates of public policy. In the strange case of *Burns* v. *Edman*[6] the income which the plaintiff widow had received from her deceased husband had come from the proceeds of crime. Her claim under the Fatal Accidents Acts was defeated on the ground that it was *ex turpi causa*. Her resort to the possibility that her husband would have returned to the straight and narrow fared no better. CRIGHTON, J. came to the pessimistic conclusion that the possibility was "entirely speculative and unproven to the point of improbability".[7]

(iii) *Amount of dependency—multiplier method* The multiplier is the favoured technique for evaluating the amount of the dependency.[8] This

---

[1] *Dolbey* v. *Goodwin*, [1955] 2 All E.R. 166; the trial judge had incorrectly treated the dependency of a widowed mother on her son aged 29 who was described as "steady, unmarried and without matrimonial intentions" as if it was a husband/wife dependency.
[2] E.g. *Barnett* v. *Cohen*, [1921] 2 K.B. 461; *Wathen* v. *Vernon*, [1970] R.T.R. 471.
[3] *Bishop* v. *Cunard White Star*, [1950] P. 240.
[4] *Piggott* v. *Fancy Woods Products*, [1958] C.L.Y. 897.
[5] *Viz* spouse, parent and child, 1846 Act, s. 2; grandparents and grandchildren, 1846 Act, s. 5; brother, sister, uncle and aunt and issue of any of them, 1959 Act, s. 1(1). These classes are then enlarged by s. 1(2) of the 1959 Act so that (a) an adopted child is treated as the child of his adopter, (b) an illegitimate child is related to his mother and reputed father, (c) a half-blood relationship is equivalent to a whole-blood relationship and (d) a relationship by affinity is equivalent to a relationship by consanguinity.
[6] [1970] 2 Q.B. 541.
[7] *Ibid.*, at p. 546.
[8] *Davies* v. *Powell Duffryn Collieries*, [1942] A.C. 601, at p. 617; *Taylor* v. *O'Connor*, [1971] A.C. 115, at pp. 128, 134, 135, 140.

method has already been described in relation to personal injury claims.[1]
Here the *multiplicand* is the net average annual benefit which would
have accrued to the dependant had the deceased lived and the *multiplier* is based on the number of years during which the benefit would
have been paid.

The multiplicand   The starting point is the lost earnings of the
deceased.   This naturally includes not only income from salaried employment but also the profits from a business.[2]   As in personal injury
cases,[3] a prediction must be made as to the future employment prospects
of the deceased, for example promotion,[4] overtime,[5] and an increase in
real earnings.[6]   The figure is to be assessed on the *net* average earnings
of the deceased: thus national insurance contributions[7] and tax
liability[8] will be taken into account.   Out of this sum is to be assessed
the pecuniary benefit regularly accruing to the plaintiff dependants.
In some cases this may be calculated simply by taking the sum which
the husband paid over to the wife and deducting from it the sums which
the wife spent on the husband (e.g. food and clothing).[9]   But the domestic financial arrangements may well be more complex.   In the first
place, the court should taken into account any savings from his salary
that the deceased would have accumulated in order to confer a benefit
on his dependants on his (natural) death.[10]   Secondly, there is to be
considered any benefits which the deceased conferred on his dependants
indirectly through, for example, mortgage payments, rent or rates,
lighting, heating, clothes and a car.[11]   Conversely the fact that the wife
was also an earner[12] or had a private income[13] is relevant only to the
extent that it would have made her or her children less dependent on
the husband during his lifetime.

The multiplier   Here the basis is the working-life expectancy of
the deceased,[14] but again modification to accommodate the variety of

---

[1] *Supra*, pp. 188–189.
[2] E.g. *Malyon* v. *Plummer*, [1964] 1 Q.B. 330.
[3] *Supra*, pp. 187–188.
[4] E.g. *Roughead* v. *Railway Executive* (1949), 65 T.L.R. 535.
[5] E.g. *Bath* v. *British Transport Commission*, [1954] 2 All E.R. 542.
[6] E.g. *Moore* v. *Moore* (1965), 109 Sol. Jo. 317.
[7] *Cooper* v. *Firth Brown*, [1963] 2 All E.R. 31.
[8] *Zinovieff* v. *British Transport Commission* (1954) *Times*, 1st April, affirmed
British Transport Commission v. *Gourley*, [1956] A.C. 185, *supra*, pp. 107–115.
[9] Per LORD WRIGHT, *Davies* v. *Powell Duffryn Collieries*, [1942] A.C. 601, at
p. 617.
[10] *Nance* v. *British Columbia Electric Rail Co.*, [1951] A.C. 601.
[11] *Roughead* v. *Railway Executive*, *supra*; *Taylor* v. *O'Connor*, *supra*.
[12] *Howitt* v. *Heads*, [1973] 1 Q.B. 64.
[13] *Shiels* v. *Cruikshank*, [1953] 1 All E.R. 874.
[14] The extent to which actuarial evidence may be admitted to determine this
figure is considered *infra*, p. 271.

factors involved in calculation is inevitable. In estimating the working-life expectancy, the court should take into account such contingencies as ill health, an early death, unemployment.[1] The prospects of the dependants' lives are as relevant as those of the deceased in determining the duration of the dependency, for the benefit would have been paid only so long as the dependency would have continued. The multiplier in the case of a dependent parent whose son may marry or of children who are likely soon to be self-supporting is smaller than that adopted in an action by a widow.[2] Among the factors which are obviously relevant in determining the duration of the dependency is the prospect of the plaintiff dependant remarrying. In the case of a *widower*, it has never been doubted that this should properly be taken into account.[3] There must be, according to one judge,[4] plenty of women who would be prepared to look after a house and children in exchange for a marriage and a home.

But consideration of a *widow's* remarriage potential has given rise to a passionate controversy. Although the principle was clear—remarriage prospects so obviously affect the duration of the dependency relationship that they had to be taken into account[5]—delicate problems were posed for the judge who had to determine the issue:

"Am I to ask her to put on a bathing-dress; because the witness-box is calculated to disguise the figure?... Am I to label the lady to her face as attractive or unattractive? If I have the temerity to apply the label, am I likely to be right? Supposing I say she is unattractive; it may well be that she has a friend who disagrees and has looked below the surface and found a charming character."[6]

Outside the courts feelings, especially those of women's organizations, ran high.[7] There were references to "slave markets"[8] and "cattle auctions";[9] There were cries of "Out, out damned spot!"[10] The campaign succeeded. Section 4(1) of the Law Reform (Miscellaneous Provisions) Act 1971 provides that

"in assessing damages payable to a widow ... there shall not be taken into account the remarriage of the widow or her prospects of remarriage".

---

[1] *Roughead* v. *Railway Executive, supra*; *Mallet* v. *McMonagle*, [1970] A.C. 166.

[2] *Supra*, p. 267.

[3] *Hurt* v. *Murphy*, [1971] R.T.R. 186.

[4] PAULL, J. in *Collins* v. *Noma Electric* (1962), 106 Sol. Jo. 431.

[5] *Goodburn* v. *Cotton*, [1968] 1 Q.B. 845 among several others.

[6] PHILLIMORE, J. in *Buckley* v. *John Allen and Ford (Oxford)*, [1967] 2 Q.B. 637, at pp. 644–645.

[7] See especially the Conservative Party paper "Fair Deal for the Fair Sex" and the Winn Committee Report on Personal Injury Litigation Cmnd. 691 (1968), paras. 378–379.

[8] Baroness Emmet, H.L. Deb., Vol. 277, col. 1323.

[9] Lord Stow-Hill, *ibid.*, Vol. 317, col. 532.

[10] Lord Stow-Hill, *ibid.*, col. 567.

On the scope of the subsection two observations must be made. First, it does not expressly extend to cases where the action is brought on behalf of dependent children. Remarriage of the widowed mother would most probably create a new dependency relationship and the prospect is therefore *prima facie* relevant in determining the children's loss. In *Howitt* v. *Heads*[1] CUMMING-BRUCE, J. thought that in some cases the distinction between a widow's action and one brought for the children might be significant[2] but in assessing an award in the latter situation he was not prepared to investigate the widow's prospects of remarriage. Secondly, the subsection excludes from the court's consideration not only the possibility of remarriage but also cases where remarriage has already taken place.[3] The reason for this extension is not hard to find: it would be unfair to draw a distinction between the widow who, at the time of the action, has just remarried, and the widow who is merely engaged.[4] But it does mean, of course, that the court in quantifying the award is moving further and further from the widow's actual loss. It is this that clearly was of concern to the Law Lords who spoke in the Parliamentary debates.[5]

There is no easy solution to the problem[6] but there would seem to be two possibilities which would avoid the extremes of the common law principle and the statutory rule.[7] The first is that the judge should not admit evidence on the question but should simply reduce the damages by a standard amount according to the plaintiff's age.[8] This is subject to the objections that on the one hand it would never represent the plaintiff's actual loss (either she will remarry or she will not—she will never remarry to the extent of say 25 per cent.!), and on the other hand it would not take account of the cultural, moral and religious dictates of individual plaintiffs. The second solution sees the question as simply part of the universal problem of future uncertainty in damages

---

[1] [1973] 1 Q.B. 64.

[2] Remarriage prospects were taken into account in *Fox* v. *Sidney Ross*, [1972] 4 C.L. 82 but there appears to be no obvious features to distinguish the case from that of *Howitt* v. *Heads*, *supra*.

[3] Thus abrogating the decisions in *Mead* v. *Clarke Chapman & Co.*, [1956] 1 All E.R. 44, and *Curwen* v. *James*, [1963] 2 All E.R. 619.

[4] See Lord Stow-Hill, H.L. Deb., Vol. 317, col. 534.

[5] H.L. Deb., Vol. 318; LORD DIPLOCK, cols. 522–531, LORD PEARSON, cols. 531–533, LORD DENNING, cols. 541–542; VISCOUNT DILHORNE, cols. 1526–1533; LORD DONOVAN, cols. 1548–1550, LORD MORRIS, cols. 1555–1559; LORD HAILSHAM, L.C., cols. 1559–1572; LORD SIMON, cols. 1573–1576. See also CUMMING-BRUCE, J., in *Howitt* v. *Heads*, *supra*, at p. 70.

[6] "I do not know any legal problem that has presented greater difficulty to me than this rather limited but extremely important matter": Lord Goodman, H.L. Deb., Vol. 318, col. 1576.

[7] These possibilities were originally considered by the present author in a note on *Goodburn* v. *Cotton* in (1968), 31 M.L.R. 339.

[8] The statistical tables available may offer some guidance: *ibid.*, at p. 341.

awards the real solution for which would lie only in the introduction of a system of periodical payments, so that an award may be modified to take account of changes in the plaintiff's position, including remarriage. This was indeed the basis of the amendment moved by LORD DIPLOCK in the debate on the Law Reform Bill of 1971,[1] but later withdrawn as the machinery for implementing the reform was not then available. The merits and demerits of the periodical payments system have already been considered.[2]

The final element to be taken into account in selecting the multiplier is the capitalization of the lost income. The court must make a discount for the fact that the dependent plaintiff is receiving a lump sum which may be invested instead of income over a substantial period of time. The purpose of the award is

> "to provide the widow and other dependants . . . with a capital sum which with prudent management will be sufficient to supply them with material benefits of the same standard and duration as would have been provided for them out of the earnings of the deceased had he not been killed".[3]

But the dependants are not entitled to live off the interest of the sum invested leaving the capital untouched. Assessment of the lump sum should be such that the capital will gradually be dissipated.[4] To counterbalance this element, the fact that income on the invested capital will be subject to tax should also be taken into account.[5]

(iv) *Critique of multiplier method—actuarial evidence* The shortcomings of the multiplier method and the judicial reluctance to pay heed to actuarial techniques have been fully discussed.[6] Similar considerations apply to Fatal Accidents claims.[7] In particular it is to be noted that in recent years judges have been reluctant to select a multiplier greater than sixteen even in cases when the working-life expectancy of the deceased exceeded thirty-five years.[8] The suspicion remains that some widows are under-compensated.

(v) *Apportioning awards* However many dependants may claim under the Fatal Accidents Acts only one action may be brought and one lump sum awarded.[9] But section 2 of the 1846 Act directed that "the amount

---

[1] The amendment is set out in H.L. Deb., Vol. 318, cols. 522–523.
[2] *Supra*, pp. 12–14.
[3] LORD DIPLOCK in *Mallett* v. *McMonagle*, [1970] A.C. 166, at p. 174.
[4] *Per* LORD PEARSON, *Taylor* v. *O'Connor*, [1971] A.C. 115, at pp. 143–144.
[5] *Taylor* v. *O'Connor, supra*.
[6] *Supra*, pp. 189–192.
[7] See *Taylor* v. *O'Connor, supra*.
[8] E.g. *Mallett* v. *McMonagle, supra* (deceased aged 25—multiplier 16).
[9] See *Kassam* v. *Kampala Aerated Water Co.*, [1965] 2 All E.R. 875.

so recovered . . . shall be divided amongst the . . . parties in such shares as the jury by their verdict shall find and direct".[1]   The method of apportioning damages has not been fully expounded and it is not a ground on which the defendant may complain.[2]   However, certain vague guidelines exist.   Where a claim is brought for the widow and children, the practice is to award the greater part to the widow, on the assumption that she will care for the childern so long as they are dependent.[3]   But a larger proportion may be conferred on the children (which sums will be in the custody of the court until majority) on the ground either that the widow prefers it that way[4] or because the court fears that in the light of the widow's (or widower's) character and/or prospects or remarriage[5] the children require greater protection.[6]   As between child dependants, the younger are generally given more since they will remain dependent longer,[7] but an older child may receive preferential treatment if he needs capital to set himself up in life.[8]

(d) Non-pecuniary losses[9]

Claims for non-pecuniary loss in the form of grief or pain and suffering were rejected in the very early decisions on the 1846 Act[10] and the position has been rigidly maintained ever since.[11]   In contrast, other legal systems have been more generous.[12]   The arguments against the award of a "solatium" in cases of death can be considered under three heads.

(i) *Construction of statute*   The nineteenth-century cases tended to rely on the wording of the Fatal Accidents Act 1846.   As COLERIDGE, J. observed,

---

[1] Unless there is a jury, this is now a task for the trial judge: R.S.C. Ord. 18, r. 15(2).

[2] *Eifert* v. *Holt's Transport Co.*, [1951] W.N. 467.

[3] Report of the Pearson Committee on Funds in Court, Cmnd. 818 (1959), para. 15.

[4] *Eifert* v. *Holt's Transport, supra.*

[5] But see *supra*, pp. 269–270.

[6] *Tatana* v. *McDonald*, [1959] N.Z.L.R. 353; *Howitt* v. *Heads*, [1,73] 1 Q.B. 64.

[7] Report of the Pearson Committee, *supra.*

[8] *Heatley* v. *Steel Co. of Wales*, [1953] 1 All E.R. 489.

[9] Law Commission Working Paper No. 41, paras. 197–203.

[10] *Gillard* v. *Lancashire and Yorkshire Rail Co.* (1848), 12 L.T.O.S. 356; *Blake* v. *Midland Rail Co.* (1852), 18 Q.B. 93.

[11] *Davies* v. *Powell Duffryn Collieries*, [1942] A.C. 601; *Taylor* v. *O'Connor*, [1971] A.C. 115.

[12] The right to solatium has always existed in Scots Law; see Walker, *Law of Damages in Scotland*, pp. 616–620.   Legislation introduced the remedy in Eire (Civil Liability Act 1961, s. 49) and in S. Australia (Wrongs Act 1936, s. 23).   For French law see Mazeaud/Tunc, *Responsibilité Civile* (6th Edn.), nos. 320–328.

"the language (of section 2) seems more appropriate to a loss of which some estimate may be made than to an indefinite sum, independent of all pecuniary estimate, to sooth the feelings; and the division of the amount strongly leads to the same conclusion".[1]

But it seems unnecessary to draw such an inference from the vague formula "to give such damages as (the jury) may think proportioned to the injury resulting from such death" and the direction as to apportionment adds no further weight to the argument. Apportionment of pecuniary benefits is no less difficult than apportionment of solatium. In truth, the conclusion seems to result not from the intention of the legislature but rather from the general policy of the courts in the middle of the last century. On the one hand there was the popular maxim of statutory interpretation that where a statute modifies a common law principle it is to be construed narrowly.[2] On the other hand, the Act imposed a new burden on the emerging industries, especially the railways, and there was a natural reluctance to add to that burden. It is far from clear that the same policy considerations apply today.

(ii) *Impracticability* The problem of proof is an obvious objection. How can it be established with certainty that a dependant has suffered grief? Must there be evidence of tears shed or moans uttered? How is the court to distinguish between the different categories of dependant now recognized by the Fatal Accidents Act 1956? Might any obscure uncle, step-child or brother-in-law turn up to court and demand his share? The answer is that though proof is nigh impossible, in many cases real grief is manifestly suffered by members of the victim's family. The award could be restricted to those dependants who were living with the victim at the time of his death.[3] It seems unjust that personal representatives may claim for the non-pecuniary losses sustained not by themselves but by the deceased,[4] while a dependant under the Fatal Accidents Acts may recover nothing for his own loss.

(iii) *Quantification* The third argument rests on the impossibility of quantifying solatium. But this has never been a legitimate ground for refusing a remedy[5] and the problem arises in determining all awards for non-pecuniary loss. Then it is said that the evidence on which the court must attempt to fix a sum would involve embarrassment and irritation to the dependants who bring the action. It would, of course,

---

[1] *Blake* v. *Midland Rail Co.*, *supra*, at p. 110. See also *Gillard's* case *supra*, *per* POLLOCK, C.B., at p. 356.

[2] See Maxwell, *Interpretation of Statutes* (12th Edn.), pp. 116–123.

[3] This seems, in practice, to apply in Scotland although because of the proclivity for the jury trial, reliable authority is scarce. In S. Australia recovery of solatium is limited to the parents of a deceased child (max. $1000) or a surviving spouse (max. $1400).

[4] Cf. *supra*, p. 118.

[5] *Supra*, p. 194.

be undesirable for the genuineness of the dependant's claim to be tested by lengthy cross-examination or the furtive investigations of inquiry agents. The solution must lie in a sum fixed by the legislature[1] so that evidence as to grief will not be required. On the functional view,[2] this sum would reflect what a reasonable person, grief-stricken at the loss of a member of the family circle might reasonable require to provide himself with some form of alternative happiness.

(e)   Deduction for compensating advantages[3]

The general principle is that there should be set off against the sum awarded any compensating advantages accruing to the dependants on the death of the victim.[4]   There are, however, several important exceptions.   These arise either because the compensating advantage was not substantially caused by the accident for which the tortfeasor is liable, or because some legislative rule or policy consideration prohibits its application.

(i) *Saving of expenses*   Clearly a deduction must be made to account for those expenses which would have been incurred by the dependants if the victim had lived, but which as a result of his death will no longer arise. For example, the cost of feeding a husband may no longer be a charge on the housekeeping money.   As has been seen,[5] however, this is usually taken into account in assessing the net dependency.[6]   If so, no further deduction need be made.

(ii) *Benefits voluntarily conferred by third parties*   As in a personal injury claim,[7] a benefit voluntarily conferred on the dependant by a third party will generally not be taken into account.   This was the position at common law,[8] and the exception seems to have been affirmed by statute.[9]   It has been sought to justify this exception on the ground

---

[1] Law Commission Working Paper No. 41, para. 201, cf. the Civil Liability Act 1961 (Eire), s. 49(2); and *supra*, n. 3, p. 273.

[2] *Supra*, pp. 195–196.

[3] Boberg (1964) 81 S.A.L.J. 194, 346, (1965) 82 S.A.L.J. 96, 247, 324.

[4] *Davies* v. *Powell Duffryn Collieries*, [1942] A.C. 601.

[5] *Supra*, p. 268.

[6] See, e.g. *Heatley* v. *Steel Co. of Wales*, [1953] 1 All E.R. 489; *Taylor* v. *O'Connor*, [1971] A.C. 115.

[7] *Supra*, p. 223.

[8] *Redpath* v. *Belfast and County Down Ry.*, [1947] N.I. 167; *Peacock* v. *Amusement Equipment Co.*, [1954] 2 Q.B. 347.

[9] Fatal Accidents Act 1959, s. 2(1), *infra*, p. 277.   The subsection was not applied in *Rawlinson* v. *Babcock and Wilcox*, [1966] 3 All E.R. 882 but Parliament appears to have intended that it should extend generally to gratuitous benefits conferred by third parties.

that being a *gratuitous* benefit it was not causally linked to the loss which is the subject-matter of the action:[1]

> "the operative cause . . . for the payment of money in such a case is not the fact of death . . . but the voluntary, spontaneous decision of a donor or donors activated by motives of compassion towards a person in distress".[2]

The difficulty with this rationalization of the exception has been the vagueness of the causal test. Before the legislature intervened in 1971 a widow's remarriage was taken into account and even after the Act a *widower's* remarriage is taken into account but in both cases it can be persuasively argued that the operative cause of the marriage was not the death of former spouse.[3] A second ground is that of public policy. For the charitable provision to enure for the benefit of the defendant rather than of the plaintiff is repugnant to the court's moral sense.[4] Further such a result would discourage charity and benevolence.[5] Legitimate though these arguments sound, there is always the danger of them sliding into a punitive condemnation of the defendant's conduct.[6] The safest justification lies in the purpose of the benefit:[7] it is, presumably, a benefit which it is intended that the recipient should enjoy in addition to any money recoverable from the tortfeasor.

(iii) *Inheritance of deceased's money and other property* The general principle applies to those benefits which pass to the dependants by the deceased's will or on intestacy.[8] But contrary to the impression given in earlier cases,[9] this does not mean that the whole value of property so conferred is to be deducted from an award. In the first place, allowance is to be made for the incidence of estate duty and other debts and expenses chargeable on the estate.[10] Secondly, no deduction is to be made for any benefit which would in any case (i.e. if the victim had survived) have been enjoyed by the plaintiffs. Thus the value of the matrimonial home which passes to the dependants on death but in which they will continue to live is not deductible.[11] It follows, too, that the court must take into account the likelihood that the dependants

---

[1] *Peacock* v. *Amusement Equipment, supra.*
[2] *Per* CHAPMAN, J., *Rawlinson* v. *Babcock and Wilcox, supra,* at p. 887.
[3] Cf. *Rawlinson's* case, *supra.*
[4] *Redpath's* case *supra.*
[5] *Rawlinson's* case, *supra,* at p. 887.
[6] E.g. *Redpath's* case, *supra,* at p. 175; see also *supra,* pp. 225–226.
[7] Cf. *supra,* pp. 228–230.
[8] *Bishop* v. *Cunard White Star,* [1950] P. 240.
[9] E.g. *Grand Trunk Rail Co. of Canada* v. *Jennings* (1888), 13 App. Cas. 800, *obiter per* LORD WATSON, at p. 804.
[10] *Roughead* v. *Railway Executive* (1949), 65 T.L.R. 435; *Baker* v. *T. E. Hopkins & Son, Ltd.,* [1958] 3 All E.R. 147.
[11] *Heatley* v. *Steel Co. of Wales,* [1953] 1 All E.R. 489.

would have benefited from the estate on the *natural* death of the deceased. In most cases, therefore, the benefit to be taken into account is not the value of the inheritance *per se*, but the value of the *acceleration* of the inheritance,[1] that is the value of having the property now instead of a mere expectation which is subject to all the uncertainties of the future. Against this must be set off the possibility that the deceased, during his lifetime, would have set aside additional moneys which would have increased the size of his estate on death.[2]

(iv) *Awards under survival actions* The justification for taking into account inheritances—advantages resulting from death and mitigating the plaintiff's loss—applies also to awards under the survival actions. In many cases a claimant under the Fatal Accidents Acts will also be a person who will take a share in the proceeds of a successful claim against the tortfeasor brought by the representatives of the estate. To the extent that this share will indemnify him against the losses remediable under the Fatal Accidents, to that extent will damages under the latter action be reduced.[3] Thus where an award under the Law Reform Act 1934 has been made the court will attempt to assess what proportion of that sum will enure for the benefit of the Fatal Accidents Act claimant, having deducted for death duties, debts and administrative expenses.[4] It must be clear, however, that the claimant's share in the award results from the death of the accident victim and not from another cause. In *Rawlinson v. Babcock and Wilcox*[5]

> W, a widow, brought proceedings (1) under the F.A. Acts on behalf of herself and her daughter D and (2) under the 1934 Act as administratrix of H her deceased husband's estate. She died before the hearing, and the actions were continued by her administrators. Under (2) Chapman, J. awarded £1000. That sum was deducted from W's claim under (1)[6] but was ignored in relation to D's claim under (1) since the benefit accrued to D as a result of W's death and not H's death.

---

[1] *Nance v. British Columbia Electric Rail Co.*, [1951] A.C. 601.
[2] *Kassam v. Kampala Aerated Water Co.*, [1965] 2 All E.R. 875; *Public Trustee v. Nickisson* (1964), 111 C.L.R. 500.
[3] *Davies v. Powell Duffryn Associated Collieries, Ltd.*, [1942] A.C. 601; affirming the decision of the Court of Appeal (*sub. nom. Yelland v. Powell Duffryn Collieries*, [1941] 1 K.B. 519) which had rejected the contention that since s. 1(5) of the Law Reform Act 1934 provided for a cause of action "in addition to and not in derogation of any rights conferred on the dependants of deceased persons by the Fatal Accidents Acts . . ." no deduction ought to be made. The subsection created an independent *right to sue*—it did not govern the measure of damages.
[4] *Feay v. Barnwell*, [1938] 1 All E.R. 31.
[5] [1966] 3 All E.R. 882.
[6] In fact since the Law Reform award exceeded the sum *prima facie* assessed under the Fatal Accidents Acts, no award was made under the latter head.

A problem will arise if at the time of the Fatal Accident claim no survival action has yet been brought. It is now clear that the existence of a parallel Fatal Accident claim is not a ground for reducing a survival action award:[1] the estate does not benefit, even indirectly, from a Fatal Accident award. The court must therefore attempt to prophesy first whether a survival action can and will be brought, secondly, how much is likely to be awarded, and thirdly what proportion of that sum will enure for the benefit of the plaintiff in the Fatal Accident claim.[2]

(v) *Insurance and pension moneys* At common law, the general principle of deduction applied to life insurance[3] and pension benefits.[4] But the rule was reversed by a series of legislative measures[5] culminating in section 2(1) of the Fatal Accidents Act 1959 which provides that

"in assessing damages in respect of a person's death in any action under the Fatal Accidents Act 1846 . . . there shall not be taken into account any insurance money, benefit, pension or gratuity which has been or will or may be paid as a result of the death".

The provision is most widely drawn and covers life insurance and social security benefits (including the return of premiums), payments by friendly societies and trade unions for the relief or maintenance of members' dependants,[6] benefits from pension schemes (including the return of contributions) and gratuities.[7]

The extent to which these major exceptions to the general rule of deduction may be justified on policy grounds rests on those considerations which were fully analysed in relation to personal injury claims.[8] There are only three special features which may qualify the conclusions drawn in that context. First, it is more difficult to justify the exceptions according to the *source of the benefit*:[9] in no case has the person claiming the award directly provided for the benefit, though in some cases it might be more realistic to suggest that the family as a whole undertook the financial sacrifice necessary to procure the benefit. Secondly, as regards the *purpose of the benefit*,[10] it would seem that life insurance

---

[1] *Davies v. Powell Duffryn Collieries, supra*, affirming a dictum of LORD ATKIN in *Rose v. Ford*, [1937] A.C. 826, at p. 835 and correcting a dictum of LORD WRIGHT in the same case (*ibid.*, at pp. 852–853).

[2] *Per* BRANSON, J., *May v. McAlpine & Sons (London), Ltd.*, [1938] 3 All E.R. 85, at p. 87; *per* LORD WRIGHT, *Davies'* case, *supra*, at p. 608.

[3] *Grand Trunk Rail Co. of Canada v. Jennings* (1888), 13 App. Cas. 800.

[4] *Carling v. Lebbon*, [1927] 2 K.B. 108.

[5] Notably Fatal Accidents (Damages) Act 1948, s. 1, Widows', Orphans' and Old Age Contributory Pensions Act 1929, s. 22.

[6] Fatal Accidents Act 1959, s. 2(2).

[7] Cf. *supra*, p. 274.

[8] *Supra*, pp. 225–230.

[9] Cf. *supra*, p. 226.

[10] Cf. *supra*, p. 228.

benefits more easily than accident insurance benefits may be fitted into the category of "investments" the proceeds of which are to be payable in addition to any other remedy which may accrue. Thirdly, it should be noted that at present social security benefits for dependants are relatively less generous than those to which a disabled person is entitled,[1] and that therefore the degree of overcompensation (if any) resulting from the rule of no deduction is likely to be small.

3   Losses consequent on disability of another

(a)   General

The Fatal Accidents Acts do not of course extend to persons who incur losses as a result of the disability (as opposed to the death) of another. Certain remedies are available at common law but their operation is both restrictive and uncertain. Discussion may conveniently be divided into (A) losses incurred by members of the injured person's family and (B) losses incurred by his employer.

(b)   Family losses

(i) *Loss of consortium* The one remaining tortious action for interference in a family relationship is the old remedy for loss of consortium,[2] that is the services and society of a wife. Viewed as an adjunct of the feudal proprietary right which a husband had in his wife, the action is clearly anachronistic. It was for this reason that the House of Lords in *Best* v. *Samuel Fox & Co.*[3] refused to extend the action to a wife whose husband had been injured by the defendant's tort. Yet independently of its origin, and failing any more general remedy, it may be regarded as a useful means of securing compensation for a husband whose wife can no longer care for him.[4] As regards the measure of damages, suggestions have been made that the primary item is for expenditure reasonably incurred and that only a moderate sum should be awarded for the loss of society and services,[5] but some courts, taking a different view, have been prepared to award substantial sums under this head.[6] Although there is little mention of this in the judgments,

---

[1] Atiyah, *Accidents, Compensation and the Law*, pp. 376–379.
[2] The Law Reform (Miscellaneous Provisions) Act 1970 abolished the right to damages for adultery, enticement, harbouring and seduction.
[3] [1952] A.C. 716.
[4] *Per* LORD PORTER, *Best* v. *Samuel Fox & Co.*, *ibid.*, at p. 728; *per* DIPLOCK, J., *Kirkham* v. *Boughey*, [1958] 2 Q.B. 338, at p. 343.
[5] *Per* LORD GODDARD, C.J., *Hare* v. *British Transport Commission*, [1956] 1 All E.R. 578 (£20 awarded); *per* BRABIN, J., *Lawrence* v. *Biddle*, [1966] 2 Q.B. 504, at p. 509.
[6] In *Cutts* v. *Chumley*, [1967] 2 All E.R. 89, £5000 was awarded for permanent loss of services and society. See also the Australian cases *Birch* v. *Taubmans*, [1957] S.R. (N.S.W.) 93 and *Bresatz* v. *Przibilla* (1962), 108 C.L.R. 541.

it seems legitimate to infer that for the *services* element assessment is based on the cost of a substitute housekeeper,[1] and a small sum is awarded for the non-pecuniary loss of society.[2] Again, despite dicta to the contrary,[3] it seems that the plaintiff may recover for an impairment of as well as for a total loss of consortium. [4]

(ii) *Loss of services*   It will be seen that subject to important limitations an employer can recover for the loss of services of his employee.[5] If a parent can show that a child, at the time of his injury, was in his "service", damages representing expenses reasonably incurred and the "value" of the services lost, measured by the cost of a substitute servant, may be awarded.[6]

(iii) *Losses incurred on behalf of the injured person*   It will be recalled[7] that in general an injured person may recover as part of *his own* award compensation for losses incurred by a third party only where he is under a legal (or possibly moral) obligation to indemnify that third person. The question now arises whether a third person sustaining losses on behalf of the injured person may recover them directly from the tortfeasor. Within the action for consortium, the husband may recover for the expense of caring for his wife. This will involve whatever is reasonably necessary for the welfare of the injured spouse: thus not only medical and travelling expenses[8] but also any loss of earnings consequent on the husband giving up his work or changing his job so that he might attend her.[9] It seems, however, that this latter item is recoverable not as an independent item[10] but only as part of the reasonable and necessary cost of caring for the injured spouse.[11] Beyond the consortium action, recovery is limited, and where it does exist its theoretical basis is uncertain. It is established law that a parent may recover for reasonable medical expenses incurred on behalf of an injured child.[12] It is often said that this is because the parent is under a legal obligation to care for the child with the consequence that no

---

[1] Cf. under the Fatal Accidents Acts, *supra*, p. 265.
[2] Cf. DEVLIN, J. in *McNeill* v. *Johnstone*, [1958] 1 W.L.R. 888, at p. 892.
[3] See the judgments of the Court of Appeal in *Best* v. *Samuel Fox & Co.*, [1951] 2 K.B. 639, at pp. 661, 665, 669 and on appeal, [1952] A.C. 716, *per* LORD PORTER at p. 728, *per* LORD GODDARD, at pp. 733–734 (*contra*, LORD REID, with LORD OAKSEY concurring, at p. 736).
[4] *Lawrence* v. *Biddle*, [1966] 2 Q.B. 504.
[5] *Infra*, p. 280.
[6] *Flemington* v. *Smithers* (1826), 2 C. & P. 292.
[7] *Supra*, pp. 175–177.
[8] *Kirkham* v. *Boughey*, [1958] 2 Q.B. 338.
[9] *McNeill* v. *Johnstone*, *supra*.
[10] *Kirkham* v. *Boughey*, *supra*, doubting *Behrens* v. *Bertram Mills Circus*, [1957] 2 Q.B. 1; and see n. 3, p. 280, *infra*.
[11] Per DEVLIN, J., *McNeill* v. *Johnstone*, *supra*, at pp. 892–893.
[12] *Barnes* v. *Pooley* (1935), 51 T.L.R. 391; *Read* v. *Croydon Corporation*, [1938] 4 All E.R. 631.

liability will arise if the expenses were incurred voluntarily.[1]   On this basis, liability depends on some quasi-contractual right to restitution for expenses incurred in pursuance of a legal obligation.[2]   On the other hand, a member of the victim's family giving up his job in order to attend the injured person may not, outside the consortium action, recover his lost earnings,[3] although there is some authority for the proposition that the injured party may in such circumstances himself recover compensation for the loss where it is a reasonable alternative to medical expenses which otherwise would have been incurred.[4]

(iv) *Non-pecuniary losses*   It is manifestly clear that beyond the small non-pecuniary element in a consortium action, no solatium claim for grief sustained by persons other than the victim will be countenanced.

(c) Losses incurred by employers[5]

The employer's right to compensation for loss of services has like the consortium action been regarded as anachronistic in modern times, and in *I.R. Comrs.* v. *Hambrook*[6] was restricted by the Court of Appeal to cases of domestic employment.   An attempt to base the claim on a quasi-contractual remedy for unjust enrichment failed in *Metropolitan Police District Receiver* v. *Croydon Corporation*.[7]   The recommendations for excluding the employer's rights altogether[8] have not been implemented.   It remains therefore to consider the measure of damages for cases within the narrow scope of the *Hambrook* decision.

(i) *Losses incurred on the victim's account*   Where the employer is legally bound to defray his employee's medical expenses or provide him with sick pay during disability, the losses so incurred may be recovered from the tortfeasor.[9]   Claims for benefits voluntarily conferred have generally failed.[10]

---

[1] *Square* v. *Model Farm Dairies (Bournemouth), Ltd.*, [1938] 2 All E.R. 740 affirmed on other grounds, [1939] 2 K.B. 365.

[2] *Per* WILD, C.J., *Cook* v. *Wright*, [1967] N.Z.L.R. 1034, at p. 1036.

[3] *McNeill* v. *Johnstone*, [1958] 3 All E.R. 16.   In that case DEVLIN, J. explained away his apparently conflicting decision in *Behrens* v. *Bertram Mills*, [1957] 2 Q.B. 1 on the ground that that too was a consortium award.   See also *Kirkham* v. *Boughey*, [1958] 2 Q.B. 338.

[4] Discussed *supra*, pp. 175–177.

[5] Luntz (1970), 2 Aus. C.L.R. 35.

[6] [1956] 2 Q.B. 641; followed in Canada (*Pagan* v. *Leifer* (1969), 6 D.L.R. (3d) 714) but not in Australia (*Railways Commissioner* v. *Scott* (1959), 102 C.L.R. 392).

[7] [1957] 2 Q.B. 154, *supra*, pp. 180–181.   The only other possibility is that the employee may himself recover for his employer's loss: e.g. *Dennis* v. *London Passenger Transport Board*, [1948] 1 All E.R. 779, *supra*, p. 181.

[8] Law Reform Committee 11th Report Cmnd. 2017 (1963);   Law Commission Working Papers Nos. 19 and 41.

[9] *A.-G.* v. *Valle Jones*, [1935] 2 K.B. 209;   *Metropolitan Police District Receiver* v. *Tatum*, [1948] 2 K.B. 68.

[10] *I.R. Comrs.* v. *Hambrook, supra*;   *Commonwealth* v. *Quince* (1944), 68 C.L.R.

(ii) *Losses incurred on the employer's own account*   An employer may recover for loss of profits where he is unable to mitigate the loss by employing a substitute. In *Mankin* v. *Scala Theodrome Co.*[1]

> P and his employee X were a music-hall double act. P was paid £40 per week out of which he paid X £10 per week. During X's period of disability, P could earn nothing.[2] P was awarded damages on the basis of £30 per week.

The corollary is that where the employer reasonably mitigates by employing a substitute the measure of damages is the difference (if any) between the remuneration paid to the injured employee when fit and that paid to his substitute.[3]

(d) Critique

It should be clear from the brief description offered above that this area of the law is in an unsatisfactory state. There are several criticisms that may be made.

(i) The law is uncertain. The exact extent of the remedies available is obscure.

(ii) There is no direct remedy to compensate the losses considered above. The courts have to make use of the antiquated actions for loss of consortium and services and the obscure quasi-contractual remedy. Benefactors who are neither members of the family nor employers (e.g. charities) have no action.

(iii) Certain obvious anomalies exist. Most prominent are the restrictions of loss of services to domestic employers and loss of consortium to husbands. As regards losses incurred on behalf of the victim, in general these may be recovered only where the third party was legally bound to assist the victim. The distinction between legal and voluntary benefits is unsatisfactory.[4]

(iv) The relationship between the third party's claim and the accident victim's own action remain obscure. In particular the courts have never rationalized (A) the extent to which the victim may in his own

---

227. Among English authorities, the only case which offers any support for recovery is *A.-G.* v. *Valle Jones, supra*, in which ATKINSON, J. allowed a claim for the indemnity of sick pay, notwithstanding the argument that since the employers could have terminated the contract of employment, the payment of the benefit was in effect voluntary.
[1] [1947] K.B. 257.
[2] STABLE, J. held that it was reasonable during this period (i) not to train a substitute (ii) not to perform a solo act.
[3] *Martinez* v. *Gerber* (1841), 3 Man. & G. 88.
[4] The distinction is usually justified on the grounds that either (a) the voluntary benefit is caused by the third party's generosity not the tort; or (b) the benefit is not deducted from the victim's own award (see *supra*, pp. 223–224). The inadequacy of (a) has already been demonstrated and (b) is not a necessary consequence: see n. 5, p. 282, *infra*.

action recover for the third party's loss;[1] (B) the extent to which a rule of deducting the value of the third party's benefit from the victim's own award should indirectly give rise to a right in the third party himself to claim the value of the benefit in an action against the tortfeasor.[2]

The Law Reform Committee[3] and now the Law Commission[4] have recommended that third parties should have a general remedy for losses incurred as a consequence of the accident victim's injuries. They should recover for assistance given to the victim whether such action was taken voluntarily or not[5] and for any loss of earnings or profits where this was a reasonably necessary consequence of the accident.[6] It is not thought desirable to restrict the remedy to any specific category of claimant (as under the Fatal Accidents Acts)[7] but the suggestion is that no compensation should be awarded for non-pecuniary losses, unless, perhaps in the form of a small sum fixed by the legislature.[8]

---

[1] *Supra*, pp. 175–177.
[2] *Supra*, pp. 229–230.
[3] 11th Report, Cmnd. 2017 (1963).
[4] Working Papers Nos. 19 and 41.
[5] Working Paper No. 41, para. 195. The result would be that if the victim were himself to recover for the "value" of the assistance, he would hold the sum for the benefit of the third party as in *Dennis* v. *London Transport Passenger Board*, [1948] 1 All E.R. 779.
[6] Working Paper No. 41, paras. 113–115.
[7] *Ibid.*, para. 204.
[8] *Ibid.*, para. 203.

CHAPTER EIGHT

Breach of Contract (I)

A INTRODUCTION

I THE OBJECT OF DAMAGES

1 The indemnity measure in tort

The object of compensation depends in the first place on the nature of the obligation which the defendant has failed adequately to perform. In tort, liability is consequent on the failure to observe a *negative* obligation: the defendant is enjoined by the law not to act in such a way as will injure the plaintiff's body, property, reputation or other interest. To compensate the plaintiff for the defendant's breach of this obligation involves putting him in the position he would have been in if the injury caused by the tort had not occurred. This measure has been referred to as *restitutio in integrum*[1] or the *indemnity measure*.

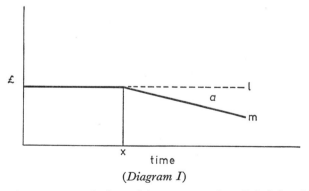

(*Diagram I*)

The graph represents P's financial resources. At *x* P is injured by D's tort. *l* represents what would have been his position if the tort had not been committed, *m* his actual position resulting from D's tort.

---

[1] *Supra*, p. 18.

The court will award P the difference between *l* and $m = £a$ (the indemnity measure).

2 Expectation interest in contract

In contract, on the other hand, the obligation on the promisor is most often, though not always, a positive one: D promises to do something for or convey something to P. Performance of this obligation will most often confer some benefit on P. Thus D may promise to deliver a chattel, build a house, or perform a service. If he fails to carry out his promise, P is deprived of the financial benefits which would have accrued to him if the chattel had been delivered, the house built, or the service performed. The object of compensation is to put him in the position he would have been in if the contract had been performed and if the benefits had accrued. He will be entitled, in other words, to the economic "value" of the bargain: this may be described as his *expectation interest*.

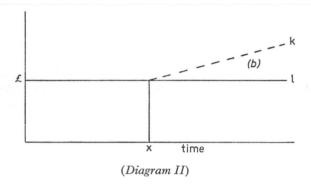

(*Diagram II*)

At *x* P enters into his contract with D. *k* represents what would have been his position if D had performed his contract, and *l* his position if he had not entered into the contract with D. In an action for breach of contract, P will be entitled to the difference between *k* and $l = £b$ (expectation interest).

In short, the difference between the indemnity measure in tort and the expectation interest in contract is that the former is concerned with the extent to which the plaintiff's assets have been *diminished* by the tort, while the latter prescribes compensation for the amount by which his assets would have been *increased* if the contract had been duly performed. The question may legitimately be posed why in a contractual action the law is prepared to adopt a measure which seeks to do more than merely to restore the plaintiff to the *status quo ante* as in tort. The answer lies deeply rooted in the economic foundations of the law of contract in Western capitalist societies.[1] Enforcement of the expectation interest, it has been said, stimulates economic activity, facilitates reliance on business agreements and protects the "credit system."[2] Indeed, in societies which do not share the same economic philosophies it is by no means obvious that recovery of lost anticipated profits is always to be tolerated.[3]

3 "Positive" losses in contract

But while the expectation interest is the primary item of damages in most actions for breach of contract, it is by no means the only one. The breach of contract may have resulted not only in the plaintiff's failure to acquire benefits to have been secured on performance, but also in his sustaining "positive" pecuniary losses: that is, his financial position is worse than it would have been if he had not entered into the contract.

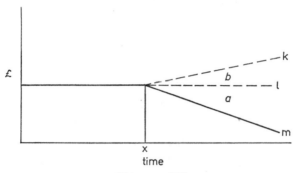

(*Diagram III*)

Here k represents what would have been P's position if D had performed his contract, l his position if he had not entered into the contract with D, and m his actual position resulting from D's breach of contract. Although the matter is complex—it will be fully discussed in Chapter Nine—it may be said that in general, in an action for breach of contract, P will be entitled to the difference between k and $m = £a$ ("positive" losses) $+ £b$ (expectation interest).

The "positive losses" represented by $£a$ themselves may be subdivided into three categories. First, in reliance on D's promise to per-

---

[1] See, e.g. Cohen (1933), 46 Harv. L.R. 553.
[2] Fuller & Perdue (1936), 46 Yale L.J. 52, at pp. 57–66.
[3] In medieval England, the efforts to restrain usury in some situations inhibited the award of the expectation interest: See Holdsworth, *H.E.L.* vol. VIII, pp. 103–104. In Soviet Russia, the right of a promisee to lost profits seems at one time to have been somewhat circumscribed: **Gsovski**, *Soviet Civil Law*, vol. I, pp. 441–444.

form his contract P may have incurred certain expenses. If the contract is duly performed he will not expect to be reimbursed for these expenses, but if it is not performed, the expenses will be wasted, and he may seek to recover what he has spent. This may be referred to as his *reliance interest*. Secondly, also in reliance on D's promise to perform, P may have conferred some benefit on D (usually the contract price). If the contract wholly fails, he will be entitled to recover that benefit. This may be described as his *restitution interest* but it is not generally recoverable in an action for damages. Strictly speaking, therefore, it does not come within the scope of this work, but it has been included for the sake of completeness. Thirdly, as a result of D's breach of contract, P may have made a payment to a third party, or himself may have suffered a pecuniary or non-pecuniary disadvantage. This may be described as his *indemnity interest*. The similarity to the tort measure will be as apparent as it was intentional, for the indemnity interest arises most often in contracts where the defendant's obligation is a negative one: not to cause injury or loss to the plaintiff.

The various interests outlined above may be illustrated by reference to a hypothetical case.

> D agrees to sell a horse to P, who in his turn resells it to X. P agrees to collect the horse from D's farm, but when he arrives D is unable to deliver the horse. In consequence P is unable to perform his contract with X and has to pay compensation to X.

P's *expectation interest* is the profit he will make on the resale to X. His *reliance interest* will be the wasted expense of transport to and from D's farm. He will claim as his *restitution interest* the price he paid D for the horse, and as his *indemnity interest* the amount of compensation he has paid to X. It must not, however, be imagined that P will recover the gross amount of all these sums. In the following pages it will be seen how various doctrines are applied generally to limit a plaintiff's recovery.

4 Tort and contract generally

It might appear from the above analysis as if the contractual damages will invariably be greater than tortious damages. There are indeed cases where this will be so, where the plaintiff's expectation interest exceeds his "positive losses". For example,

> D fraudulently sells to P for £10 a manuscript which he represents to be an historical document but which he knows to be a worthless forgery. If the manuscript had been genuine P could have resold it for £30.
>
> If P sues D in *tort*, he is to be put in the position he would have been in if no tort had been committed, and hence if he had not bought the manuscript. He will be awarded his loss on the transaction which is

the difference between the price he paid for the manuscript (£10) and its value in his hand (£0)=£10.

If P is able to prove that D warranted the manuscript was genuine, that is that D promised to deliver a valuable document, in an action for *breach of contract*, P will recover his expectation interest, which is the difference between the selling price of the manuscript as it exists (£0) and as it would have been if it had corresponded to the contractual description (£30)=£30.

But damages in contract are not always larger than in tort, and this for several reasons.

(a) Net loss on transaction

The plaintiff may have made a bad bargain. Performance of the contract would have resulted in a net loss to him. In such circumstances, he may recover more in tort than in contract.

As in the hypothetical case above, but P paid D £30 for the manuscript and even if it had been genuine it would only have fetched £10 on resale. In tort, P will recover his loss on the transaction =£30. In contract, he will be limited to his expectation interest =£10.[1]

(b) Expectation interest as tort loss

What is regarded as part of the expectation interest for the purposes of an action for breach of contract may in some cases be recovered in tort as a "positive loss", because it is a benefit or a profit which the plaintiff would have enjoyed if the tort had not been committed. In other words, the process of restoring the plaintiff to the *status quo ante* in tort will arrive at the same result as putting him in the position he would have been in if the contract had been performed.

Under a contract of sale, D promises to deliver to P a valuable historical document. As D knows, P intends to resell it to X. D wrongfully refuses to deliver the document and converts it to his own purposes. In contract, P will recover as his expectation interest the profit he would have made on the subsale. But he will recover the same amount if he sues D in tort for conversion. He would have made the same profit if the article had not been converted.

(c) Exemplary damages

Provided the case comes within one of Lord Devlin's categories,[2] in tort the plaintiff may exceptionally recover exemplary damages. The award is not available in an action for breach of contract.[3]

---

[1] Though on the authority of *Anglia Television, Ltd.* v. *Reed*, [1972] 1 Q.B. 60, it seems that he may elect to sue for his reliance interest. See *infra*, pp. 350–352.

[2] *Supra*, pp. 34–37.

[3] *Addis* v. *Gramophone Co.*, [1909] A.C. 488.

(d) Liquidated damages

In contract, the plaintiff's remedy may be limited by agreement.[1] *Ex hypothesi*, this cannot apply where the action is not based on a contract.

(e) Non-pecuniary losses

The plaintiff's right to compensation for non-pecuniary losses is more limited in contract than in tort.[2]

(f) Remoteness

The doctrine of remoteness is more restrictive in contract than in tort.[3] A greater degree of "foreseeability" is necessary in contract as a condition of recovery.

(g) Certainty

In contract, the plaintiff may not recover for the loss of any benefits which were at the discretion of the defendant.[4] The same limit appears not to apply to actions in tort.[5]

(h) Election

It appears from recent authority,[6] that in a contractual action a plaintiff may elect to sue for his reliance interest rather than his expectation interest. If so he will recover the compensation which he would have recovered if he had sued in tort.

II THE PURPOSES AND PROBLEMS OF CLASSIFICATION

There is no general agreement among authors as to the way in which losses arising from a breach of contract are to be classified. Even more disturbing is the fact that the courts seem reluctant to recognize any form of classification. There would seem to be a twofold purpose to classification. On the one hand, it facilitates the exposition of principles by distinguishing between different *factual* situations even though the same general principle might be applied to those different classes. In

---

[1] *Supra*, pp. 38–59.
[2] *Infra*, pp. 307–309.
[3] *Supra*, pp. 75–76.
[4] *Infra*, pp. 309–314.
[5] *Supra*, p. 262.
[6] *Anglia Television, Ltd.* v. *Reed*, [1972] 1 Q.B. 60, *infra*, pp. 350–352.

order to reach a decision on a given set of facts it is not necessary for the court to recognize such classifications.   But when *different* principles are to be applied to *different* factual situations, then, of course, classification becomes crucial.   The distinction between the expectation and the reliance interest is one such classification, yet it has been curiously ignored by the courts in this country,[1] with a consequent uncertainty over certain major problems.[2]   Judges and some influential writers have for a long time been almost totally preoccupied with the rule in *Hadley* v. *Baxendale* and the doctrine of remoteness.[3]   One of the purposes of the adopted classification is to reassert the importance of the distinctions of principle which exist.

In the light of these observations we may consider certain objections which might be raised against the classification adopted in this work. In the first place, it is arguable that the restitution interest is simply one aspect of the reliance interest: P has incurred expenditure through reliance on D's performance.   Since however English law employs a different remedy for restitution it would seem convenient to keep these two interests separate.   Secondly, it is apparent that the line to be drawn between the expectation and the indemnity interest is not always easy to draw.[4]   For example, if D fails to complete the building of P's house, and P employs another to execute the unfinished work, P will be able to recover the cost of this substitute performance.   In one sense, this may be regarded as the recovery of the indemnity measure: an expense made necessary by the breach.   But it is in reality a substitute to the benefit which the defendant should have conferred on performance, and thus is more properly treated as part of the expectation interest.   The indemnity interest is not concerned with the benefits of performance (or their equivalents).   It deals with "positive losses". It measures the extent to which the plaintiff is put in a worse position than if he had not entered into a contract with the defendant.

III   LAW OF CONTRACT OR LAW OF CONTRACTS

Any author who purports to state general principles governing contractual agreements is confronted with the objection that there is in

---

[1] It has been discussed in only two reported cases: *Cullinane* v. *British "Rema" Manufacturing Co.*, [1954] 1 Q.B. 292, *infra*, p. 354 and *Anglia Television, Ltd.* v. *Reed*, [1972] 1 Q.B. 60, *infra*, p. 350 but in neither case was the analysis successful: Macleod, [1970] J.B.L. 19; Ogus (1972), 35 M.L.R. 423.

[2] *Infra*, pp. 350–354.

[3] "One might get the impression that all problems of damages in contract were capable of being answered by the rule."; Street, pp. 236–237.

[4] The distinction and the objection to it are considered further *infra*, pp. 364–365.

reality not a law of contract, only a law of contracts,[1] that it is dangerous to argue from one particular type of contract to another. Some judges have gone so far as to question whether any general principles of damages do exist: "cases of damage differ as much as the leaves of a tree differ from each other, or rather the leaves of different trees. . . . No precise positive rule can embrace all cases."[2] Others have feared to venture beyond the broadest of general principles, such as remoteness ("the assessment of damages must vary so much with the particular circumstances of each case that justice can only be done by applying the broad principles laid down in *Hadley* v. *Baxendale*,"[3]) or the general compensatory principle of putting the plaintiff in the position he would have been in if the contract had been performed.[4] It is of course true that there is a great multitude of situations which come within this area of the law: there are various types of contract and various types of obligation within each such contract; there are various types of breaches and various types of loss arising from each such breach. But the basic premise of this work is that general principles do exist and need to be stated. The "rules" for measuring damages for specific contracts should not, it is contended, be considered in isolation from one another, but within the context of a broad normative structure. In each section, therefore, it is proposed to state a general principle, and then to illustrate it with reference to certain categories of specific contracts.

B THE EXPECTATION INTEREST

I INTRODUCTION

The expectation interest, most broadly described, embraces all the pecuniary and non-pecuniary advantages which the plaintiff would have enjoyed if the defendant's obligation had been duly performed. It is, however, rare for the plaintiff to recover damages for his full expectation interest. The reason is that in order to award a sum which might be deemed "just and reasonable" the court applies a number of doctrines which limit the measure of compensation. There are rules: to construe the advantage promised as narrowly as possible, to exclude uncertain, remote and non-pecuniary advantages, and in some special

---

[1] The problem is particularly acute for those who are attempting to draft a code. See Gower (1967), 30 M.L.R. 259, at p. 261.

[2] *Per* POLLOCK, C. B., *Wilson* v. *Newport Dock* (1866), L.R. 1 Ex. 177 at p. 190.

[3] (1854), 9 Exch. 341; *per* UPJOHN, L.J., *Charterhouse Credit* v. *Tolly*, [1963] 2 Q.B. 683, at p. 712.

[4] E.g. LORD DUNEDIN in *Watts, Watts & Co., Ltd.* v. *Mitsui & Co.*, [1917] A.C. 227, at p. 241.

cases for the purposes of public policy to exclude compensation for the expectation interest altogether. Most important of all, there is the doctrine of mitigation which forbids the recovery of compensation for those losses which the plaintiff might reasonably have avoided. At the end, four different measures for the lost expectation interest will emerge. If the doctrine of mitigation does not apply (because it was impossible or unreasonable for the plaintiff to avoid the loss) he will be entitled to (A) his *lost profits*. In the ordinary case, however, he must mitigate his loss and the sum awarded will be further reduced to either (B) the *substitution cost* or (C) the *completion cost* or (D) *diminished profits*.

The starting point of the exposition will be the factual benefits which the defendant should have conferred on performance. It will then be seen how the limiting doctrines apply to scale down this figure to the *exceptional* measure of lost profits. The more *normal* measures consequent on the doctrine of mitigation will then be analysed. The process may be illustrated in diagrammatic form.

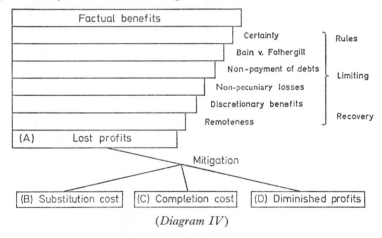

(*Diagram IV*)

II FACTUAL BENEFITS AND THE DOCTRINE OF CERTAINTY

1 General

In this section, an account will be given of the factual benefits which are likely to arise on complete performance of the defendant's obligation, and how the doctrine of certainty[1] reduces each such benefit to an ascertainable monetary sum. The notion of factual benefits has sometimes been paraphrased as the "value" of the defendant's obligation.[2] This is not a helpful formulation. The ambiguities which are

---

[1] See generally *supra*, pp. 79–85.
[2] E.g. *per* MEGAW, L.J. in *The Mihalis Angelos*, [1971] 1 Q.B. 164, at p. 210.

created by the use of the term "value" have been described in another chapter.[1] The embarrassments are equally acute in cases of breach of contract and the remedy is the same: a suspicion of rules couched solely in terms of the "value" of property to be transferred or services to be performed, and a concern instead to indicate with greater particularity the exact meaning to be given to "value" appropriate to the rule in question.[2]

The factual nature of an inquiry into the benefits arising on performance means that any exhaustive analysis is impossible. The variety of contracts, and of obligations within contracts, is infinite. The consequences will differ widely from case to case. Nevertheless, certain groups of obligation tend to give rise to certain categories of benefit. It is therefore proposed to give an account of the benefits arising from four different classes of contractual obligation: (I) delivery of a chattel; (II) transfer of an interest in land; (III) performance of a service; (IV) acceptance of performance.

2　Obligation to deliver a chattel

The obligation to deliver a chattel arises under such contracts as sale, hire, hire-purchase, carriage, bailment, repairs.

(a)　Profit on resale

Where the plaintiff is a trader, the benefit he will derive from the delivery or redelivery of the chattel will be the profit he will make on the sale of it. If the subcontract was made before the breach, there will be evidence of an *actual* profit, that is, the resale price less the expenses necessary to secure that profit,[3] usually the price that was paid for the article plus overheads.[4] Conversely, if at the time of breach the plaintiff had not yet entered into a contract to sell the article but had the intention of doing so the court will have regard to his *notional* profit, that is the difference between the price he paid for it (plus overheads) and the price at which he might reasonably have sold it. In the ordinary case this will be assessed on the basis of the market *selling* price at the time when the resale might reasonably have taken place if the article had been duly delivered.[5] Alternatively, if there is no market for the goods in question, a figure representing a reasonable percentage of the price the plaintiff paid for the goods might be selected.[6] Where either

---

[1] Tortious damages for injury to property, *supra*, pp. 121–123.
[2] The various possible interpretations of "value" are set out, *ibid.*
[3] This is the reliance interest: see, generally, *infra*, pp. 346–354.
[4] E.g. *Patrick* v. *Russo-British Grain Export Co.*, [1927] 2 K.B. 535.
[5] E.g. *Koufos* v. *Czarnikow*, [1969] 1 A.C. 350.
[6] E.g. *Household Machines* v. *Cosmos Exporters*, [1947] K.B. 217: 10 per cent.

the resale itself, or the number of articles to be resold, remains uncertain, the doctrine of certainty will enjoin the court to do the best it can to establish the amount of trade lost through the breach.[1] The plaintiff must, however, produce evidence sufficient to satisfy the court on the probability of the loss: a claim for "general loss of business" is generally inadequate without specific proof.[2]

(b) Profit through use

In other cases, the profit will be derived from the use of the article rather than from its resale. The defendant may fail to deliver a profit-earning chattel, for example a ship or a piece of machinery. Here the benefit will be the profits to be earned on the basis either of contracts already made,[3] or of contracts which the plaintiff would have made if the article had been delivered,[4] or failing either, the average earnings of the chattel in question.[5] "Profits" in this context means, generally, net profits after deducting the cost of the article and necessary overheads.[6] The same principles of certainty apply to this as to the previous category of profit.

(c) Possession or use

In the cases described above, where the plaintiff's sole interest in the delivery of the chattel is the profit he can make from it, it may be said that he has no particular interest in possession or use of the article itself. Possession and use are only the means by which the end, the financial profit, might be secured. Where, in contrast, the plaintiff is a consumer, the ultimate purpose of the transaction is mere possession and use. The benefit arising from the contract, then, is the advantage (if any) in having secured delivery of the particular article at the particular price. This advantage may involve both pecuniary and non-pecuniary elements. The most important pecuniary advantage will be the difference (if any) between the price which the plaintiff paid for the article and the buying price of the same article or its nearest equivalent in the market. This is, in fact, the substitution cost, perhaps the most common measure in all cases of breach of contract after the doctrine of mitigation has been applied. For this reason, discussion of the notion of

---

[1] *Cointat* v. *Myham & Son*, [1913] 2 K.B. 220. In the nineteenth century it was not so clear that prospective profits could be recovered, see *Wilson* v. *Lancashire and Yorkshire Rail Co.* (1861), 9 C.B.N.S. 632. Cf. in tort, *supra*, p. 126.

[2] *Watson* v. *Gray* (1900), 16 T.L.R. 308.

[3] E.g. *T.C. Industrial Plant* v. *Robert's* (1964), 37 A.L.J.R. 289.

[4] E.g. *Victoria Laundry (Windsor)* v. *Newman Industries*, [1949] 2 K.B. 528.

[5] E.g. *Elliott Steam Tug Co., Ltd.* v. *Shipping Controller*, [1922] 1 K.B. 127.

[6] *Cullinane* v. *British "Rema" Manufacturing*, [1954] 1 Q.B. 292; cf. *infra*, pp. 352–354.

substitution cost will be reserved.[1] Another form of pecuniary advantage may exist where the use of the chattel has some "commercial value" even though it cannot be translated into "profits". In such cases, the courts tend to evaluate the advantage as interest on the capital invested in the goods.[2] The non-pecuniary element will exist where the chattel has unique qualities which cannot be expressed in pecuniary terms, for example, a wedding ring or an heirloom.

3 Obligation to transfer an interest in real property

Under this heading are included the obligations to complete the sale of a freehold or leasehold interest in land (including options to purchase or to renew), covenants for title, covenants in a lease to deliver up the property at the end of the term, and in a good condition (with analogous covenants to repair). The benefits which may arise on due performance of these obligations follow a similar pattern to those described above, but the modes of dealing with land present such special features that separate treatment seems desirable.

(a) Profit on resale

Unlike contracts involving chattels, it is not common for the transferee to purchase land (or buildings) for the sole purpose of immediate resale. Where the phenomenon does occur, the benefit is the same: the difference between the contract (plus necessary expenses) and the resale price.[3] The true equivalent of the trader in goods is the property developer who seeks to buy, improve and resell at a profit. His benefit will be the profit to be made on dealing with the land,[4] taking into account all the necessary expenses (to include, *inter alia*, purchase price and development costs).

(b) Profit through letting

More frequently the plaintiff on obtaining possession intends to let the property. His interest in the defendant's performance will then be the profit to be obtained: the rent.[5] The plaintiff need not, of course, prove the existence of an actual contract to grant a lease: it is sufficient if he can produce evidence of an intention to let, and the profit lost

---

[1] *Infra*, pp. 322–335.
[2] E.g. *B. Sunley & Co., Ltd.* v. *Cunard White Star, Ltd.*, [1940] 1 K.B. 740 (the features of this measure have already been described in the context of tortious damages: *supra*, p. 140). Alternatively, the advantage can be evaluated as the rent payable for the use of the article in question: e.g. *Charterhouse Credit* v. *Tolly*, [1963] 2 Q.B. 683.
[3] *Goffin* v. *Houlder* (1921), 90 L.J.Ch. 488.
[4] *Diamond* v. *Campbell-Jones*, [1961] Ch. 22.
[5] *Royal Bristol Permanent Building Society* v. *Bomash* (1887), 35 Ch.D. 390.

will be the rent that would have been obtained in the market.[1] But at
the same time it seems that the court will not always take the trouble to
ascertain whether the plaintiff's intention was to sell or to let.   Where a
tenant fails in his obligation to deliver up premises in good repair,
according to section 18(1) of the Landlord and Tenant Act, 1927
damages should not "exceed the amount (if any) by which the value
of the reversion ... is diminished."   The courts have always interpreted the word "value" in this provision as referring to the *saleable*
value of the reversion rather than the *lettable* value,[2] even though in
most cases it would seem fairly clear on the facts that the reversioner's
intention was to relet rather than to sell the premises at the end of the
defendant's term.

(c)   Profit through use

The plaintiff may wish to use the property for the purposes of a
profitable business.   His benefit will be the profits to be made on the
business less the necessary expenses.[3] Of course, the ordinary rules of
certainty apply, and where the plaintiff has not yet set up the business,
the possibility of profits is even more speculative than usual.[4]

(d)   Use or possession

The requirement of the property for the transferee's own use and
enjoyment is even more common than in the corresponding contracts
for the delivery of chattels and the benefits are the same: the advantage
of the bargain, measured by the substitution cost,[5] and the use of the
property measured by the rent obtainable on letting it out.[6] Presumably also the plaintiff has a non-pecuniary interest in having transferred
to him a property which has for him some sentimental value.

4   Obligation to perform a service

The obligation to perform a service or services arises in a variety of
contractual agreements.   The types of benefit accruing therefrom are
correspondingly numerous.   At a general level of analysis, however,
four categories may be distinguished.

---

[1] *Jones* v. *Gardiner*, [1902] 1 Ch. 191.
[2] E.g. *Jaquin* v. *Holland*, [1960] 1 All E.R. 402; *Re King, Robinson* v. *Gray*,
[1962] 2 All E.R. 66. Of course, the saleable value of property may represent a
capitalization of its letting potential: Cf. *supra* p. 123.
[3] *Phillips* v. *Lamdin*, [1949] 2 K.B. 33.
[4] See e.g. *Cottrill* v. *Steyning and Littlehampton Building Society*, [1966] 2 All
E.R. 295.
[5] *Re Daniel*, [1917] 2 Ch. 405.
[6] *Royal Bristol Permanent Building Society* v. *Bomash* (1887), 35 Ch.D. 39.

(a) Profit from service

The object of the contract may be that the defendant is to secure a pecuniary benefit for the plaintiff. Thus in a contract of employment, the benefit accruing to the employer is often the profit that will result from the employee's work, or if the employee acts with others to produce the profit, then a proportionate part of that profit.[1] Similarly, under a charterparty, a charterer is often under a duty to load a full and complete cargo. The benefit to the shipowner will be the freight which will be payable.[2] Also under this head may be included those cases in which the defendant is charged with the duty of selling the plaintiff's property. The benefit here will be the financial advantage accruing to the plaintiff if the defendant sells at the proper time.[3]

(b) Opportunity to make a profit

In other cases, the defendant does not himself acquire the profit for the plaintiff but provides him with an opportunity of making a profit. The classic case of *Chaplin* v. *Hicks*[4] in which the plaintiff was deprived of the chance of winning a beauty competition is one example. But there are other more common if less colourful illustrations: an advertising agent publicizing products,[5] a theatrical agent procuring an engagement,[6] a solicitor advising on legal rights[7] or pursuing a claim for damages,[8] a financier advising on investments.[9] In all these cases the profit-making transaction is not a necessary consequence of the defendant's proper performance. The benefit is not the profit but the chance of making a profit. This is evaluated by applying the doctrine of certainty. From the profit which would have been made if the venture had been successfully accomplished there is deducted an amount representing the degree of uncertainty.[10] Thus if the plaintiff has a fifty per cent chance of making £100, the "value" of his chance is £50.

(c) Use or possession of property

Performance by the defendant may not procure any financial advantage for the plaintiff. Its object may be the acquisition of property for the plaintiff's use and enjoyment: an agent procuring the purchase of

---

[1] *Ebbw Vale Steel, Iron and Coal Co.* v. *Tew* (1935), 79 Sol. Jo. 593.
[2] E.g. *Heimdal* v. *Questier & Co.* (1949), 82 Ll.L.Rep. 452.
[3] *Michael* v. *Hart & Co.*, [1902] 1 K.B. 482.
[4] [1911] 2 K.B. 786, *supra*, p. 83.
[5] *Marcus* v. *Myers* (1895), 11 T.L.R. 327.
[6] *Johnston* v. *Braham and Campbell, Ltd.*, [1917] 1 K.B. 586.
[7] *Cook* v. *S.*, [1966] 1 All E.R. 248.
[8] *Yardley* v. *Coombes* (1963), 107 Sol. Jo. 575.
[9] *Woods* v. *Martins Bank*, [1958] 3 All E.R. 166.
[10] See, e.g. *Otter* v. *Church, Adams, Tatham & Co.*, [1953] Ch. 280 and *supra* pp. 83–84.

goods,[1] a solicitor effecting the conveyance of land,[2] a surveyor or estate agent advising on the merits of a house to be bought.[3] The benefits to be derived on performance are the same as those described in relation to the obligation to deliver chattels (2) (c) and real property (3) (d).

(d) Non-pecuniary benefits

There are many contracts one of whose objects is to promote a non-pecuniary benefit. A bride employing a photographer to take photographs at her wedding expects more than the mere pecuniary value of the pictures.[4] A traveller booking a holiday through travel agents anticipates a certain amount of pleasure.[5] A man entering into a restaurant and ordering a meal looks forward to savouring the results. In all these cases, it is difficult to equate the "value" of the promisee's performance with the price that he was paid for it. However the non-pecuniary benefit is described, it forms part of the plaintiff's expectation interest.

5 Obligation to accept promisee's performance

Where A is under an obligation to deliver property to B or perform a service for B, B is generally bound by at least two reciprocal obligations: to accept performance by A and to pay him the contract price. In English law, an action for the non-payment of money is not an action for damages and different rules apply: in particular a plaintiff cannot recover what in an action for damages would be regarded as the expectation interest.[6] Thus should he wish to claim compensation for the various benefits which flow from the prompt payment of a contract debt, he will do better if he is able to prove that the defendant was in breach of his obligation to accept performance. The benefits arising from the due execution of this obligation may now be considered.

(a) Profit from performance

The plaintiff who has at his disposal certain property which he is able to deliver to the defendant or who is able to perform some service for the defendant possesses a valuable asset which through the performance of the contract he is able to translate into a financial advantage. This advantage will therefore constitute the benefit to be derived from the successful execution of the contract. In the case of non-

---

[1] *Cassaboglou* v. *Gibb* (1883), 11 Q.B.D. 797.
[2] *Pilkington* v. *Wood*, [1953] Ch. 770.
[3] *Philips* v. *Ward*, [1956] 1 All E.R. 874.
[4] *Diesen* v. *Samson*, 1971 S.L.T. (Sh. Ct.) 49.
[5] *Jarvis* v. *Swans Tours Ltd.*, [1973] 1 All E.R. 71.
[6] *Infra*, pp. 369–370.

acceptance of goods which have been sold, this is calculated by the difference between (i) the contract price and (ii) the price which the plaintiff paid for it or the cost of manufacture plus overheads.[1] The calculation is the same in hire-purchase contracts except that (i) becomes the full hire-purchase price, that is deposit and instalments and fee for exercising the option to purchase,[2] while in contracts for hire alone, the benefit is the total amount of rent payable less expenses and depreciation.[3] In employment contracts, it is the earning capacity of the plaintiff who has been wrongfully dismissed. The analogy with tortious damages for personal injuries[4] is obvious. Included are not only wages, which, if the rate was variable (e.g. piece work) are based on the plaintiff's average earnings,[5] but also bonuses,[6] commission,[7] payments in kind (e.g. board and lodging)[8] and pension and life insurance rights.[9] In a contract of apprenticeship, the primary object of which is the training of the plaintiff for more lucrative employment, the benefits include the plaintiff's future prospects of employment, in short his labour potential.[10]

(b) Use of money

It must not be forgotten that the prompt payment of the contractual price itself represents a financial advantage to the recipient. Money may be invested either in the plaintiff's own profit-making enterprise or in other securities. The former possibility tends to be speculative, and for the court to be able to quantify the amount, evidence of a specific project is generally required.[11] The normal measure of the benefit accruing from the use of money is the current rate of interest on loans.[12]

(c) Advancement of reputation

Acceptance of the plaintiff's performance may advance his reputation both in a pecuniary and in a non-pecuniary sense. A man's social reputation or prestige will doubtlessly be advanced should he be engaged in certain esteemed activities. From a pecuniary point of view,

---

[1] *Re Vic Mill, Ltd.,* [1913] 1 Ch. 465.
[2] *Yeoman Credit* v. *Waragowski,* [1961] 3 All E.R. 145.
[3] *Interoffice Telephones* v. *Freeman,* [1958] 1 Q.B. 190.
[4] *Supra,* pp. 187–188.
[5] *Devonald* v. *Rosser & Sons,* [1906] 2 K.B. 728.
[6] *Powell* v. *Braun,* [1954] 1 All E.R. 484.
[7] *Reigate* v. *Union Manufacturing Co.,* [1918] 1 K.B. 592.
[8] *Lindsay* v. *Queens Hotel Co.,* [1919] 1 K.B. 212.
[9] *Bold* v. *Brough, Nicholson and Hall,* [1963] 3 All E.R. 849.
[10] *Dunk* v. *Waller & Son,* [1970] 2 Q.B. 163.
[11] See, e.g. *Manchester and Oldham Bank* v. *W. A. Cook* (1883), 49 L.T. 674.
[12] *Supra,* pp. 99–100.

the plaintiff's prospects of future financial gain may depend on reputation and publicity. Thus an actor's or author's chance of future employment will be vitally affected by the reception of his present activities.[1] In a similar way a trader's hold over customers in the market and his prospects of expanding his custom will depend on the reputation as to his creditworthiness.[2] In all such cases, it seems legitimate to assume that the benefits accruing from due acceptance of the plaintiff's performance include the chance of future, though necessarily speculative-profits.

(III) THE DOCTRINES LIMITING RECOVERY AND THE LOST PROFITS MEASURE

1 Introduction

Having ascertained the full extent of the *factual* benefits which would have accrued on performance, the court must, in accordance with the doctrines now to be described, reduce the sum to the *legally recoverable* amount. It is proposed to begin with those doctrines which apply only in special areas of the law of contract.

2 The Rule in *Bain* v. *Fothergill*

The first such rule is one of public policy. It excludes altogether the right to compensation for loss of the expectation interest where a vendor of land fails to complete the sale through a defect in title. The rule was first established in the eighteenth-century decision of *Flureau* v. *Thornhill*[3] and was confirmed a century later by the House of Lords[4] in *Bain* v. *Fothergill*.[5] It has been accepted in the major Commonwealth jurisdictions,[6] but many (though apparently not the majority of) American jurisdictions have rejected what is referred to as the "English rule".[7]

(a) Scope of rule

For the rule to be applied certain conditions must be fulfilled.

---

[1] *Clayton and Waller, Ltd.* v. *Oliver*, [1930] A.C. 209.
[2] *Rolin* v. *Steward* (1854), 14 C.B. 595.
[3] (1776), 2 Wm. Bl. 1078.
[4] Six common law judges attending the hearing to offer their advice.
[5] (1874), L.R. 7 H.L. 158.
[6] See, e.g. for Australia, *Coronet Homes* v. *Bankstown Finance and Investment Co., Ltd.*, [1966] 2 N.S.W.R. 351; for New Zealand, *Jacobs* v. *Bills*, [1967] N.Z.L.R. 249; for Canada, *Resume* v. *Lalonde*, [1939] 3 D.L.R. 270.
[7] McCormick, pp. 686–692; 55 Am. Jur. pp. 951–952.

(i) *The contract must be for the conveyance of an interest in land*   This includes not only sales of freehold land[1] but also leases[2] and easements.[3]   It does not apply to the sale of personalty. [4]

(ii) *The breach must consist of the vendor's failure to complete or his delay in completing.*   One curious feature of the rule is that, though it applies where the defendant's failure to make good title causes loss to the plaintiff *before* the conveyance is complete, should he be ousted *after* completion the rule will not apply and he will recover[5] substantial damages for the loss of his expectation interest.[6]   This would seem to be an aberration on the part of the judges for in the cases falling within the latter category, with a single exception,[7] the rule is not even mentioned. Moreover there is no obvious explanation for the distinction.[8]   Whatever be the policy reasons for the rule,[9] the mere passing of ownership seems hardly sufficient to justify a substantially different award of damages.[10]

(iii) *The breach must substantially result from a defect of title*   The principle rationale for the rule in *Bain* v. *Fothergill*, as will be seen,[11] is the complexity and uncertainties of title.   It follows that the substantial cause of the breach must be a defect in title.   A vendor who simply refuses to complete cannot take advantage of the rule.[12]   Nor can a

---

[1] E.g. *Bain* v. *Fothergill, supra.*
[2] *J. W. Cafés* v. *Brownlow Trust,* [1950] 1 All E.R. 894.
[3] *Morgan* v. *Russell & Sons,* [1909] 1 K.B. 357.
[4] *Bain* v. *Fothergill, supra,* at pp. 172, 211.
[5] In actions for breach of quiet enjoyment or the analogous actions for breaches of covenant (i) for a good right to convey or (ii) against encumbrances.
[6] E.g. *Beard* v. *Porter,* [1948] 1 K.B. 321.
[7] BLACKBURN, J. in *Lock* v. *Furze* (1866), L.R. 1 C.P. 441, at p. 454, but although the distinction is made no reasons for it are given.
[8] Those American jurisdictions which have accepted the rule in *Bain* v. *Fothergill* apply it (with some exceptions) equally to breaches of covenant of title: McCormick, pp. 702–704; 61 A.L.R. 10.   An Australian judge has attempted to rationalize the rule on the ground that in cases of sale of land the making of title is a condition precedent for the existence of the contract.   On the failure to make title, therefore, the plaintiff is not entitled to damages for the breach of contract since no contract has come into existence but is restricted to a restitutionary remedy: ISAAC, J. in *Coronet Homes* v. *Bankstown Finance and Investment Co., Ltd.,* [1966] 2 N.S.W.R. 351.   This would certainly explain the distinction stated in the text but for reasons given below (pp. 303–304) the theory is untenable.
[9] *Infra,* p. 304.
[10] If prevention of hardship to the defendant is the reason for the rule, then the distinction becomes even more irrational since to recover lost profits against someone who has already conveyed land may be harsher than against someone who has only promised to do so: Fuller & Perdue (1936), 46 Yale L.J. 373, at p. 378.
[11] *Infra,* p. 304.
[12] *Diamond* v. *Campbell-Jones,* [1961] Ch. 22.

vendor who has already sold the property to a third party:[1] the breach results not from the defect of title but from the defendant's own act rendering completion of the contract impossible. Further, if the defendant could by his own efforts have removed the obstacle to completion then this too will exclude the rule.[2] This includes cases where it is theoretically possible for the defendant to cure the defect but he has not the financial means to do so. In *Re Daniel, Daniel v. Vassall*[3]

> T agreed to sell certain mortgaged property to P. T died. The mortgagees refused to release the property from the mortgage and T's executors did not have sufficient funds to redeem the property. It was held that since the failure to complete was "due, not to any defect in title, but to the refusal of the mortgagees to release, and to the pecuniary inability of the testator and his estate to pay the mortgagees off,"[4] the rule in *Bain v. Fothergill* was to be excluded.

(iv) *The defendant must act in good faith* If the vendor fraudulently represents that he has a good title to the land, but has not, the rule does not apply.[5] The same is true where the vendor deliberately abstains from making title,[6] and where he knows that there is no hope of making title by the completion date.[7] But the rule will apply where he knows at the time of entering the contract that he has no title and merely believes bona fide that he will have it by completion date,[8] or where he has been mistaken as to the validity of the title.[9]

(b) Effect of rule

Where the rule applies, the plaintiff may not recover damages for any part of his expectation interest. He has a restitutionary remedy: return of the deposit plus interest. His right to recover for his full reliance interest is somewhat uncertain. He is certainly entitled to the expenses wasted in investigating title[10] and in preparing the contract.[11] The plaintiff has never been permitted to recover other wasted expenses, but significantly all the cases denying compensation[12] preceded *Hadley v. Baxendale*[13] and may perhaps be explained away as an appli-

---

[1] *Goffin v. Houlder* (1920), L.J. Ch. 488.
[2] *Braybrooks v. Whaley*, [1919] 1 K.B. 435.
[3] [1917] 2 Ch. 405.
[4] *Ibid., per* SARGANT, J., at p. 409.
[5] There is no direct English authority for this but it is implicit in dicta in *Bain v. Fothergill, supra*, at pp. 173–175, 183–184, 200, 206–207; and in *Re Daniel, Daniel v. Vassall, supra*, at p. 410. See California Civil Code, § 3306.
[6] *Day v. Singleton*, [1899] 2 Ch. 320.
[7] Again this is implicit in the dicta in *Bain v. Fothergill, supra*, n. 5.
[8] *Bain v. Fothergill, supra.*
[9] *J.W. Cafés v. Brownlow Trust*, [1950] 1 All E.R. 894.
[10] *Flureau v. Thornhill* (1776), Wm. Bl. 1078.
[11] *Hanslip v. Padwick* (1850), 5 Exch. 615.
[12] See McGregor, § 677.
[13] (1854), 9 Exch. 341.

cation of the remoteness doctrine before it was fully developed. It is submitted that where the rule does apply, in principle the plaintiff should be entitled to his full reliance interest, subject to the ordinary limitations which are placed on that measure.

A question also arises as to the measure of damages where the rule does not apply. The reasonable assumption is that the plaintiff should be entitled to his lost expectation interest, generally loss of the bargain. But where the rule does not apply because the defendant acts in bad faith, it is arguable[1] that the plaintiff must bring the tortious action for deceit, with the result that he will not recover damages for his lost expectation interest. This view is prompted by a dictum of Lord Chelmsford in *Bain* v. *Fothergill* in which he refers to the possibility of obtaining "other damages by an action for deceit."[2] But it may be doubted[3] whether the learned judge intended to countenance a measure of damages different from that which ordinarily applies to breaches of contract.[4] The phrase is thrown in at the end of a paragraph without any elaboration. The distinction between tortious and contractual measure of damages was not fully grasped by the English courts until some time later.[5]

(c) Rationale of the rule

No less than six different reasons have been proffered to justify what judges are inclined to refer to as an "anomalous" rule.[6] None of them seems to be adequate.

(i) *Certainty* One argument put forward is that the expectation interest is too speculative for the purposes of evaluation:

> "'The fancied goodness of the bargain' must be a matter of a purely speculative character, and in most cases would probably be very difficult to determine."[7]

But difficulty of evaluation is not a ground for refusing to award damages, and equal or even more acute difficulties of quantification pervade the law of damages.[8]

---

[1] E.g. Treitel, p. 816.
[2] (1874), L.R. 7 H.L. 158, at p. 207.
[3] See also McGregor, § 669.
[4] This view is supported by the opinion of DENMAN, J. in *Bain* v. *Fothergill supra*, at pp. 181–182.
[5] See *supra*, p. 249.
[6] E.g. LINDLEY, L.J. in *Day* v. *Singleton*, [1899] 2 Ch. 320, at p. 329; KE-KEWICH, J. in *Rowe* v. *School Board for London* (1887), 36 Ch.D. 619, at p. 625.
[7] *Per* LORD CHELMSFORD, *Bain* v. *Fothergill* (1874), L.R. 7 H.L. 158, at p. 202.
[8] *Supra*, p. 82.

(ii) *Remoteness*

"Even if it could be proved to have been a beneficial purchase, the loss of the pecuniary advantage to be derived from a resale appears to me to be a consequence too remote from the breach of contract."[1]

There are two objections to this argument. First, the question whether a loss is too remote is a question of fact, determinable according to the circumstances of the particular case. It cannot be used as a ground for excluding damages as a matter of law for breaches of certain contractual obligations. Secondly, the pecuniary advantage may accrue to the purchaser not only by means of a resale. The benefit may lie in the price secured for the property in the particular transaction.[2]

(iii) *Intention of the parties* It has been said that it is the intention of the parties entering into a contract for the sale of land to limit compensation for the breach of it in this way.[3] But this will not suffice. If the test is truly that of the intention of the parties, then the courts should conduct a proper inquiry in every case to see whether such was indeed their intention. This they manifestly neglect to do. If the test is not that of the intention of the parties, then to try to justify the rule by reference to it is plainly fruitless.

(iv) *Breach of condition precedent* The rule has been defended by one Australian judge[4] on the ground that the action to which it applies is not one of damages for breach of contract but rather an action for the breach of a condition precedent: that is, it is a condition precedent of the *existence* of the contract that the vendor should have a good title. Should the condition not be fulfilled the contract fails to come into existence, and the purchaser is entitled only to the restitution of the benefits he has conferred on the vendor. This ingenious rationalization cannot, however, be allowed to stand. In terms of authority there is little or no support for it,[5] and there are many judicial statements, especially in *Bain* v. *Fothergill*[6] which are quite irreconcilable with it. In terms of principle, the argument must presuppose that the vendor is under no *duty* to make title, but such a duty clearly exists.[7] The word "condition" as used in *Flureau* v. *Thornhill*[8] and *Bain* v. *Fothergill*[9]

---

[1] *Per* Lord Chelmsford, *Bain* v. *Fothergill*, *supra*, at p. 202.
[2] *Supra*, p. 293.
[3] E.g. Pollock, B. in *Bain* v. *Fothergill*, *supra*, at p. 171.
[4] Isaac, J. in *Coronet Homes* v. *Bankstown Finance and Investment Co., Ltd.*, [1966] 2 N.S.W.R. 351.
[5] There is but one paragraph in Pollock, B.'s opinion in *Bain* v. *Fothergill* which can be interpreted in this light: (1874), L.R. 7. H.L. 158, at pp. 173–174.
[6] Apart from the isolated paragraph (n. 5 *supra*), throughout the case the rule is treated as one of "assessment of damages for breach of contract"; *ibid.*, at pp. 173, 177, 194, 200, 206.
[7] See *Williams on Title* (3rd Edn.) pp. 526–528 and the cases there cited.
[8] (1776), 2 Wm. Bl. 1078.
[9] (1874), L.R. 7 H.L. 158.

indicates that the vendor promises to make title rather than that the contract is contingent on the existence of the title.[1] Even with the rule, the disappointed purchaser is entitled to some compensation for his reliance interest,[2] which is more than he should recover under a restitutionary remedy.

(v) *Difficulty of making title* The most frequently adduced reason for the rule is the difficulty of making title.[3] Conveyancing is a complex business suitable only for the specialists. Investigation of title usually does not take place until the contract to convey has already been entered into. This is clearly the most potent argument and it involves policy issues over which opinions may differ. But it is difficult to resist the objection that this rationale has largely been overtaken by legal developments.[4] The rule was established (and confirmed) at a time when titles to land were notoriously uncertain and when the conveyance of land could be subject to formidable risks.[5] The 1925 property legislation and the expansion of registration have reduced considerably the risks of failure of title.[6] It is submitted that the need to protect the vendor is no longer so great as to maintain a rule which conflicts with the ordinary principles of damages for breach of contract.

(vi) *Longstanding adherence to rule* The last and least respectable reason for retaining the rule is the fact that it has existed in England for nearly two hundred years and has thereby become accepted in practice by those who deal in conveyances of land.[7] This argument, as so often, tends to be the last resort of the conservative lawyer, and will not stand alone as sufficient justification.[8]

3 Actions for non-payment of money

The second rule limits the recovery of the expectation interest in actions for the non-payment of money. The starting point is the basic proposition that in an action for the non-payment of a debt at common law a plaintiff can recover neither interest nor damages for the detention of the debt.[9] In fact the rule has been considerably undermined by

---

[1] See, in general, for the ambiguities of "condition": Reynolds, (1963), 79 L.Q.R. 534.

[2] *Supra*, p. 301.

[3] E.g. KELLY, C.B. in *Engell* v. *Fitch* (1869), L.R. 4 Q.B. 659, 666; LORD HATHERLEY in *Bain* v. *Fothergill, supra,* at p. 210.

[4] See J.M.J., (1934) 77 L.J. 169.

[5] See Cheshire, *Modern Law of Real Property*, (11th Edn.) pp. 63–64.

[6] See, generally, Glasgow, *A Modern View of Conveyancing.*

[7] *Bain* v. *Fothergill* (1874), L.R. 7 H.L. 158, *per* POLLOCK, B. at p. 174, *per* DENMAN, J. at p. 177, *per* PIGOTT, B. at pp. 194–195, *per* LORD HATHERLEY at p. 209. For an anecodotal account of this aspect of the case see Hollams, *The Jottings of an Old Solicitor* (1906) at pp. 132–134, 208–210.

[8] Cf. Mr. Justice Holmes (1897), 10 Harv. L.R. 457, at p. 469.

[9] *London, Chatham and Dover Rail Co.* v. *South East Rail. Co.*, [1893] A.C. 429.

exceptions both statutory and judicial. It is proposed first to give a brief historical introduction to the rule, then to examine its scope, finally to consider its rationale.

(a) History[1]

The general disinclination to favour the creditor in these actions was part of a general attack on usury,[2] and in the medieval period recovery of the expectation interest was strictly barred.[3] But the specific rule that in an action for the non-payment of money only nominal damages might be recovered appears to date only from the eighteenth century as a result of the complex feud between the old action for debt and the ever-expanding action of assumpsit.[4] In the area of commerce the rule was clearly of great inconvenience and could not survive. As has already been seen,[5] the law by gradual steps overcame its inhibitions sufficiently to permit the award of interest, but since the sixteenth century all claims for compensation beyond this have failed.[6] The ghost of usury appears still to loom in the distance, though in a recent case the Court of Appeal appeared willing to rid themselves of it.[7]

(b) Exceptions to rule

If, in theory, the principle still prevails that damages for the expectation interest may not be awarded in cases where the defendant fails to pay a sum due, its impact has been substantially reduced by exceptions.

(i) *Breach of a different obligation*   If the creditor is able to characterize his action as one for the breach of another contractual obligation the rule will not apply. In *Trans Trust S.P.R.L.* v. *Danubian Trading*[8]

> Ds contracted to buy steel from Ps. For the purposes of payment, Ds also agreed to procure credit in favour of X from whom Ps were to buy the steel. Ds failed to procure the opening of credit and repudiated the contract. Ds argued that their breach was a failure to pay money and that damages beyond interest could not be awarded. But it was held that substantial damages could be awarded: Ds were in

---

[1] Washington (1931), 47 L.Q.R. 345, 366–369; (1932), 48 L.Q.R. 90, 93–94.
[2] Holdsworth, H.E.L. vol. VIII, pp. 100–113.
[3] *Ibid.*, at p. 103. It is interesting to note that in this context as early as the 13th century a distinction was drawn between *damnum emergens* (which was recoverable) and *lucrum cessans* (which was not).
[4] Washington (1931), 47 L.Q.R. 345, 367–369. Before this period consequential damages had been awarded for the non-payment of a debt; *ibid.*, at pp. 366–367.
[5] *Supra*, pp. 97–99.
[6] Washington (1931), 47 L.Q.R. at pp. 345, 366–368.
[7] *Trans Trust S.P.R.L.* v. *Danubian Trading Co.*, [1952] 2 Q.B. 297, *infra*.
[8] *Ibid.*

breach not of an obligation to pay money, but of an obligation to open credit.

Similarly expectation interest damages can be awarded for failure to maintain[1] or honour[2] the plaintiff's credit, and for breach of a promise to lend the plaintiff money.[3] A purchaser of goods who has repudiated the contract may be sued for damages in an action for non-acceptance of the goods.[4] An improperly dismissed employee will recover his lost earnings by claiming in an action for wrongful dismissal that the employer refused to accept performance.[5] There are special statutory provisions governing actions for dishonouring bills of exchange and promissory notes.[6]

(ii) *Interest* Interest may be recovered *as of right* where the parties have expressly or impliedly agreed[7] that it should be paid, or *at the court's discretion* under section 3(1) of the Law Reform (Miscellaneous Provisions) Act 1934.[8]

(iii) *Exceptional cases* In the *Trans Trust* case[9] two members of the Court of Appeal *obiter* questioned whether the rule that prohibited the award of substantial damages for the non-payment of a debt was an absolute one. DENNING, L.J. did not think "that the law has ever taken up such a rigid standpoint." Remoteness is "the only real ground on which damages can be refused for non-payment of money."[10] ROMER, L.J. agreed: he was not "as at present advised, prepared to subscribe to the view that in no case can damages be recovered for non-payment of money."[11] The door has been opened. It remains to be seen whether a judge will be prepared to venture through it.

(c) Rationale

The alleged reasons for the existence of the rule tend to be even more unsatisfactory than those adduced for the rule in *Bain* v. *Fothergill*.

---

[1] *Wilson* v. *United Counties Bank, Ltd.*, [1920] A.C. 102.
[2] *Rolin* v. *Steward* (1854), 14 C.B. 595.
[3] E.g. *Astor Properties* v. *Tunbridge Wells Equitable Friendly Society*, [1936] 1 All E.R. 531.
[4] See, in general, *infra*, pp. 326–329.
[5] See, further, *infra*, pp. 329–330.
[6] Bills of Exchange Act 1882 s. 57 (1), which, however, limits recovery to the amount of the bill or note plus interest plus the expense of noting and protest. For details see McGregor §§ 795–813.
[7] For the circumstances in which it is likely to be implied see *De Havilland* v. *Bowerbank* (1807), 1 Camp. 50 and *supra*, p. 97.
[8] See, generally, *supra*, pp. 98–103.
[9] [1952] 2 Q.B. 297.
[10] *Ibid.*, at p. 306.
[11] *Ibid.*, at p. 307.

(i) It has been argued[1] that it is merely an illustration of the remoteness doctrine. This ignores the historical background to the rule and the plain language of the judges applying it. The rationale of the rule certainly has deeper foundations than this. (ii) One writer attributes it to "the policy of having a measure of damages of easy and certain application."[2] It may be conceded that this is indeed the chief historical reason for the rule.[3] But the desire to facilitate procedure should not by itself be a ground for refusing to award damages for provable losses, and is, in any case, hardly appropriate in modern conditions where the doctrine of certainty exists to deal with this same difficulty. (iii) Doubtless, at one time[4] the rule was an effective weapon against usury, but today more sophisticated armoury exists.[5] (iv) All that remains is the disturbing fact that if the plaintiff is able to characterize his action in terms of the breach of a different obligation his award is not so limited. The method of pleading a case is an improper criterion for any rule of substantive law. The forms of action should not continue to rule us from the grave.

4 Non-pecuniary benefits

(a) Introduction

There are many contracts the primary object of which is to provide happiness, pleasure or enjoyment rather than a purely pecuniary benefit. The extent to which compensation may be awarded for the failure to confer such benefits is somewhat speculative. Until 1972, English law was not prepared in general to recognize that non-pecuniary elements in the expectation interest might properly be made the subject of an award. But in the recent case of *Jarvis* v. *Swans Tours Ltd.*,[6] the Court of Appeal appears to have swept away such limitations on the award of non-pecuniary damages as it had previously favoured. Whether or nor a plaintiff may recover damages for the loss of a non-pecuniary benefit in all types of contract is as yet uncertain. In the circumstances, the impact of the *Jarvis* decision is best viewed in the light of the previous law.

(b) Pre-Jarvis limitations on non-pecuniary awards

Under the old action for breach of promise to marry, damages were at large[7] and may well have included an element for lost expectation of

---

[1] *Per* DENNING, L.J., *ibid.*, at p. 306, citing Bullen & Leake, *Precedents of Pleading*, (3rd Edn.) p. 51.
[2] *Williston on Contracts*, § 1410.
[3] See Washington (1931), 47 L.Q.R. 345, at p. 365.
[4] *Supra*, p. 305.
[5] See *Meston on Moneylenders* (5th Edn.).
[6] [1973] 1 All E.R. 71.
[7] *Finlay* v. *Chirney* (1888), 20 Q.B.D. 494.

happiness. But the action has been abolished.[1] Beyond this, non-pecuniary damages seem to have been awarded in only two types of case, and the first of these on closer examination reveals itself as more properly concerned with pecuniary losses.

(i) *Loss of reputation and credit* An actor[2] or author[3] who had been denied publicity by the defendant's breach might recover as compensation for his expectation interest damages for loss of "reputation". But this did not refer to "reputation" in its social or moral sense, which could not be made the subject of an award.[4] It was concerned solely with the future earning potential of the plaintiff. In contracts, the performance of which was intended to attract public esteem, the prospect of future engagements and the level of fees to be earned might depend as much on reputation and publicity as on vocational skill. A similar award might be made in cases which did not involve any element of publicity but where the plaintiff claimed a general loss of custom consequent on the non-acceptance of performance. Thus a failure to honour the credit of a trader would give rise to a claim for substantial damages for the loss of custom without requiring specific proof.[5] But this, too, was manifestly a pecuniary loss.

(ii) *Physical injury, discomfort and inconvenience* For the breach of certain types of contract, damages for non-pecuniary losses, such as pain and suffering and inconvenience were regularly awarded. A person physically injured as a result of the defendant's breach would be awarded the same damages as if he had claimed in tort.[6] A non-pecuniary award might also be made for physical discomfiture if, for example, the plaintiff was forced by the defendant's breach to reside in inferior or unpleasant premises.[7]

(c) A new approach?

Damages under this latter head fell short of a general recognition of non-pecuniary benefits as part of the expectation interest in two respects. First, they seem to have been limited to cases of *physical* discomfort or inconvenience.[8] There was no compensation for loss of happiness. Secondly, the awards were really part of the plaintiff's *indemnity* interest not his *expectation* interest, that is, they compensated for

---

[1] Law Reform (Miscellaneous Provisions) Act 1970, s. 1(1).
[2] *Clayton* v. *Oliver*, [1930] A.C. 209.
[3] *Tolnay* v. *Criterion Film Productions*, [1936] 2 All E.R. 1625.
[4] *Addis* v. *Gramophone Co.*, [1909] A.C. 488.
[5] *Rolin* v. *Steward* (1854), 14 C.B. 595.
[6] E.g. *Summers* v. *Salford Corporation*, [1943] A.C. 283.
[7] *Bailey* v. *Bullock*, [1950] 2 All E.R. 1167; *Feldman* v. *Allways Travel Service*, [1957] C.L.Y. 934.
[8] Per MELLOR, J., *Hobbs* v. *London and South Western Rail. Co.* (1875), L.R. 10 Q.B. 111, at p. 122.

"positive losses" sustained, rather than for the deprivation of benefits which should have been enjoyed. A hint of a new approach first appeared in Scotland. In *Diesen* v. *Samson*[1]

> P, a bride, employed D to take photographs at her wedding. D failed to appear. P was awarded £30 damages.

The Sheriff-Substitute said:

> "Wedding photographs generally are of no interest to anyone except the bride and bridegroom and their relatives and friends, and then only because they serve to stimulate recollection of a happy occasion and so give pleasure. What both parties obviously had in their contemplation was that the pursuer would be enabled to enjoy such pleasure in the years ahead. This has been permanently denied her by the defender's breach of contract and in my opinion it is a fitting case for the award of damages."[2]

In England, a confident attack on the previous position was launched in *Jarvis* v. *Swans Tours Ltd.*[3]

> P booked with Ds, travel agents, a winter sports holiday in Switzerland. The brochure on which he placed reliance promised many attractive facilities, both sporting and social. In the event, what was provided for him was greatly inferior to that which he had been led to expect. The trial judge limited P's award for breach of warranty to £31.72, as being the difference in the value of the holiday he had paid for, and the holiday he had got, on the ground that he had suffered no real physical inconvenience. The Court of Appeal held that the basis of the award should have been for "loss of entertainment and enjoyment" and increased it to £125.

(d) Conclusion

This welcome decision appears to have removed the obstacles to awarding non-pecuniary damages generally as part of the expectation interest. Presumably, the award is to be made only in cases where the plaintiff has a primary non-commercial interest in performance. It will, of course, give rise to problems of quantification but these will be no greater than those with which the court is accustomed to deal in tort actions.[4]

5 Discretionary benefits

(a) The principle

It has already been indicated[5] that when ascertaining the factual benefit implicit in the expectation interest the courts take into account

---

[1] 1971 S.L.T. (Sh.Ct.) 49.
[2] *Ibid.*, at p. 50.
[3] [1973] 1 All E.R. 71.
[4] *Per* LORD DENNING, M.R., *ibid.*, at p. 74.
[5] *Supra*, p. 291.

the certainty or uncertainty of that benefit. The expectation interest in a "possible" profit will be only a proportion of that in a "certain" profit. Where, however, the realization of a benefit is dependent on the discretion of the defendant promisor, then a special rule prevails. The plaintiff promisee is entitled to no more than the defendant was legally *bound* to do or to convey.

> "The first task of the assessor of damages is to estimate as best he can what the plaintiff would have gained . . . if the defendant had fulfilled his legal obligation and had done no more."[1]

> "Generally speaking, where there are several ways in which the contract might be performed, that mode is adopted which is the least profitable to the plaintiff and the least burthensome to the defendant."[2]

The word "performed" in this dictum must not, it seems, be taken too literally, for if the defendant has a right under the contract lawfully to terminate, then the case must be treated as if he had exercised that right on the assumption that to do so would be most favourable to him.[3] In this wider form the principle may be reformulated as follows:

> "Where the obligations under a contract are not firm but qualified, the damages must be assessed with the qualification in mind so that in the result that measure should be adopted which is the least burdensome to the defendant."[4]

(b) Application of the principle

In certain contracts, especially commercial contracts, the application of the principle might be regarded as obvious and necessary. In others, for example contracts of employment, it may produce hardship. The principle has been developed in four main types of contract.

(i) *Sale of goods* If a contract for the sale of goods provides for the delivery of "200 tons, 5 per cent more or less", then, should the vendor fail to deliver, he will be liable only for the loss of 190 tons, since that was his minimum legal obligation.[5]

(ii) *Carriage of goods* Where charterers under a charterparty have the option of discharging the cargo at a number of ports, should they fail to load the cargo the damages recoverable by the owners will be calculated

---

[1] *Per* DIPLOCK, L.J., *Lavarack v. Woods of Colchester*, [1967] 1 Q.B. 278, at p. 294.

[2] *Per* MAULE, J., *Cockburn v. Alexander* (1818), 6 C.B. 791, at p. 814. In the U.S.A. the same principle is known as "the measure of damages for the breach of alternative contracts". See Corbin, § 1079.

[3] *British Guiana Credit* v. *Da Silva*, [1965] 1 W.L.R. 248; *The Mihalis Angelos*, [1971] 1 Q.B. 164.

[4] *Per* HYATALI, J. A., *Gomez* v. *Olds Discount Co. (T.C.C.), Ltd.* (1964), 7 W.I.R. 98, at p. 111.

[5] *Re Thornett and Fehr and Yuills, Ltd.*, [1921] 1 K.B. 219.

on the assumption that the charterers would have discharged the cargo at the port most favourable to them and least favourable to the owners.[1] The wider interpretation of the principle was applied in *The Mihalis Angelos*[2]

> Ds, charterers under a charterparty made with Ps, shipowners, had the option of cancelling the contract if the vessel failed to arrive at the port of loading before 20 July. Ds purported to cancel on 17 July. It was held that this was a lawful termination of the contract, but even if it had been an anticipatory breach which Ps had accepted, Ps would have been entitled only to nominal damages, since it was to be assumed that Ds would in any event have exercised their option of cancelling on 20 July: the vessel would not have been ready to load on that date.

(iii) *Hire-purchase*   Under a contract of hire-purchase the hirer may have a right to terminate the contract. If the wider form of the principle is recognized[3] the result should be that if the hirer is in breach of his contract, the owner's remedy must be limited to whichever course would be more favourable to the hirer: damages for the owner's full expectation interest or the money payable on lawful termination of the contract. Such was the approach taken in a West Indian case.[4] But English law seems to accord only partial recognition to the principle in its wider form. In those cases in which the hirer has *repudiated* the contract, the owner has recovered his expectation interest,[5] unaffected by the principle.[6] The failure to take into consideration the hirer's right to terminate the contract has been criticized[7] but must still be regarded as good law.

(iv) *Contracts of employment*   The principle has had its greatest impact in contracts of employment. In three principal ways may it affect the measure of damages for wrongful dismissal. First, if the exact mode of the plaintiff's profit-making activity is at the discretion of the employer, then damages for breach must be assessed on the basis of a mode of

---

[1] *Kaye Steam Navigation Co., Ltd., v. Barnett, Ltd.* (1932), 48 T.L.R. 440.

[2] [1971] 1 Q.B. 164

[3] *Supra*, p. 310.

[4] *Gomez* v. *Olds Discount, supra.*

[5] *Viz.* the unpaid balance of hire purchase price less (i) the price at which the article was resold plus (ii) the fee for exercising the option to purchase. Deduction of (ii) represents an application of the principle in its narrow form since it is at the discretion of the hirer whether or not to exercise his option to purchase.

[6] *Yeoman Credit* v. *Waragowski*, [1961] 3 All E.R. 145.

[7] Notably by Lord Denning, M.R. in *Financings* v. *Baldock*, [1963] 2 Q.B. 104, at p. 113. The observations were *obiter* since in that case it was the *owner* who terminated. In such circumstances recovery for loss of profit is denied on the different ground that once the owner terminates there are no more obligations for the breach of which the hirer can be made liable. See also the criticisms of Goode, *Hire-Purchase Law & Practice* (2nd Edn.) pp. 401–402 and Guest, *Law of Hire-Purchase*, § 620.

performance consistent with the employer's obligations but least profitable to the plaintiff. Thus the employer may have the discretion at which of a number of theatres an artist should appear. Should the employer wrongfully dismiss the artist, the latter's damages will be based on the least profitable theatrical engagement.[1] Secondly, the principle prevents the award of compensation for the loss of those financial benefits which are payable at the discretion of the employer, for example, directors' fees,[2] and bonuses.[3] Thirdly, it is the basis of the rule that where contracts are terminable on notice, damages for lost earnings are restricted to those which would have been payable during the period of notice.[4]

(c) Limitations to the principle

The principle does not apply where the benefit is at the discretion of a third party. Thus in *Manubens* v. *Leon*[5] the plaintiff, dismissed from his position as a hairdresser's assistant, was able to recover compensation for the gratuities he would have received. Nor does it apply where, on construction of the contract, the court concludes that it was the intention of the parties that the discretion in the promisor should be exercised "reasonably".[6] In such circumstances, the plaintiff would be entitled to such a benefit as would have accrued to him if the defendant had exercised his discretion reasonably.[7] Even in circumstances where the defendant is under no legal obligation to act reasonably, commercial or social considerations may give him little alternative. In other words, in considering what is "least burdensome to the defendant", the court must take into account the position of the defendant generally, not merely his relationship with the plaintiff. He would not be expected to act in such a way as would seriously prejudice his dealings with others:

> "one must not assume that he will cut off his nose to spite his face and so (act) as to reduce his legal obligations to the plaintiff by incurring greater loss in other respects."[8]

The decision in *Bold* v. *Brough, Nicholson and Hall*[9] may be explained on this basis.

---

[1] *Withers* v. *General Theatre Corporation, Ltd.*, [1933] 2 K.B. 536.
[2] *Beach* v. *Reed Corrugated Cases*, [1956] 2 All E.R. 652.
[3] *Lavarack* v. *Woods of Colchester*, [1967] 1 Q.B. 278.
[4] *British Guiana Credit Corporation* v. *Da Silva*, [1965] 1 W.L.R. 248.
[5] [1919] 1 K.B. 208. See also *Fraser* v. *B. N. Furnam Productions*, [1967] 3 All E.R. 57.
[6] *Per* BANKES, L.J., *Abrahams* v. *Reiach, Ltd.*, [1922] 1 K.B. 477, at p. 480; and see the cases of the remuneration of agents where the amount is left to the discretion of the employer, e.g. *Bryant* v. *Flight* (1839), 5 M. & W. 114.
[7] *Abrahams* v. *Reiach, supra.*
[8] *Per* DIPLOCK, L.J., *Lavarack* v. *Woods of Colchester*, [1967] 1 Q.B. 278, at p. 295.
[9] [1963] 3 All E.R. 849.

P, wrongfully dismissed by Ds, claimed *inter alia* for the loss of certain pension rights. The pension scheme was run by Ds for the benefit of their employees, and one clause gave them the right to terminate the scheme on six months notice. It was held that they could not rely on this clause to reduce P's award. It was unlikely that they would have taken "a step so disastrous to its relations with all its employees solely to defeat a claim by this plaintiff . . ."[1]

Finally, it is worth reiterating that in hire-purchase contracts, the courts have not applied the principle where the discretion exercised by the defendant would amount to a non-performance of the contract, as opposed to a different mode of performing it.[2] In employment contracts, the courts, with the dissent of one judge,[3] have applied the principle in these circumstances.[4]

(d) Critique—principle of reasonable expectation?

That the doctrine may operate harshly is evident from the case-law. In *Lavarack* v. *Woods of Colchester*[5]

The master assessing damages clearly found it highly probable that the employers Ds would pay P the bonuses, for in awarding P a sum for the loss of this financial advantage he made no deduction for uncertainty. Yet when his award was adjusted by the Court of Appeal to conform to the doctrine, P recovered nothing for something which he had every reason to expect would have been paid to him.

As in other areas of the law of damages,[6] the courts are here sadly failing to come to terms with modern economic realities. In employment contracts today benefits are frequently made discretionary in order to add a flavour of incentive to the ordinary remuneration. They are nevertheless regarded as a very real part of the consideration in the employment relationship.

Where the eventual financial benefit is to be derived from a transaction with a third party, then the plaintiff may often recover this even though the defendant does not promise that the performance of his obligation will result in that benefit. Thus in an ordinary sale of goods case a disappointed buyer may recover his lost profits on resale pro-

---

[1] *Per* PHILLIMORE, J., *ibid.*, at p. 856.
[2] *Supra*, p. 311.
[3] LORD DENNING, M.R. in *Lavarack's* case, *supra*, p. 288. It is ironical to note that it was the same judge who criticized the non-application of the "wider principle" in hire-purchase contracts: *supra*, n. 7, p. 311.
[4] *Supra*, pp. 311–312.
[5] [1967] 1 Q.B. 278.
[6] E.g. the law of compensating advantages as applied by the House of Lords in *Parry* v. *Cleaver*, [1970] 1 A.C. 1, *supra*, p. 227.

vided the loss is not too remote.[1] Yet this benefit may be more "contingent" than a so-called discretionary benefit within the defendant's control.

It might be argued that to abolish the rule would be to interfere with the contractual agreement freely entered into by the parties. This argument may be discredited on grounds both of principle and of practice. In principle, it may be argued that the discretion conferred on the defendant by the contract controls the nature of his obligation rather than the extent of the plaintiff's remedy; that is, that it determines whether or not the defendant is in breach—but once he is in breach it should not limit the measure of the plaintiff's recovery. In practice, it can be shown that on analogous questions the courts are not prepared to adhere too rigidly to a consensualist approach. As has been seen,[2] where compensation is agreed by the parties, the courts will not uphold an estimate which is out of reasonable proportion to the loss which was likely to result from the breach. In contracts of agency, where the amount of remuneration is left to the discretion of one of the parties, the courts are sometimes prepared to allow an action of quantum meruit for a reasonable amount,[3] ignoring the argument that they are thereby exercising a discretion properly vested in another.[4]

It is submitted that a realistic application of the basic compensatory principle of putting the plaintiff in the position he would have been in if the contract had been performed conflicts with the doctrine discussed in this section. The plaintiff should be entitled to what benefits he might reasonably have acquired if the contract had been performed.

6   Remoteness

(a)   General

The principles of the fifth doctrine which may operate to restrict an award of the expectation interest have already been described in some detail.[5] Briefly restated, the doctrine of remoteness confines the award of compensation to those losses which are to be considered reasonably to have been within the contemplation of the parties, at the time of the contract, as liable (or not unlikely) to result from the breach. The determination of what is to be regarded as within the contemplation of the contracting parties is, in theory, a question of fact for the trial judge, having regard to the circumstances of the case, in particular the

---

[1] *Infra*, p. 316.
[2] *Supra*, pp. 41–51.
[3] *Powell* v. *Braun*, [1954] 1 All E.R. 484; cf. *Kofi Sunkersette Obu* v. *Strauss*, [1951] A.C. 243 and see generally Bowstead, *Agency* (13th Edn.) pp. 175–177.
[4] See, e.g. *Re Richmond Gate Property Co.*, [1964] 3 All E.R. 936.
[5] *Supra*, pp. 71–79.

terms of the contract.   Nevertheless, in practice, uniform standards are applied to certain categories of expectation interest arising in certain categories of agreements.   To begin with, it may be observed that loss of an expectation interest which depends for its realization wholly on the promisor/defendant and not on any third person (for example, wages in an employment contract) will never be too remote.   This follows from the doctrine propounded in the last section.   Either the promisor will be bound under the contract to confer such a benefit, in which case, *ex hypothesi*, it cannot be too remote;   or assignment of the benefit is at his discretion, in which case the doctrine described above will prevent compensation for the loss of it.[1]   It follows that in this context the doctrine of remoteness is concerned with those cases where the pecuniary benefit is to be derived from one or more strangers to the contract.   The application of the doctrine of remoteness to these benefits may be illustrated under three heads: loss of profit from resale, loss of profit from use, and loss of uncertain profits.

(b)   Loss of profit on resale

The problem has been considered mainly in relation to three types of contract.

(i) *Sale of goods—breach by vendor*   Where a seller delivers goods late, in an improper condition, or not at all, the buyer may lose the profit he would have made on a subsale.   At first the courts were inclined to treat this loss as too remote:[2] it did not follow as "a natural consequence of the breach";   it would not be proper to throw on the defendants the risk of the lost profit.[3]   This harsh attitude did not prevail for long.   The first inroad was made when damages were awarded in circumstances in which the vendor knew of the existence of the subcontract.[4]   This was then extended to cases where the defendant did not have actual notice but should reasonably have considered a subsale probable from the circumstances of the contract and his knowledge of trade custom generally.[5]   In *R. and H. Hall, Ltd.* v. *W. H. Pim*[6]

Ps bought from Ds an unascertained cargo of Australian wheat and without waiting for delivery resold it to X.   Although Ds did not know

---

[1] Of course, if the writer's suggestion that the doctrine should be abolished were to be accepted, it would have to be replaced by the doctrine of remoteness which would then apply to all categories of expectation interest.

[2] *Williams* v. *Reynolds* (1865), 6 B. & S. 495.

[3] *Per* BLACKBURN, J., *ibid.*, at p. 505.

[4] *Grébert-Borgnis* v. *Nugent* (1885), 25 Q.B.D. 85; *Mott & Co., Ltd.* v. *Muller & Co., Ltd.* (1922), 13 Ll.L. Rep. 492.

[5] *Patrick* v. *Russo-British Grain Export*, [1927] 2 K.B. 535.

[6] (1928), 33 Com. Cas. 324.

of the sale to X, they were held liable for the loss of profit since "it was well known to both parties that it was a common practice in the trade to resell cargoes whilst still afloat, and the contract itself . . . shows this distinctly."[1]

A buyer's anticipated profits may be reduced through a fall in the market price between the date when the seller should have delivered and the date when he actually delivered. He may recover this so-called "loss of a market"[2] unless (which is rare) the court holds that owing to special circumstances prevailing in the trade a fall in the market price was not foreseeable.[3]

There are, however, two qualifications that should be made to these principles. First, although a subsale may itself reasonably be within the contemplation of the parties, profits at an unusually high rate may not be. In such a case the plaintiff's remedy will be limited to the ordinary foreseeable rate of profits.[4] Secondly, if it is reasonably to be contemplated that on the defendant's failure to deliver the buyer will go into the market and purchase a substitute, then he cannot recover for lost profits.[5] This is really an application of the doctrine of mitigation and will be considered below.[6]

(ii) *Carriage of goods—breach by carrier*   The position of a defaulting carrier of goods is significantly different from that of a seller of goods. A carrier who has no notice that the buyer has sold or intends to sell the goods will not be liable for the loss of profits on resale.[7] The reason is that

"a carrier commonly know less than a seller about the purposes for which the buyer or consignee needs the goods, or about other 'special circumstances' which may cause exceptional loss if due delivery is withheld."[8]

The risk of such a loss is not one which the carrier in the ordinary case will reflect in his rates of carriage.[9] For a long time it was also true that where delivery of goods by sea was delayed a consignee could

---

[1] *Per* Viscount Dunedin, *ibid.*, at p. 328.

[2] There is, surprisingly, no direct English authority for this in a sale of goods contract but it was assumed to be the rule in *Taylor & Sons, Ltd.* v. *Bank of Athens* (1922), 91 L.J.K.B. 776, and it was applied to a carriage of goods contract in *Koufos* v. *C. Czarnikow*, [1969] 1 A.C. 350. See also *Aruna Mills, Ltd.* v. *Dhanrajmal Gobindram*, [1968] 1 Q.B. 655 where the plaintiff recovered for loss of profits resulting from a revaluation of currency.

[3] *Andre et Cie, S. A.* v. *Vantol*, [1952] 2 Lloyd's Rep. 282.

[4] E.g. *Household Machines* v. *Cosmos Exporters*, [1947] 1 K.B. 217: rate of profit reduced from 12 per cent to 10 per cent.

[5] *Kwei Tek Chao* v. *British Traders and Shippers*, [1954] 2 Q.B. 459.

[6] Pp. 323–330.

[7] *The Arpad*, [1934] P. 189.

[8] *Per* Asquith, L.J., *Victoria Laundry (Windsor)* v. *Newman Industries*, [1949] 2 K.B. 528, at p. 537.

[9] Atiyah, *Introduction to the Law of Contract* (2nd Edn.) pp. 272–273.

not, in general, recover for loss of market.[1] In *Koufos* v. *Czarnikow*,[2] however, the House of Lords held that since it was common knowledge that prices fluctuate in a commodity market the defendant shipowners should reasonably have contemplated the likelihood of a fall in the market and a consequent loss of profit on resale. To what extent this decision may be regarded as setting a new trend in contracts of carriage of goods and generating a possibility that loss of profits may more frequently be recovered remains a matter for speculation. The House of Lords was quick to stress that it was a question of fact.[3] But, at the same time, it is also clear that they expected the shipowner to be more ready to take the risks of such losses than his counterpart in the nineteenth century when voyages were subject to much greater uncertainty.[4]

In those cases in which it has been held that loss of profit on resale was not reasonably within the contemplation of the parties at the time of contracting, the question arises whether the position will be affected if the carrier is given *actual* notice of the resale. According to the orthodox view of the principles of remoteness he should be liable. Any different result can be justified only on either of two grounds. (A) Consistent with the doctrine of remoteness, to hold the defendant liable for a special loss that loss must not merely be within his contemplation at the time of the contract but in addition he must be said to have assumed the risk of that special loss by, for example, a special term to that effect. Alternatively (B) it must be argued that there exists a special rule limiting liability for the carriage of goods. It has already been suggested[5] that mere knowledge is sufficient for the rule in *Hadley* v. *Baxendale* to be satisfied and (A) is not supported by authority.[6] As for (B) the House of Lords in *Koufos* v. *Czarnikow* was at pains to point out that the ordinary principles of remoteness applied to carriage of goods by sea as to other contracts.[7]

The final question then remains whether knowledge or notice of an exceptional loss is sufficient to fix liability for that exceptional loss. Here there are dicta suggesting that the defendant should indicate by a term of the contract that he is assuming the risk of liability for such

---

[1] *The Parana* (1877), 2 P.D. 118.
[2] [1969] 1 A.C. 350.
[3] E.g. LORD PEARCE, *ibid.*, at p. 419.
[4] *Per* LORD REID, *ibid.*, at p. 392; *per* LORD PEARCE, *ibid.*, at p. 418; *per* LORD UPJOHN, *ibid.*, at p. 428.
[5] *Supra*, p. 77.
[6] In *Simpson* v. *London and North Western Rail. Co.* (1876), 1 Q.B.D. 274 lost profits were recovered although it certainly could not be said on the facts as reported that the defendants had assumed the risk of those losses.
[7] [1969] 1 A.C. 350, *per* LORD REID at p. 392, *per* LORD MORRIS at pp. 402–403, *per* LORD HODSON at p. 420, *per* LORD UPJOHN at p. 428.

losses.[1] Such a view seems contrary to principle: where it is clear that the defendant has notice (and of course it is a question of fact to be decided by the court in all the circumstances whether he had such notice) before or at the time of entering the contract, then should he find the risk too onerous he will always have the opportunity to resist the contract on such terms. He will also have the opportunity to adjust the rates charged for carriage in the instant or in subsequent contracts.[2] The view expressed in these dicta dates from a time when the theoretical basis of the rule in *Hadley* v. *Baxendale* was still a matter of some doubt.[3]

(iii) *Sale of land—breach by vendor*   In the few cases of sale of land where there is a likelihood of immediate or imminent resale by the purchaser, the position is the same as that in the sale of goods: the profit lost on resale is recoverable provided that it was reasonably within the contemplation of the vendor that the purchaser was likely to deal with the land in this way.[4]

(c) Loss of profit on use

(i) *Sale of goods—breach by vendor*   Damages for the loss of user profits are recoverable where the seller either knew or should have known that the article to be sold was likely to be used in a profit-making capacity. For some time the courts seemed ready to award damages on this basis only in the case of ships, but the modern cases show that the courts are ready to infer such knowledge in contracts dealing with a variety of chattels.[5] The fact that the chattel forms only a part (as opposed to the whole) of a profit-making process is of no significance.[6] The same two qualifications which were made in relation to resale profits apply equally here. On the one hand, reasonable expectation that a replacement of the profit-earning chattel would be readily available on the market is generally sufficient to support the doctrine of mitigation.[7] On the other hand, where the vendor is aware that the purchaser intends to use the chattel in a profit-earning capacity

---

[1] *Horne* v. *Midland Rail Co.* (1873), L.R. 8 C.P. 131, *per* MARTIN, B. at p. 139, and *per* LUSH, B. [at p. 145; *Elbinger Actien-Gesellschaft* v. *Armstrong* (1874), L.R. 9 Q.B. 473, *per* BLACKBURN, J. at p. 478.

[2] Cf. Atiyah, *op. cit.* p. 273.

[3] *Supra*, p. 77.

[4] *Cottrill* v. *Steyning and Littlehampton Building Society*, [1966] 2 All E.R. 295.

[5] E.g. *Victoria Laundry (Windsor)* v. *Newman Industries*, [1949] 2 K.B. 528 (boilers); *Cullinane* v. *British "Rema" Manufacturing Co.*, [1954] 1 Q.B. 292 (pulverizing plant).

[6] *Per* ASQUITH, L.J., *Victoria Laundry* case, *supra* at pp. 543–544. STREATFIELD, J. at first instance had thought that this was an important consideration [1948] W.N. 397.

[7] *Infra*, p. 322.

but a special use to which the chattel is to be put is beyond his reasonable contemplation, then the disappointed buyer will recover only such profits as would have been made if the chattel had been put to its ordinary foreseeable use. The well-known case of *Cory v. Thames Ironworks*[1] provides a good illustration of this.

> Ds sold a floating boom derrick to Ps, coal merchants, assuming that it would be employed for its usual purpose of storing coal. In fact Ps wished to use it for the novel purpose of carrying cranes to convey coal from colliers into barges. If the derrick had been delivered on time, Ps would have made a special, if unforeseeable, profit. Ps were awarded the profit they would have made if they had used the derrick to store coal even though they had not actually sustained that loss.

(ii) *Carriage of goods—breach by carrier* As with resale profits, the courts are reluctant to hold a carrier liable for loss of user profits. Without knowledge of the way in which the profit-making activity of the plaintiff might be affected by the late delivery or non-delivery of the chattel the defendant carrier will not be liable for such losses.[2] Thus in *British Columbia and Vancouver Island Spar Lumber and Saw Mill Co., Ltd. v. Nettleship*[3]

> D agreed to carry for Ps machinery for the purposes of constructing a saw-mill. On arrival some of the machinery was missing and Ps had to wait a year before substitute parts could be found. They did not succeed in their claim for a year's loss of profits. Although D knew that he was carrying machinery, he did not know for what purpose it was to be used, nor that it would be so difficult to find replacements.

Cases in which user profits have been recovered are rare because generally the carrier does not possess the requisite knowledge, but one example is *Montevideo Gas v. Clan Line Steamers*[4]

> Ds agreed to deliver to Ps 1471 tons of gas coal but instead delivered 1037 tons of steam coal. There was no market for gas coal in Montevideo and Ps had to do the best they could with the steam coal. The production of gas and other by-products was seriously affected. It was held that Ps were entitled to recover for the consequent loss of profit since Ds clearly knew that gas coal was required by Ps for manufacturing gas, and that substitute coal might be unobtainable and "they must have known" that steam coal would make less gas than gas coal.[5]

---

[1] (1868), L.R. 3 Q.B. 181.
[2] *Hadley v. Baxendale* (1854), 9 Exch. 341 is itself authority for this.
[3] (1868), L.R. 3 C.P. 499.
[4] (1921), 37 T.L.R. 866.
[5] These latter findings of fact emerge clearly in ROCHE, J.'s judgment at 37 T.L.R. 544, at p. 545. The C.A. upheld his decision.

(iii) *Leases—breach by lessor*   Where the defendant fails to complete an agreement for the leasing of premises to the plaintiff, and he knows that the plaintiff intends to carry on a particular trade there, the plaintiff may recover for the loss of profits.[1]

(d) Loss of uncertain profits

In the cases considered above the plaintiff was able to prove with sufficient certainty that had the defendant fulfilled his obligation the plaintiff would have secured definite and quantifiable profits from his transactions with one or more strangers to the contract. In other cases, there is much less degree of certainty. The plaintiff is unable to offer the court specific proof of contracts, but contends that, if the defendant had performed, his profit-making activities generally would have benefited. This type of claim has been variously described as "loss of business", "loss of custom", "loss of goodwill" and "loss of (commercial) reputation". It might be thought that the problem is wholly one of certainty. Such heads of damage do indeed arise for consideration from that point of view,[2] but the courts, perhaps from a confusion between the two doctrines are also inclined to treat it as a question of remoteness. This is, it is submitted, an unfortunate tendency, for, although the loss is described as being "too remote", in many cases it would seem that recovery is denied not so much because the loss was not reasonably within the contemplation of the parties but rather than the court is unhappy with the lack of direct evidence that the plaintiff is able to produce.

(i) *Sale of goods—breach by vendor*   The situation arises most frequently in contracts for the sale of goods as where the plaintiff is a trader who pleads loss of customers as a consequence of breach. It would seem unrealistic to suppose that such consequences are not generally within the contemplation of a vendor who fails to deliver goods or delivers them in a defective condition, but in only one case has the loss been recovered[3] and that, a decision at first instance, was later criticized by the Court of Appeal.[4] A claim for the loss of business generally was described by one judge as being "far outside the region of damages as recognized by the law."[5] Other attempts have been dismissed on more moderate grounds. In *Simons v. Pawsons and Leafs, Ltd.*[6]

---

[1] *Jaques v. Millar* (1877), 6 Ch.D. 153.
[2] *Supra*, p. 293.
[3] *Cointat v. Myham*, [1913] 2 K.B. 220.
[4] *Simon v. Pawson and Leafs, Ltd.* (1932), 38 Com. Cas. 151.
[5] Per KENNEDY, J., *Watson v. Gray* (1900), 16 T.L.R. 308.
[6] (1933), 38 Com. Cas. 151.

P alleged that as a result of Ds' breach of contract to supply dress materials she had lost an appointment as school outfitter and with it the profit from repeat orders. In dismissing the claim, SCRUTTON L.J. referred to the fact that Ds had had no notice of the appointment but then went on to observe that "in a considerable experience of contracts of sale of goods I do not remember cases of claim for loss of repeat orders from the customer."[1] The implication would seem to be that as a *general* principle they ought not to be recovered. SLESSER L.J. found the whole matter "one entirely of speculation" and "impossible to say that the alleged loss was in fact actually in the contemplation, or ought to be taken to have been in the contemplation, of the wholesaler at the time of making the contract"; but he found it unnecessary to decide in what circumstances damages might be awarded for loss of prospective custom.[2]

Mere knowledge that the plaintiff runs a business is insufficient to impose liability for this head of loss,[3] but circumstances may perhaps be envisaged in which the defendant knows that his breach is likely to lead to a general loss of trade.[4] It remains to be seen whether the court will be prepared to allow recovery on this basis.

(ii) *Carriage of goods—breach by carrier* With the reluctance of the courts to award damages for loss of general business in cases of *sale*, it is not surprising that in carriage cases there is no decision authorizing recovery. Indeed, it seems only to have been discussed in one case, and was there firmly rejected.[5]

(iii) *Contracts of employment—breach by employer* Future but uncertain pecuniary advantages have been recovered in different types of employment contract. In certain jobs the expected remuneration includes the uncertain element of gratuities from satisfied customers. A wrongfully dismissed employee may recover for the loss of these benefits provided they were within the contemplation of the parties.[6] In other categories of employment the plaintiff's future earning potential may depend on his reputation or on the publicity which the defendant agrees to confer on him. As has been seen,[7] an actor or author may recover for the defendant's failure to confer this kind of benefit. The loss is essentially one of future but uncertain profitable engagements.[8] The restriction on this head of compensation to artistic professions depends not on the application of the remoteness doctrine but on a direct and inflexible

---

[1] *Ibid.*, at p. 157.
[2] *Ibid.*, at p. 165.
[3] *Doe* v. *Bowater, Ltd.*, [1916] W.N. 185.
[4] *Per* ROWLATT, J. *ibid.*
[5] *Mann* v. *General Steam Navigation* (1856), 26 L.T. O.S. 247.
[6] *Manubens* v. *Leon*, [1919] 1 K.B. 208.
[7] *Supra*, p. 308.
[8] *Withers* v. *General Theatre Corporation*, [1933] 2 K.B. 536.

rule of law.[1] Nevertheless those within the special class must still show that the loss was reasonably within the contemplation of the parties at the time of the contract.[2]

7 The lost profits measure

If a factual benefit survives the limitations imposed by the doctrines which have been considered above, it will constitute what has been described as the *lost profits measure*. This will be awarded in the exceptional cases where the doctrine of mitigation has no application because it is either impossible or unreasonable for the plaintiff to avoid that loss. In the ordinary case, the doctrine of mitigation does apply, and the measure of the plaintiff's recovery will be further limited.

(IV) MITIGATION AND THE NORMAL MEASURES OF COMPENSATION

1 Modes of mitigation

The doctrine of mitigation, it will be recalled,[3] prevents the recovery of those losses which the plaintiff might reasonably have avoided. In a contractual situation the doctrine has a vigorous role to play: a disappointed promisee is not encouraged to remain inactive and then claim his lost profits. He is expected on breach to take such steps as are reasonable to neutralize the effects of the defendant's failure. Whether or not these steps are actually taken, the plaintiff will recover compensation only for such losses as he would have sustained if he had acted reasonably in mitigation. There are three ways in which he may be expected to mitigate.

(a) Substitute performance

In the first, the plaintiff is expected to go into the market to find an alternative (should one be available) to that which the defendant promised to confer on, or do for, him. Provided that he could have secured an exact or near equivalent, the benefit which would have been derived from the defendant's performance should remain unimpaired, and the plaintiff's loss will be the difference (if any) between the price he was bound to pay for performance under his contract with the defendant, and the price for which he is able to secure this alternative performance.

---

[1] *Addis v. Gramophone Co., Ltd.,* [1909] A.C. 488.
[2] *Clayton and Waller, Ltd. v. Oliver,* [1930] A.C. 209.
[3] *Supra,* pp. 85–93.

(b) Complementary performance

The second mode of mitigation arises where the defendant's performance is not so substantially defective that the plaintiff may reasonably reject it altogether and seek an alternative in the market. Here he is expected to accept the partial performance and complete it by what he can obtain in the market. If he is able by this means, to transform what the defendant has done into what the latter had, in law, promised to perform, the benefit which would have resulted will remain unimpaired and the loss will be the cost of completing performance.

(c) Accepting partial performance

Although it may be reasonable for the plaintiff to accept partial performance, the cost of completing or modifying it may be unreasonable relative to the nature and extent of the anticipated benefit. In such circumstances the court will expect the plaintiff to derive what benefit he can from the use or disposal of what was conveyed to him. His loss will be the difference between the benefits he would have acquired on complete performance of the contract, and the benefits which he is reasonably able to secure on the use or disposal of what the defendant has in fact conferred on him.

The measures of compensating from these three modes of mitigation may be described respectively as:

(i) substitution cost
(ii) completion cost
(iii) diminished profit

The questions whether the plaintiff is under a duty to mitigate, and, if so, which method is appropriate, depend on a number of factors, the most important of which is the nature of the breach. It is therefore proposed to discuss the principles under three categories of breach: non-performance, defective performance and delayed performance.

2 Non-performance

(a) The principle of substitute performance

The type of breach first to be envisaged occurs where either the defendant has wholly failed to perform his obligation—he has conferred nothing of value on the plaintiff—or the breach is so substantial that the plaintiff has legitimately exercised his right to reject performance. In such circumstances the plaintiff is under a duty to look for *substitute performance.* If some equivalent to what the defendant promised to perform is readily available on the market, the plaintiff is treated as if he had gone to the market at the time of breach and secured it.

He will then recover the substitution cost, that is the difference between the contract price and the price of the substitute.

(b) Illustrations

Several points arising from this principle require closer examination, but it may be found convenient, first to illustrate it by reference to typical contractual situations.

(i) *Sale of goods* Where a seller fails to deliver goods the buyer is entitled to the difference between the contract price and the *buying* price of the goods on the market at the time when delivery was due.[1] Where, on the other hand, the buyer refuses to accept delivery, the seller is expected to go into the market and find a substitute buyer, and his damages will be the difference between the contract price and the *selling* price of those goods at the time when delivery should have been accepted.[2]

(ii) *Sale of land* The rules here are analogous to those in (i). In those cases in which the rule in *Bain* v. *Fothergill* does not apply,[3] the seller of land who fails to complete is liable for the difference between the contract price and the market buying price of the land at the date when completion was due.[4] A buyer failing to accept is liable for the difference between the contract price and the market selling price at the same date.[5]

(iii) *Lease* Again where *Bain* v. *Fothergill* does not apply, a lessor who refuses to complete must account for the difference between the rent payable under the contract and that which the lessee would have to pay for equivalent property.[6] Where a lessee fails to accept, the lessor's damages are the difference between the contractual rent and the rent he may obtain on finding another tenant.[7]

(iv) *Carriage of goods* A failure by a carrier to deliver goods gives rise to two different methods of mitigating the consignee's loss. On the one hand, he may find an alternative carrier to transport the goods.[8] On the other hand, he may go into the market at the place of delivery

---

[1] Sale of Goods Act 1893, s. 51(3). The statutory provision refers to the "market or current price". That the *buying* price is intended is clear not only on the principle of mitigation stated in the text but also from the previous case-law on which the legislation was based: see, e.g. *Barrow* v. *Arnaud* (1846), 8 Q.B. 595.
[2] S.G.A. 1893, s. 50(3). Cf. n. 1 *supra*: the same comments *mutatis mutandis* apply.
[3] *Supra*, pp. 299–301.
[4] *Diamond* v. *Campbell-Jones*, [1961] Ch. 22.
[5] *Per* PARKE, B., *Laird* v. *Pim* (1841), 7 M. & W. 474, at p. 478.
[6] There is no direct authority for this but it must follow from the sale of land cases: Hill & Redman, *Law of Landlord and Tenant* (14th Edn.) p. 116.
[7] *Marshall* v. *Mackintosh* (1898), 78 L.T. 750.
[8] *Romulus Films* v. *Dempster*, [1952] 2 Lloyd's Rep. 535.

and purchase suitable goods there. The measure would then be the same as that applied in a sale of goods case for non-delivery.[1] The reasons for selecting one measure rather than the other are not made explicit in the cases, but according to the ordinary rules of mitigation the choice must depend on which method of mitigating the loss is more reasonable in the circumstances. The first method can clearly not apply in cases where the carrier takes up the goods but loses them en route.[2] Nor will it apply where, though the carrier fails to take up the goods, the plaintiff has no control over them until they reach their destination:[3] the plaintiff is in no position to find alternative transport. It can only apply where the plaintiff has the goods at his disposal at the place of dispatch.[4]

(v) *Carriage of persons*   For the failure to convey a person, a carrier is liable for the difference between the contract price and the cost of alternative transport.[5]

(vi) *Employment*   In an action for wrongful dismissal (i.e. non-acceptance of performance) the employee is entitled to the difference between what he would have earned under the contract and what he is able to earn when he offers his services on the employment market.[6] In the converse situation where the employee fails to carry out his contractual duties, the employer is entitled to the difference between the remuneration he would have paid the defendant and that which he has to pay for a substitute.[7]

(vii) *Loan*   On the failure of a lender to transfer money, the borrower is entitled to the difference between the rate of interest payable under the contract and that payable on a substitute loan.[8]

(c)   Repudiation of substantially defective performance

The substitute cost is the appropriate measure not only in cases where the defendant has wholly failed to perform but also where his performance is so defective that the plaintiff is entitled to repudiate. The criteria for determining whether the plaintiff is entitled to repudiate are fully considered in the standard textbooks on the law of contract and do not call for discussion here.

(d)   Reasonable substitute available

For the substitution cost to provide the measure of damages, the court must be satisfied that the plaintiff could reasonably have acquired a

---

[1] *Rodocanachi* v. *Milburn* (1886), 18 Q.B.D. 67.
[2] *Ibid.*
[3] *Nissho Co., Ltd.* v. *Livanos* (1941), 57 T.L.R. 400.
[4] *Romulus Films* v. *William Dempster, supra.*
[5] Per BLACKBURN, J., *Hinde* v. *Liddell* (1875), L.R. 10 Q.B. 265, at p. 268.
[6] *Jackson* v. *Hayes*, [1938] 4 All E.R. 587.
[7] *Richards* v. *Hayward, Candy & Co., Ltd.* (1841), 2 Man. & G. 574.
[8] Per CHITTY, L.J., *South African Territories* v. *Wallington*, [1897] 1 Q.B. 692, at pp. 696–697.

substitute; otherwise it must award the lost profits measure. To determine whether or not a substitute was readily available involves a consideration of various factors. These include: how long the plaintiff would have to wait for the substitute; how far he would have to travel to acquire it; whether the substitute was sufficiently similar in kind and price to that promised by the defendant. Exposition of these matters is rarely explicit in the case-law outside two areas: sale of goods contracts, where discussion has been extensive, and employment contracts where it has been spasmodic. The reason for the special scrutiny in sale of goods is that the formulation of the statutory measure of damages obliges the court to ascertain whether there was an "available market" for the goods. In employment contracts other factors must be taken into account, notably the very personal nature of the employee's obligations. Nevertheless, the principles emerging in these two areas may serve to guide the court in other contractual situations.

(i) *Sale of goods*[1]   Inquiry is here prompted by the language of section 50(3) and section 51(3) of the Sale of Goods Act 1893 which prescribes the substitution cost as the prima facie measure of damages for the non-acceptance and non-delivery of goods respectively. The measure is in both cases conditional on the existence of "an available market for the goods in question". In interpreting these words, the courts have tended to lose sight of the fact that the doctrine of mitigation lies behind the rule. Thus the suggestion[2] that the meaning of "available market" in section 50(3) is not materially different from that in section 51(3) can hardly be accurate. For the purposes of section 50(3) there must be a market in which the plaintiff can *sell* his article, whereas section 51(3) requires a market in which he can *buy* an equivalent article. Again in attempting to define "market" the courts have been distracted from the relatively simple proposition of mitigation that a substitute should be reasonably available to the plaintiff, and instead concentrated on the more technical aspects of the word. Thus in *Dunkirk Colliery Co.* v. *Lever*[3] JAMES L.J. implied that there must be something like an official exchange for the goods in question and in *Charter* v. *Sullivan*[4] JENKINS, L.J. considered that a "market" would exist only where the price of the goods fluctuated according to supply and demand—a fixed retail price prevented the application of section 50(3). These limitations are, it is respectfully suggested, too rigid for the purposes of the inquiry which is to determine whether or not the plaintiff might reasonably have ac-

---

[1] Lawson (1969), 43 A.L.J. 52.
[2] SELLERS, J. in *A.B.D.* (*Metals and Waste*) v. *Anglo Chemical and Ore Co.*, [1955] 2 Lloyd's Rep. 456, at p. 464.
[3] (1878), 9 Ch. D. 20, 25 preceding the S.G.A. but concerned to apply the same "market" rule.
[4] [1957] 2 Q.B. 117, at p. 128.

quired a substitute. Certainly the place and the price at which the goods might be bought (or sold) are among the relevant considerations but they should not in themselves be regarded as conclusive. It is the use of the term "available . . ." "rather than . . . market" which is crucial in this context and it would therefore seem that if a definition of "market" is thought necessary, then, for this reason, the widest is to be preferred. In a case of breach by non-acceptance of goods UPJOHN, J. propounded what might from this point of view be regarded as the most satisfactory definition:

> "an available market merely means that the situation in the particular trade in the particular area was such that the particular goods could freely be sold, and that there was a demand sufficient to absorb readily all the goods that were thrust on it."[1]

In deciding whether a market is "available" the court must take into account several factors.

Time The goods must be available within a reasonable period of time from the breach. In *Lester Leather and Skin Co., Ltd.* v. *Home and Overseas Brokers, Ltd.*[2] the plaintiff would have to wait for eight or nine months which was clearly unreasonable. What is too long is of course a question of fact which will vary according to the needs of the particular plaintiff.

Place The plaintiff should be able to find his substitute without travelling an unreasonable distance. It was argued in the *Lester Leather* case that there was a market for the goods in question in India, but the contract stipulated delivery in the United Kingdom and the plaintiffs were not bound "to go hunting the globe" for replacements.[3] The question may often be determined by the scope of the plaintiff's business. In *Thompson* v. *Robinson*[4] the fact that no purchaser could be found within the East Riding of Yorkshire was regarded as conclusive since the plaintiff was restricted in his dealings to that particular area.

Supply and demand The fact that the plaintiff was able to find a substitute is not always conclusive. If he is a trader and supply exceeds demand, the dealing may be ignored for it may be assumed that the plaintiff would in any event have dealt with the third party. The latter was not in reality a *substitute*.[5]

Similar goods Where the seller is in breach, the goods available to the buyer in the market must be reasonably similar to those offered

---

[1] *W. L. Thompson* v. *Robinson (Gunmakers)*, [1955] Ch. 177, at p. 187. The definition was *obiter* as UPJOHN, J. felt himself bound to accept the C.A.'s definition in *Dunkirk Colliery* v. *Lever, supra.*

[2] (1948) 64 T.L.R. 569.

[3] *Ibid.*

[4] [1955] Ch. 177.

[5] *Charter* v. *Sullivan*, [1957] 2 Q.B. 117.

under the contract. Of course, this is a question of degree, and much will depend on the construction of the contract. In extreme cases,[1] the court may find that the plaintiff intended to buy *only* the particular merchandise offered by the defendant and no other, in which case the buyer cannot mitigate by finding a substitute. Where such an intention is not inferred, the courts tend to say that it is unreasonable for the plaintiff to purchase goods of a different kind or character[2] but that a mere difference in quality will not matter.[3] Of course, as with other principles of law which rely on such a distinction,[4] this test is highly elusive and little more by way of guidance can be offered here.

Price To be consistent with the doctrine of mitigation, the price which the plaintiff must pay for the substitute must be reasonable. In *Diamond Cutting Works Federation* v. *Triefus & Co.*[5] the defendants sought to argue that where the contract price for the diamonds which they had promised to deliver was 24*s*. 6*d*. per carat, a price of 40*s*. at which the plaintiffs purchased a substitute was unreasonable. The argument was rejected. But in *Le Blanche* v. *London and North Western Rail Co.*

> In breach of contract the D ry. co. failed to deliver a passenger P at his destination in time to catch a connection. Instead of waiting an hour for the next ordinary train to complete his journey P caught a special train at the additional expense of £11 10*s*. The court held that in the circumstances this was an extravagant mode of mitigating his loss.

The test applied by MELLISH, L.J. was

> "whether the expenditure was one which any person in the position of the plaintiff would have been likely to incur if he had missed the train through his own fault, and not through the fault of the railway company."[7]

The principle is often stated in a different form by stipulating that the existence of an excessive price indicates that there is not a sufficient availability of the substitute to constitute "an available market" for the purposes of, for example, section 51(3) of the Sale of Goods Act.[8] It is generally also the reason why in practice the plaintiff is rarely expected or entitled to order the manufacture of the substitute where

---

[1] E.g. *R. and H. Hall, Ltd.* v. *W. H. Pim* (1928), 33 Com. Cas, 324, *infra*, pp. 334–335.
[2] Where the plaintiff is only able to purchase a substitute of inferior quality, he will recover any loss of benefit resulting therefrom: cf. *infra*, pp. 340–342.
[3] See, e.g. *Sharpe & Co.* v. *Nosawa & Co.*, [1917] 2 K.B. 814.
[4] E.g. the doctrine of mistake in the law of contract: Treitel, pp. 216–218.
[5] [1956] 1 Lloyd's Rep. 216.
[6] (1876), 1 C.P.D. 286.
[7] *Ibid.*, at p. 313.
[8] E.g. (by analogy) *O'Hanlon* v. *Great Western Rail Co.* (1865), 6 B. & S. 484.

there is none for ready purchase.[1] It would seem to be wrong to lay down that as a matter of law a plaintiff may not mitigate by ordering the manufacture of goods but in general it will be unreasonable on the grounds either of price, or of time.

(ii) *Employment* The special feature of contracts of employment is that substitute performance entails the plaintiff tendering his own personality. Psychological and social factors therefore may go to the question of what is reasonable.[2]

Time In contrast to sale of goods and other contracts time is unimportant in employment contracts in the sense that *whenever* a reasonable alternative is available the plaintiff is expected to take advantage of it. In another sense, however, it may be relevant in determining whether the plaintiff's conduct was reasonable. Immediately after breach he may aim at a job of equivalent status and remuneration to that from which he was dismissed. But after some time it may become apparent that his efforts to find employment of that quality are unlikely to succeed. The court may then expect him to lower his ambitions and accept an offer of a somewhat inferior post.[3]

---

[1] E.g. *Elbinger Actien-Gesellschaft* v. *Armstrong* (1874), L.R. 9 Q.B. 473.

[2] It is of interest to note that the doctrine of mitigation is applied to unemployment benefits under the National Insurance scheme. Section 22(2) of the National Insurance Act 1965 disqualifies a person from receiving a benefit if "he has neglected to avail himself of a reasonable opportunity of suitable employment." Section 22(5) provides that employment shall not be "suitable" where, *inter alia*, it is:
(I) "employment in his usual occupation in the district where he was last ordinarily employed at a rate of remuneration lower, or on conditions less favourable, than those which he might reasonably have expected to obtain having regard to those which he habitually obtained in his usual occupation in that district . . ." *or*
(II) "employment in his usual occupation in any other district at a rate of remuneration lower, or in conditions less favourable, than those generally observed in that district between associations of employers and employees, or, failing any such agreement, than those generally recognized in that district by good employers;" but
(III) "after the lapse of such an interval from the date on which he becomes unemployed as in the circumstances of the case is reasonable, employment shall not be deemed to be unsuitable by reason only that it is employment of a kind other than employment in his usual occupation if it is employment at a rate of remuneration not lower, and on conditions not less favourable, than those generally observed by agreement between associations of employers and employees or, failing any such agreements, than those generally recognized by good employers."
It would seem, however, that the standard of reasonableness required of a claimant under these provisions is generally higher than that required of a plaintiff in a common law action for wrongful dismissal. See, e.g. the cases in the Digest of Commissioner's Decisions (H.M.S.O.). If this is right, it would follow that the statutory principles above can only be used as a guide to the *maximum* that may be required of a plaintiff in a common law action.

[3] *Yetton* v. *Eastwoods Froy*, [1967] 3 All E.R. 353. See also n. 2 (III) *supra*, for analogous considerations under the N.I. scheme.

Place   Again, this factor will vary according to the nature of the employment, but in general a plaintiff is not expected to uproot his home and family in order to find a job in another area.[1]

Remuneration   The standard of remuneration offered in the alternative employment in comparison with that obtainable under the contract with the defendant is of course an important factor in deciding whether the plaintiff should reasonably accept an offer.[2]   Any generalization is bound to be inadequate but it may be suggested with hesitation that a difference of over 30 per cent in earnings and other benefits is too great to make refusal unreasonable.[3]

Similar employment   A skilled man is not expected to abandon his technical proficiency to take a post requiring quite different abilities.[4] At the same time, a consideration peculiar to the employment contract should also be taken into account.   Owing to the fact that employment invariably involves a *personal* relationship, the plaintiff may reasonably refuse an offer by the defendant himself on the ground that the strained relations resulting from the breach are not the best foundation for a future employment relationship.[5]

(e)   Assessment of substitution cost

The substitution cost is the difference between the contract price and the price for which the substitute might reasonably have been procured.

(i) *Market buying price*   Most often evidence is required of the market buying price of the service or property promised.   The court may, it seems, include for this purpose prices to be paid in "black-market" conditions.   In *Mouat* v. *Betts Motors*[6]

> Ps sold a car to D subject to a condition of no resale within 2 years, except back to Ps at a stipulated price.   D, in breach of this condition, sold the car to X on the "black market".   It was held that Ps were entitled to the difference between the "black-market" price and the price Ps would have to pay D for it on lawful resale.   Ps were entitled to mitigate by going into the "black-market" in order to purchase their substitute.

(ii) *Necessary and reasonable expenses*   The substitution cost includes not only the price which the plaintiff pays (or in the case of non-acceptance receives) for the substitute, but also any necessary and reasonable

---

[1] Cf. n. 2(III), p. 329, *supra*, and see decisions R(U) 41/52 and R(U) 34/58 in the Digest there cited.

[2] *Dunk* v. *Waller & Son*, [1970] 2 Q.B. 163.

[3] See, e.g. R(U) 14/54.

[4] *Yetton* v. *Eastwoods Froy supra*, cf. n. 2, p. 329, and see R(U) 18/55.

[5] *Shindler* v. *Northern Raincoat*, [1960] 2 All E.R. 239.

[6] [1959] A.C. 71.   See also *British Motor Trade Association* v. *Gilbert*, [1951] 2 All E.R. 641.

expenses involved in securing it. These may, of course, be reflected in the "market price". Thus in a carriage of goods case BRAMWELL, B. referred to the "value of the goods" as being "the price for which they can be got to the place of consignment."[1] Alternatively the expenses incurred may be subsumed under an independent head of damages. In *Cranston v. Marshall*[2]

> Ds' ship failed to arrive as promised at Plymouth en route to Australia. P who had reserved passage for himself and his family recovered a sum for the expenses incurred while waiting for substitute passage.

In circumstances in which the substitute is not the exact equivalent of what the defendant promised to provide, the plaintiff may, where it is deemed reasonable, purchase the nearest equivalent and then adapt it at the defendant's expense to suit his particular requirements. The substitution cost as the measure of compensation will comprise both the market price of the substitute and the cost of adaptation. In *Blackburn Bobbin Co. v. Allen & Sons*[3]

> Ds sold to Ps an amount of timber to be imported from Finland. Ds were unable to acquire Finnish timber with the result that Ps accepted English timber as the best available substitute. This involved greater expense and more waste in cutting. Ps recovered compensation for these losses.

That the expenses incurred in finding or adapting must be reasonable follows from the general principles of mitigation to which reference should be made.[4]

(iii) *Time* The principle is that the substitution cost must be assessed at the time when the plaintiff might reasonably have procured the substitute. In the ordinary case this is at the time of the defendant's breach. It thus becomes a question on the construction of each contract or each type of contract as to when the breach takes place. In contracts for the sale of goods statutory provisions lay down the prima facie rule. For failure to deliver the court should award:

> "the difference between the contract price and the market or current price of the goods at the time or times when they ought to have been delivered, or, if no time was fixed, then at the time of the refusal to deliver."[5]

---

[1] *Rice v. Baxendale* (1861), 7 H. & N. 96, at p. 102. See also *Rodocanachi v. Milburn* (1886), 18 Q.B.D. 67.

[2] (1850), 5 Exch. 395.

[3] [1918] 1 K.B. 540 affirmed without discussion of the point [1918] 2 K.B. 467.

[4] *Supra*, pp. 85–93 and see also pp. 132–134 for the cost of repairs as the tortious measure in cases of injury to chattels.

[5] Sale of Goods Act 1893, s. 51(3).

Conversely where the seller sues for non-acceptance the time of breach is usually the date of the buyer's refusal to accept the goods.[1]   In an instalment contract there is a breach on the failure to deliver or accept each instalment and consequently the market price for the amount of each instalment is taken at its delivery date.[2]

In other contracts the common law rules follow a similar pattern.[3] But the existence of special circumstances may displace the ordinary rules.   First, it may be reasonable for the plaintiff to wait for a time after breach to see whether the defendant will in fact perform.   This is particularly true where the defendant requests an extension of time to discharge his obligations.   In such cases the court will assess the substitution cost as at the date when it becomes reasonably clear to the plaintiff that the defendant is unlikely to perform.[4]   Secondly, the defendant may have indicated before the contract date that he would not perform —an anticipatory breach.   Here the plaintiff has the choice whether to affirm (i.e. wait for the contract date to pass before repudiating) or repudiate (i.e. bring the contract to an end before the contract date). If he takes the former course the court will, as in the cases of an ordinary breach, take the market price at the date when the obligation should have been performed, for the plaintiff is under no duty to mitigate before that date.[5]   If, on the other hand, he repudiates, then the doctrine of mitigation will at once apply, and he will be expected to go into the market and procure a substitute as soon as one is readily available.[6] The onus is on the defendant to show that the plaintiff should have taken advantage of more favourable market conditions before the contract date.[7]

(iv) *Relevance of subcontracts*   The question next arises whether the award of the substitution cost will be affected by any subcontracts that the plaintiff may have made.   To put this in a different form, is the award always to be regarded as referring to the *notional* cost of substitution, or may it be calculated on the basis of *actual* dealings with

---

[1] *Ibid.*, s. 50(3).

[2] *Re Voss, ex p. Llansamlet Tin Plate Co.* (1873), L.R. 16 Eq. 155.

[3] For carriage of goods see *Rodocanachi* v. *Milburn* (1886), 18 Q.B.D. 67; for sale of land see *Engell* v. *Fitch* (1869), L.R. 4 Q.B. 659; and for sale of shares see *Shaw* v. *Holland* (1846), 15 L.J. Ex. 87.

[4] *Ogle* v. *Earl Vane* (1868), L.R. 3 Q.B. 272 (sale of goods); *Wilson* v. *London and Globe Finance* (1897), 14 T.L.R. 15 (sale of shares).

[5] *Brown* v. *Muller* (1872), L.R. 7 Exch. 319 (sale of goods: non-delivery); *Tredegar Iron* v. *Hawthorn* (1902), 18 T.L.R. 716 (sale of goods: non-acceptance).

[6] *Melachrino* v. *Nickoll and Knight*, [1920] 1 K.B. 693 (sale of goods: non-delivery); *Sudan Import and Export* v. *Société Generale de Compensation* [1958] 1 Lloyd's Rep. 310 (sale of goods: non-acceptance).

[7] *Roper* v. *Johnson* (1873), L.R. 8 C.P. 167.

the subject-matter? Two different situations must be carefully distinguished.

Actual substitute   In the first, the plaintiff has actually gone into the market and secured for himself a substitute. The price which he paid may constitute the substitution cost on two different bases. On the one hand, it may be regarded as evidence of the market price at the time of breach.[1]   On the other hand, it may itself constitute the measure where it is deemed to have been a reasonable act in mitigation: it represents the plaintiff's real loss.   In *ex parte Stapleton*[2] a disappointed seller found a buyer who was willing to pay "the best price which he could then obtain".   He was allowed to recover the difference between that price and the price at which he had sold to the defendant.   If, however, the court decides that the plaintiff's act in securing a substitute was in the circumstances unreasonable, then the notional market price will prevail. Thus in *Diamond Cutting Works* v. *Triefus*[3] the price which the plaintiff buyer had paid for substitute goods was considered excessive in the light of the market conditions then prevailing and his award of damages was reduced.

Contract of resale   The second situation is very different from the first and has given rise to extensive judicial[4] and academic[5] discussion. In fact, it is submitted that the problem is not so difficult as it is made to appear from these sources.   The solution lies, as so often, in a careful consideration of the general principles of quantification, with particular reference to the doctrine of mitigation.   The situation arises where a seller (or carrier) fails to deliver to a purchaser (or consignee) who has resold the property to a third party.   For example,

> D sells an article to P for £a and P resells it to X for £b.   The ordinary measure of damages, should D fail to deliver the goods, is the difference between the market price of the goods at the time of the breach (£c) and the contract price (£a).   But the suggestion is that instead the court should award the difference between the contract price (£a) and the resale price (£b) on the ground that this represents P's true loss.

The first response to this suggestion is that to adopt the resale price as "representing" or as "evidence of" the market price[6] may be erroneous for this is to ignore the fact that the "market price" which constitutes

---

[1] *Hong Guan & Co.* v. *Jumabhoy & Sons*, [1960] A.C. 684.
[2] (1879), 10 Ch.D. 586.
[3] [1956] 1 Lloyd's Rep. 216.
[4] There are lengthy discussions in *Rodocanachi* v. *Milburn* (1886), 18 Q.B.D. 67; *Wertheim* v. *Chicoutimi Pulp*, [1911] A.C. 301, *infra*, p. 345; *Williams Brothers, Ltd.* v. *Agius*, [1914] A.C. 510; *R. & H. Hall, Ltd.* v. *W. H. Pim* (1928), 33 Com. Cas. 324; *Finlay & Co., Ltd.* v. *Kwik Hoo Tong*, [1929] K.B. 400; *The Arpad*, [1934] P. 189.
[5] McGregor, §§ 552–555; Treitel, pp. 789–791.
[6] McGregor, § 552.

the measure of damages in cases of non-delivery refers to the price at which a substitute might be *bought* in the market and this is not necessarily linked to the price at which the plaintiff *sold* the goods. The difference between the resale price and the contract price represents indeed not the substitution cost but the profit which the plaintiff would have made if the contract had been performed. As such it may be recovered only if it satisfies the requirements of remoteness and mitigation. The remoteness aspects of the problem have already been discussed,[1] and some cases have been decided almost wholly on this ground.[2] But it is submitted that the solution to the difficulties created by the subsale should be sought rather in the doctrine of mitigation. As has been seen, the lost profit measure ($£b-a$) is not awarded if the plaintiff might reasonably have secured a substitute, for had he done so, the profit on the subcontract would not have been lost. The lost profit will be awarded to the plaintiff only if, in the circumstances of the case, he might not reasonably have procured a substitute. Where, on the other hand, the court awards the substitution cost ($£c-a$), it does so not because the sum will necessarily represent the plaintiff's actual loss (for he may not in fact have procured a substitute) but because it represents the loss which he would have sustained if he had acted reasonably in mitigation. Whether it was reasonable for the plaintiff to secure a substitute must, of course, depend on the facts of the case. In *Williams Brothers* v. *Ed. T. Agius*[3]

> D agreed to sell to P a cargo of coal at 16s 3d. per ton. P sold the same amount of coal of the same description to X at 19s. per ton. D failed to deliver. At the date of breach the market price of the coal was 23s. 6d. It was held that P was entitled to recover the substitution cost *viz.* the difference between the contract price (16s. 3d.) and the market price at the time of breach (23s. 6d.) and the price of the resale contract was irrelevant.

In the circumstances of the case P was reasonably expected to purchase a substitute cargo: "he is entitled to recover the expense of putting himself into the position of having these goods, and this he can do by going into the market and purchasing them at the market price."[4] In contrast, in *R. & H. Hall, Ltd.* v. *W. H. Pim*[5]

> Ds agreed to sell to Ps a cargo of wheat at 51s. 9d. per quarter. Ps resold the *identical* cargo to X at 56s. 9d. per quarter. Ds failed to deliver.

---

[1] *Supra*, pp. 315–316.
[2] E.g. *R. & H. Hall* v. *W. H. Pim.*, *supra*.
[3] [1914] A.C. 510.
[4] *Per* LORD MOULTON *ibid.*, at p. 531. For analogous decisions see, on carriage of goods, *Rodocanachi* v. *Milburn* (1886), 18 Q.B.D. 67, and on sale of land, *Brading* v. *McNeill*, [1946] Ch. 145.
[5] (1928), 33 Com. Cas. 324. For the remoteness aspect of the case, see *supra*, p. 315.

The arbitrators awarded Ps the difference between the contract price (51*s*. 9*d*.) and the market price of similar quality wheat at the time the delivery should have been made (55*s*.). ROWLATT, J. substituted for this award the lost profits measure, viz. the difference between the contract price and the resale price. His decision was upheld by the House of Lords.

Here it would have been of no avail for Ps to have purchased substitute wheat since they had promised to sell to X not a certain amount of wheat but the particular cargo of wheat purchased from Ds.[1] As was remarked in another case, if "the sub-sale is a sale of the self-same thing, that involves the fact that there is no market in which the thing sold can be bought."[2] If there is no market for a substitute, the doctrine of mitigation cannot apply and subject to the loss being held not too remote, the plaintiff is allowed to claim his lost profit.

3 Defective performance

(a) Completion cost or diminished profit

Where a defendant's performance of his obligations does not reach the standard required by the terms of the contract, then, should the plaintiff accept the defective performance,[3] the doctrine of mitigation may require him to act in one of two ways. Either the plaintiff will be expected to seek for himself complete performance through implementation or repair, in which case he will recover the cost of this undertaking or he will be expected to use or dispose of what the defendant has conveyed in its defective condition, in which case he will recover his diminished profit, that is the difference between the benefits he would have acquired on complete performance of the defendant's obligation and what benefits he is reasonably able to secure after the defective performance. Apart from a few statutory provisions there are no rules of law which compel the court to chose one or other of these measures. It is a question which in all the circumstances the court considers the more appropriate.[4] At the same time it is clear that certain factors exist which should, and do, influence the court in reaching its

---

[1] See, especially, the opinion of LORD PHILLIMORE: (1928). 33 Com. Cas. 324, at p. 338.

[2] *Per* GREER, L.J., *The Arpad*, [1934] P. 189, at p. 215.

[3] Should the breach be so substantial that the plaintiff is entitled to and does reject performance, the case is treated as one of non-performance, *supra*, pp. 323–335.

[4] See WIDGERY, L.J. in *Harbutt's Plasticine* v. *Wayne Tank*, [1970] 1 Q.B. 447, at pp. 472–473.

decision on the point. These have never been comprehensively stated. The following is a tentative list of what may be regarded as the relevant criteria.

(i) *General doctrine of mitigation* At the heart of the matter is the doctrine of mitigation.[1] The court must in all cases ask itself whether it was reasonable in the circumstances for the plaintiff to seek to complete or adapt performance, or whether he should have resigned himself to dealing with the effects of defective performance as best he could.

(ii) *Completion impossible* The choice of measure may be dictated by the fact that from the nature of the contract or of the breach it is impossible to complete or rectify what has gone wrong. If the defendant sells a lame horse instead of a sound one all the endeavours of veterinary science may be insufficient to cure the defect: the court will be bound to award to the plaintiff his diminished profit, that is the difference in the selling price of the horse as warranted and as in fact delivered.[2]

(iii) *Market conditions* If completion of performance is not readily available,[3] or if, though available, it would be unreasonably expensive,[4] the court will award the diminished profit. Conversely, if there is no market for the disposal of a defective article, this might be used as an argument for adopting the completion cost as measure.[5]

(iv) *Whether plaintiff a trader* In dealing with a similar question regarding tortious damages for injuries to property, it was suggested[6] that a distinction should be made as to whether or not the plaintiff held the property primarily as an economic asset. The same considerations apply here. If the plaintiff's interest in the contract is primarily a trading one, that is he seeks to make a profit on the *disposal* of what he receives from the defendant, then damages based on the diminished profit will provide him with adequate compensation.[7] If, on the other hand, the plaintiff wishes himself to use what the defendant conveys, he will have a greater interest in having performance completed, and the completion cost will be the better remedy.[8]

(v) *Liability to third parties* The plaintiff may at the time of breach have already entered into a contract with a third party for the discharge

---

[1] *British Westinghouse Electric and Manufacturing Co.* v. *Underground Electric Railways Co. of London, Ltd.*, [1912] A.C. 673.
[2] *Couchman* v. *Hill*, [1947] K.B. 554.
[3] *Monte Video Gas and Dry Dock Co., Ltd.* v. *Clan Line* (1921), 37 T.L.R. 866.
[4] COLLINS, M.R. in *Holden* v. *Bostock* (1902), 18 T.L.R. 317, at p. 318.
[5] *Per* LORD DENNING, M.R. in *Harbutt's Plasticine* v. *Wayne Tank*, [1970] 1 Q.B. 447, at p. 468.
[6] *Supra*, p. 129.
[7] The rules governing breaches of covenants to repair in leases (*infra*, p. 338) illustrate this.
[8] *Harbutt's Plasticine* case *supra*.

of which he is dependent on complete performance by the defendant. Although the defendant may be liable to indemnify against any liability to the third party,[1] the plaintiff has an additional interest based on his commercial reputation in seeing the subcontract performed. This consideration also adds weight to a claim for the completion cost measure.[2]

(vi) *Whether plaintiff intends to complete* Finally the court may look to the plaintiff's actual intentions. If he has already completed or he clearly intends to do so, then the courts obviously prefer to award damages on that basis.[3] If, on the other hand, it is unlikely that the plaintiff will proceed with the undertaking, the courts will be reluctant to award him compensation as if he were to do so.[4]

(b) Illustrations

(i) *Sale of goods* In contracts for the sale of goods the diminished profit measure is favoured. Section 53(3) of the 1893 Act provides that in the case of a breach of warranty of quality *prima facie* the measure of damages shall be:

> "the difference between the value of the goods at the time of delivery to the buyer and the value they would have had if they had answered to the warranty."

Awards on this basis have dominated the case law, but the completion cost has been applied where there has been no market for the disposal of goods,[5] or where the plaintiff has reasonably employed a third party to remedy the defect or clearly intended to do so.[6]

(ii) *Carriage* In contracts of carriage the question has largely turned on whether or not completion was possible. In a case where goods were delivered to the wrong port the court was clearly justified in awarding the cost of shipping the goods from that port to the contractual place of discharge.[7] Where, however, a carrier delivers goods of the wrong description which cannot be adapted to the contractual requirements an award based on the diminished profit is appropriate.[8]

(iii) *Building* Where premises are defectively constructed the courts tend to favour the completion or reinstatement cost.[9] This is because

---

[1] *Infra*, pp. 355–356.
[2] *Ebbetts* v. *Conquest*, [1895] 2 Ch. 377.
[3] *Haviland* v. *Long*, [1952] 2 Q.B. 80.
[4] *Smiley* v. *Townshend*, [1950] 2 K.B. 311.
[5] *Minster Trust* v. *Traps Tractors*, [1954] 3 All E.R. 136.
[6] *Gull* v. *Saunders and Stuart* (1913), 17 C.L.R. 82.
[7] *Monarch S.S.* v. *Karlshamns Oljefabriker*, [1949] A.C. 196.
[8] *Monte Video Gas and Dry Dock Co., Ltd.* v. *Clan Line* (1921), 37 T.L.R. 866.
[9] *Mertens* v. *Home Freeholders*, [1921] 2 K.B. 526; *Harbutt's Plasticine* v. *Wayne Tank*, [1970] 1 Q.B. 447 and see Pickering and Legh-Jones (1970), 86 L.Q.R. 513, at pp. 524–527. See also on tort, *supra*, pp. 163–165.

most often the premises are required for residential or business purposes and in these circumstances it is reasonable to reinstate.[1] Where
the plaintiff desires the property as an economic asset, that is he wishes
to make a profit on an early sale, there will be a strong argument for
awarding damages on his diminished profit.

(iv) *Lease*[2]   The choice between the two measures has received greatest attention in cases of breach of covenant to repair.   Where the lessor
is bound by such a covenant, the meagre authority available favours the
diminished profit, that is the diminution in the value of the premises to
the lessee.[3] The reason for this is presumably that the tenant may have
no long-term interest in the property and he may not intend himself to
execute the necessary repairs.   Where the lessee is in breach of the
covenant the position is more complicated.   In the nineteenth century
three situations were distinguished.

(A) Where the action was brought by the lessor at the end of the
lessee's term, the cost of repairs was the usual measure.[4]   It was
assumed that the lessor intended to restore the premises to their original
condition.
(B) Where the action was brought during the currency of the lease
the measure was the diminished profit (reduction in the value of the
reversion).[5]   The lessor was not bound to carry out the repairs until the
end of the term and often he did not have the power to enter the
premises and execute them.[6]
(C) Where the lessor was himself liable to a superior landlord, the
cost of repairs was preferred[7] for the plaintiff was likely to take steps to
repair the premises during the currency of the term.

These principles were somewhat affected by section 18(1) of the
Landlord and Tenant Act 1927 which provided that damages for
breach of a covenant to repair should

"in no case exceed the amount (if any) by which the value of the reversion (whether immediate or not) in the premises is diminished owing to
the breach."[8]

---

[1] *Harbutt's Plasticine* case *supra*, *per* LORD DENNING, M.R. at p. 465, *per*
WIDGERY, L.J. at pp. 472–473, *per* CROSS, L.J. at pp. 476–477.
[2] For a detailed account of the rules in this area see McGregor, §§ 730–765.
[3] *Hewitt* v. *Rowlands* (1924), 93 L.J.K.B. 1080; but see also the judgments in
the Divisional Court in the same case, *ibid.*, at p. 729, which envisaged that in
certain cases the cost of repairs might be appropriate.
[4] *Morgan* v. *Hardy* (1886), 17 Q.B.D. 770.
[5] *Doe d. Worcester School Trustees* v. *Rowlands* (1841), 9 C. & P. 734.
[6] *Per* COLERIDGE, J., *ibid.*, at p. 739.   But where he did not reserve power of
entry and did carry out the repairs, the cost of repairs might be awarded:
Joyner v. *Weeks*, [1891] 2 Q.B. 31.
[7] *Conquest* v. *Ebbetts*, [1896] A.C. 490.
[8] The object of the subsection was to avoid the possibility of the lessor reaping
an unjustifiable benefit where he did not intend to repair.

The effect of this is not that the diminished profit measure must always prevail over the completion cost but that the former is to be regarded as the ceiling of the award. The completion cost may still constitute the measure in situations (A) and (C) where the cost does not exceed the reduction in the value of the reversion.[1] But even in situation (B) it seems that the courts are sometimes prepared to use the cost of repairs as evidence of the diminution in the value of the reversion.[2] This is particularly evident where the lessor has actually executed the repairs or has a clear intention to do so.[3]

(c) Assessment of completion cost

The basic item in assessing the completion cost is the amount payable to bring the effects of the defendant's defective performance as close as possible to what he promised to do or convey. Several points require elaboration.

(i) *Expenses* The cost of completion includes, of course, any necessary but reasonable incidental expenses, for example those arising from transport, administration, or surveying.[4]

(ii) *Loss of use* During completion or repairs the plaintiff may be deprived (wholly or partly) of those advantages which he would have acquired if the defendant's performance had been satisfactory and timely. The methods for compensating for loss of use have been most comprehensively worked out in cases of tortious injuries to property.[5] The principles analysed in that context apply equally here.[6] Briefly restated, for the loss of use of profit-earning property, a plaintiff may recover either the loss of his profits or the cost of hiring a substitute. In the case of non-profit-earning property the court may award either the cost of hiring a substitute or interest on the capital invested in the property.

(iii) *Time* The completion cost should be estimated as at the time when the defects might reasonably have been discovered.[7] Of course, if the plaintiff has already executed the work the price he paid will probably constitute the measure but this is subject to the condition that the work done and the price paid were both reasonable.[8]

---

[1] *Jaquin* v. *Holland*, [1960] 1 All E.R. 402.
[2] *Smiley* v. *Townshend*, [1950] 2 K.B. 311.
[3] *Haviland* v. *Long*, [1952] 2 Q.B. 80.
[4] In *Maud* v. *Sandars*, [1943] 2 All E.R. 783 this item was disallowed but the appropriate measure in that case was not the completion cost but the diminished profit.
[5] *Supra*, pp. 135–140.
[6] See, e.g. *Birch* v. *Clifford* (1891), 8 T.L.R. 103 and *Harbutt's Plasticine* v. *Wayne Tank*, [1970] 1 Q.B. 447.
[7] *East Ham Corporation* v. *Sunley & Sons*, [1966] A.C. 406.
[8] *Harbutt's Plasticine* case *supra*.

(iv) *Standard of repairs* The principle is that the plaintiff should seek
to procure performance as similar in kind and degree to that promised
by the defendant.[1] Yet differences may remain. The result of his
intervention may either fall short of or exceed in quality the standard
required of the defendant. In the former case, theoretically the plaintiff should be entitled not only to the completion cost but also to any
consequent diminution of his expectation interest.[2] In practice, however, the fact that complete reinstatement is impracticable may tempt
the court to hold that the completion cost is not the appropriate
measure.[3] Should the results exceed those that would have ensued
from complete performance by the defendant, the English position is
that no deduction for "betterment" should be made.[4] The merits of
this rule as applied to tortious damages for injury to property has already been considered.[5]

(d) Assessment of diminished profit

The alternative measure is assessed by taking the difference between
the benefits which would have accrued if the defendant had satisfactorily performed his duties, and the benefits which have resulted
from defective performance. The modes of ascertaining the benefits
accruing have already been considered[6] but two problems deserve
special attention here: first, the extent to which actual dealings with the
subject-matter of the contract may affect the award; secondly, the time
when the evaluation should be made.

(i) *Relevance of subcontracts* In contracts involving the delivery of
property for resale, the measure is often described as the difference
between the "market value" of the property according with this contractual description, and that of the property in its actual condition as
delivered by the defendant. In other words the basis is the *notional*
diminution of profits: the difference in the profit which would have
been made *if* the plaintiff had sold it in its proper condition and *if* he had
sold it in its defective condition.

Illustration (A) D a wholesaler agrees to sell a car to P, a trader, for
£800. The retail market price for the model in perfect condition is

---

[1] The fact that to furnish performance in its complete condition will be of no
greater value to the plaintiff (i.e. will not affect his expectation interest) than
performance in its defective condition may be a ground for preferring the diminished measure, but should the court adopt the cost of repairs measure this
factor will not go to reduce damages: *Anstruther–Gough–Calthorpe* v. *McOscar*,
[1924] 1 K.B. 716.
[2] *The Georgina* v. *The Anglican* (1872), 21 W.R. 280.
[3] *Supra*, p. 338.
[4] *Harbutt's Plasticine* case, *supra*.
[5] *Supra*, p. 134.
[6] *Supra*, pp. 291–299.

£1,000. P's notional profit is therefore £200. The car delivered has defective bodywork and the market price is in fact £600. P's notional profit has been reduced to £ – 200. He is therefore entitled to £400 for the diminution in profits.

But the retail prices might have been real rather than hypothetical. In the first place, the profit to have been made on sale according to contractual description might be determined by an actual rather than a notional sale.[1] Thus before delivery, the plaintiff may have entered into a contract to resell the property to a third person.

Illustration (B) As in (A) but P has resold the car to X for £1,100. The profit to be secured on performance is now £300. The diminution in profit resulting from D's breach is now £500.

To take cognizance of the resale price in this sense, however, the court must be satisfied that the subcontract related to the very thing which was the subject-matter of the contract for the breach of which the defendant is liable. In other words, the plaintiff must prove the specific causal connection between what the defendant promised to convey and what he promised to sell to a third party. If he fails to do this, the doctrine of mitigation will apply to the effect that the damages will be awarded on the basis that he was able to go into the market and obtain a satisfactory substitute which he might have delivered to the third party: the substitution cost.[2]

Alternatively, the diminished profit may be determined by an actual rather than a notional sale.[3] The plaintiff may have sold the article with all its faults to a third party after acceptance.

Illustration (C) As in (A) but P resells the car with its defective bodywork to Y for £500. The diminution in profits is now £500.

But before the award can be based on the actual subsale, the requirements of mitigation must be satisfied: the plaintiff must be able to show that the price he obtained was reasonable in the circumstances. In practice, the courts are reluctant to award damages on this basis where the subsale was not made within a reasonable time of acceptance of the defective goods.[4] Where the requirements of mitigation are not met, the court must fall back on the notional market value of the defective goods.[5]

---

[1] E.g. *Slater* v. *Hoyle and Smith*, [1920] 2 K.B. 11.
[2] Cf. *supra*, p. 334.
[3] E.g. *Biggin & Co.* v. *Permanite*, [1951] 1 K.B. 422.
[4] *Loder* v. *Kekulé* (1857), 3 C.B.N.S. 128.
[5] *Slater* v. *Hoyle & Smith, supra*.

(ii) *Time*   In the ordinary case, the diminished profit is assessed at the time when performance is accepted in its defective state.[1] Where the defect was not patent, it follows that the appropriate date will be when the defect was discovered, or would have been discoverable on reasonable inspection.[2]

4   Delayed performance

(a)   Diminished profit or substitution cost

A delay in performance by the promisor may give the promisee a right to repudiate the contract. Where he does so, the breach is treated as one of non-performance and compensation is assessed accordingly. Where a promisee does not repudiate, or has no right to do so,[3] in most cases the doctrine of mitigation will require nothing more of the plaintiff than to sit and wait for the defendant to perform, and then to secure what financial benefit he may. The measure will then be the difference between the benefits he would have acquired on timely performance, and those he is able to acquire on late performance: the *diminished profit*. In exceptional circumstances, however, where the plaintiff requires the subject-matter of the contract for his own use, he may reasonably hire a substitute for the period of delay and his award will be based on the *substitution cost*. There have been no attempts by the courts to lay down in any general terms when such exceptional circumstances might exist, but proceeding from the ordinary principles of mitigation and the little authority that does exist, it may be suggested that the right to damages based on the substitution cost will exist where the following conditions are satisfied.

(i) A reasonable equivalent substitute must be readily available on the market. Three factors should be considered: what is sought must be the rough equivalent of what was promised; it must be readily available to the plaintiff in the sense that he can hire it without excessive delay or trouble; the price to be paid for the hiring must be reasonable relative to the use required of the substitute.[4]

(ii) The plaintiff must require the subject-matter of the contract for his own use. Excluded from this measure is the trader whose interest in timely performance is concerned only with the rise and fall in the market, and hence with his profit on resale. Damages based on the

---

[1] *Ibid.*

[2] *Kwei Tek Chao* v. *British Traders and Shippers*, [1954] 2 Q.B. 459 (by analogy).

[3] E.g. because time is not construed as being of the essence: see Treitel, pp. 720–724.

[4] Cf. *supra* pp. 325–330 for a discussion of these factors in cases of non-performance.

diminished profit will be an adequate remedy for this plaintiff.[1] However, the fact that the plaintiff requires the subject-matter for his own use is not in itself conclusive. Where the defendant is late in delivering a profit-earner, the court still has the option of awarding loss of profits,[2] and even where a chattel is not a profit-earner, the choice is still open to the court to award damages based on interest on the capital invested.[3]

(iii) It must be reasonable to hire a substitute. This condition provides a greater obstacle for the plaintiff suing for late performance than does the equivalent condition for a plaintiff who sues for defective performance and seeks to persuade the court that the completion cost should be awarded.[4] Here there must be special circumstances making an award of the diminished profit an inadequate remedy. Such circumstances may well exist where the plaintiff's commercial reputation is at stake, where other transactions are contingent on the prompt performance of the contract, or where the losses resulting from the delay would multiply at an alarming rate. The court should also take into account how long the delay was likely to last. These points are well illustrated by two contrasting decisions. In *Romulus Films* v. *William Dempster*[5]

> Ps, producing a film partly in East Africa and partly in the U.K., engaged Ds to convey their equipment and two of their staff from Uganda to London. The aircraft was not available for two weeks after the contract date. As a result of the delay, Ps felt themselves obliged (A) to fly out one of their staff to London by alternative means, (B) to extend the hire of cameras since they would be unable to return them on time, (C) to duplicate in London certain "properties and wardrobe" which they required for shooting there and which were held up in Uganda. It was held that the cost of all three items was reasonably incurred though (C) was not recoverable as being too remote.[6]

In *Le Blanche* v. *London and North Western Rail Co.*[7]

> P bought a railway ticket from Ds to convey him from Liverpool to Scarborough. The journey involved changing trains at Leeds and York. Ds' train arrived too late at Leeds for the intended connection to York, and the train he travelled on from Leeds arrived too late at

---

[1] See, e.g. *Koufos* v. *C. Czarnikow*, [1969] 1 A.C. 350.
[2] *B. Sunley* v. *Cunard White Star Ltd.*, [1940] 1 K.B. 740.
[3] *Ibid.*
[4] *Supra*, p. 336.
[5] [1952] 2 Lloyd's Rep. 535.
[6] It is suggested with respect that it is unnecessary to bring in remoteness as well as mitigation to bear on the issue: the question whether the procuring of the substitute was reasonably within the contemplation of the contracting parties may itself be answered by the doctrine of mitigation—if the act was reasonable, then it should not be too remote and *vice versa*.
[7] (1876), 1 C.P.D. 286.

York for the intended connection to Scarborough. At York instead of waiting an hour for the next ordinary train to Scarborough, P caught a special train at additional expense. It was held that since P had no special business in Scarborough which required him to be there at any particular time, his action in taking the special train was not reasonable, and the additional expense was not recoverable.

(b) Assessment of substitution cost

The substitution cost when awarded is comprised of three different elements: first, the cost of hiring a substitute during the period of delay; second, any necessary but reasonable incidental expenses; third, any loss of profits pending delivery of the substitute. The principles governing the assessment of these items have been fully considered in relation to tortious damages for injury to property,[1] and further discussion is not required.

(c) Assessment of diminished profit

The method of assessing the diminished profit is similar to that described above with regard to cases of defective performance.[2] The court must award the difference between the financial benefit which would have accrued to the plaintiff on timely performance and that which has accrued on later performance. In contracts involving the delivery of a chattel, this difference is often referred to as "loss of market": the plaintiff, intending to sell the chattel immediately on receipt, is awarded the difference between the market selling price of the goods if they had arrived on time, and the market selling price at the time of actual delivery.[3] As with other measures based on the expectation interest, the question arises whether actual subcontracts made by the plaintiff should be taken into account. The position is the same as that described above with regard to cases of defective performance.[4] The price received on an actual sale may be relevant for either of two purposes. On the one hand (A) it may determine the extent of the benefits accruing on timely performance. But again,[5] for this purpose it must be shown that the defendant was bound to deliver to the plaintiff the very thing which the plaintiff had promised to sell. On the other hand (B) it may be taken as evidence of the actual diminution of profits: the price which the plaintiff actually gets for the property when he sells it on late delivery. For this to apply the standard of reasonableness must be complied with.

---

[1] *Supra*, pp. 138–139.
[2] *Supra*, pp. 340–342.
[3] *Koufos v. C. Czarnikow*, [1969] 1 A.C. 350.
[4] Pp. 340–341.
[5] Cf. *supra*, p. 334.

In the light of these propositions, the curious and controversial decision in *Wertheim* v. *Chicoutimi Pulp Co.*[1] may be visited.

Ds agreed to deliver to P, in September to November 1900, 3,000 tons of wood pulp at 25s. per ton. In a series of agreements with sub-buyers, some before and some after the above agreement P sold the pulp at 65s. per ton. The market price at the date of delivery was 70s. per ton. Delivery was not made until July 1901 when the market price was 42s. 6d. The subbuyers were still prepared to accept the pulp.

Now there are two possible constructions of the facts of this case. On one view, the plaintiff was bound to deliver to the subbuyers the specific wood pulp sold to him by the defendants. If this was the case, the price which he obtained on the subcontracts would determine the extent of the benefits accruing on prompt performance. But since the profit of the subcontracts actually accrued, he sustained no loss of profits and his damages must be nominal. On an alternative view, the plaintiff was not bound to deliver the specific goods to the third parties. The resale price then becomes irrelevant for determining the extent of the expectation interest, and the court must fall back on the notional diminished profit, that is, the difference between the market value at the time when delivery should have been made (70s.) and when it was made (42s. 6d.). If the resale price is to be regarded as irrelevant for purpose (A), it must be equally irrelevant for purpose (B). The plaintiff did not sell the property to the third parties *as a result of* late delivery (if he had done so at a time when the market price was 42s. 6d. he would hardly have been able to make a bargain at 65s.). A subcontract cannot serve both purposes (A) and (B). On these grounds it is impossible to defend the decision of the Privy Council in the *Wertheim* case that the plaintiff should be awarded the difference between the market price at the date when delivery was due (70s.) and the resale price (65s.) since this was based on the view that though the resale price was irrelevant for ascertaining the extent of the breach (purpose (A)), it could nevertheless be relevant for determining the diminished profit (purpose (B)).

---

[1] [1911] A.C. 301.

CHAPTER NINE

Breach of Contract (II)

OTHER ASPECTS OF COMPENSATION

I THE RELIANCE INTEREST

1 Introduction

An inquiry into the role of the reliance interest in the English law of damages involves entering into a murky area where only a few outlines are visible and where much remains uncharted. For some considerable time judicial discussion of the question was non-existent. So-called damages for "wasted expenses" were often awarded but more often instinctively than in accordance with established legal principles. In the United States of America the subject has been extensively treated.[1] It is only within recent years that it has received academic[2] and judicial[3] attention in this country.

The basic notion of the reliance interest is a simple one: in relying on the defendant's promise to perform, the plaintiff has acted to his own detriment usually by the outlay of some money. While awaiting completion of a conveyance the purchaser of a house may have purchased furniture or fittings. A manufacturer, while awaiting delivery of special parts, may have commenced work on a machine, or engaged special labour forces. Should the defendant fail to perform, these expenses will be wasted.

It is important to appreciate that damages for the plaintiff's reliance interest may be awarded for two different purposes: (i) they may be awarded as an *alternative* to damages for loss of the expectation interest; or (ii) they may be awarded to *complement* damages for the loss of the expectation interest. In (i) the object of compensation will not be, as with the expectation interest, to put the plaintiff in the position he

---

[1] See, especially Fuller & Perdue (1936), 46 Yale L.J. 52, and *Corbin on Contracts* §§ 1031–1036.

[2] Street, pp. 240–245; Macleod, [1970] J.B.L. 16.

[3] *Cullinane* v. *British "Rema" Manufacturing Co.*, [1954] 1 Q.B. 292; *Lloyd* v. *Stanbury*, [1971] 2 All E.R. 267; *Anglia Television, Ltd.* v. *Reed*, [1972] 1 Q.B. 60.

would have been in if the defendant had satisfactorily performed his contract. Instead it will be to put him in the position he would have been *if he had not entered into the contract.* It is the basic compensatory principle of actions in tort: *restitutio in integrum.* As measure of damages in a contractual situation it is a double-edged sword, for it can operate either to the advantage or to the disadvantage of the plaintiff. If he has made a profitable bargain, then should it replace compensation based on the expectation interest, it will prevent him reaping the benefits. If, on the other hand, he has made a bad bargain, as against expectation interest damages, it will protect him against the consequences of his folly. It is necessary to add, however, that if the law considers the latter consequence to be undesirable—if, in short, it seeks never to put the plaintiff in a better position than he would have been in if the contract had been performed—then it will place a limit on recovery of the reliance interest, such that a plaintiff may never recover more than the extent of his expectation interest. As will appear, it is not yet clear whether English law imposes this limitation, and as a result the policy considerations behind the award of the reliance interest remain largely unexplored. As regards (ii) where the reliance interest is used to complement the expectation interest, there can be no doubt that the object of the award is the more effectively to put the plaintiff in the position he would have been in if the contract had been performed. It deals, in such circumstances, with losses which on another view might well have entered into the calculation of the expectation interest itself. Where the reliance interest is used for this purpose care must be taken that the plaintiff does not benefit from double recovery.

2 Reliance interest as alternative to expectation interest

It is proposed first to consider the scope and recoverability of the reliance interest as an alternative to the expectation interest.

(a) Losses other than expenses

In most cases the loss for compensation of which the defendant is sued comprises money spent by the plaintiff in reliance on the defendant's promise to perform. But the remedy will extend to cases where he assigns some valuable property to or performs some valuable service for another. In *Hydraulic Engineering Co.* v. *McHaffie*[1]

> Ps contracted to deliver to X a piece of machinery part of which was to be manufactured by Ds. Ds failed to deliver on time. Ps lost the contract with X. They recovered damages *inter alia* for the cost of making other parts of the machinery and also for painting it.

---

[1] (1878), 4 Q.B.D. 670.

(b) Overlap with restitution interest

The plaintiff usually changes his position by paying money to or conferring something of value on a third party. Yet during the currency of the contract he is, of course, also likely to confer something of value on the defendant himself. This, though it may be regarded as part of the reliance interest, is treated under the restitution interest.[1]

(c) Time and purpose of expenses

The most important category of loss which directly comes within the ambit of the reliance interest covers those expenses which were necessarily incurred by the plaintiff in performance of his part of the contract, and the payments of which took place during the currency of the contract. It is sometimes said that in order to recover compensation for the reliance interest, the doctrine of remoteness must be satisfied. In the ordinary case of expenses necessary for performance (what have conveniently been described as constituting the "essential reliance interest")[2] the requirement will always be satisfied. A defendant should always foresee what the plaintiff *must* do under the contract. Recovery of other losses is less certain.

(i) *Incidental expenses* The expenses incurred may be incidental to, rather than necessary for, performance of the contract: for example, a purchaser of land acquiring stock or furniture.[3] The principle emerging clearly from the case-law is that compensation for these wasted expenses is recoverable provided they were reasonably within the contemplation of the defendant at the time of making the contract. This is well illustrated by *Lloyd* v. *Stanbury*[4]

> D agreed to sell to P a plot of land, knowing that P intended to use it for poultry farming. It was a term of the contract that D could occupy a caravan to be brought onto the land by P until alternative accommodation was ready. In anticipation of completion by D,[5] P (a) moved the caravan onto the land, (b) installed a chemical toilet for use in connection with it, (c) purchased a chicken house and wire netting for use on the land, (d) transported some of his furniture, (e) spent some money in improving the roadway and cutting the grass. The expenses in-

---

[1] *Infra*, pp. 367–370.
[2] Fuller and Perdue *supra*, at p. 78.
[3] It is interesting to note that for the purposes of assessing income tax, the Inland Revenue has to draw a distinction similar to that between "necessary" and "incidental" expenses. Under Income and Corporation Taxes Act 1970, s. 189, deductions from taxable income are made for expenses incurred wholly exclusively and necessarily in the performance of the taxpayer's duties.
[4] [1971] 2 All E.R. 267.
[5] Some of the steps were taken before the making of the contract. This is considered *infra*, pp. 349–350.

curred in (a) and (b) were recoverable as being items of essential reliance interest. The remaining items were incidental to P's performance of the contract and of these only (c) and (d) were recovered as (e) was not reasonably within the contemplation of D at the time of the contract.

(ii) *Expenses incurred after breach* Any reliance interest expenses which the plaintiff incurs after breach are governed by the doctrine of mitigation.[1] Once he has notice of breach he may not reasonably incur expenses in reliance on the defendant's performance, and such expenses if incurred will not be recoverable. Thus in *Lloyd v. Stanbury* (above) when the plaintiff had already issued a writ for breach of contract, hoping for a decree of specific performance, he installed a power control, a television aerial and a telephone. It was, however, held that he had already repudiated the contract, and hence that these expenses were unreasonable and could not be recovered.[2]

(iii) *Expenses incurred before contract*[3] The question then arises whether the plaintiff might recover any expenses incurred before the contract with the defendant was made. It must first be observed that where a plaintiff claims the expenses *in addition* to profits, that is as part of his expectation interest, they should be taken into account. In the calculation of lost profits, an allowance is made for expenses necessarily incurred,[4] and it would seem unreasonable to exclude consideration of overheads and other expenses which related to the profitable transaction but which were incurred before the contract. Where, however, the reliance interest is claimed as an *alternative* to the expectation interest, the position appears to be different. Here the object is to put the plaintiff in the position he would have been in if the contract had not been made, and on that hypothesis the expenses would still have been incurred. There is, indeed, no causal connection between the loss (the wasted expenses) and either the making of the contract or its breach. On these grounds American authorities have rejected claims for pre-contract expenditure.[5] English law seems to have taken a different path. Until recently, recovery was allowed only within very narrow limits. In contracts for the sale of land where a vendor had failed to complete, the disappointed purchaser could recover the

---

[1] Such expenses are sharply to be distinguished from those which are incurred *as a result of* the breach: these are governed by the indemnity interest, *infra*, pp. 354–367.
[2] [1971] 1 W.L.R. 535, at p. 547.
[3] See the author's casenote on *Anglia Television v. Reed*, *infra*, at (1972), 35 M.L.R. 423.
[4] *Infra*, p. 352.
[5] See 22 Am. Jur. 2d 226–227 and *Corbin on Contracts*, § 1934. See also *per* TINDAL C.J., *Hodges v. Earl of Litchfield* (1835), 1 Bing. N.C. 492, at p. 498.

expenses of executing the contract.[1] In a recent case within this area,[2] BRIGHTMAN, J. extended the ambit of recovery to cover "the costs of performing an act required to be done by the contract".[3] Finally in *Anglia Television* v. *Reed*[4] a completely new principle was introduced. On the breach of *any* class of contract, the plaintiff could recover *all* pre-contract expenditure which "was such as would reasonably be in the contemplation of the parties as likely to be wasted if the contract was broken".[5] Now it may be conceded that dogmatically to insist that there may be recovery of expenditure incurred only from the moment that the contract was complete might lead to artificial results. If the parties had clearly reached agreement on the substance of the contract and all that remained was for their legal advisers to draft and execute the contract, it would be unfair to the plaintiff to disallow a claim for expenses which had been incurred at this stage. But the broad principle of *Reed's* case surely goes too far. The doctrine of *restitutio in integrum* which lies at the heart of the reliance interest award dictates that while a contract is still being negotiated a party who incurs expenditure does so at his own risk. Perhaps the best solution would be for the reliance interest award to comprise those expenses incurred as from the time when there was substantial agreement between the parties.[6]

(d) Election and limitation by the expectation interest

Although this section deals with the reliance interest as an "alternative" to expectation interest damages, it is to be observed that in certain circumstances it will represent the plaintiff's only chance of substantial damages. Such is the case where there is a rule of law preventing the award of the expectation interest, as under *Bain* v. *Fothergill*.[7] But the same is also true where loss of profits is too remote, or the existence and extent of the expectation interest remain so speculative and uncertain that the court is not prepared to award damages on this basis. The well-known Australian case of *McRae* v. *Commonwealth Disposals Commission*[8] provides an excellent illustration.

Ds sold to Ps the wreck of an oil tanker lying on a reef about 100 miles north of Samarai. At considerable expense Ps fitted out a salvage

---

[1] E.g. *Hanslip* v. *Padwick* (1850), 5 Exch. 615. The costs of investigating title were also allowed (*ibid.*, at p. 624) but *semble* this referred to those investigations which took place after the contract.

[2] *Lloyd* v. *Stanbury*, [1971] 1 W.L.R. 535, *supra*, pp. 348–349.

[3] *Ibid.*, at p. 546.

[4] [1972] 1 Q.B. 60.

[5] *Per* LORD DENNING, M.R., *ibid.*, at p. 64.

[6] The old rule that a disappointed purchaser of land could recover the cost of executing the contract (*supra*) would be consistent with the suggested modification.

[7] (1874), L.R. 7 H.L. 158, *supra*, pp. 299–304.

[8] (1951), 84 C.L.R. 377.

expedition and proceeded to the location but found no tanker there. They successfully sued Ds for breach of contract. Ps were awarded not their expectation interest (the value of the ship and its contents) which was so speculative as to make quantification impossible, but their reliance interest: the wasted expenditure.

The principle has recently been asserted that a plaintiff may elect between expectation interest damages and reliance interest damages.[1] If the plaintiff claims his reliance interest, the question then arises as to whether his remedy should in any way be limited by reference to his expectation interest. English case-law provides no guidance on the point and yet it goes to the very root of the reliance interest and its rationale. The objection to allowing recovery unaffected by the expectation interest is that it may be too generous to the plaintiff. By seeking to put the plaintiff in the position he would have been in if the contract had not been made, it may protect him against the consequences of having entered into a bad bargain. He may be put in a better position than if the defendant had performed his contract. For example:

D agrees to supply materials for P, a property developer, to build a house. In necessary preparation for the work P spends £3,000. Because of prevailing market conditions, D is able to show that P would have made a net loss on the sale of the house of £200 (i.e. P's expectation interest is £ − 200). On breach by D, P elects to claim his wasted expenditure of £3,000. If he recovers this sum he will be in the position he would have been in if he had not entered into the contract with D, but he will be £200 better off than if D had performed his contract.

It may be sought to defend this result on the ground that it does not lie in the mouth of a person who has broken his contract to complain if the plaintiff is put in the position he would have been in if he had not entered into a contract with the defendant.[2] But this view involves by implication some punitive consideration. The opposing view that a plaintiff should never be put in a better position than if the contract had been performed, seems to be more consistent with the true principle of compensation.[3] If this conclusion is accepted, the principle emerges, as formulated by the American Restatement that "if full performance would have resulted in a net loss to the plaintiff, the amount of this loss must be deducted . . .".[4] The objection might then be brought that

---

[1] *Anglia Television* v. *Reed*, [1972] 1 Q.B. 60, 64. The case-law prior to this decision was uncertain on the point.

[2] Cf. LORD DENNING, M.R. in *Anglia Television* v. *Reed, supra.*

[3] This is the position taken in the U.S.A.: see *Corbin on Contracts*, § 1033.

[4] § 333(d). An alternative formulation of the principle is that recovery of reliance interest damages should not exceed the value of the expectancy: see

if damages are to be assessed on this basis, there would be no point in the plaintiff electing to sue for his reliance interest—the remedy would have no advantage over expectation interest damages. If the expectation interest shows a net profit, he might as well sue for that, while if it shows a net loss, the rule will compel the court to take it into account in assessing reliance interest damages. The answer to this objection is that, when suing for his reliance interest, the plaintiff will have the advantage of the burden of proof. In a claim for expectation interest damages the plaintiff must prove to the satisfaction of the court that he has sustained a loss which is capable of quantification. Where, in the alternative, the reliance interest is claimed, then should the defendant seek to limit the award on the principle stated above, it will be for him to prove that the plaintiff would have made a net loss on the transaction.[1]

3　Reliance interest as a complement to expectation interest

It cannot be doubted that when the reliance interest is used to complement the expectation interest the ordinary object of putting the plaintiff in the position he would have been in if the contract had been performed is to be pursued. It may at first sight seem strange that if that be the object of damages the plaintiff should be entitled to both his reliance and his expectation interest. It would seem that the plaintiff has to spend the reliance interest in order to earn the expectation interest, and therefore to award both would amount to a double recovery. It is on this ground that the courts have insisted that the plaintiff is not entitled to *both* wasted expenditure *and* loss of profits.[2] But this principle, as stated, is ambiguous and misleading for in every case whether or not the reliance interest may complement the expectation interest depends on how the expectation interest has been calculated, in short on what is meant by "profits" in this context.

(i) Where the expectation interest is based on the "net profit", that is, where the plaintiff's expenses have been deducted from his receipts he will be entitled both to his wasted expenses and to the "net profit" lost, for clearly the "net profit" does not allow for the fact that the price he will get on eventual sale or dealing will include reimbursement of the expenses.

Fuller & Perdue *loc. cit*, at p. 75 and the German Civil Code, arts. 122, 179, 307. This is perfectly acceptable provided that it is appreciated that the "value of the expectancy" refers to the *gross* profits to be earned on the transaction, i.e. without deduction of the necessary expenses. See *infra*, pp. 353–354.

[1] U.S. Restatement § 333(d).

[2] *Cullinane* v. *British "Rema" Manufacturing Co.*, [1954] 1 Q.B. 292, *per* EVERSHED, M.R. at p. 303, *per* JENKINS, L.J. at p. 308; *Anglia Television* v. *Reed*, [1972] 1 Q.B. 60, *per* LORD DENNING, M.R. at p. 64.

(ii) Where the expectation interest is calculated simply by reference to "gross profit", that is to receipts on eventual sale or dealings without deduction for expenses, then the plaintiff is not entitled to both the "gross profit" and the wasted expenses, for, in order to earn that profit those expenses would have been incurred.

There are, therefore, two methods of calculating damages. Their contrasting application may be seen in the following illustration (based on the facts in *Hydraulic Engineering Co.* v. *McHaffie*[1])

> D agrees to supply materials to P for £100. P is to incorporate these materials in the manufacture of machine which he will sell to X for £1,200. In addition to the price of the materials P must spend another £900 in part performance of his contract with X, but as D fails to deliver the special materials, the machine is useless and the contract with X is lost.

On *Method* (i) it would be said that P's "net profit" is:

$$£1,200 - (£900 + £100) = £200$$

Assuming that P has paid £100 to D for the materials, he will be entitled to compensation for his real loss which is wasted expenses plus "net profit":

$$£900 + £100^2 + £200 = £1,200$$

On *Method* (ii) it would be said that P's "gross profit" is £1,200 (his receipts on sale of the machine to X). Assuming that P has paid £100 to D for the materials, he will be entitled only to his "gross profit" without any addition for his wasted expenses = £1,200.[3]

Whether in any given case, the expectation interest will be calculated on the basis of the "net profits" or the "gross profits" will depend on various factors including the nature of the contract, the nature of the expenses, the nature of the eventual profit, and accountancy practice.[4] Unhappily it is not always clear in the decided cases on what basis "profits" have been calculated. The result has been some considerable confusion. The award of both "profits" and expenses in *Hydraulic Engineering* v. *McHaffie*[5] has been criticized for allowing double recovery[6] and yet defended by an Australian court on the ground that the "profits" referred to in the judgments were "net profits" and not

---

[1] (1878), 4 Q.B.D. 670.
[2] Strictly speaking, this is recoverable as the restitution interest, *infra*, pp. 367–370.
[3] A simple set of figures has deliberately been chosen to facilitate comprehension, but it should be borne in mind that in the ordinary commercial case the situation is likely to be much more complex. See, e.g. *Cullinane* v. *British "Rema" Manufacturing*, *supra* and Macleod [1970] J.B.L. 19.
[4] In formulating the principles for quantifying the expectation interest the author suggested that as a general rule the calculation should be made on the basis of "net profits", *supra*, p. 292.
[5] (1878), 4 Q.B.D. 670.
[6] McGregor, § 42.

"gross profits".[1] In truth, it is impossible to ascertain from the facts as reported which was intended. Even greater difficulty arises from *Cullinane* v. *British "Rema" Manufacturing Co.*[2]

> Ds sold and delivered to P a clay pulverizing plant warranting that it would process clay at six tons per hour. In fact it could handle clay at only two tons per hour. P claimed (a) wasted expenditure *viz.* the capital cost of the plant, the cost of installing it, and the cost of an ancillary plant less the residual value of the plant *and* (b) loss of "net profits"[3] *viz.* estimated receipts after deducting for depreciation, interest, maintenance and other expenses.

Now clearly in accordance with the principles discussed above, the claim did not infringe the double recovery rule: it sought to recover damages on the basis of method (i) and not method (ii). However the majority of the Court of Appeal refused to allow recovery of both heads of damages. They seemingly failed to appreciate that there was any difference between the two methods for, having made the unexceptional statement that a plaintiff cannot recover for both wasted expenditure and "gross profits",[4] they concluded that this was a conclusive ground for rejecting the plaintiff's claim. The point was, however, taken by MORRIS, L.J. in his dissenting judgment: the plaintiff might claim either his "gross profits" or his "net profits" plus expenditure. In this case, he claimed the latter, and as such his claim was "permissible and logical".[5] It is to be hoped that in future cases the courts will adopt his reasoning rather than that of the majority.

II THE INDEMNITY INTEREST

1 Introduction

The indemnity interest embraces all *positive* pecuniary losses which flow from the breach of contract. To the extent that the breach has put the plaintiff in a worse position than if he had not entered into the contract with the defendant, then, subject to the limitations to be discussed below, he may recover compensation for all such losses.

Described in these terms the indemnity interest may be distinguished from both the expectation and the reliance interests.

---

[1] *T.C. Industrial Plant* v. *Robert's*, [1964] A.L.R. 1083, at p. 1091.

[2] [1954] 1 Q.B. 292. See Street, pp. 242–245, and the penetrating analysis by Macleod [1970] J.B.L. 19.

[3] Some of the difficulty is caused by the fact that though the loss of profits claimed was over a three-year period, the majority in their calculations seemed to have treated it as a ten-year claim: Macleod, *ibid.*, at pp. 30–32.

[4] [1954] 1 Q.B. 292, *per* EVERSHED, M.R., at p. 302, *per* JENKINS, L.J. at p. 308.

[5] *Ibid.*, at p. 315.

(1) It differs from the expectation interest in that the latter is concerned with the gains prevented by the breach—the pecuniary advantages which would have been conferred on the plaintiff if the defendant had satisfactorily performed his contract. Thus, for example where D sells goods to P who resells them to X, and D fails to deliver, P's *expectation interest* will include the profit to be made on his contract with X. His *indemnity interest* will include any compensation payable to X as a result of his consequent failure to deliver to X.

(2) It differs from the reliance interest in that damages for the latter provide compensation for those expenses which the plaintiff incurred in reliance on performance by the defendant and which therefore would have been incurred if the defendant had performed his contract. Indemnity expenses, on the other hand, are caused not by the making of the contract, but by the defendant's breach. They would not have been incurred if the defendant had satisfactorily performed his contract. The difference may be illustrated by *Molling & Co. v. Dean & Son, Ltd.*[1]

Ds, printers in Germany, contracted to supply Ps in England with a quantity of books, some of which, as Ds knew, were for resale in the United States. The quality of the books did not reach the required standard and were rejected by the American buyers. Ps were entitled, *inter alia*, to (a) the cost of sending the books to the U.S.A.—reliance interest—and (b) the cost of bringing them back from U.S.A.—indemnity interest.

2   Illustrations

The types of losses covered by the indemnity interest are many and various. To illustrate this head of damages, however, certain important categories may be selected. It must be stressed that what follows is a summary of some *factual* indemnity interests which may arise on breach of contract. Whether or not they are recoverable in law depends on principles an account of which will follow the illustrations.

(a)   Civil or criminal liability

As a result of the defendant's breach, the plaintiff may be liable in contract or in tort to a third party.[2] Similarly, he may be made liable in a criminal court, and any fine he must pay may also qualify for compensation.[3] Complementary to these losses are the plaintiff's own

---

[1] (1901), 18 T.L.R. 217.
[2] E.g. *Hammond & Co. v. Bussey* (1888), 20 Q.B.D. 79.
[3] E.g. *Osman v. Moss*, [1970] 1 Lloyd's Rep. 313.

costs in defending the action and the costs of his opponent should he be ordered to pay them.[1]

(b)   Property or personal injury

The defendant's breach may cause some physical injury to the plaintiff's property[2] or to his person.[3]   The losses consequent on such injuries will be identical to those resulting from a tortious injury.[4]

(c)   Out-of-pocket expenses

There is a great variety of miscellaneous expenses which may be subsumed under this heading.   Where the defendant is late in performing, the plaintiff may incur expenses in inquiring after performance,[5] or accommodation expenses.[6]   In other cases of breach he may, for example, have to convey himself[7] or his property[8] back from a place where performance was anticipated.

(d)   Non-pecuniary losses

In addition to pecuniary losses, the plaintiff may sustain certain non-pecuniary losses.   Where these are consequent on physical injury, then these are covered under (b) above.   But quite apart from physical injury, the defendant's breach may result in inconvenience, discomfort or loss of happiness generally.   Thus where a railway company failed to carry the plaintiff to his destination, he had to complete the journey on foot[9] and where a solicitor failed to take the proper steps to evict persons from the plaintiff's property, he was obliged to live under uncomfortable circumstances.[10]

3   Limitations on recovery

The general principle is that the plaintiff can recover for all such losses subject to the following limitations.

(a)   Causation and remoteness

The causal link between the breach and the loss must, of course, satisfy the *sine qua non* test.[11]   Further generalization is difficult

---

[1] E.g. *Kasler and Cohen* v. *Slavouski*, [1928] 1 K.B. 78.
[2] E.g. *Smith* v. *Green* (1875), 1 C.P.D. 92.   See also for a misappropriation consequent on breach *Stansbie* v. *Troman*, [1948] 2 K.B. 48.
[3] E.g. *Andrews* v. *Hopkinson*, [1957] 1 Q.B. 229.
[4] *Supra*, Chaps 5–6.
[5] E.g. *Woodger* v. *Great Western Rail. Co.* (1867), L.R. 2 C.P. 318.
[6] E.g. *Beard* v. *Porter*, [1948] 1 K.B. 321.
[7] E.g. *Rice* v. *Baxendale* (1861), 7 H. & N. 96.
[8] E.g. *Molling* v. *Dean* (1901), 18 T.L.R. 217, *supra*, p. 355.
[9] *Hobbs* v. *London and South Western Rail. Co.* (1875), L.R. 10 Q.B. 111.
[10] *Bailey* v. *Bullock*, [1950] 1 All E.R. 1167.
[11] *Supra*, pp. 62–67.

except to reiterate that the defendant's breach must be the "substantial cause" of the loss.[1] To escape liability it will not be sufficient for the defendant to show that other events (or breaches of contract) concurrently caused the losses.[2] Nor is the position different if the plaintiff himself had been in breach of contract or committed a tort,—indeed, this will invariably be the case where the plaintiff seeks an indemnity for his liability to a third party.[3] The court must instead inquire whether the plaintiff's conduct (as opposed to his legal liability) was such as to break the causal link between the defendant's breach and his own loss. This problem has attracted greatest attention in contracts for the sale of goods where the buyer has paid compensation to a sub-buyer for breach of a warranty of quality and himself sues the vendor for an indemnity. It is established law that if the buyer ought, on reasonable examination, to have discovered the defect he alone is liable for the loss sustained by the sub-buyer. His act or omission broke the chain of causation linking the defendant's breach with the sub-buyer's loss.[4]

The ordinary rules of remoteness[5] apply to prevent recovery of losses which were not within the contemplation of the parties at the time of contract as liable (or not unlikely) to result from the breach. Thus in *Burton* v. *Pinkerton*[6]

> P, employed to serve on D's ship, left the ship when he became aware that it was being used, in breach of his contract, for the "extraordinary" purpose of supplying ammunition to countries at war. On leaving the ship he was imprisoned by the Brazilian authorities in the belief that he was a Peruvian deserter. By the time he was released, D's ship had left with some of P's clothes on board. It was held that P could not recover either for the imprisonment or for the loss of his clothes as both events were too remote.

The cases on indemnity in a contract of sale for liability to third persons again call for special mention. Here two sub-rules have their origin in, or are sometimes justified by reference to, the remoteness doctrine.

(i) In order that the vendor should be liable for losses resulting from the resale, it must reasonably have been within the contemplation of the vendor that the buyer would enter into a contract to resell the goods.[7] This requirement, made most explicit in the important deci-

---

[1] Cf. *supra*, pp. 67–68.
[2] See, e.g. *Williams* v. *Earle* (1868), L.R. 3 Q.B. 739.
[3] E.g. *A.M.F. International* v. *Magnet Bowling*, [1968] 2 All E.R. 789.
[4] See among many others *Biggin & Co.* v. *Permanite*, [1951] 1 K.B. 422, reversed on another ground [1951] 2 K.B. 314.
[5] *Supra*, pp. 71–74.
[6] (1867), L.R. 2 Ex. 340.
[7] Cf. *supra*, pp. 315–316.

sion of *Hammond* v. *Bussey*,[1] proved unexpectedly decisive in *Bostock &*
Co., Ltd. v. *Nicholson & Sons, Ltd.*[2]

> Ds agreed to supply Ps with sulphuric acid, warranting it to be free
> from arsenic. Ps used the acid in the manufacturing of brewing sugar
> which they sold to X. The acid contained arsenic and X successfully
> sued Ps. Ds had no notice of the particular use to be made of the acid
> but nevertheless its use in the manufacture of brewing sugar could not
> "be said to be other than a well-recognized and ordinary use."[3]
> BRUCE J. held that Ds were not liable to indemnify Ps since they had no
> notice of the contract with X.

This decision is undoubtedly harsh for, on the facts, it would not have
been difficult for the learned judge to have found that it was reasonably
within the contemplation of Ds that Ps would use it to manufacture
brewing sugar, which in due course would be sold to a brewer. The
case seems to fall in line with those which, in applying the *Hadley* v.
Baxendale rules, required express notice of special purposes.[4] As explained elsewhere,[5] this notion has now fallen out of favour, and it
seems that the courts are now prepared to apply the doctrine more
liberally in this area. Typical is *Pinnock Brothers* v. *Lewis and Peat*[6]

> Ds sold 100 bags of copra cake to Ps who resold them to X who manu-
> factured part of them into cakettes and dairy meal. These were then
> sold by X to Ys, farmers. The cake proved to be poisonous and Ys
> brought an action against X who claimed against Ps. Ds were held
> liable for the damages and costs down the line. Although Ds had no
> specific notice of (i) the particular use made of the cake by X, or (ii) the
> various subcontracts, both were "within the contemplation of the par-
> ties."

Of course, what is to be regarded as within the contemplation of the
parties is a question of fact, and all the circumstances of the case may
be taken into account, but it would seem, following the traditional
approach, that the vendor (or trader) is presumed to have a more extensive knowledge of the market than the carrier.[7]

(ii) The second principle is that for the vendor to be liable for any
compensation paid for breaches of warranty in sub-sales the terms of
the warranty must be the same as in the principal contract between the
defendant and plaintiff. The rationale is clear: if the plaintiff is not
bound to pass on to his sub-buyer the very same thing which he has

---

[1] (1889), 20 Q.B.D. 79, *per* LORD ESHER, M.R., at p. 88, *per* BOWEN, L.J., at
p. 94–95, *per* FRY, L.J. at pp. 99–100.
[2] [1904] 1 K.B. 725.
[3] *Per* BRUCE, J., *ibid.*, at p. 736.
[4] *Supra*, pp. 77–78.
[5] *Supra*, p. 78.
[6] [1923] 1 K.B. 690.
[7] *Supra*, p. 316.

acquired from the defendant, there is no necessary connection between the goods which the defendant supplied to him and those which were the subject-matter of his dispute with the sub-buyer.[1] Further,

> "if the variation to a description is such that it is impossible to say whether the injury that ultimately results would have flowed from the breach of the original warranty, the parties must as reasonable men be presumed to have put the liability for the injury outside their contemplation as a measure of compensation."[2]

The principle emerges most clearly from *Dexters* v. *Hill Crest Oil Co. (Bradford) Ltd.*[3]

> Ds sold "250 tons of dark cotton seed grease as per sample no. 9536" to Ps. Ps sold the goods to X and X sold them to Y. Y sold them to Z as "black cotton seed grease". The latter but not the former was a recognized trade description. *Obiter* it was said that this difference was sufficient to repudiate P's claim for an indemnity.[4]

The question then arises as to the extent of variation necessary for this principle to apply. Some assistance on this point was given by DEVLIN, J. in his most comprehensive judgment in *Biggin* v. *Permanite*.[5] Since the basis of the rule is foreseeability of the ultimate injury, the nature of that injury will be a material consideration in determining whether or not a variation in terms was sufficient to prevent recovery. If the injury is an economic one, resulting from, for example, a fall in the market value (as in *Dexters*' case), "any variation that is more than a mere matter of words is likely to be fatal, because there is no way of telling its effect on the market value." In the case of physical injury, however, some variation may not be fatal. The particular type of physical injury ultimately sustained may more easily be contemplated as flowing from the breach of warranty. The crucial question is whether the whole of the liability for the injury flows from the warranty as made by the defendant or whether it flows more from a variation in terms of the sub-sale.

(b) Mitigation

The principle that the plaintiff shall not recover for those losses which he might reasonably have avoided when applied to the indemnity interest gives rise to two further rules.

---

[1] Cf. *supra*, pp. 334–335.
[2] *Per* DEVLIN, J., *Biggin & Co.* v. *Permanite*, [1951] 1 K.B. 422, at p. 433.
[3] [1926] 1 K.B. 348.
[4] *Ibid.*, *per* WARRINGTON, L.J. at p. 357, *per* SCRUTTON, L.J. at p. 359.
[5] *Supra*, at p. 433–434.

(i) The plaintiff must have acted reasonably in sustaining the loss. Confronted with the defendant's breach of contract, the plaintiff may feel it incumbent on him to take certain action to his own detriment. For compensation to be recovered for the consequences of such action it must be shown that the action was, in the circumstances, reasonable. In *Aerial Advertising Co.* v. *Bachelor Peas, Ltd.*[1]

> Ps employed Ds to fly above certain towns trailing a streamer advertising Ps' goods. In breach of contract Ds executed their obligation while Armistice services were in progress to "the horror and indignation (of) thousands of people congregated."[2] Ps were denounced in the local press and elsewhere and threats to boycott their goods were made. Ps at once inserted advertisements in the local newspapers containing apologies etc. They were allowed to recover the cost of such advertisements (£70): in the circumstances, it was "a wholly reasonable thing that they should want to get their advertisements into the press as quickly as they could."[3]

In cases where the plaintiff is sued on a subcontract by a third party, to recover the costs of litigation he must be able to show that it was reasonable to defend the case. The question will often turn on the extent to which the defect giving rise to the action should have been apparent to the plaintiff. In many cases of sales of goods, the plaintiff/buyer is a "middleman" whose knowledge of the condition of the goods is slight compared with that of the defendant/seller who has warranted their soundness. Should a sub-buyer claim against him, the plaintiff may, on the strength of the defendant's warranty, be entitled to assume that the case is worth defending.[4] In most cases, however, he would be expected to give notice of the claim to the defendant/seller[5] and only if the latter were then to reassert the soundness of the article would it be reasonable for the plaintiff to dispute his own liability with the sub-buyer.[6] Moreover, if the court concludes that the plaintiff was under a duty to examine the goods before he passed them onto his sub-buyer, defending the action may be deemed unreasonable.[7] Where, too, the facts of the plaintiff's position fully emerge in arbitration proceedings, it will rarely be reasonable for the plaintiff to appeal against the arbitration award.[8]

(ii) It is a corollary of the first principle that when the plaintiff as a consequence of a breach of contract acts to his own detriment, the

---

[1] [1938] 2 All E.R. 788.
[2] *Per* ATKINSON, J., *ibid.*, at p. 792.
[3] *Ibid.*, at p. 794.
[4] E.g. *Scott* v. *Foley* (1899), 5 Com. Cas. 53.
[5] *Hammond* v. *Bussey* (1888), 20 Q.B.D. 79, *per* LORD ESHER, M.R., at p. 90.
[6] *Hammond* v. *Bussey, supra*; *Bennett, Ltd.* v. *Kreeger* (1925), 41 T.L.R. 609.
[7] *Wrightup* v. *Chamberlain* (1839), 7 Scott 598.
[8] *G.W.R.* v. *Fisher*, [1905] 1 Ch. 316.

amount of expenditure incurred or loss sustained must be reasonable.[1] Where, for example, a plaintiff/buyer compromises a claim brought by a sub-buyer, to recover the amount paid he must be prepared to show that the settlement was not, in the circumstances, unreasonably high.[2] The onus is on the plaintiff to show that it was reasonable.[3] In deciding the point the court is entitled to consider what sum would have been paid by way of damages if the action had gone to judgment.[4]

(c) Policy

Public policy considerations may operate to defeat a plaintiff's claim to recover his indemnity interest. The most important instance of policy being pleaded is where as a result of the defendant's breach of contract the plaintiff is convicted of a criminal offence and seeks to recover from the defendant an indemnity for the fine and costs. It is at least arguable that on grounds of public policy a convicted person should not be allowed to pass the burden of criminal liability onto another person. The principle was most broadly stated by DENNING, J. in *Askey* v. *Golden Wine Co., Ltd.*[5]: "the punishment inflicted by a criminal court is personal to the offender and . . . the civil courts will not entertain an action by the offender to recover an indemnity against the consequences of that punishment."

In fact, there is some divergence of opinion as to the extent to which that principle should apply. Two decisions early in this century allowed recovery of fine and costs without reference to the policy considerations.[6] In *Leslie, Ltd.* v. *Reliable Advertising, Ltd.*[7] ROWLATT, J. clearly thought that to allow the claim would be contrary to public policy, but he did not have to decide the point as he found that the loss was in any event too remote. On the other hand, in *Askey* v. *Golden Wine Co., Ltd.*[8] and in *Payne* v. *Ministry of Food*[9] the broad principle of policy enunciated by DENNING, J. was regarded as decisive and the plaintiffs' claims were dismissed on that ground. A compromise solution is suggested by the most recent decision on the point: *Osman* v. *Ralph Moss.*[10] The amount paid as a fine may be recovered unless the defendant is able to show "that there was on the part of the person fined a degree of *mens rea* or of culpable negligence in the matter which resulted in the fine."[11]

---

[1] Cf. *supra*, p. 90.
[2] *Biggin* v. *Permanite*, [1951] 2 K.B. 314.
[3] *Ibid., per* SINGLETON, L.J., at p. 325.
[4] *Ibid., per* SOMERVELL, L.J., at p. 322.
[5] [1948] 2 All E.R. 35, at p. 38.
[6] *Crage* v. *Fry* (1903), 67 J.P. 240; *Cointat* v. *Myham*, [1913] 2 K.B. 220.
[7] [1915] 1 K.B. 652.
[8] *Supra*, n. 57.
[9] (1953), 103 L.Jo. 141.
[10] [1970] 1 Lloyd's Rep. 313.
[11] *Ibid., per* SACHS, L.J., at p. 316.

The question arises whether this solution is compatible both with previous authority and with the policy considerations which provoke the limitation of awards of damages. In terms of authority, there would seem to be no problem. The cases in which the plaintiff has recovered an indemnity were cases of strict liability and in neither case was evidence of "mens rea or culpable negligence adduced."[1] In *Leslie* v. *Reliable Advertising*[2] the plaintiffs were convicted of sending a moneylender's circular to an infant without reasonable ground for believing him to be of full age and there was a clear inference of "culpable negligence". Finally in *Askey* v. *Golden Wine Co., Ltd.*[3] DENNING, J. found that the plaintiff had been grossly negligent in selling cocktails unfit for human consumption.

The policy issues are more problematical. The solution in *Osman* v. *Ralph Moss* may appear as an attractive compromise, but if it is to be justified certain premises must be accepted. These are: first, that in the words of DENNING, J.

> "in every criminal court the punishment is fixed having regard to the personal responsibility of the offender in respect of the offence, to the necessity of deterring him and others from doing the same thing again, to reform him, and . . . to make him and others more careful in their dealings, to make him choose with more discrimination his suppliers or his servants, and to make him more exact and scrupulous in his supervision of the matters for which he is responsible;"[4]

secondly, that if an offender were able to assign the burden of his criminal liability these objects would be defeated; thirdly, that this deterrence argument (if accepted) is not effective where the offender is held strictly liable, in the sense that "guilty knowledge" not being required the existence of an indemnity is unlikely to affect whether or not he commits the offence. The first and second premises have been generally accepted.[5] But the third is more doubtful. Recent empirical investigation tends to suggest that strict liability offences are effective as deterrents.[6] If this is, indeed, the case the arguments for deciding the issue according to the mens rea of the offence in question do not carry the same weight.

The final point to be determined under the head of public policy is whether it should in any circumstances impede the recovery of an

---

[1] *Crage* v. *Fry*; *Cointat* v. *Myham, supra,* n. 6, p. 361.
[2] *Supra,* n. 7, p. 361.
[3] [1948] 2 All E.R. 35.
[4] *Ibid.,* at p. 38.
[5] See, e.g. *Beresford* v. *Royal Insurance,* [1938] A.C. 586, though the implications of the decision should not be drawn too widely: Furmston (1966) 16 U. of Toronto L.J. 267.
[6] "The existence of strict liability does induce organisations to aim at higher and higher standards": Smith and Pearson, [1969] Crim. L.R. 5, 16.

indemnity for compensation payable as a result of *civil liability*. In the ordinary case it is not a defence to a plaintiff's claim that he himself has committed a tort or a breach of contract but the policy considerations described above may be invoked in cases where the civil liability of the plaintiff arose on facts which would, in addition, have supported a criminal prosecution. In *Askey's* case, an additional claim for indemnifying a settlement made with a third party was also repudiated on the ground that "public policy requires that no right of indemnity or contribution or damages should be enforced in respect of expenses which the plaintiff has incurred by reason of being compelled to make reparation for his own crime."[1]   But even though the ruling in that case was posited on the plaintiff's degree of fault, the rule as stated is a harsh one.   The claim by the third party, it may be suggested, is consequent not on the criminal act but on the failure to fulfil his contractual undertakings, and if this is itself the result of the defendant's breach of contract, the defendant should be liable for an indemnity.

(d) Non-pecuniary losses

It has been seen that until recently[2] courts have not been prepared to include non-pecuniary items as part of the legally recoverable expectation interest.   Despite the occasional dictum to the contrary,[3] it is quite clear that this reluctance did not extend to the indemnity interest.   Where a breach of contract results in physical injury, damages are assessed as in a tort action.[4]   It follows that where, for example, a plaintiff sustains personal injuries he can claim in an action for breach of contract for loss of amenities, pain and suffering and loss of expectation of life.[5]   Independently of physical injuries, compensation may also be awarded for physical inconvenience and discomfort. Such losses were recovered in *Hobbs* v. *London and South Western Rail Co.*[6] and in *Bailey* v. *Bullock*,[7] the facts of which two cases have already been given.[8]

4   Quantification of indemnity interest damages

The general principle of compensation for breach of contract is to put the plaintiff in the position he would have been in if the contract

---

[1] [1948] 2 All E.R. 35, at p. 38.
[2] *Jarvis* v. *Swans Tours, Ltd.*, [1973] 1 All E.R. 71, *supra*, pp. 307–309.
[3] E.g. HALLETT, J. in *Sunley & Co., Ltd.* v. *Cunard White Star*, [1939] 2 K.B. 791, at p. 799.
[4] *Supra*, Chap. 6.
[5] E.g. *Summers* v. *Salford Corporation* [1943] A.C. 283.
[6] (1875), L.R. 10 Q.B. 111.
[7] [1950] 2 All E.R. 1167.
[8] *Supra*, p. 356.

had satisfactorily been performed. Now it has been seen that a contractual obligation may serve either of two functions: it may confer benefits or it may prevent losses. The expectation interest covers the former and the indemnity interest the latter. It follows that in assessing damages for the indemnity interest, the court must calculate the extent to which the plaintiff's patrimony and person have suffered detriment as a result of the defendant's breach. The measure is the equivalent of the *restitutio in integrum* doctrine in tort, for, in effect, the plaintiff is being restored to the *status quo ante*: his position before he entered into a transaction with the defendant.

Once it is clear that the *restitutio in integrum* doctrine is the basis of the award, the methods of quantifying it pose no new problems. There are three stages in the process of assessment.

(a) The first is to ascertain whether the breach of contract gave rise to personal injury, property injury or mere economic injury.

(b) Once the category of injury is clear, the court simply applies the principles governing the awards of damages for tortiously-caused injuries.[1]

(c) The only qualification to the sum arrived at by this method is that recoverability may be affected by the doctrines of causation, remoteness, mitigation and public policy as elaborated above. The court must, therefore, determine whether or not these doctrines are applicable, and adjust or annul the award accordingly.

5 Overlap with other interests

The question finally arises whether a plaintiff may recover compensation for his indemnity interest in addition to compensation for other interests.

(a) Indemnity interest and expectation interest

The general rule is that there may be recovery for both interests but there are cases of both direct and indirect overlap where the court must be careful lest it allows the plaintiff a double recovery.

(i) *Direct overlap* There are some losses which on the face of them might seem to fit appropriately under either the indemnity or the expectation interest: this is because a "loss of profits" may include a "positive loss". Many expectation interests may on an alternative though perhaps artificial construction be regarded as indemnity interests. If D agrees to deliver P's goods safely to him but damages them, this injury to P's property might be treated as an indemnity interest, and P would claim the tortious measure for his losses. Were

---

[1] See, e.g. *Godley* v. *Perry*, [1960] 1 All E.R. 36.

this approach to be taken it would, of course, be wrong to award P his expectation interest, *viz.* his loss of profit on selling the damaged article, and his indemnity interest, *viz.* the pecuniary losses flowing from the injury to his property. Indeed it may be conceded that the division between the expectation interest and the indemnity interest is neither perfect nor logically necessary. Yet the principles and policies which affect the measure of compensation for the two interests are best treated separately. In the first place, the measure of damages for the indemnity interest is the tortious measure of *restitutio in integrum.* Secondly, the rules relating to the recovery of non-pecuniary loss are somewhat different. Thirdly, the defences of causation, remoteness, mitigation and public policy reveal different aspects depending on whether they are to be applied to an expectation interest or to an indemnity interest. Fourthly, there are circumstances when the indemnity interest but not the expectation interest may supplement an award of the reliance interest. A workable distinction between the two interests may be based on the following propositions.

(A) Where the obligation for the breach of which the plaintiff is seeking compensation was not intended to add something of value to the plaintiff's patrimony, then any loss which is consequent on that breach may be treated as an indemnity interest loss.

(B) Where, on the other hand, the obligation in question was to add something of value to the plaintiff's patrimony, then all losses consequent on the breach should be treated as expectation interest losses, except those resulting from the plaintiff changing his position by, for example, settling a valid claim brought by a third party or incurring certain out of pocket expenses—these latter should always be treated as indemnity interest losses.

(ii) *Indirect overlap* Even if cases of direct overlap are avoided, difficulty may arise where an indemnity interest indirectly represents an expectation interest. This may occur, where, for example, a sum paid to a third party as a result of the breach includes something which, if the contract had been performed, the plaintiff would have retained as profit. A set of hypothetical facts may illustrate this.

> D contracts to sell and deliver an article to P at £100. P with the knowledge of D resells it to X for £130. P pays £100 to D and D delivers the article to him. X pays £130 to P who delivers the article to him. X repudiates the contract when he discovers that it does not accord with the contractual standard of quality. X successfully recovers £200 from P representing recovery of £130 + £70 other damages. P, subject to the rules described above, may recover the £200 paid to X but he may not in addition recover the £30 profit he would have made on the contract since that has already been accounted for in the indemnity measure.

(b) Indemnity interest and reliance interest

When the relationship between the reliance interest and the expectation interest was examined,[1] it was seen that reliance interest compensation might serve two different purposes. Either the object is to put the plaintiff in the position he would have been in if the contract had been performed, in which case the reliance interest if it is awarded at all must *complement* expectation interest damages, or the object is to put the plaintiff in the position he would have been in if he had never entered into the contract with the defendant, in which case the reliance interest is awarded as an *alternative* to the expectation interest. The same distinction is relevant to the relationship between the reliance interest and the indemnity interest.

(i) *Reliance interest as complement*   The extent to which a plaintiff may accumulate compensation for his indemnity and reliance interests on this first hypothesis, is determined on the basis of principles already discussed.[2] If the object is to put the plaintiff in the position he would have been in if the contract had been performed, compensation for reliance interest may only supplement expectation and indemnity interest damages where the reliance interest has already been taken into account in the calculation of the expectation interest, that is where the latter is assessed on the basis of "net profits" rather than on "gross profits". For example in *Molling* v. *Dean*[3] on the facts which were set out above[4]

> Ps were entitled to (A) their *expectation* interest, their lost "net profits", that is the profits they would have secured after a deduction had been made for the expenses necessary to secure that profit, including the cost of transporting the books to the U.S.A. *plus* (B) their *reliance* interest, the cost of sending the books to the U.S.A. *plus* (C) their *indemnity* interest, the cost of bringing them back from the U.S.A.

Where, on the other hand, the expectation interest has been calculated on the basis of "gross profits", without account being taken of the reliance interest, the remedies may not be accumulated. In *Howell* v. *St. Louis Ry*[5]

> Ds promised to carry P's mules to market. P drove his mules to Ds' station but could not find there a suitable truck. P then drove the mules back to his farm and then to another station. As a result of the trek, the mules arrived at the market in gaunt condition. It was held that P was entitled to recover both (A) his *expectation* interest, the

---

[1] *Supra*, pp. 346–354.
[2] *Supra*, pp. 352–354.
[3] (1901) 18 T.L.R. 217.
[4] *Supra*, p. 355.
[5] 153 S.W. 578 (1913).

diminution in the selling price of the mules, and (B) his *indemnity* interest, the cost of driving them back to the farm, but not (C) his *reliance* interest, the wasted expense of driving them to the station. The latter item would have been incurred if the contract had been performed, and it was not reflected in the expectation interest award.

(ii) *Reliance interest as alternative*   If the court allows the reliance interest as a true alternative to the expectation interest, that is without limiting the award by any reference to a net loss on the expectation interest,[1] the object of the award must be to put the plaintiff in the position he would have been in if he had not entered into a contract with the defendant. It follows that though, on such a basis, he will not be allowed any part of his expectation interest, he will be entitled to recover his indemnity interest, for the object of that measure is to restore him to the *status quo ante*.   Thus in *Lloyd* v. *Stanbury*[2] on the facts which were set out above[3]

> P recovered damages both for his reliance interest, the expenses incurred in anticipation of completion (e.g. the cost of moving the caravan onto the land) and for his indemnity interest, the expenses caused by the breach (e.g. the cost of removing the caravan).

III   THE RESTITUTION INTEREST

1   Introduction

The restitution interest comprises those benefits which the plaintiff has conferred on the defendant in part performance of the contract. In many cases this will be a sum of money—the contract price.   But it may include the conveyance of property or the performance of a valuable service.   The restitution interest may form part of the ordinary award of damages, but it may, in the alternative be claimed in an independent quasi-contractual action for money had and received. Neither case requires elaborate discussion for when it forms part of an ordinary damages action the restitution interest is treated as part of the reliance interest, and no new principles are involved, while the action in quasi-contract is not an action for damages and thus does not, strictly, come within the scope of this book.

2   Restitution interest as part of a damages award

Factually, the restitution interest differs from the reliance interest in that something of value is conferred on the defendant rather than

---

[1] See *supra*, pp. 351–352.
[2] [1971] 2 All E.R. 267.
[3] *Supra*, pp. 348–349.

on a third party.   The only significant consequence of this is that the doctrine of remoteness can never bar recovery of the restitution interest: it must always be within the contemplation of the defendant that the plaintiff will confer benefits on him.   Apart from this, it would seem[1] that the principles governing recovery of the restitution interest are the same as those governing the award of the reliance interest. Thus in cases where the reliance interest is claimed as an alternative to the expectation interest,[2] the plaintiff may recover as part of his wasted expenses the value of anything which he conferred on the defendant.[3]   Where, however, the expectation interest is the basis of the award, the plaintiff may recover his restitution interest only if it has been deducted in the calculation of the expectation interest, that is, only if the expectation interest was estimated on the basis of "net profits" rather than "gross profits".[4]   Analogous principles apply where the plaintiff seeks to recover his restitution interest and his indemnity interest: he will be barred from accumulating both only where he recovers also for his expectation interest, the calculation of which does not account for the payment of the restitution interest.[5]

3   Restitution interest in an action for quasi-contract

In certain circumstances, the plaintiff may elect to claim his restitution interest not in an action for damages but in a quasi-contractual action for money had and received.   For a full account of this action reference should be made to the standard works on restitution.[6]   The sole object of the limited discussion in this paragraph is to highlight those aspects of the remedy which differ from a damages award, and thus to consider when it will be to the plaintiff's advantage to exercise his right to opt for the restitutionary remedy.

(a)   Total failure of consideration

The plaintiff may only claim under a restitutionary action where there has been a total failure of consideration.[7]   An action in damages will of course arise on any breach of contract.

---

[1] There is no explicit judicial statement on this, but the practice of the courts may provide sufficient evidence.   See also Fuller & Perdue (1936), 46 Yale L.J. 52, at p. 55.

[2] *Supra*, p. 347.

[3] E.g. *McRae* v. *Commonwealth Disposals Commission* (1951), 84 C.L.R. 377; *Engell* v. *Fitch* (1869), L.R. 4 Q.B. 659.

[4] *Supra*, pp. 352–354.

[5] Cf. *supra*, p. 353.

[6] Goff and Jones, *The Law of Restitution*;   Stoljar, *The Law of Quasi-Contract*.

[7] See in general *Fibrosa Spolka Akcyjna* v. *Fairbairn Lawson Combe Barbour, Ltd.*, [1943] A.C. 32 and Stoljar (1959), 75 L.Q.R. 53.   It may also be available

(b) Object of recovery

The object of the restitutionary action is to restore to the plaintiff the value of those benefits which he has conferred on the defendant: his restitution interest.[1] As such the amount recovered will differ from the ordinary measure in an action for damages. It does not seek to put the plaintiff in the position he would have been in if the contract had been performed; it does not take account of his expectation interest. At the same time it is only a partial recognition of the *restitutio in integrum* doctrine since it is concerned only with the plaintiff's dealings with the defendant, and does not extend to those losses incurred in relation to third parties such as are covered by the reliance and indemnity interests.

(c) Limitations

While the action for money had and received is confined to recovery of the restitution interest, it has a compensating advantage over a damages award in that it is not subject to the same limitations.

(i) Although in the restitutionary action a plaintiff is bound to restore to the defendant any benefit received from him by way of part performance,[2] he may retain the value of any benefit which was not part of the consideration of the contract. In *Rowland* v. *Divall*[3]

> D sold a car to P, who used it for several months and then sold it to X. It emerged that the car had been stolen from Y. The police seized the car from X and returned it to Y. P repaid to X the price that he had been paid for the car, and then sought to recover against D the price he had been paid on the ground of total failure of consideration. P succeeded in his claim despite the fact that he had used the car for the several months: "the buyer (P) had not received any part of that which he contracted to receive—namely, the property and right to possession —and, that being so, there has been a total failure of consideration."[4]

In an action for damages, on the other hand, it is clear that the value of any such benefit is to be deducted from the award.[5]

(ii) It is not, as yet, clear in English law whether the reliance interest may be recovered as a "true" alternative to the expectation interest,

---

where there has been a breach of a divisible contract and part of the consideration relating to one of the divisible parts of the contract has wholly failed: e.g. *Devaux* v. *Conolly* (1849), 8 C.B. 640.
  [1] The exact nature of the quasi-contractual action has been a rich source of academic dispute: see, especially, Goff & Jones, *op. cit.*, Chap. 1.
  [2] *Towers* v. *Barrett* (1786), 1 Term Rep. 133.
  [3] [1923] 2 K.B. 500.
  [4] *Per* ATKIN, L.J., *ibid.*, at p. 507. The Law Reform Committee has described the result as "unjust" and has recommended that account be taken of any such benefit accruing to the plaintiff: Cmnd. 2958 (1966), para. 36.
  [5] *Charterhouse Credit* v. *Tolly* [1963] 2 Q.B. 683 and *infra*, p. 371.

that is without being limited by the extent of the expectation interest.[1]
It was suggested that a damages award should not operate so as to put
the plaintiff in a better position than he would have been in if the contract had been performed, and hence that the reliance interest award
should be limited by the extent of the expectation interest.[2] Whatever
be the principle governing the damages award, it is manifestly clear that
no such limitation is applied to the restitutionary remedy.   In an action
for money had and received the courts regard as irrelevant the argument
that unless a deduction is made the plaintiff will be put in a better position than if the contract had been performed.   It follows that where the
plaintiff has made a bad bargain, it may be to his advantage to claim
in a restitutionary action.   Thus in *Wilkinson* v. *Lloyd*[3]

> D sold to P shares in a mining company.   The deed of settlement
> under which the company was established required that to execute a
> valid transfer of shares the directors must approve of the prospective
> transferee.   The directors did not approve of the transfer of shares to
> P.   P thereupon brought against D an action for money had and
> received to recover the purchase money.   The value of the shares had
> dropped since the time of the transfer.   It was held that D as vendor
> was in breach of contract for failing to obtain the approval of the
> directors, that there had been a total failure of consideration, and that P
> was entitled to recover his purchase money, notwithstanding the fall in
> the value of the shares.

Clearly, if the plaintiff had sued in a contractual action for damages his
remedy would have been limited to the value of the shares, as representing the extent of his expectation interest.[4] The success of his restitutionary action protected him against the consequences of a bad bargain.

IV   DEDUCTION FOR COMPENSATING
ADVANTAGES

1   Introduction

If the law of damages is to take its stand on a pure principle of compensation, it is clear that in assessing an award a court should take into
account not only the losses but also the compensating advantages which
result from a breach of contract.

In two special cases the principles developed in tortious actions are
applied by analogy.   These are: (i) actions for wrongful dismissal
where the dismissed employee recovers some benefit from a collateral

---

[1] *Supra*, pp. 351–352.
[2] *Supra*, p. 352.
[3] (1845), 7 Q.B. 27.
[4] *Supra*, p. 324.

source;[1] and (ii) actions for losses arising out of damage to property where reinstatement makes the property more valuable than it was before the breach.[2] For an account of the doctrine as applied to these situations, therefore, reference should be made to the analogy in tort.[3]

Discussion of the remaining categories of compensating advantage will be subsumed under four heads: (i) in part performance of the contract, the defendant has conferred on the plaintiff some part of the consideration for the contract; (ii) the defendant has failed to perform according to the contract but has conferred on the plaintiff some alternative benefit; (iii) the plaintiff by his own efforts has procured a substitute benefit; (iv) the termination of the contract has saved the plaintiff from an expense which otherwise he would have incurred.

2 Part of the consideration

The plaintiff should account for the value of anything which the defendant has conferred on him as part of the consideration for the contract. The most important application of this principle is implicit in a rule of quantification which has already been discussed. In cases of defective or delayed performance where the breach is not sufficiently fundamental for the plaintiff to repudiate, he is expected to accept partial performance and derive what benefit he may from it. In such circumstances the measure of his compensation is the *diminished profit*: that is, the benefits which would have accrued on complete performance less the value of those benefits which he is reasonably able to secure on the use or disposal of what the defendant has conferred on him.[4]

The deduction rule becomes more explicit in cases where the defect is so substantial that the plaintiff repudiates. Here a deduction is made for such benefits as have already been conferred on him by the defendant. This may be part of the contract price: in a hire-purchase contract, for example, where the owner terminates on the hirer's breach, he may recover his lost profit, *viz.* the full hire-purchase price, but from this will be deducted, *inter alia*, the deposit and those instalments already paid.[5] But it may also be for the use of an article during the currency of the contract. In *Charterhouse Credit* v. *Tolly*[6]

D, in a h.p. contract, delivered to P a second-hand car which was seriously defective. On rescission of the contract P recovered all the money paid or payable under the contract but a deduction was made for the use he had had of the car while in his possession[7]

---

[1] E.g. *Dunk* v. *Waller*, [1970] 2 Q.B. 163 (unemployment benefit).
[2] E.g. *Harbutt's Plasticine* v. *Wayne Tank*, [1970] 1 Q.B. 447.
[3] *Supra*, pp. 222–230, and p. 234 respectively.
[4] *Supra*, pp. 335 and 340.
[5] E.g. *Yeoman Credit* v. *Waragowski*, [1961] 3 All E.R. 145.
[6] [1963] 2 Q.B. 683.
[7] For the method of quantifying loss of use, see *supra*, pp. 139–140.

3   Defendant confers some alternative benefit

Whilst unable to confer the promised benefit on the plaintiff, the defendant may, through his efforts to perform, confer some alternative benefit.   In general, it is in accord with the compensatory principle that if the benefit is accepted, it should be deducted.   Thus in *Smith, Edwards & Co.* v. *Tregarthen*[1]

> D, a carrier, signed bills of lading for 400 bales of cotton to be de-
> livered at Liverpool.   He did not have enough room on his own ship,
> and so 235 bales were carried on another vessel.   Although Ps, in-
> dorsees, had an action for the non-delivery of 235 bales, the award of
> the market price of the cotton on the delivery date was reduced by the
> value of the cotton when it arrived on the substitute ship.

However, there will be no deduction where the plaintiff not unreason-ably refuses to accept the benefit of the substitute.   This seems to have been the reason for the decision in *Eyre* v. *Rea*[2]

> D, the assignee of a lease, in breach of covenant, converted the leased
> premises into flats.   P, the lessor, was granted a decree of forfeiture and
> in an action for damages was awarded the cost of restoring the premises
> to their original condition.   ATKINSON, J. refused to take account of the
> fact that the conversion had rendered the property of greater economic
> value than it had been in its unconverted state.

From a purely economic point of view, the decision may seem a doubtful one.   As a result of the conversion, the plaintiff had been put in a better financial position than he would have been in if the covenant had been observed.   But the award may be justified on the ground that the plain-tiff had a *non-pecuniary* interest in maintaining the property in its unconverted state.[3]

4   Plaintiff by his own efforts acquires a substitute benefit

It is a corollary of the doctrine of mitigation that if the plaintiff, confronted by the defendant's failure to perform, should act to his own advantage by procuring a substitute, the value of that advantage should be deducted from his award against the defendant.[4]   The principle is, of course, the basis of the measure of damages where the plaintiff is under a duty to mitigate and he is awarded the cost of substi-tute performance.   In a sale of goods contract where the seller has

---

[1] (1887), 56 L.J.Q.B. 437.
[2] [1947] K.B. 567.
[3] Cf. *supra*, pp. 337–338. On the facts as reported in *Eyre* v. *Rea*, however, it is far from clear that the plaintiff had such a non-pecuniary interest.
[4] See, generally, *British Westinghouse* v. *Underground Ry.*, [1912] A.C. 673.

failed to deliver the buyer is awarded the market buying price of the goods.[1] In an action for wrongful dismissal the plaintiff employee is awarded his lost earnings less anything which he has or should have earned in alternative employment.[2] But even where the plaintiff is not under a legal duty to mitigate, the value of any benefit which he has in fact acquired in an act of mitigation will be deducted from his award. Thus in *Erie County Natural Gas* v. *Carroll*[3]

> Ps transferred gas leases to Ds reserving the use of such gas as would be sufficient to supply a plant operated by them. Ds cut off the supply reserved. Ps managed to obtain substitute gas by acquiring other gas leases and from the construction of works to procure gas. Ps eventually sold the substitute leases and works at a profit. It was held by the Privy Council that, though Ps had been under no duty to mitigate (i.e. they could simply have done nothing and sued for breach of contract), the fact that they *did* mitigate and emerge with a net profit was a bar to recovering substantial damages.

For this principle of deduction to apply, there must be a substantial causal link between the breach of contract and the plaintiff's act in securing the benefit: the benefit must arise out of an act of mitigation.[4] Where, therefore, the benefit is secured *before* the breach of contract, in general it will not be deducted because it is not an act of mitigation which is causally connected to the defendant's breach. In *Joyner* v. *Weeks*[5]

> P granted a lease of premises to D for 21 years from 1868 to 1889, D covenanting to deliver up the premises at the end of the term in good repair. In 1887 P executed a lease of the same house to X with the same covenants to run from the end of D's term. D failed to deliver up the premises in good repair but in an action brought by P he claimed that P was in fact no worse off than he would have been if the contract had been performed and that therefore his damages should be nominal. The argument was rejected by the Court of Appeal: the claim by P could not be affected by his agreement with a third party made before the expiry of D's term.

Where the benefit arises from an act subsequent to the breach it will be easier to prove that it was causally linked to the breach. In *Lavarack* v. *Woods of Colchester*[6]

> Ds wrongfully dismissed P from their employment. P, in consequence, entered the employment of X co. at a comparatively low salary but he

---

[1] Sale of Goods Act 1893, s. 51(3).
[2] E.g. *Collier* v. *Sunday Referee Publishing*, [1940] 2 K.B. 647.
[3] [1911] A.C. 105.
[4] McGregor, § 246.
[5] [1891] 2 Q.B. 31.
[6] [1967] 1 Q.B. 278.

bought half of X co.'s share capital. He also invested a large sum of money in a new company (Y) which was in competition with Ds. It was held that the profits from P's investment in (as well as his salary from) X co. should be deducted from the award of his lost earnings: it was in the nature of remuneration[1] for the post and was therefore part of the act of mitigation. But profits from his investment with Y co. were not deductible. Although P was only allowed to invest in them once he had been dismissed by Ds, the investment was not by way of mitigation: "it was not a direct result of his dismissal. It was an entirely collateral benefit, for which he need not account to his employers."[2]

A less obvious decision was *Jebsen* v. *East and West India Dock Co.*[3]

Ds were late in performing their contractual obligation to discharge cargo from P's ship. As a result P's ship was unable to carry 240 passengers from Bergen to New York. 227 of these passengers were, however, carried on other ships belonging to Ps.[4] It was held that the profit made on the substitute contracts should not be deducted.

The case could, perhaps, have been decided on the ground that the defendants failed to prove that the places in the substitute ships would otherwise have remained empty. But the decision was not so restricted, and as such, it is, with respect, difficult to support.[5] There was an obvious causal connection between the failure of the first ship to carry the passengers and the securing of their passage in the later ships.

5 Saving of expenses

On complete performance of the contract the plaintiff may have incurred expenditure or some liability to a third party. If the object of compensation is to put the plaintiff in the position he would have been in if the contract had been performed, it is clear that allowance must be made in the award for the saving of these expenses. In most cases, the saving of such expenses will have been accounted for in the assessment of the expectation interest: this is especially likely where the interest has been quantified on the basis of "net profits".[6] In other cases a

---

[1] *Ibid., per* LORD DENNING, M.R. at p. 291, *per* RUSSELL, L.J. at p. 301.
[2] *Ibid., per* LORD DENNING, M.R. at p. 290.
[3] (1875), L.R. 10 C.P. 300.
[4] In fact these other ships were only partly owned by Ps, but the point was not regarded by the court as decisive: *ibid.*, at p. 305.
[5] In *The World Beauty*, [1970] P. 144, Ps chartered a substitute when their own vessel had been injured by Ds. The profit made by the substitute ship was deducted. Although *Jebsen* was cited in argument, it was not considered in the judgments of the C.A. It is difficult to reconcile the two decisions. Cf, McGregor, § 251.
[6] Cf *supra*, pp. 352–354.

separate deduction must be made.   In *Watts, Watts & Co., Ltd.* v. *Mitsui & Co.*[1]

> Ds agreed to provide Ps with a steamer to carry goods to Japan.   If the ship had been delivered on time it was established that, because of the outbreak of war, the ship would not have been able to reach Japan, but that Ps would have insured against war risks and would have recovered on their insurance policy.   It was held that they were entitled to what they would have recovered under an insurance policy (the value of the goods on arrival in Japan) but that a deduction should be made for the insurance premium and the other expenses they would have incurred if the ship had sailed.

Finally, an allowance must be made for the tax which would have been paid on benefits for the loss of which compensation is payable.   The question has been fully discussed in an earlier chapter.[2]

---

[1] [1917] A.C. 227.
[2] *Supra*, pp. 107–115.

Index

377